FROM QUILLS TO TWEETS

To Dave,

Thank you for all the support and
encouragement,
Best regards,
Andrea, Marc & Sally

FROM QUILLS TO TWEETS

HOW AMERICA COMMUNICATES ABOUT WAR AND REVOLUTION

ANDREA J. DEW, MARC A. GENEST, and S. C. M. PAINE
EDITORS

Georgetown University Press
Washington, DC

Library of Congress Cataloging-in-Publication Data

Names: Dew, Andrea J., editor. | Genest, Marc A., 1958– editor. | Paine, S. C. M., 1957– editor.
Title: From Quills to Tweets : How America Communicates about War and Revolution / Andrea J. Dew, Marc A. Genest, and S.C.M. Paine, editors.
Description: Washington, D.C. : Georgetown University Press, 2020. | Includes bibliographical references and index. |
Identifiers: LCCN 2019003697 (print) | LCCN 2019018836 (ebook) | ISBN 9781626167117 (hardcover : alk. paper) | ISBN 9781626167124 (pbk.: alk. paper) | ISBN 9781626167131 (ebook : alk. paper)
Subjects: LCSH: Mass media and war—United States. | Mass media—Political aspects—United States. | Communication in politics—United States. | Social media—Political aspects—United States.
Classification: LCC P96.W352 (ebook) | LCC P96.W352 U5556 2020 (print) | DDC 070.4/49355020973—dc23
LC record available at https://lccn.loc.gov/2019003697

21 20 19   9 8 7 6 5 4 3 2 First printing

Printed in the United States of America.

Cover design by Jeremy Parker.
Cover images courtesy of shutterstock (Condoleeza Rice); iStock (Morse Code & Telegraph, msnbc.com main page, hashtag image, Walter printing press, quill & inkwell, soldiers against a sunset); Library of Congress (President Franklin D. Roosevelt, "Ultimatum!" newspaper clipping, telegraph operator, Theodore Roosevelt leading the Rough Riders); U.S. National Archives & Records Administration (President Lyndon B. Johnson)

To our students and military teaching partners—thank you for the education.

*To our families—John E., Sheila, Bev, Caroline, and our newest reader, Alexander—
thank you for your support and encouragement; to Pauline, Nate, and Caroline—
thank for your love and inspiration; and to Bruce, Anna, and Steven—
thank you for the support and patience.*

Contents

Acknowledgments

The analysis and opinions expressed by the authors and editors of this book do not represent the views of the Department of Defense, the US Naval War College, or any government agency.

The editors would like to express their sincere thanks to Donald Jacobs and the staff at Georgetown University Press for all their support and encouragement. We would also like to thank our very talented copy editor, Julie Kimmel, and the anonymous reviewers who helped to strengthen the manuscript.

Introduction: Message, Messenger, Medium, and Political Environment

Andrea J. Dew, Marc A. Genest, and S. C. M. Paine

War is the most consequential form of communication engaged in by human beings. It is a lethal form of political messaging that relies on violence to defend one's interests or compel others to accept one's ideological, social, economic, or territorial aims. Given the enormous stakes, it is little wonder that scholars have riveted their attention on the violence of warfare. This book, however, tacks in a different direction by exploring the role that information, political narratives, and the evolving nature of communications technology have played in precipitating, prolonging, and concluding wars over the course of American history.

From Quills to Tweets examines the changing role that information, rhetoric, and communications technology have played in shaping the American political landscape. From the rebellion against Great Britain to contemporary conflicts in Iraq and Afghanistan, one thing remains clear: war is a political campaign in which violence plays a necessary but not sufficient role in the outcome. Since war is suffused with politics, its conduct requires all the tools associated with waging a political campaign. The management of war entails more than just military acumen; it requires effective messengers, messages, and media and skillful management to construct and disseminate compelling arguments justifying the costs both at home and abroad. Adversaries must communicate their aims, actions, and decisions to a wide variety of audiences. To accomplish this task, belligerents build communications networks, construct narratives, circulate messages, defend their supporters, and attack their opponents. The pen may not be mightier than the sword, but success in war is often as dependent on the pen (or quill, telegraph, newspaper, television, or tweet) as it is on traditional military means.

1

This edited volume examines the American way of "communicating war." We look at the impact that the messengers, messages, mechanisms, and management of information and persuasion have on the course and conduct of warfare throughout American history. We consider a wide array of topics, all of which touch on important issues associated with political communication preceding and during hostilities. What effect do civilian and military leaders as well as journalists have on creating war narratives? How has press coverage of political squabbles between military and political leaders affected popular support? How have advances in communications technologies influenced the conduct of war? Has the internet allowed non-state actors to compete with the United States on a level playing field in the information game? If so, how has that influenced the ability of the United States to achieve its aims in Afghanistan, Iraq, and elsewhere? We examine these and many other questions in this book.

We do not attempt to provide a comprehensive assessment of all the various components that make up the art and science of "communicating war." Rather, each reading takes a different conflict and offers a unique assessment of a particular aspect of the communication battle. While we investigate the impact of technological advances on warfare, we focus primarily on the political and military implications rather than delving into the science behind the technology.

We divide the book into five sections. Part 1 covers early America, when committees of correspondence, pamphlets, and newspapers were the dominant information outlets. Marc Genest shows how Samuel Adams and the Sons of Liberty constructed and implemented a propaganda network that incited rebellion in Boston and spread word of the uprising against Great Britain. Troy Bickham provides an account of how both the American and British press covered the War of 1812 and shaped public perceptions of the conflict in both countries.

Part 2 investigates the era of mass circulation newspapers and the telegraph. Martin Manning's Civil War chapter reviews the groundbreaking effects the telegraph had on reporting and the dissemination and control of information during this conflict. Michelle Getchell highlights the role of the Cuban revolutionaries in shaping US press coverage of the war for Cuban independence. Ironically, Cuban propaganda drove the American public into supporting military intervention leading to the marginalization of the revolutionaries. David Silbey discusses how the advent of mass newspaper circulation and rapidly rising rates of literacy compelled US civilian and military leaders to develop more sophisticated communication strategies to justify their actions to the public in the Philippine-American War. Bruce Elleman's chapter examines how journalist John Reed's writing influenced American perceptions of the Russian Revolution for generations to come. J. Lee Thompson's World War I chapter reviews the media battle waged between President Woodrow Wilson and former president Theodore Roosevelt that undermined US foreign policy.

Part 3 covers the period when radio and newsreels competed with newspapers for public attention. S. C. M. Paine focuses on the books and articles of another American journalist, Edgar Snow, and his role in glorifying Mao Zedong and the Chinese Communists. Mike Carew reviews Franklin Roosevelt's remarkably successful fireside-chat strategy, which galvanized and maintained strong public support during World War II despite the enormous costs associated with the war effort. Next, Steven Casey compares and contrasts the Truman and Eisenhower communication strategies in a limited war in Korea.

Part 4 assesses the period of mass media when newspapers, radio, television, and eventually cable networks reached global audiences with increasing speed. David Kaiser analyzes the narratives five presidents used to frame and justify US intervention in Vietnam, culminating with Gerald Ford's acceptance of America's defeat. Judith Baroody's chapter on the Gulf War reviews the Bush administration's struggle with the press over management of real-time information about the war in the new age of global cable media.

Part 5 covers conflicts occurring in the contemporary dynamic environment of ubiquitous mass communications outlets, when cable television, radio, and newspapers now compete on an increasingly level playing field alongside the internet and social media. Thomas Johnson and Matthew DuPée provide a pessimistic assessment of the communication strategies of the United States and its allies in developing effective narratives to combat the influence of the Taliban in Afghanistan. Haroro Ingram and Craig Whiteside document how the Islamic State's slick media campaign and use of semiautonomous regional and local cells have allowed it, thus far, to withstand American counterpropaganda and cyberattacks. Andrea Dew's evaluation of the various US efforts to counter al Qaeda's jihadist propaganda network offers an equally pessimistic account of the continuing battle against radical jihadists.

We end with an analytical chapter drawing conclusions based on the preceding chapters. It suggests both the value and dangers of disseminating information during wartime, the circumstances most and least conducive to successful information campaigns, the dangers of ceding the battle of perceptions to the opposition, the audiences most and least receptive to messaging, and the problem of reaching intended as well as unintended audiences. In doing so, we show both the power and the limitations of words.

PART I. Introduction

Committees of Correspondence and Early Newspapers

Marc A. Genest

There are three vital steps for information technology to have a profound influence on society. First, the innovation must be more efficient and cost-effective than what was currently available. Second, the technology must be available to enough people to have a broad impact. Third, individuals or groups must find practical and imaginative means to exploit the new technology. No better example illustrates these three points than the invention of the printing press.

Sometime between 1440 and 1450, Johann Gutenberg revolutionized printing by creating a "movable type machine." This simple innovation dramatically increased efficiency and lowered the cost of printing. Before Gutenberg's invention, texts were handwritten by monks, making them rare and very expensive. Gutenberg's press greatly expanded the supply of books and reduced the cost of printing. Within only a few decades, printing presses were operating in many European countries. The written word no longer was confined to a small number of wealthy and elite individuals as literacy began expanding across Europe.

The first printing press was introduced to the Massachusetts Bay Colony in 1638. Once the technology arrived in New England, it quickly spread to other areas as ambitious publishers began producing newspapers, pamphlets, and books in all thirteen colonies. There was also a high demand for written materials among the colonists. By the dawn of the American Revolution, scholars estimate that between 85 and 90 percent of white males could read and write, and in cities like Boston, the rate was close to 100 percent. Sadly, the literacy rate for women was less than half that of men, and for nonwhites, literacy was relatively rare.[1]

It is fair to say that without printing presses, the rebel uprising in Boston would have remained localized and far less effective in spurring the American rebellion against the British Empire. Chapter 1, written by Marc Genest, argues that newspapers, broadsheets, and pamphlets played a crucial role in inciting the mutiny against the British. Samuel Adams and the Sons of Liberty deftly exploited the printed word to spread news of the rebellion while also ensuring that their unique spin on breaking events dominated stories across British colonial America and in Europe.

By 1800 there were over two hundred weekly newspapers in the United States, and even daily broadsheets were flourishing in many American cities. The expansion of newspapers had a significant impact on American politics. Journalists became essential players in partisan warfare. The two major US political parties, the Federalists and the Republicans, each sponsored newspapers, using them as mouthpieces to get their views out to the public. This highly competitive and charged information environment is the focus of chapter 2. In this chapter Troy Bickham investigates the role that newspapers played in the course and conduct of the War of 1812. Bickham notes that the war dominated public discourse in both nations as newspaper reports of individual battles and domestic political debates shaped public perception in the United States as well as Great Britain. Ironically, leading newspapers in both countries commonly reprinted articles that appeared in their enemy's papers across the Atlantic. Indeed, Bickham concludes by stating unequivocally that "the press both manipulated perceptions and played on expectations."

Note

1. See Jack Lynch, "Every Man Able to Read," *Colonial Williamsburg Journal*, Winter 2011, http://www.history.org/foundation/journal/winter11/literacy.cfm#top; and Joel Perlmann and Dennis Shirley, "When Did New England Women Acquire Literacy?" *William and Mary Quarterly*, 3rd ser., 48, no. 1 (January 1991): 50–67.

1.

The Message Heard "Round the World" and the First American Political Campaign

Marc A. Genest

Insurrections often build for years, as the number of protests and violent confrontations escalate tensions, setting the stage for open rebellion. This slow, simmering revolt epitomized the decade leading up to the American War for Independence. During the 1760s radicals in Boston repeatedly tried to entice British authorities to overreact to their protests. Despite the best efforts of the militants, the city remained firmly under the control of the British Crown. During this time, however, Boston's revolutionary leaders began designing and implementing a strategy to defeat the British in the battle of ideas and perceptions. The rebels' communication plan depended on their ability to accomplish two critical tasks. First, they needed a coherent and marketable message to justify the revolt against Britain. Second, a communications network had to be built to ensure the rebel viewpoint dominated the information environment.

The Americans continued to refine their radical political narrative and the communications channels expanded during the revolt, but the essential groundwork was laid years before the first shot was fired in Lexington. In the words of John Adams, "The revolution was in the minds of the people . . . before a drop of blood was shed at Lexington."[1] All the rebels needed to do was wait for the right incident to put their communication plan into action.

The ideal opportunity arrived on the bitterly cold evening of March 5, 1770. British sentries guarding the Customs House on King Street became targets of some rabble-rousers looking for an excuse to vent their frustrations over British rule. A crowd gathered and began insulting the sentries. By most accounts the soldiers acted with remarkable restraint, doing their best to ignore the taunts. Nonetheless, as the crowd grew, it became more aggressive. Several began flinging snowballs and then bricks at the guards. Around 8 p.m. one of the sentries had had enough and struck a particularly aggressive local on the side of the head.

The crowd seized the moment. Some surrounded the offending soldier while others ran to nearby churches to sound the alarm. Bells, the public alarm for fire, rang across the city. Over three hundred people quickly assembled but mysteriously brought sticks and clubs instead of water buckets and blankets. It is as if the incident were preplanned, with locals prepared for a fight rather than a fire. The sentries called for reinforcements. Eight more soldiers, led by Capt. Thomas Preston, soon arrived. Preston drew his sword, ordered his men to fix bayonets, and repeatedly commanded the mob to "clear the way." He issued a final warning: "Boys stand off or we shall wound you, you had better stand off." Instead, the mob hurled snowballs, rocks, and coal at the soldiers. Several sentries opened fire, killing three instantly and wounding several more, two mortally. Thereafter civil unrest in Boston exploded.

American revolutionaries soon labeled the event "the Boston Massacre" and considered it the beginning of colonial Boston's uprising against the British Empire. The rebels had finally manufactured an incident that would ignite a shockingly successful rebellion against the most powerful empire of the day.[2]

Other incidents followed: the *Gaspee* affair in 1772 (the looting of a British customs schooner), the Boston Tea Party in late 1773 (the looting of British tea imports), and other confrontations that American insurgents manufactured to incite self-destructive British responses that would weaken loyalties to the crown. Thus, a radical political minority transformed street brawls and looting into a vehicle for rebellion.

The rebels built their uprising on four pillars that remain essential for any political campaign. First, campaigns require a standard-bearer or a group of individuals willing to lead the political battle. Skilled candidates or messengers are necessary to deliver persuasive arguments and convince others to adopt their cause. It is also important to recruit credible messengers such as established community leaders whose opinions are already widely respected. Second, marketable messages must be constructed to resonate with a significant percentage of the population. The most fruitful political campaigns are those that identify and exploit legitimate grievances. Grievances enable leaders to inflame popular passions and attract supporters. Third, spreading the word to attract support requires gaining control over the major communications outlets. Finally, an effective political campaign requires an organization capable of managing operations, crafting strategies, and responding to new developments. The rebels became skilled operatives in all these areas.

Samuel Adams: Rebel Campaign Manager

Rebellions against great powers are difficult under any circumstances, and they often fail. The American Revolution could not have succeeded without the many remarkable people attracted to the cause. Effective political campaigns require individuals who are willing and able to lead the way. At its very essence, politics is about converting ideas into action. This conversion process depends on people who can marshal the power of ideas to inspire people to act when they otherwise would not do so. Leaders are the architects and artisans of politics. Without them, political movements cannot be built.

A diverse array of highly skilled and dedicated individuals, including John Adams, John Hancock, James Otis, Patrick Henry, Joseph Warren, and Paul Revere, risked their lives to play critical roles in the initial stages of the uprising in the Massachusetts Bay Colony. One person is especially worthy of highlighting—Samuel Adams, the unofficial campaign manager of the first stage of the American Revolution.[3] London's annotated list of the Continental Congress's instigators behind the boycott of British merchandise labeled Samuel Adams as "the principal spring and manager of plots and conspiracies against the State."[4]

Adams played two essential roles in initiating and sustaining the insurrection. First, he used his formidable gifts as a political philosopher and essayist to produce some of the most provocative and highly respected intellectual arguments justifying the rebellion. In many ways he was born for this role. Adams studied political theory at Harvard College and wrote his master's thesis on "Whether it be lawful to resist the Supreme Magistrate, if the Commonwealth cannot be otherwise preserved."[5]

By the 1760s Samuel Adams was an influential and well-known member of the Massachusetts House of Representatives. At the outset of the uprising, he used his education in political theory to make the case against British authority. Samuel Adams circulated letters and pamphlets throughout the colonies promoting his radical positions regarding the rights of colonial subjects. His influential 1772 essay, "The Rights of Colonists," drew heavily on Thomas Hobbes, John Locke, and other great political philosophers to legitimize and defend the insurrection. His sharp pen spared neither Parliament nor King George III; he wrote that Parliament "has no right to absolute, arbitrary power over the lives and fortunes of the people" and that even the king "cannot justly take from any man any part of his property, without his consent in person or by his representative."[6]

Adams assumed a far less highbrow demeanor in his other role as the chief political agitator or spinmaster of the rebellion. In the weeks and months leading up to the Boston Massacre, he produced a steady stream of articles in the *Boston Gazette* accusing British troops of committing "piping hot atrocities" against the good towns-folk.[7] The point of the propaganda campaign was evident: Adams and his coconspirators sought to exacerbate the already tense relationship between British authorities and the Massachusetts Bay colonists.

Adams also had an uncanny knack of positioning himself in the right place at the right time. The day after the Boston Massacre a large group of concerned citizens met at Boston's Faneuil Hall, where they formed a committee to investigate the incident and made Adams the chairman. The committee immediately demanded what he had been advocating since the arrival of British forces, that British governor Thomas Hutchinson order the removal of all troops from Boston.[8] When the governor refused, the propaganda onslaught escalated. Within a week the committee issued a report that offered a biased account of the Boston Massacre. Soon afterward "A Short Narrative of the Horrid Massacre" was printed by order of the town of Boston. Adams later used its title to coin the phrase "Boston Massacre"—a catchy sound bite to rally the public.

With tensions mounting, Governor Hutchinson finally agreed to remove British troops to Castle Island in Boston Harbor. Back in London, Prime Minister Lord North mockingly referred to the two British regiments exiled to the middle of the harbor as "Sam Adams' Regiments."[9] Throughout the prewar period Adams played a key role as the chief propagandist. Often operating behind the scenes, he and his collaborators orchestrated well-coordinated and efficient propaganda campaigns. They exploited local grievances and wrapped the rebel cause in eloquent political rhetoric that justified their actions and mobilized popular support. In 1768 Hutchinson's predecessor, Governor Francis Bernard, had already identified Samuel Adams as "the most dangerous man in Massachusetts, a man dedicated to the perpetrations of mischief." Hutchinson later called Adams "the Grand Incendiary" and the "master of the Puppets."[10]

Winning the Message Battle

The most adroit political rhetoric is a careful blend of intellectual and emotional arguments calculated to resonate with specific audiences. The rebels tailored their message to attract two important demographic groups: elites at home and abroad and the general population of the American colonies.

To attract support from political and intellectual elites living in the colonies as well as Europe, rebel leaders framed their narrative as a legitimate protest movement. They portrayed themselves as loyal subjects forced to stand against a tyrannical Parliament that wantonly violated their rights. Their reliance on traditional values grounded in English law and classical political philosophy immunized them against British accusations that ruffians ruled the streets of Boston. Rebel leaders needed to make clear that Bostonians were not hooligans. Instead, the colonists were civilized people standing up for their rights as British citizens. The rebels understood that effective political propaganda was vital to galvanize colonialists while simultaneously undercutting British popular support for the war. Boston leaders, such as Samuel Adams, John Adams, James Otis, and Dr. Joseph Warren, constructed political arguments to attract British intellectuals. Edmund Burke, the great conservative British philosopher and member of Parliament, was one of the first to empathize with the colonists.

Burke argued against the British use of force, preferring a negotiated settlement. According to Burke, Americans were merely defending their inalienable rights as Englishmen. "Taxation without representation" was a principle codified in the 1689 English Bill of Rights, which forbade the imposition of taxes without the consent of Parliament. This principle was the foundation of the British parliamentary system, so the demands of the colonists were not unreasonable.[11] Burke's stirring comments helped form the Whig Party's position toward British colonial policy.

The second set of arguments rested on pragmatic appeals intended to sway colonists to rebel against British authorities. To incite the public, the revolutionaries encapsulated their justification for rebellion in sharp slogans like "Taxation without representation is tyranny" and "Give me liberty or give me death." They made the case for revolution in simple terms that focused on the so-called tyrannical acts of British authorities.

The rebels needed a powerful grievance to rally public support for their cause, but living conditions in the colonies were better than those in Britain. White males living in the American colonies enjoyed more liberties, paid lower taxes, owned more land, and had a much higher literacy rate than did their counterparts living in Britain.[12] Moreover, Britain had imposed the taxes to defray the massive costs of defending the colonies during the French and Indian War (1754–63). Many British leaders and even many colonists considered the rebels ungrateful louts. British chancellor of the exchequer Charles Townshend echoed these sentiments before Parliament in support of the Stamp Act, which raised taxes on the colonists. He called the colonists "children planted by our care, nourished up by our indulgence and protected by our arms—will they grudge to contribute their mite?"[13]

The rebels evaded these inconvenient facts by focusing on specific imperial policies that angered most colonists. The British unwittingly played into this strategy with taxes that antagonized colonial elites. The 1765 Stamp Act imposed a tax by requiring all legal documents, newspapers, magazines, and even playing cards be printed on paper stamped with an official seal. While designed to offset the costs of British troops stationed to protect the colonists, the act infuriated the people most capable of leading a tax revolt.[14] It was no coincidence that elites involved in publishing newspapers and magazines, as well as the lawyers whose job it was to produce legal documents, were the first and most vocal opponents of the new laws. Attorneys such as John Adams, Patrick Henry, and James Otis and newspaper publishers like Benjamin Edes, John Gill, and Isaiah Thomas were drawn into the conflict by these threats to their livelihood. Their professions and notable reputations within Boston society allowed them to exert considerable influence over public opinion. These were the men who led the charge and crafted many of the arguments that would become the mainstay of the American Revolution.

The British also alienated American merchants, one of the wealthiest groups in colonial society and so most capable of funding an insurgency. The Townshend Acts infuriated them by imposing external taxes on goods such as tea and paper.[15] Further fueling tensions, the Indemnity Act of 1767 allowed customs officials to search shops and homes for smuggled wares, a widespread source of income in the Massachusetts Bay Colony. Britain undertook these measures because colonial juries rarely convicted their peers on smuggling charges.

These highly unpopular measures propelled many wealthy and powerful colonists into the rebel camp. For example, the Sugar Act and Townshend Acts incensed John Hancock because they cut his business profits. Hancock's radicalization occurred in June 1768, when British officials charged him with smuggling and seized his ship, *Liberty*. Although the British later dropped the charges, the event drew him closer to Samuel Adams, who then recruited Hancock to the rebel cause.[16] One of the most affluent and influential men in all thirteen colonies, Hancock placed his considerable wealth and influence into the hands of Samuel Adams and the insurgency.

Later in 1774 the British again unwittingly exacerbated tensions by passing the Coercive Acts, which closed Boston Harbor, ended elections, and made all councilors and assistants in the Massachusetts Bay Colony subject to appointment by the Crown. The colonists soon labeled these laws the "intolerable acts." Most unpopular of all, the British passed the Quartering Act, which forced Bostonians to house British troops. Britain had become a grievance-making machine, which the rebels fully exploited.

Communications Outlets

Legitimate grievances and appealing political rhetoric were important, but as with any political movement, they required a marketing mechanism to rally the public. The rebel campaign relied primarily on four essential communications outlets: committees of correspondence, newspapers, pamphlets, and speeches.

Committees of correspondence, formed in towns across New England, connected rebel leaders throughout the colonies. They were perfect mechanisms to deliver subversive propaganda. Meetings were commonly conducted in secret. Most groups maintained a flexible organizational structure, allowing each to "function in a modular fashion by breaking itself into sub-committees for its central purpose of composing communications."[17] These groups played a vital role by providing crucial information, and at times disinformation, to cities and towns outside Boston.

Samuel Adams formed the first committee of correspondence in 1764, when he organized letter-writing campaigns by friends, family, and acquaintances living outside Boston to encourage resistance to British customs enforcement and the prohibition of American paper money. Initially, committees of correspondence were formed on an ad hoc basis, starting and disbanding in response to specific British provocations. This informal and decentralized nature kept them outside the purview of British authorities.

The Boston Massacre precipitated a proliferation of committees of correspondence. For the insurrection to succeed, Samuel Adams and the insurgents had to ensure that their version of the event became widely publicized. After the Boston Massacre they raced to spread the word, knowing that the first account would remain the most powerful in the public mind. So they formed new committees of correspondence to spread the news of the "horrid massacre" and stoke anti-British resentment throughout the colonies.

In 1772 another Boston committee of correspondence was organized to publish a circular letter written by Samuel Adams to all the towns in Massachusetts as well as "the World." The letter excoriated a new British policy that undermined the colonists' leverage over their leaders by mandating that the Crown, not the colonial legislature, pay the governor and judges of the Massachusetts Bay Colony. More than 260 towns formed committees and replied to the circular letter.[18]

By 1774 nearly all the colonies had joined the communications network, and more committees formed at the town and county levels. The correspondence helped build a sense of community among the colonies, allowing them to share common grievances and negotiate cohesive responses to British authorities. The First Continental Congress could not have been established in 1774 without the groundwork laid by the committees of correspondence coordinating different parts of British America to speak with one voice.

The second important rebel channel of communications was more conventional but even more effective. Americans were among the most literate people in the world, and their thirst for local, regional, and international news led to the proliferation of newspapers and pamphlets throughout the colonies. In reflecting on the early period of the rebellion, John Adams, a second cousin of Samuel, highlighted the critical role of the press in shaping public opinion from 1760 to 1775: "The pamphlets, newspapers in all the colonies, ought to be consulted during that period, to ascertain the steps by which the public opinion was enlightened and informed concerning the authority of parliament over the colonies."[19] Much of Samuel Adams' most influential work appeared in newsprint around Boston.

The publishers Benjamin Edes and John Gill, as well as Samuel and John Adams, directly connected the rebels to Boston's most influential media outlet, the *Boston Gazette* newspaper. Edes and Gill allegedly ceded editorial control over the paper to Samuel Adams, who wrote many of its pseudonymous articles.[20] On September 3, 1769, John Adams wrote in his diary, "Spent the remainder of the evening and supped with Mr. Otis, in company with Mr. Adams, Mr. William Davies, and Mr. John Gill. The night spent in preparing for the next day's newspaper—a curious employment, cooking up paragraphs, articles, occurrences, &c., working the political engine!"[21]

Governor Hutchinson complained, "For news I refer to you to Edes and Gill. I am grown callous and all they say about me makes no impression. Otis and the two Adams, Cooper & Church go regularly every Saturday in the afternoon to set the Press."[22] In his opinion Edes and Gill "may be said to be no more than mercenary printers, but they have been and still are the trumpeters of sedition."[23] Back in London many considered the *Boston Gazette* to be the most subversive paper in the colonies, christening it "the weekly dung barge" and labeling Benjamin Edes, Samuel Adams, and all associated with the paper as "Trumpeters of Sedition."[24]

This vitriolic response of British authorities was well placed. The *Boston Gazette* served as a mouthpiece for Samuel Adams and those determined to drum up public support for the insurrection. Like most effective information campaigns, the propaganda was an entertaining mix of fact, exaggeration, and outright fiction. The *Gazette* article on the Boston Massacre is a case in point. Samuel Adams, the probable author, laid full blame on the British soldiers. Adams defended Crispus Attucks, one of the first killed, against reports of his complicity in the violence, writing that Attucks "had as good a right to carry a stick, even a bludgeon, as the soldier who shot him had to be armed with musket and ball."[25] The *Gazette*'s March 12, 1770, issue portrayed the soldiers as undisciplined hooligans bent on hurting innocent bystanders:

> On hearing the noise, one Samuel Atwood came up to see what was the matter; and entering the alley from dock square, heard the latter part of the combat; and when the boys had dispersed he met the ten or twelve soldiers aforesaid rushing down the alley towards the square and asked them if they intended to murder people? They answered Yes, by G-d, root and branch! With that one of them struck Mr. Atwood with a club which was repeated by another; and being unarmed, he turned to go off and received a wound on the left shoulder which reached the bone and gave him much pain.[26]

The New World's most famous journalist, Benjamin Franklin, aptly described both the power of the press and Samuel Adams' communication strategy when he quipped, "And we now find, that it is not only right to strike while the iron is hot, but that it may be very practicable to heat it by continually striking."[27] Samuel Adams used the *Gazette* to wage unrelenting attacks against the Crown, composing at least sixty pseudonymous articles. Adams' writing style blended polemical attacks with reasoned legal and philosophical arguments. He defined his enemy from the outset, always portraying the British in the most negative light possible. As he wrote, "It is a good Maxim in Politicks as well as in War to put & keep the Enemy in the Wrong."[28] A frequent target of Adams' propaganda assaults, the exasperated Governor Hutchinson asked, "[Is] there a greater incendiary than he in the King's dominions[?]"[29] There is little doubt that Hutchinson knew the answer to his question.

The final channel of communications, available to any political campaign, was oratory. Samuel Adams, John Adams, Dr. Joseph Warren, James Otis, and Patrick Henry were all gifted speakers. In the 1760s James Otis, a prominent lawyer, delivered powerful courtroom arguments defending Boston merchants against the despised writs of assistance issued by British customs officials. He challenged the legality of the search warrants, labeling them the "worst instrument of arbitrary power." Otis also coined the slogan "Taxation without representation is tyranny."[30]

The widely respected physician Joseph Warren was one of the most talented speakers of all. On March 5, 1772, he stood before a huge crowd to memorialize the second anniversary of the Boston Massacre. He railed against the "ruinous consequences of standing armies to free communities . . . and we, my fellow citizens, have seen, we have felt the tragical effects!" He warned the crowd that "the fatal fifth of March, 1770, can never be forgotten. . . . The horrors of that dreadful night are but too deeply impressed on our hearts." Warren evoked gruesome images that doubtlessly remained on the minds of the audience for years: "Language is too feeble to paint the emotion of our souls, when our streets were stained with the blood of our brethren—when our ears were wounded by the groans of the dying, and our eyes were tormented with the sight of the mangled bodies of the dead."[31] The rebels made sure that the speech appeared in the *Boston Gazette* and was reprinted annually on the anniversary of the Boston Massacre.

Just before the Boston Tea Party on December 16, 1773, Samuel Adams and Joseph Warren delivered addresses at the Old South Meeting House before a throng of hundreds, if not thousands, of people.[32] By many accounts their speeches were instrumental in convincing the crowd to ransack the three ships and throw more than three hundred chests of British-taxed tea into the harbor. The estimated value of the cargo was £15,000 or roughly $3.5 million in today's dollars.

Therefore, even in the early stages of the Boston uprising, the rebels had a diverse array of eloquent and charismatic orators who articulated the principles behind the rebellion and rallied the crowds to the cause. As the insurgency grew and spread to other colonies, the number of great communicators expanded exponentially as

Benjamin Franklin, Thomas Jefferson, Patrick Henry, Alexander Hamilton, Fisher Ames, Richard Henry Lee, and a slew of other gifted speakers fed the revolt.

A Covert Campaign Organization: The Sons of Liberty

All the speeches, articles, and legal arguments would have amounted to little without a campaign organization to transform these ideas into a successful political movement. The role of the Sons of Liberty and particularly its Boston chapter was critical. Like any covert group, the Sons of Liberty concealed their organizational structure, the names of their leaders, and the way they operated. Enough evidence remains to make a compelling case that the organization formed the centerpiece of the rebellion. This well-organized, skillfully led, often ruthless, and exceptionally competent group of insurgents drove the public agenda, intimidated foes, and out-foxed British authorities.

The Sons of Liberty originated from a group known as the Loyal Nine, who joined in protest against the 1765 Stamp Act. While Samuel Adams was not publicly associated with the Loyal Nine, his friend Benjamin Edes and cousin Henry Bass were founding members.[33] The Sons plucked their name from the debate on the Stamp Act in Parliament. Speaking in defense of the colonists, Isaac Barre, a member of the Whig Party in Parliament, cautioned that "these Sons of Liberty" would bitterly oppose the Stamp Act. The Sons of Liberty took its name from Barre's words and rapidly organized into chapters.[34] Soon its activities became the focus of pamphlets, newspapers, and people across the colonies. Some groups created their own versions of the title, calling themselves the "True Born Sons of Liberty" or "Sons of Freedom." Women formed chapters called the "Daughters of Liberty." The moniker conferred a certain cult status to members and the self-appointed authority to summon people to public meetings at a "Liberty Tree" or "Liberty Pole." Community elites secretly led these groups. As a testament to their effectiveness, British authorities labeled them as "The Sons of Violence" and "The Sons of Iniquity."[35]

Because the covert nature of the work required operatives to shield their organizational makeup from both authorities and the public, the Boston chapter of the Sons of Liberty had a political and a military wing, each tasked with separate responsibilities. The political wing provided the public face of the movement, operating within the legal system. It was dominated by many of the social and economic elite of Boston. Samuel Adams, John Adams, Dr. Joseph Warren, John Hancock, and James Otis as community leaders eschewed association with the less "respectable" activities of the Sons of Liberty. Individuals like Samuel Adams and John Hancock used their positions as representatives to the Massachusetts colonial legislature to make the philosophical case against British colonial policies. These leaders made speeches, wrote articles, and published pamphlets articulating the principles of the uprising. They also financed the insurgency. John Hancock and James Swan contributed substantial sums to fund day-to-day operations. By the 1780s Swan's financial commitment to the Boston uprising and, later, to the war effort led to his financial ruin.

The military wing of the Sons of Liberty supplied the violence and intimidation. All rebellions entail a degree of thuggery to coerce opponents and keep followers in line. Samuel Adams frequently incited the mobs with stories printed in Boston newspapers and circulated by the committees of correspondence. The military wing carried out a campaign of intimidation that included burning effigies of British tax administrators, tarring and feathering local officials, and setting fire to the property of authorities while forcing the owner to watch. As with any uprising, uncontrolled acts of violence and vandalism also occurred. For the most part, however, the violence was discriminate, focusing on specific targets symbolizing British authority.

One of the first coercive acts committed by the Sons of Liberty occurred on August 14, 1765, against Andrew Oliver, the new distributor of stamps for Massachusetts. The Sons of Liberty communicated their displeasure with his choice of occupation. On a downtown Boston tree, they hung his effigy along with a devil climbing out of a large boot. The boot represented John Stuart, the Earl of Bute, who was prime minister under King George III. The symbolism linked Oliver to the unpopular Stamp Act. British authorities ordered the sheriffs to remove the display, but they refused to intervene against the large, unruly mob gathered around the tree. When the throng proceeded to Oliver's house, some beheaded the effigy and threw stones at the residence. Oliver and his family fled in fear for their lives. The mob then moved to nearby Fort Hill and lit a huge fire to burn the headless effigy. Later that night, the Sons of Liberty sent a group led by Ebenezer Mackintosh to loot Oliver's abandoned home. Oliver apparently fled Boston the next day, signaling the total success of the intimidation campaign.[36] British authorities had dared not interfere even though it was widely understood that Samuel Adams had orchestrated the thuggery. Andrew Oliver's brother, Peter, who served as the last royal chief justice of Massachusetts, encapsulated the British authorities' view, writing that "If he wished to draw the Picture of the Devil, that he would get Sam Adams to sit for him."[37]

Criminal behavior like the Oliver episode did not occur spontaneously but was part of a strategy to augment political protests with systematic intimidation and violence. To wage a successful insurgency, rebel leaders had to create or tap into networks to organize effective coercive actions. Samuel Adams exploited four crucial strategies to recruit, motivate, and organize his cadres.

First, Adams used his position as tax collector to assemble a group of men he could organize and manage to carry out the less seemly acts needed to wage rebellion. For example, Ebenezer Mackintosh, one of the first to be targeted by the "rebel tax assessor," soon turned coat to become a key leader of the Sons of Liberty's military wing. The original tax records listed Mackintosh in default of his taxes, yet Adams withdrew the warrant issued against Mackintosh despite no receipt of the back taxes. Two days later Mackintosh was terrorizing Andrew Oliver. Apparently, this was the beginning of a beautiful relationship between Mackintosh and Adams.[38]

Second, Adams' recruitment of Mackintosh was part of a grander plan to assemble a group of thugs willing to and capable of carrying out such acts of violence. While Adams developed the strategy and arranged the meetings, John Hancock footed the bill. They hosted a series of dinners known as the "union feast" between rival Boston gangs. There was a long history of animosity between the South Enders, led by Ebenezer Mackintosh, and the North Enders, led by Henry Swift. Both gangs were known for their tough and lawless behavior, ideal characteristics for the military wing of the Sons of Liberty. Over food and ale Adams and Hancock convinced both gangs to put aside their differences to focus their aggression on the "lobsterbacks" and British authorities. Mackintosh and Swift soon received "fancy new uniforms and speaking trumpets," and the military wing of the Sons of Liberty was born.[39]

Third, Adams exploited existing municipal organizations to position rebels to incite insurrection and respond quickly to opportunities that arose. For example, the Sons of Liberty used the fire warden system to summon supporters during the Boston Massacre. Ringing church bells ostensibly warned of fire; in fact, the alarm also signaled the Sons of Liberty attached to the fire brigades that something was afoot. Both Samuel Adams and John Hancock were leaders of fire companies in Boston. So were other conspirators such as Ebenezer Mackintosh.[40] The fire wardens system formed an ideal cover for conspirators to meet secretly and to use fires to coerce others. At fires, secret watchwords allowed them to identify other members.[41]

The fourth organizational strategy combined Adams' interests in music and revolution. The son of a church deacon, by all accounts with a beautiful singing voice on public display in church every Sunday, Adams gradually built a reputation around Boston as a skilled singer and choir director. Royal Chief Justice Peter Oliver conceded that Adams had "a good voice & was a Master in vocal Musick" but recognized that "this genius he improved, by instituting singing Societys of Mechanicks where he presided and embraced such Opportunities to ye inculcating sedition." Adams formed "Societys of Mechanicks" or choirs to serve as fronts to organize rebel cells throughout Boston to build the military wing of the Sons of Liberty. The choirs were made up of artisans and tradesmen, the very people Adams needed to perform his more muscular overtures. Reportedly, the recitals improved each year, with choirmaster Adams conducting their "Psalm singing" as well as arranging their covert performances against the British. Chief Justice Oliver labeled them "Mr. Saml. Adams' Psalm-singing Myrmidons [warriors]."[42]

The division of the Sons of Liberty into political and military wings reflected shrewd operational and strategic planning. The leaders understood that to be effective the revolt required two faces, with each appearing distinct from the other. People like the Adams cousins and Hancock knew that to be taken seriously by elites in both America and England, they had to separate themselves from the most unseemly acts committed by the Sons of Liberty. They defended the principles behind the revolt without publicly condoning the worst of the violence. This strategy was critical, especially in the initial stages of the insurgency, when they needed to appear as legitimate spokesmen for the cause of liberty. Meanwhile, the military wing required secrecy to allow members to undermine British authorities and punish loyalists. This arrangement worked splendidly.

Conclusion

The Sons of Liberty pioneered an organizational structure emulated by such successful independence movements as the Irish Republican Army and Algeria's National Liberation Front. In many respects Samuel Adams and his coconspirators invented modern insurgency strategy with four essential contributions.

First, they understood that the American Revolution was fundamentally a struggle for the allegiance of the colonists. As John Adams wrote, "This radical change in the principles, opinions, sentiments, and affections of the people, was the real American Revolution."[43] Accordingly, the revolutionaries implemented a strategy to defeat the British in the battle of ideas and perceptions. So they focused on estranging American hearts and minds from British loyalty. In this process the Boston Massacre became a formative event. The rebels' opportunistic exploitation of British missteps allowed them to promote their views. The Boston insurgents manufactured confrontations like the Boston Massacre to incite a self-defeating overreaction by their enemies. When the abused British guards fired into the crowd, Samuel Adams was ready to shape the narrative of the "Horrid Massacre" in favor of the radicals. The ensuing interaction between British authorities and the agitators strengthened the rebel cause and weakened the ties that bound colonists to the Crown.

The second contribution to contemporary insurgency strategy involved the Americans' resourceful use of multiple channels of communications to win the information war against the British. Rebels recruited well-respected community leaders who mixed intellectual arguments and emotional appeals to attract people from diverse social and economic backgrounds. The revolutionaries then built a covert communications network of committees of correspondence to distribute the first accounts of controversial events, allowing the rebels to shape public opinion. This network proved so effective that soon other colonies formed committees of correspondence that together helped create a sense of community among the thirteen colonies. Newspapers and pamphlets also played vital roles in the propaganda war. Much of Samuel Adams' most influential work appeared in print around Boston. These pamphlets and newspaper articles were reprinted and distributed to towns outside Boston and other colonies as the rebels methodically built support and spread the rebellion.

The third innovation relevant for modern insurgency strategy was to divide political and military responsibilities into separate wings of the organization. The Boston chapter of the Sons of Liberty was the first insurgent group to make this deliberate organizational split. Highly respected and influential men like John Adams, Samuel Adams, Dr. Joseph Warren, and James Otis led the political wing of the Sons of Liberty and provided the public face of the revolt. They crafted the intellectual arguments, wrote newspaper articles, distributed pamphlets, and gave stirring speeches to justify the uprising and build public support. Meanwhile, the military wing executed covert operations to disrupt and weaken British control over the Massachusetts Bay Colony. Ebenezer Mackintosh, Henry Swift, and their bands of ruffians carried out a relentless campaign of violence and intimidation, making it impossible for the British to govern Boston. Samuel Adams and his fellow rebel leaders carefully guided both wings to ensure that all operations were coordinated to propel the rebellion forward.

Finally, the rebels never lost sight of the critical point that the American uprising against the British was a true political campaign. They built their rebellion on four pillars that remain essential for any political campaign: they recruited highly skilled leaders, developed powerful messages, created a reliable communications network, and established an organization capable of transforming ideas into successful action. Samuel Adams and his collaborators provided the inspirational and organizational talent necessary to feed and nurture the revolution. Their efforts formed the first American political campaign and helped deliver independence to the American colonies.

Notes

1. John Adams to Thomas Jefferson, August 24, 1815, in *The Works of John Adams, Second President of the United States*, ed. Charles Francis Adams (Boston: Little Brown, 1856), 10:172–73.

2. Robert Goddard, testimony, March 6, 1770, in Richard Ward, Thomas Dawes, and Samuel Gray, "Deposition about Boston Massacre," American Revolutionary War Manuscripts Collection, Boston Public Library, https://archive.org/stream /depositionaboutbo00ward/39999063782518#page/n0/mode/1up; John [Leachland], testimony, March 6, 1770, in Boston Registry Department, "Records Relating

to the Early History of Boston," Boston Public Library, https://archive.org/stream /recordsrelatingt18bost#page/2/mode/2up.

3. William V. Wells, *The Life and Public Services of Samuel Adams, Being a Narrative of His Acts and Opinions, and of His Agency in Producing and Forwarding the American Revolution* (Boston: Little, Brown, 1865), 2:250.

4. Quote found in the *Massachusetts Historical Society Proceedings* 32 (1897–99): 140; Charles W. Akers, "Review: Sam Adams—and Much More," *New England Quarterly* 47, no. 1 (1974): 120–31; Pauline Maier, "Coming to Terms with Samuel Adams," *American Historical Review* 81, no. 1 (1976): 12–37.

5. Commencement Theses, Quaestions, and Orders of Exercises, 1642–1818, Section II Quaestions, 1653–1791, Harvard University Archives, http://oasis.lib.harvard .edu/oasis/deliver/~hua03010#theses.

6. Samuel Adams, "The Rights of the Colonists, A List of Violations of Rights and a Letter of Correspondence," November 20, 1772, in *The Writings of Samuel Adams*, ed. Harry Alonzo Cushing (New York: G. P. Putnam's Sons, 1906), 2:357.

7. John C. Miller, *Sam Adams Pioneer in Propaganda* (Stanford: Stanford University Press, 1936), 174.

8. Wells, *Life and Public Services*, 1:323.

9. Richard Frothingham, "The Sam Adams Regiments in the Town of Boston," *Atlantic Monthly* 10 (August 1862): 195–96. See also Mark Puls, *Samuel Adams: Father of the American Revolution* (New York: Palgrave Macmillan, 2006), 105.

10. Quoted in Dennis B. Fradin, *Samuel Adams: The Father of American Independence* (New York: Clarion Books, 1998), 52; Carl Becker, *The Eve of Revolution: A Chronicle of the Breach with England* (New Haven, CT: Yale University Press, 1920), 175.

11. Bernard Bailyn, *The Ideological Origins of the American Revolution*, enlarged ed. (Cambridge, MA: Belknap Press, 1992), 146.

12. Samuel Eliot Morrison, *Prehistory to 1789*, vol. 1 of *The Oxford History of the American People* (New York: Meridan, 1994), 235–47; Kenneth A. Lockridge, *Literacy in Colonial New England: An Enquiry into the Social Context of Literacy in the Early Modern West* (New York: W. W. Norton, 1974) 13; Lawrence A. Cremin, *The American Education: The Colonial Experience, 1607–1783* (New York: Harper & Row, 1970).

13. *Proceedings and Debates of the British Parliaments respecting North America* (London: Parliament, 1966), 2:13.

14. For a great overview of the crisis, see Edmund S. Morgan and Helen M. Morgan, *The Stamp Act Crisis: Prologue to Revolution* (Chapel Hill: University of North Carolina Press, 1962).

15. Benjamin Woods Labaree, *The Boston Tea Party* (Boston: Northeastern University Press, 1979), 15–37; John C. Miller, *Sam Adams: Pioneer in Propaganda* (Boston: Little, Brown, 1936), 57–58.

16. William Tudor, *The Life of James Otis of Massachusetts: Containing Also, Notices of Some Contemporary Characters and Events from the Year 1760–1775* (Boston: Wells and Lilly, 1823), 262.

17. William B. Warner, "The Invention of a Public Machine for Revolutionary Emotion: The Boston Committee of Correspondence" (University of California–Santa Barbara, 2007), 20, https://escholarship.org/uc/item/8710d7mf.

18. Samuel Adams to James Warren, November 4, 1772, in the Warren-Adams Papers, Massachusetts Historical Society, http://www.masshist.org/database/438; John K. Alexander, *Samuel Adams: America's Revolutionary Politician* (Lanham, MD: Rowman & Littlefield, 2002), 52–55.

19. Adams to Jefferson, August 24, 1815.

20. Eric Burns, *Infamous Scribblers* (New York: Public Affairs, 2007), 141.

21. John Adams, diary entry from September 3, 1769, in Adams Family Papers, Massachusetts Historical Society, 9, https://www.masshist.org/digitaladams/archive/popup?id=D15&page=D15_9.

22. Rollo G. Silver, "Benjamin Edes, Trumpeter of Sedition," *Papers of the Bibliographical Society of America*, 3rd Quarter 1953, 11.

23. Quoted in Frothingham, "Sam Adams Regiments," 192.

24. See Bernard to Hillsborough, January 25, 1769, in George Bancroft, *History of the United States* (Boston: Little, Brown, 1854), 6:251.

25. Vindex, "To the Printers," *Boston-Gazette, and Country Journal*, December 31, 1770, in Annotated Newspapers of Harbottle Dorr Jr., Massachusetts Historical Society, 346–47, http://www.masshist.org/dorr/volume/3/sequence/386.

26. "Boston, March 12," *Boston-Gazette, and Country Journal*, March 12, 1770, in Annotated Newspapers of Dorr, 60, http://www.masshist.org/dorr/volume/3/sequence/101.

27. Benjamin Franklin, *The Writings of Benjamin Franklin*, ed. Albert Henry Smith (New York: Macmillan, 1906), 7:457.

28. Samuel Adams to Richard Henry Lee, March 21, 1775, in *Writings of Samuel Adams*, 3:205–9.

29. Bancroft, *History of the United States*, 6:406.

30. Tudor, *Life of James Otis*, 76, 77, 118.

31. Joseph Warren, "Boston Massacre Oration," in John Collins Warren Papers, Massachusetts Historical Society, 28, http://www.drjosephwarren.com/2015/03/1775-boston-massacre-oration-manuscript-transcription-in-full-text, http://www.masshist.org/dorr/volume/4/sequence/1162.

32. "An Impartial Observer to Messrs Edes & Gill," *Boston-Gazette, and Country Journal*, December 2, 1773, in Annotated Newspapers of Dorr, 415; Thomas Hutchinson, "To Dartmouth. Boston 17 1773," Letterbooks of Thomas Hutchinson, Massachusetts Historical Society, 1119; Labaree, *Boston Tea Party*, 140.

33. Thomas Crafts Jr. to John Adams, February 15, 1766, Adams Papers Digital Edition, Massachusetts Historical Society, http://www.masshist.org/publications/apde/portia.php?id=PJA01d088; John Adams, diary entry January 15, 1766, in *Diary and Autobiography of John Adams*, ed. L. H. Butterfield (Cambridge, MA: Belknap Press, 1962), 1:294.

34. *Proceedings and Debates*, 2:16.

35. Hutchinson to Dartmouth, June 1773, in Letterbooks of Hutchinson, 1088.

36. Hutchinson to Milton, August 16, 1765, in Letterbooks of Hutchinson, 291–95; *Boston-Gazette, and Country Journal*, December 23, 1765, in Annotated Newspapers of Dorr, 302, http://www.masshist.org/dorr/volume/1/sequence/307.

37. Douglass Adair and John A. Schutz, eds., *Peter Oliver's "Origin and Progress of the American Rebellion"* (Stanford, CA: Stanford University Press, 1961), 145–46.

38. Alfred F. Young, "Ebenezer Mackintosh: Boston's Captain General of the Liberty Tree," in *Revolutionary Founders: Rebels, Radicals, and Reformers in the Making of the Nation*, ed. Alfred F. Young, Gary B. Nash, and Ray Raphael (New York: Vintage Books, 2012), 23; Richard Archer, *As If an Enemy's Country: The British Occupation of Boston and the Origins of Revolution* (New York: Oxford University Press, 2010), 44; Russell Bourne, *Cradle of Violence: How Boston's Waterfront Mobs Ignited the American Revolution* (Hoboken, NJ: John Wiley and Sons, 2006), 102.

39. Harlow Giles Unger, *American Tempest: How the Boston Tea Party Sparked a Revolution* (Cambridge, MA: Da Capo Press, 2011), 87; Bob Rupert, "The Seed from Which the Sons of Liberty Grew," *Journal of the American Revolution*, December 8, 2014, https://allthingsliberty.com/2014/12/the-seed-from-which-the-sons-of-liberty-grew/; Benjamin L. Carp, "Fire of Liberty: Fire Fighters, Urban Voluntary Culture and the Revolutionary Movement," *William and Mary Quarterly* 58, no. 4 (October 2001): 808.

40. Arthur Wellington Brayley, *A Complete History of the Boston Fire Department* (Boston: John P. Dale, 1889), 78.

41. Carp, "Fire of Liberty," 792.

42. Adair and Schutz, *Peter Oliver's Origin*, 41, 74; J. L. Bell, "You Won't Believe How Samuel Adams Recruited Sons of Liberty," *Journal of the American Revolution*, February 5, 2014, http://allthingsliberty.com/2014/02/you-wont-believe-how-samuel-adams-recruited-sons-of-liberty/#_ftn6; John Mein, "A Key to a Certain Publication," in Sparks Manuscripts, New England Papers, 10:3, Houghton Library, Harvard University, 2007, 45–47.

43. John Adams to H. Niles, 1818, in *Works of John Adams*, 10:283.

2.

Why Communications Mattered in the War of 1812

Troy Bickham

The War of 1812, more so than many conflicts, was a matter of perceptions. Most unusually, each side believed it had won. Until the final battle the fighting took place far away from population centers and so became, for most people, a virtual war portrayed in the press. By this time the Anglophone press had become global so that American and British newspapers routinely quoted each other. In a laissez-faire era without censorship, the press informed government actions and shaped public opinion on both sides of the Atlantic. Newspaper coverage influenced both elections and recruitments. Journalists magnified unexpected victories so that the strategic importance of battles came not from their military effects but from their political effects. The press grossly exaggerated the significance of single-ship engagements, while often glossing over the major battles.

On the night of August 24, 1814, Sir George Cockburn, who had just captured the US capital, surveyed the burning city. In view were the offices of the *National Intelligencer*, the government-backed newspaper that had led the American press's attacks on the British admiral, accusing him personally of brutalities (genuine and false). The papers called him "the monster, Cockburn, who is a disgrace not only to his nation, but to the whole human race."[1] Cockburn, like most British senior officers of that era, had political ambitions and was sensitive to public opinion and press accounts about him—even American newspapers, which were reprinted throughout the British Empire. The *National Intelligencer*'s editor, Joseph Gales, had already fled, but Cockburn ordered the newspaper's building burned. Several women pleaded with him to desist, fearful that the fire would take their buildings with it. Cockburn relented and ordered the destruction of just the printing press and all papers of "Dear

24

Josey" (his name for Joseph Gales), instructing his men to "be sure that all the c's are destroyed so the rascals can't abuse my name any more."[2]

Communications mattered greatly in the Anglo-American War of 1812. Fought mostly at sea and in the borderlands among the American, British, and Spanish Empires, the war was geographically distant from the belligerent nations' populations and governing centers. Problems of distance and accessibility both shaped the military struggle and allowed men and women to transform a conflict that mattered little in military terms into a major struggle in the public sphere. Compared to the casualties and duration of the French Revolutionary and Napoleonic Wars, the War of 1812 was almost insignificant.

Yet even in Britain, the war dominated the public discussion and, consequently, commanded time and energy from government leaders disproportionate to its military significance. One popular English newspaper declared in the summer of 1812, "The question of Peace or War with America takes the precedency in public importance over all other foreign news. . . . The happiness and tranquility of this country are much more closely connected with this subject, than with the victories in Spain, or the movements of contending armies in Russia."[3] The situation had changed little by the war's end. Although the peace settlement for the French wars at the Congress of Vienna transpired simultaneously, many Britons saw it as secondary to peace negotiations with the United States. As another English paper argued at the opening of the negotiations, British affairs with the United States "deserve, at present much more of our attention than any of the expected transactions [at Vienna]."[4] Thus perception, as much as action on any battlefield, determined the merit of leaders, governments, and nations, and perception was shaped by timely communications and the printed word.

Logistical Difficulties and the Power of the Press

Communications during the War of 1812 was slow and unreliable. The technologies that facilitated it (paper, ink, sail, and horses) had not changed significantly since the founding of England's New World colonies two centuries earlier. Better maps and charts facilitated travel, and the frequency of transatlantic crossings ensured a steady flow of information, but voyages were still measured in weeks and months. Dedicated riders were often available on land, but seagoing government correspondence relied on the same mixture of merchant and state vessels as private correspondents did. Even when dispatches arrived by an assigned messenger, often that messenger had traveled privately.

To stay abreast of events, the Americans and British relied on multiple channels, first and foremost, on newspapers. Cutthroat competition for readers ensured that editors went to great lengths to disseminate the latest information. Consequently, newspapers typically provided battlefront information long before official dispatches arrived. The Americans and their supporters had understood this during the American Revolution and had successfully plastered British newspapers with sympathetic accounts that had eroded British enthusiasm for that war. In 1812 both sides demonstrated their mastery of this lesson. High officials' account books and correspondence reveal their reliance on the press as a source of information. Even as president, James Madison wrote to Thomas Jefferson in early 1812 that "the Newspapers give you a sufficient insight into the measures of Congress" and regularly sent his mentor newspaper clippings.[5] This is not to suggest that readers blindly accepted anything printed as truth. Politicians, ordinary readers, public commentators, and rival editors regularly accused newspapers of lies and bias. In response to one minor affront, the *Liverpool Mercury* accused its rival in a typical dramatic fashion of "devoting a column and a half of its pages to the promulgation of as barefaced prevision of falsehood, as ever disgraced any public journal."[6]

The American and British governments had networks of informants but relied heavily on the local press, often including relevant clippings with their reports. The American delegation negotiating for peace at Ghent depended heavily on the British press for European news and information about public opinion and the disposition of their counterparts. Following the burning of Washington, Henry Clay, one of the delegates, confessed that "I tremble indeed whenever I take up a late News paper" for fear of bad news.[7] While some informants were official, working as diplomats and consuls, others were private citizens living and working in cosmopolitan port cities. The opportunity for interception made ciphers essential. These were unique to one person or a small group.[8]

By the mid-eighteenth century the Anglophone press had established itself as a commercially viable, reliable source of global information that connected port cities and towns and their respective hinterlands with the rest of the world. It was not unusual for a prime minister to read about a battle in a local newspaper before official dispatches arrived. This was almost invariably the case for members of Parliament and later Congress, who routinely cited newspapers in debates as reliable sources of information. During the war, most small towns had access both to a local weekly paper (or two) as well as subscription services to newspapers from urban centers. In consequence, a single issue of small-town Williamsburg, Ohio's *Western American* carried news from London, Tennessee, Virginia, France, Spain, New York, South Carolina, Massachusetts, Canada, Maryland, Connecticut, and Washington.[9]

That most news articles were cut and pasted from other newspapers mattered little to readers, who were more interested in timeliness—prompting editors routinely to pledge their commitment to swiftness, something reinforced in every issue by a date above external articles. The *Dublin Evening Post* highlighted that "news from America, which will be considered of some importance, reached this office yesterday. For this we are indebted to those *private* and *authentic* sources of information, which give our Paper so pre-eminent a rank in public opinion."[10] The competition for the freshest information compelled editors relentlessly to seek new sources for information. In the Caribbean, where privateers and naval vessels of all sides ravaged the normal flow of communications and goods, savvy editors turned to neutral Havana and paid privateers for American newspapers found on board enemy prizes. As the *Bahama Gazette* informed its readers in March 1813, "We are indebted to lieutenant Yates for New York papers to the 20th ult. Received by him from the prize brig Clarissa; and nearly the whole contents of this day's Gazette are taken from that file."[11]

Throughout the war, newspapers routinely printed articles from the enemy's newspapers. Canadian newspapers, particularly those in Upper Canada, relied heavily on American sources even for European news, and British newspapers regularly printed articles from the Canadian press that had reached them as reprints in American newspapers that flowed into Britain. The *York Gazette* of Upper Canada even synchronized its publication date with the arrival of American newspapers, explaining to readers in January 1812, "Circumstances have obliged us to alter the issuing day of the Gazette, which will be hereafter, ordinarily, the day after the Receipt of the U. States papers."[12]

Equally important, war information was not censored. Libel laws applied to the portrayal of individuals and were rarely enforced. When they were, the more established operations in London considered bail and fines as routine expenses, with editors running newspapers from comfortable cells provided by shareholders.[13] Newspapers unabashedly printed troop numbers and movements, casualty lists, and information on ships down to the names of the captains and number of crew and guns. Huge tables, analyzing the strengths of each side as a whole and in individual encounters, abounded. In consequence, readers and officials could be equally well informed because often they were relying on the same sources of information.

Secrecy of any major operations became all but impossible. American battle plans rarely surprised the inhabitants of Canada, who read detailed reprinted American press reports on troop, naval, and supply movements in the local press. In early 1812, in response to the widely reprinted congressional debates on war preparation, a reader's letter to the editor of the *Quebec Mercury* declared, "Every man may soon have his doubts cleared up (if he entertains any) by a reference to the American journals, where no secret is made of the 'ways and means' by which this war is to be carried on."[14] Many newspapers on both sides of the Atlantic even kept score in the naval war with tallies of prizes that editors gleaned from an array of international sources, including classified advertisements selling the captured ships. Baltimore's *Niles' Weekly Register* provided a weekly tally, reprinted throughout North America, the Caribbean, and the

British Isles. For those unfamiliar with naval warfare, newspapers provided terminology cheat sheets, such as the *Register's* popular December 1812 question-and-answer interview with Charles Stewart, captain of USS *Constellation*, about frigates.[15] Perhaps in no previous war were the civilian populations on both sides better informed.

Both in the British Empire and in the United States, governments, political groups, lobbyists, and businesses all used the press to advance their goals. In some instances this was overt, such as the government-owned *London Gazette's* printing of official decrees. In other instances pens-for-hire and politicians themselves made their cases to the public under the veil of assumed names. They did so because the press was an established tool for both measuring and influencing public opinion.

The Baltimore riots in the summer of 1812 illustrated that people from all walks of life recognized the significance of the press.[16] In June a mob attacked and destroyed the press of the *Federal Republican* when its Federalist editor, Alexander Contee Hanson, responded to the US declaration of war with a scathing editorial. Although Hanson had fled Baltimore in June, he returned in July to resume the attack on Madison. Hanson followed up with an announcement that he and two dozen armed supporters would defend the paper's offices. After an initial melee in which Hanson's group fired on the gathering angry mob, killing one and wounding others, the mob returned with an artillery piece manned by the editor of the *Baltimore Sun*, a rival paper. By the next morning the crowd neared two thousand. Outgunned and outnumbered, Hanson's group surrendered, but the mob broke into the local jail the next evening and assaulted the men before a cheering crowd, leaving one dead and eleven, including Hanson, physically broken. The rioters went unpunished, and Baltimore endured the name "mobtown" for decades.

The war's critics then seized every opportunity to link their opponents with mob violence. A town meeting in Boston that August made a typical attempt to link the riots with Madison's presidency, calling them a "prelude to the dissolution of all free government" with interchangeable government-supported mobs and the governors themselves. The solution, they resolved, required "a change of our present rulers."[17] Festus Foster of Vermont, a state with a government divided between Federalists and Republicans, called the pro-Madison press "the mercenary scribblers in every prostitute Gazette" that justified the "Presidential mob" that "most inhumanly mangled and massacred some of our best and worthiest citizens."[18] The funeral of James Lingan, the Revolutionary War veteran and former senior officer of the Maryland State Militia whom the Baltimore rioters had tortured and killed, became a national media event. Outrage over the riots boosted the Federalists in elections in New England and New York and enabled them to win control of the House of Delegates in Maryland.[19]

Governments wanted to influence public opinion not only to secure votes but also to secure enlistments and financing. Votes in elections mattered, but corruption, the party system, and complex safeguards, such as the rotten boroughs in Britain and the Electoral College in the United States, precluded true democracy. More important was the dependence on voluntarism for war recruitments and financing. The professional soldier was something of a rarity in the War of 1812, as both sides in North America relied heavily on local militia and other volunteers to do the fighting—and struggled to secure reliable recruits. Private banks could, and did, cripple the US ability to wage war, while Britain depended on the honesty of private citizens in voluntarily reporting their own income for the new property tax. At times, citizens on both sides had voted with their wallets by boycotting goods they associated with unsavory policies, such as tea with British taxation in North America in the 1770s and sugar with the slave trade in Britain in the 1790s.[20]

Each newspaper's political independence varied. Overt government ownership was limited to official gazettes, such as the *London Gazette*, which printed official speeches and announcements and did not take advertisements. Other newspapers fell under the sway of men in government who provided subsidies, either directly via payments or ownership of shares or indirectly through government stationery contracts with the printer. In small markets such as Upper Canada, where the *York Gazette* operated, newspapers could not survive without such subsidies. Washington's *National Intelligencer* was known internationally as the more-or-less official mouthpiece of the Madison administration, although it technically was a private newspaper that carried advertising. In other instances, governments and officials apparently bribed editors. Although incontrovertible evidence is typically in short supply, contemporary accusations are not.

By the end of the eighteenth century, the major urban newspapers, the news sources for local newspapers, were profitable commercial ventures that relied on advertisements and subscriptions rather than subsidies.[21] Their bias was intertwined with profit. More than one editor switched allegiances to see readership soar, and many investors backed newspapers expressing political opinions contrary to their own. Governments lamented their lack of control over their national, state, or colonial presses. Government opponents, however, reveled in it. One such opponent was William Ellery Channing, a leading outspoken opponent of the war and minister of the Federal Street Church in Boston who declared in a widely reprinted sermon that "Freedom of opinion, of speech, and of the press, is our most valuable privilege . . . the safeguard of all other rights."[22]

Imagined Communities

Some discourses clearly transcended local and national boundaries to create "imagined communities." Readership was widespread, with ample evidence of the literate reading to the illiterate and newspapers being shared in coffeehouses and taverns and between families. A single London newspaper could reach as many as forty readers, and a single, well-placed article in a major newspaper could reach a global audience. The press was a major forum for public debate. While pamphlets offered greater space for more detailed and nuanced arguments, only a handful commanded a larger readership than a single, badly distributed, small-town paper. Commentators and politicians knew this, and they relied on the press to gauge both domestic and foreign opinion. It is no accident that governments and individual politicians had multiple newspapers subscriptions.[23]

USS *Constitution*'s defeat of HMS *Guerrière* in August 1812 illustrates how a single event could create an international discussion. All sides assumed at the outbreak of war that the Royal Navy was invincible on every level. After all, it was the Goliath of the sea, boasting some 584 warships, including 102 ships of the line and 124 frigates; the Americans had no ships of the line, a mere eight frigates, and a total of seventeen ships fit for service.[24] Not surprisingly, the American war strategy did not rely on the Navy, and the Republican neglect of the Navy continued through the outbreak of war, despite some failed late efforts by members of Congress.[25] A minister's remarks to his Salem congregation on the national fast day in August 1812 epitomized the prevailing sense of impending maritime doom: "Where are the fleets and navies of those nations of Europe? In their fate we may read an instructive lesson."[26] The British generally dismissed the American Navy on the eve of war, having grown accustomed to naval success that spanned generations.[27] As the *Ipswich Journal* mockingly remarked, "With all due deference to the sagacity of the American Legislature, it seems rather an inversion of the natural order of proceeding, first to recommend a Maritime War with Great Britain, and then to set about building a Navy."[28]

Despite an operationally insignificant two-ship encounter that could not possibly affect the outcome of the naval war, *Constitution*'s victory provoked public euphoria in the United States and outright despair in Britain. For example, the Baltimore-based national news magazine *Niles' Weekly Register* called *Constitution*'s victory over *Guerrière* "one of the most splendid naval achievements in maritime history." At the end of the year, the *Register* likened America's success at sea to Britain's victory at Trafalgar, a clash of over seventy warships producing more combat casualties than for the entire War of 1812.[29] Songs, plays, and prints celebrating the success abounded. During the usual Fourth of July festivities in 1814, the people of Waterville, Maine, raised their glasses in celebration of "Our Navy—The gallant exploits of which, cover its commanders with glory, and reflect a luster on the nation."[30]

In Britain the reaction was equally out of proportion. The news of the loss of the single frigate *Guerrière* arrived at the same time as word of Britain's far more important victory on the Canadian border, where both sides expected the Americans to overwhelm the British, who instead easily thwarted the invasion and then shockingly captured the entire Michigan Territory. Yet the Navy-obsessed nation ignored the land success and indulged in a national lament over the naval defeat. As Henry Goulburn, the undersecretary for war and the colonies in charge of the day-to-day running of the war, reflected, the "public . . . scarcely appreciated this success as the ship which brought [it] home brought also the intelligence of the capture of the British frigate *Guerrière*. . . . The feeling in the British Public in favor of the Navy rendered in their eyes the military triumph no compensation for the Naval disaster."[31] The *Times of London* called the loss of *Guerrière* a "disaster" with which "England is but little familiar." While admitting the "loss of a single frigate by us, when we consider how all the other navies of the world have been dealt by, is, it is true, a small one . . . it is almost nothing," the *Times* confessed that "we know not any calamity of twenty times its amount."[32]

What followed was a multiyear, multinational debate that rehashed the outcome. Adding further fuel to the fire were two more American ship-on-ship victories over the next few months—three times as many such victories as the French had experienced in the previous two decades of war. Not until the following summer was the US Navy satisfactorily neutralized. "Any one who had predicted such a result of an American war, this time last year, would have been treated as a madman or a traitor," the *Times* raged. In a fit of exaggeration, the *Times* proclaimed that consequence of the naval embarrassments would be ruinous: "It will waste away the strength of the country, and what is worse, it will break down the national spirit, so that gallant enterprise and far-sighted undertakings will become foreign to our very nature, and the English character will dwindle into effeminacy and decrepitude."[33]

Blame first fell on the captain and crew of *Guerrière*, but then attention shifted to the inequity of the battle. A slew of editorials throughout the British Empire noted, correctly, that the American frigates encountered were larger, sleeker, and, therefore, effectively another class of ship. As the *Kingston Gazette* of Upper Canada explained to its readers, who were hundreds of miles from the sea, the British were outnumbered almost two-to-one in crew and completely outgunned.[34] Even so, the *Jamaica Magazine* declared, Britain has lost "on *our own element*, as we modestly term it." Sarcastically referring to the American boasts that peppered newspapers throughout the empire, the magazine declared that any admiration it expressed would pale in comparison as they had "already exultingly heaped the honours due to a Nelson [the victor at Trafalgar] on their conquering hero."[35] The *Quebec Mercury* concurred, dismissing Madison's celebratory speech, which appeared in an early issue, "We will allow Mr. Madison to vaunt himself, for a short time, of his reprisals and success on the Ocean; the British lion is not yet roused."[36] In Britain, blame ultimately shifted to the government for allowing the situation to occur in the first place. "The reply to this [that the American ships were larger] is very obvious," the *Times* declared. "Why, then, had not we line-of-battle ships to fight them?"[37] Under mounting pressure,

John Wilson Croker, secretary to the Admiralty, in 1813 wrote ten letters for the *London Courier*, which were reprinted across the Atlantic. Croker defended the actions of the Admiralty and Liverpool ministry, insisting that adequate ships were in American waters and that Britain's defeats were cases of chance encounters.[38] For its part the American press delighted in the British anguish, joyfully reprinting British articles under such headings as "Groans of the Britons."[39]

While *Constitution*'s victory over *Guerrière* demonstrates how international discussions in the press transpired, the success of the Loyal and Patriotic Society highlights their impact. Among the most effective tools in bringing Upper Canada to the wider public consciousness was the empire-wide charity drive to aid its suffering civilian inhabitants. Organized by the Loyal and Patriotic Society of Upper Canada in late December 1812, the drive brought in well over £10,000 in the first year alone—or roughly two and a half times the annual, prewar government revenue of Upper Canada and exceeding the previous totals for any charitable drives in the British Empire for an American-related cause. Although begun as a modest shirt-making campaign by the "young ladies" of York, the province's male loyalist elite identified the promotional opportunity and seized control, promptly choosing a name, designing a strategy, crafting its publicity, distributing the proceeds, and excluding women from the organization's leadership.[40]

Publicity for the charity emphasized that Upper Canada's inhabitants were loyal subjects of the Crown suffering at the hands of the United States. While the misery is manifest in contemporary accounts, the inhabitants were anything but steadfastly loyal, with pitiful turnouts for militia service, high desertion rates, and turncoat assemblymen who had defected to the United States and led fellow subjects in raids across Canada.[41] This was hardly surprising considering that most inhabitants were recent economic migrants from the United States rather than the original core group of refugees from the American Revolution. So widespread was the assumption of tenuous Upper Canadian loyalties for Britain at the start of the war that Thomas Jefferson predicted that the conquest of Canada would be a "matter of marching."[42] The charity's intense publicity campaign attempted to dispel such notions by highlighting tales of grief and heroism in service to the Crown. Therefore, as the charity's leaders styled it, a donation represented an act of both kindness and patriotism. As one of the London advertisements in the *Times* noted, the relief would aid "the Inhabitants of the British North American Colonies, whose gallant exertions in defence of their country when invaded by the enemy, have subjected themselves and their families to severe sacrifices and distress."[43]

The drive succeeded, with donors from across the social and political spectrum contributing. In Lower Canada the people of Montreal and Quebec mounted effective nonsectarian campaigns, securing endorsements from both the Catholic and Church of England bishops, who became members of the society. In Jamaica, planters and merchants donated cash as well as coffee, sugar, and rum for sale in Lower Canada to benefit the charity. When the goods arrived, the brokers, printers, "and even the bell-men who announced the day of the sale throughout the city and its environs, spurned at remuneration." In London, Prince Edward chaired the subscription drive, hosting the meeting in July 1813 at the City of London Tavern, one of the most famous eateries in the city. The prince appropriately gave the largest individual donation at £105, but merchant firms dominated the list, and the Bank of England outdid all by pledging £1,000. The famous Lloyd's coffeehouse, whose patrons invested heavily in maritime insurance, volunteered to collect donations. Not only did the charity col-lect cash, but its meetings across the empire unanimously adopted resolutions. At the London meeting, for example, those in attendance resolved to praise the "unshaken loyalty, fidelity and attachment" of the inhabitants of Upper Canada. They also gave credence to the myth of the military prowess of Canada's militia by declaring the enemies "have been repelled by the valour of the Volunteers and Militia, in aid of small numbers of His Majesty's forces" at the cost of "leaving their farms, upon the produce of which their support depend, uncultivated and neglected."[44]

The wider British public and government responded favorably to such arguments asserting Canada's importance. Although reluctant to send reinforcements at the start of the war, the British government poured in reinforcements in 1814 and pressed for concessions at the peace negotiations that would have constricted US power to the benefit of British North America. Lord Castlereagh, foreign secretary and the most reluctant major player in the British government on the issue of favoring the overseas empire over European affairs, came around to the idea of Canada's value by the end of the war. On his way to the Congress at Vienna, where the leaders of Europe were gathering to decide the fate of the Continent and much of the world controlled by Europe, Castlereagh described to Lord Bathurst, secretary for war and the colonies, how he had been studying "our system towards America for years past, as well as the growing value of Canada." From this reading, he continued, "I have certainly acquired by those researches a very increased notion of the value of our North American possessions to us."[45] The public discussion in the press agreed, with such papers as London's *Morning Post* declaring that British North America was an "invaluable resource on which can alone be founded the independence of the West Indian possessions—the independence of our Navy against defective supplies of tim-ber from the Baltic—and as the certain means, if duly cherished, of increasing our commercial wealth and maritime power."[46] The West Indian press joined the chorus and found in Canada a new ally for pressing the importance of colonial affairs. By the end of 1813, editors were flooding their pages with reports emphasizing Canada's importance. As the *Royal Gazette and Bahama Advertiser* explained to readers after reprinting petitions from Canadian merchants demanding increased protection, "We wish to press upon the minds of the colonial public, as far as in us lies, of what importance it is, that we should be prompt and united in our efforts to claim our rights."[47] With no small thanks to the press, both leaders in London and fellow colonists considered Canada to be an integral part of the British Empire.

Consequences of Lengthy Communications Lines

The Battle of New Orleans encapsulated the negative consequences of lengthy communications lines. As the standard telling of the familiar story goes, the ill-fated British attack in January 1815, resulting in a staggering 2,459 British casualties (more than half of Britain's total for the war), was a needless slaughter because, unbeknownst to either army, a peace treaty had been signed in Europe at Ghent three weeks earlier. However, a closer examination reveals this was not merely a case of tragic folly.

Commanders and politicians on both sides leveraged lengthy communications lines when developing military and diplomatic strategies. In the case of the Battle of New Orleans, the British strategy on the field proved faulty, but the decision to attack during the peace negotiations was perfectly sound. After all, delegates at Ghent signed the peace treaty on Christmas Eve, but the US Senate did not ratify it until February 18, 1815—nearly a month after the Battle of New Orleans. The distance between Ghent and Washington caused concern among Britain's leaders, who legitimately feared that the Madison administration might reject the settlement, the fate of the Monroe-Pinkney Treaty intended to resolve Anglo-American differences a decade earlier. The British also did not trust the Americans, who in June 1812 had purposely massed their troops on the Canadian border before declaring war in order to gain a strategic advantage. In fact, many British ships first learned of the war when the Americans fired upon them. In consequence, the British insisted on a provision stating that the declaration of war would continue until the treaty was ratified, and Anthony Baker, the British diplomat entrusted with conveying the treaty to Washington, was given a contingency plan in case the American government refused to sign.[48] While the terms of the treaty required both sides to return any lands seized during the war, the rules of war allowed armies and navies to keep their plunder. Therefore, if the British had taken New Orleans, they would have first plundered the wealthy port city and made the commanders some of the wealthiest men in Britain.

This is not to suggest that communications distances did not cause problems for either side. The United States declared war in June 1812 just as Britain suspended a major American grievance—the Orders in Council, which for years the British had used to interfere with US maritime trade and infringe on its neutral rights. Whether or not the Americans would have declared war if they had known of the suspension is difficult to determine. The vote in the Senate was painfully close, and great swathes of Americans opposed the war. But Madison and his supporters later dismissed the British reconciliatory move, shifting their rhetoric to a more general argument against continued British imperialism and the lack of respect for American sovereignty, which, in truth, was at the core of many Americans' abhorrence for the Orders in Council.[49] Madison justified his decision to remain at war to Congress on the logic that doing otherwise would have acknowledged Britain's right to trample America's rights. After all, Britain's impressment of sailors aboard American ships continued, and the Orders in Council were only suspended, not permanently revoked. Thus, according to Madison, ending the war in 1812 would have wrongfully yielded that on the sea, "which forms three fourths of the globe we inhabit, and where all independent nations have equal and common rights, the American people were not an independent people, but colonists and vassals."[50] Therefore, even if better communications had enabled Britain's suspension of the Orders in Council to avert war, irreconcilable differences meant that something else could just as easily have ignited the conflict. In fact, in hindsight more surprising than the continuation of the war was that it had not erupted earlier.

The communications distance played a more significant role at Ghent during the peace negotiations beginning in August 1814. The British team's proximity to home allowed the prime minister, Lord Liverpool, and his inner circle to direct the talks, whereas the Americans' distance from Washington left them largely to their own devices. Both sides played this to their advantage that summer and in the ensuing autumn. When caught off guard by a staggering list of British demands, the Americans pled that they must first consult their government, a delay that would take months. Having carefully followed public opinion via the British press, the American delegation knew that such a delay risked the British government's alienation of a war-weary public that, following the defeat of Napoleon earlier in the year, yearned for peace and the tax relief it would bring. When the war in America swung decidedly in Britain's favor following the arrival of news that Washington had been burned and British veteran troops had arrived safely in Canada for an anticipated invasion of the United States, it was Britain's turn to delay and let the war play out. But news soon arrived of Britain's failure at Plattsburgh, which set back any invasion plans from Canada until the following spring. An impatient Liverpool, aware of the fragility of his own government and growing public demands to reduce expenditures and wartime taxes, reluctantly softened. The Americans then held out with more pleas for needed government instructions.

In December the tactic paid off. Parliament would soon be back in session, and Liverpool expected his opponents to complain about war costs. "The continuance of the American war," Liverpool worried in a letter to Castlereagh, "will entail upon us a prodigious expense, much more than we had any idea of." He predicted that the opposition's first action would be to request the government's papers on the American war to go before Parliament—papers that would enable opponents to discern the real cost, which the government had disguised within the larger war effort against France. The vote could have been called as early as December, and the Liverpool ministry could very well have lost the vote and possibly its hold on power. Liverpool anticipated the opposition's line of attack: "We must expect, therefore, to hear it said that the property-tax is continued for the purpose of securing a better frontier for Canada." Liverpool expected that neither Parliament nor the greater public would make the sorts of sacrifice necessary for a colonial war.[51] He thus instructed Britain's delegates to retreat dramatically and offer generous peace terms of status quo ante bellum—an offer he knew the Americans would accept immediately.

Responses to war termination demonstrate the impact of both the distance of communications and public communication via the press. The Treaty of Ghent did not recognize a victor, leaving many people at the time (as well as historians ever since) more than a little vexed.[52] In Britain the public debated the issue. A few observers, such as Glasgow's *Caledonian Mercury*, found the subject vulgar: "As to the question so eagerly contested in some of the London newspapers, which of the two nations have done most mischief to the other in the war, we have really too much respect for the good sense of our readers to enter into such a controversy." Peace, the *Mercury* declared, "is the great object of war. This object we have attained, and it is surely not very humane to boast at what an expense of human misery it has been purchased."[53] Most were glad that a generation of warfare was finally over and focused more on the future than on counting the ship and troop losses in America. Alluding to the angelic chorus's announcement of the birth of Jesus, the *Leeds Mercury* declared its joy: "This Country, thanks to the good Providence of God, is now at Peace with Europe, with America, and with the World. . . . There is at length 'Peace on Earth,' and we trust the revival of 'Good-will among men' will quickly follow the close of national hostilities."[54] Some, however, were incensed, insisting that Britain had disgraced itself and lost. The *Times* railed against the treaty, claiming that its terms and timing made the outcome verge on a capitulation to the United States. The *Times* lamented that "the painful anticipation of vulgar and insolent triumph from adversaries on whom we had looked down with contempt" awaited the British, along with "the certainty that we should be considered both in America and Europe as partly beaten and partly intimidated into pacification."[55] The Americans, the paper declared, had bested the British, and no one mounted a convincing contrary argument.

Crucially, the epic defeat of Napoleon at Waterloo completely overshadowed any British embarrassment over the Battle of New Orleans. Waterloo enabled both the public and government conveniently to ignore the humiliation at the hands of the

Americans and celebrate for generations the mastery of British arms. In contrast, when news of the treaty reached the United States in mid-February, the nation was already celebrating Andrew Jackson's victory at New Orleans. As the British would with Waterloo, the Americans seized the image of the victory at New Orleans as evidence of their greatness.

Parades and town celebrations erupted across the nation. In a celebratory sermon Stephen Bovell challenged his Virginia congregation to "search the annals of the most celebrated heroes and conquerors from the earliest ages down to the present . . . no instance has ever occurred in which a victory so decisive was obtained at the expense of so small a number of lives."[56] The terms of the treaty mattered relatively little to the celebrating Americans. As Charles Ingersoll, a congressman from Pennsylvania, observed at the House of Representatives, "The terms of the treaty are yet unknown to us. But the victory at Orleans has rendered them glorious and honorable, be that what they may."[57]

Combined with the news of New Orleans, the conclusion of the war sent a rapid wave of jubilation across the country. Within two days of arriving at New York, the news reached Washington, Boston, and Philadelphia. Within three days it reached Maine, and within a week most Americans knew.[58] By the end of February towns and cities were advertising their celebration plans in newspapers and broadsides along with those from across the country so that the people of Hallowell, Maine, knew about the banners in Charleston, and readers of the *Western Monitor* in Kentucky had full details of the parade in Hartford, Connecticut. As the *Monitor* remarked in a March issue, "This day's mail brought us little else than universal expressions of gladness at the return of peace. Every city town and village from New-York to Lexington . . . vied with each other in manifestations of joy at the return of this inestimable blessing."[59]

In this triumphant atmosphere Madison and his supporters quickly claimed the peace as a victory. The president declared, "Peace, at all times a blessing, is peculiarly welcome, therefore, at a period when the causes for war have ceased to operate; when the government has demonstrated the efficiency of its powers of defence; and when the nation can review its conduct without regret, and without reproach."[60] The press was far bolder. The *National Intelligencer* produced a widely reprinted poetic "Tribute to American Valor" that began by mockingly asking "Where are Britannia's glories now?" and claimed that its laurels now adorn America's "Naval Band, and the Heroes of the Land."[61] As news of British disgruntlement with the peace terms spread, many American editors gleefully depicted it as further evidence of America's victory.

The sermon that John Latta gave to his parish in Newcastle, Delaware, on the national day of thanksgiving for peace on April 13 encapsulates the American narrative of victory in a second war of independence. The British, he argued, "entertained towards us a grudge" for "they had never forgiven us for what they called our rebellion." The prosperity of the United States merely filled the British with "jealousy and

envy," and so they embraced the war as an opportunity to "chastise [us] for our inso-
lence, haughtiness, and presumption." As in the revolution the Americans faced and
overcame internal divisions and escaped the indignity of being a "vassal" of Britain.
Equally important, he concluded, the United States had undeniably demonstrated its
martial prowess: "No nation can, without a miracle, expect to enjoy its independence
and its rights, unless it be respected and feared on account of its military strength."
Pointing to "the success of our arms at New Orleans," Latta asserted that the United
States had proved itself and thereby secured its independence.[62] Sermons, orations,
and newspaper columns throughout the country echoed his sentiments. Likewise, a
mass-distributed broadside poster in Boston propounded, the United States had won
independence again and its people had a new George Washington:

> Great Washington of peerless name,
> Our country gain'd immortal fame;
> Where veteran Jacksons presence cheers,
> A second Washington appears.

"This" day of celebration, the broadside announced, "is freedom's holiday."[63]

Thus, the timing of news delayed by distance of communications enabled both
nations, albeit for different reason, to emerge from the War of 1812 exuding more
confidence and optimism than ever. The war highlights the low bar for the weak
to claim victory and the much higher bar for the strong to do so. The press both
manipulated perceptions and played on expectations.

Conclusion

In the War of 1812 the newspaper was the medium through which governments
and citizens alike derived much of their information about the hostilities. Given the
remoteness of the battlefield, the press served as the connection not only between
citizens and soldiers but also between policymakers and the battlefield. Copyright
and plagiarism had yet to become issues, so papers on both sides routinely reprinted
each other's and anybody else's stories. This was the last US war before censorship.
The appearance of battle plans in print before battle ruffled militaries, but there was
no easy way to censor given the decentralized nature of the press and relative newness
of the mass readership press in wartime.

The message of the storylines reflected a mix of political and economic motives.
While the publishers wished to sell copy, governments wished to popularize policies
and showcase victories. So the messages delivered in the press reflected the ownership of the newspapers, the government officers quoted, and the marketability of

the stories. Audiences were diverse since the literate often read aloud to the illiterate. The slowness of communications allowed coverage of militarily insignificant battles to acquire political significance simply from the sheer number of stories about them rather than the actual battlefield consequences. There was no obvious messenger as stories generally lacked a byline and neither belligerent government attempted to propagandize systematically.

Notes

1. *American Mercury*, July 16, 1813.
2. Jon Latimer, *1812: War with America* (Cambridge, MA: Belknap Press, 2008), 320.
3. *Leeds Mercury*, August 8, 1812.
4. *Liverpool Mercury*, October 17, 1814.
5. James Madison to Thomas Jefferson, February 7, 1812, in James Morton Smith, ed., *The Republic of Letters: The Correspondence between Thomas Jefferson and James Madison* (New York: W. W. Norton, 1995), 1687.
6. *Liverpool Mercury*, May 13, 1814.
7. Henry Clay to William Crawford, US minister to France, October 17, 1814, in *The Papers of Henry Clay*, ed. James F. Hopkins and Robert Seager (Lexington: University Press of Kentucky, 1959), 1:989.
8. Barclay to Castlereagh, marked "Private Cypher," May 20, 1813, Foreign Office records [FO], National Archives, Kew, UK 5/95; Barclay to William Hamilton, February 16, 1814, f. 20 in cipher, FO 5/100; Barclay to Castlereagh, March 17, 1814, FO 5/100; Barclay to Castlereagh (in cipher), April 9, 1814, FO 5/100.
9. *Western American*, September 3, 1814.
10. *Dublin Evening Post*, October 15, 1812; emphasis in original.
11. *Bahama Gazette*, March 18, 1813.
12. *York Gazette* (Upper Canada), January 22, 1812.
13. Solomon Lutnick, *The American Revolution and the British Press, 1775–1783* (Columbia: University of Missouri Press, 1967), 28, 33–34; *Saint James's Chronicle*, Minute Books, Manuscripts Department, University of North Carolina Library, Chapel Hill, i: fo. 162 and ii: fo. 108–11 and 115–17.
14. Reprinted in the *York Gazette*, February 4, 1812.
15. *Niles' Weekly Register*, December 26, 1812.
16. Troy Bickham, *The Weight of Vengeance: The United States, the British Empire, and the War of 1812* (New York: Oxford University Press, 2012), 185–88; Donald Hickey, *The War of 1812: A Forgotten Conflict* (Urbana: University of Illinois Press, 1989), chap. 3; Paul A. Gilje, "The Baltimore Riots of 1812 and the Breakdown of the Anglo-American Mob Tradition," *Journal of Southern History* 13 (1980): 547–64.

17. Richard Buel Jr., *America on the Brink: How the Political Struggle over the War of 1812 Almost Destroyed the Young Republic* (New York: Palgrave Macmillan, 2005), 163–64.

18. Festus Foster, "An Oration Pronounced before the Washington Benevolent Society, of the County of Franklin in the Town of Northfield. In Commemoration of the Thirty-Seventh Anniversary of American Independence" (Brattleboro, VT, 1813), 12.

19. Hickey, *War of 1812*, 70.

20. T. H. Breen, *The Marketplace of Revolution: How Consumer Politics Shaped American Independence* (New York: Oxford University Press, 2004), chap. 6; and Clare Midgley, "Slave Sugar Boycotts, Female Activism and the Domestic Base of British Anti-Slavery Culture," *Slavery and Abolition* 17 (1996): 137–62.

21. Troy Bickham, *Making Headlines: The American Revolution in the British Press* (DeKalb: Northern Illinois University Press, 2009), chap. 2.

22. William Ellery Channing, "A Sermon Preached in Boston, August 20, 1812, The Day of Humiliation and Prayer, Appointed by the President of the United States, in Consequence of the Declaration of War against Great Britain" (Boston, 1812), 9.

23. Benedict Anderson, *Imagined Communities: Reflections on the Origin and Spread of Nationalism*, rev. ed. (London: Verso, 1991); Bickham, *Making Headlines*, chap. 1; Naomi Tadmor, "'In the Even My Wife Read to Me': Women, Reading and Household Life in the Eighteenth Century," in *The Practice and Representation of Reading in England*, ed. James Raven, Helen Small, and Naomi Tadmor (Cambridge: Cambridge University Press, 1996), 162–74; Jan Fergus, "Women, Class, and Growth of Magazine Readership in the Provinces, 1746–1780," *Studies in Eighteenth-Century Culture* 16 (1986): 41–53. See also Kathryn Shevelow, *Women and Print Culture: The Construction of Femininity in the Early Periodical* (New York: Routledge, 1989); and Alison Adburgham, *Women in Print: Writing Women and Women's Magazines from the Restoration to the Accession of Victoria* (London: Allen and Unwin, 1972), chap. 7; and Jeremy Black, *The English Press in the Eighteenth Century* (Philadelphia: University of Pennsylvania Press, 1987), 105.

24. Arthur Herman, *To Rule the Waves: How the British Navy Shaped the Modern World* (New York: HarperCollins, 2004), 413; Latimer, *1812*, 84.

25. Peter J. Kastor, "Toward 'the Maritime War Only': The Question of Naval Mobilization, 1811–1812," *Journal of Military History* 61 (1997): 455–80.

26. Brown Emerson, "The Causes and Effects of War: A Sermon, Delivered in Salem, August 20, 1812, the Day of National Humiliation and Prayer" (Salem, 1812), 11.

27. On the Royal Navy and its centrality to national British esteem and identity, see especially Margarette Lincoln, *Representing the Royal Navy: British Sea Power, 1750–1815* (London: Ashgate, 2002); and Timothy Jenks, *Naval Engagements: Patriotism, Cultural Politics, and the Royal Navy, 1793–1815* (Oxford: Oxford University Press, 2006).

28. *Ipswich Journal*, February 7, 1812.

29. *Niles' Weekly Register*, September 12, 1812, and December 26, 1812.

30. *American Advocate*, July 16, 1814.

31. Wilbur Devereaus Jones, "A British View of the War of 1812 and the Peace Negotiations," *Mississippi Valley Historical Review* 45 (1958): 481–87.

32. *Times*, October 7, 1812.

33. *Times*, March 20, 1813.

34. *Kingston Gazette*, November 11, 1812.

35. *Jamaica Magazine*, November 1812.

36. *Quebec Mercury*, December 26, 1812.

37. *Times*, December 30, 1812.

38. John Wilson Croker, *The Letters on the Subject of the Naval War with America, Which Appeared in the Courier, under the Signature of Nereus* (London: B. M. Swyny, 1813); Stephen Budiansky, *Perilous Fight: America's Intrepid War with Britain on the High Seas, 1812–1815* (New York: Vintage Books, 2011), 194–96.

39. *Niles' Weekly Register*, May 8, 1813.

40. Bickham, *Weight of Vengeance*, 150–52; *Report of the Loyal and Patriotic Society of Upper Canada with an Appendix and a List of Subscribers and Benefactors* (Montreal, 1817); P. J. Marshall, "Who Cared about the Thirteen Colonies? Some Evidence from Philanthropy," *Journal of Imperial and Commonwealth History* 27 (1999): 53–67; Troy Bickham, *Savages within the Empire: Representing American Indians in Eighteenth-Century Britain* (Oxford: Oxford University Press, 2005), chap. 6.

41. George Sheppard, *Plunder, Profit, and Paroles: A Social History of the War of 1812 in Upper Canada* (Montreal: McGill-Queen's University Press, 1994).

42. Jefferson to William Duane, August 4, 1812, in *The Writings of Thomas Jefferson*, ed. Albert Ellery Bergh (Washington, DC: Thomas Jefferson Memorial Association, 1907), 13:180–81.

43. *Times*, July 5, 1813.

44. *Report of the Loyal.*

45. Castlereagh to Bathurst, October 4, 1814, *Historical Manuscripts Commission Report on the Manuscripts of Earl Bathurst, Preserved at Cirencester Park*, ed. F. Bickley (London: HMSO, 1923), 295–96.

46. *York Gazette*, April 8, 1815.

47. *Royal Gazette and Bahama Advertiser*, December 18, 1813.

48. Bathurst to Baker, December 31, 1814, FO 5/105.

49. Bickham, *Weight of Vengeance*, chap. 1.

50. James Madison, "Message from the President of the United States to both Houses of Congress. November 4, 1812" (Washington, 1812), 15.

51. Liverpool to Castlereagh, November 2, 1814, and Liverpool to Castlereagh, October 28, 1814, in *Supplementary Despatches, Correspondence, and Memoranda of Field*

Marshal Arthur, Duke of Wellington, K.G., ed. A. R. Wellesley, 9:402, 382–83; Rory Muir, *Britain and the Defeat of Napoleon* (New Haven, CT: Yale University Press, 1996), 339–40.

52. Bickham, *Weight of Vengeance*, 262–79; Andrew Lambert, *The Challenge: Britain against America in the Naval War of 1812* (London: Faber and Faber, 2012), chaps. 11–12; Donald R. Hickey, "The War of 1812: Still a Forgotten Conflict?" *Journal of Military History* 65 (2001): 743; Latimer, *1812*, 400–401; Jeremy Black, *The War of 1812 in the Age of Napoleon* (Norman: University of Oklahoma Press, 2009), 202–3.

53. *Caledonian Mercury*, December 31, 1814.

54. *Leeds Mercury*, December 31, 1814. The reference is to Luke 2:14.

55. *Times*, December 28, 1812.

56. Stephen Bovell, "A Thanksgiving Sermon, Delivered April 13th, 1815. On Occasion of the Treaty of Peace" (Abingdon, VA, 1815), 15, 16.

57. *Annals of Congress: Debates and Proceedings in the Congress of the United States, 1789–1824* (Washington, DC: Gales and Seaton, 1834–56), 28:1159.

58. *American Advocate* (Maine), February 18, 1815.

59. *Western Monitor*, March 10, 1815.

60. James Madison, "Message from the President . . . Transmitting the Treaty of Peace and Amity between the United States and His Britannic Majesty" (Washington, 1815), preface.

61. *Western American* (Ohio), March 4, 1815.

62. John E. Latta, "A Sermon Preached at New-Castle . . . for the Restoration of Peace" (Wilmington, 1815).

63. *Peace on Honorable Terms to America Ratified* (broadside), February 17, 1815 (Boston, 1815).

PART II. Introduction

Mass Circulation Newspapers, Magazines, and the Telegraph

Marc A. Genest

Several remarkable technological advances took place in the 1800s that allowed publishers to expand the number and quality of newspapers while also reducing costs to their readers. First, by the 1840s the process of making paper from wood pulp spread to the United States, increasing the supply of paper and reducing production expenses. Second, Samuel Morse's telegraph machine made rapid, long-distance communications possible, helping newspapers bring breaking events from around the country to their readers. Third, significant improvements in technology lowered the cost while simultaneously increasing the speed and quality of printing. These cost-saving and mechanical advances enabled publishers to increase profits, expand their audience, professionalize their staff, and offer newspapers filled with pictures, large print, and colorful comic strips.

Technology provided the means for ambitious publishers to reach out to a much broader audience at precisely the right time. The United States was becoming more urban and diverse as immigrants inundated cities along the Eastern Seaboard in search of jobs and a new life. By the 1840s literacy even among first- and second-generation Americans had improved enough to entice publishers to offer newspapers that suited the interests of the middle and working class. Benjamin Day's *New York Sun* and James Gordon Bennett's *Herald* lowered the price of their dailies to one penny, hired children to hawk their papers on street corners, enlarged the newsprint, and included illustrations to make their product more appealing to the casual reader. In the 1850s Henry J. Raymond's *New York Times* brought greater professionalism and higher standards with more objective, less sensationalized news that appealed to both middle- and upper-class readers. The *New York Times* demonstrated that hard news and solid reporting could attract large audiences and be profitable as well.

The move toward more objective news was the by-product of the industry's increasing reliance on the telegraph. In 1848 the six major New York papers agreed to share the cost of telegraphing news from Washington and Europe. This agreement led to the creation of the Associated Press (AP), which quickly transformed into a national wire service whose reports were purchased by a wide variety of newspapers around the country. The telegraph remained an expensive form of communications, so reporters working for the AP had to be concise and objective, providing only critical facts such as who, what, when, and where, allowing their client newspapers to fill in the rest.

By the outbreak of the American Civil War in 1861, the information environment had grown tremendously, permeating American culture with a wide array of less expensive newspapers as well as pamphlets and magazines. Martin Manning's chapter on the Civil War focuses on how the communications revolution transformed reporting "as well as the dissemination and control of information" as both sides of the conflict tried to manage and exploit coverage of the war.

By the beginning of the twentieth century, the media environment was diverse, informative, entertaining, and prosperous as large newspaper chains and national magazines, such as *Saturday Evening Post*, *Harper's Weekly*, and *McClure's*, all competed for a share of the large American audience. Michelle Getchell's look at the origins of the Spanish-American War and David Silbey's assessment of US war in the Philippines both highlight the critical role that large newspaper chains played in shaping and disseminating political narratives about the war.

Moreover, these advances in technology enabled individuals to dramatically shape American opinions and policy through public media. Bruce Elleman's examination of John Reed's bestseller, *Ten Days That Shook the World*, examines how Reed influenced Americans' views of the 1917 Bolshevik Revolution in Russia and offers a cautionary account of how the political bias of one prominent journalist dramatically affected public opinion. And finally, J. Lee Thompson's chapter on World War I investigates the political war of words between Theodore Roosevelt and Woodrow Wilson that played out in major news outlets preceding and during the war. Their public battle began when Roosevelt wrote newspaper columns disparaging President Wilson's neutrality policy designed to prevent US entry into the war in Europe. Roosevelt's stinging reproaches continued throughout the conflict and culminated with his critique of the weak enforcement mechanisms provided in Wilson's Fourteen Points peace plan, shaping American perceptions and support for Wilson's idealist vision.

3.

The Communications Revolution during the US Civil War

Martin J. Manning

During the US Civil War the telegraph revolutionized war reporting as well as the dissemination and control of information. Telegraph lines paralleled the railways so that both people and information traveled along the same corridors. Reporters often reached the battlefield by rail, while battlefield reports reached newspaper and government offices by telegraph. For the first time in history, the almost real-time transmission of information became possible. This put telegraph offices in great demand and in a position of great control over who could transmit what.

Together the press pool, the telegraph, and the photograph transformed reporting. The press pool facilitated the deployment of journalists across the nation to cover dispersed battlefields. Telegraph transmissions allowed newspapers to assemble news from across the nation, often within the day as opposed to days, weeks, or months as in the past. Telegraph charges led to more succinct articles and the development of the pyramid style of reporting information. Photojournalism came into being with the development of photography.

In addition, the telegraph began the technologically driven trend that continues down to the present of ever more real-time information flowing to civil leaders, who could then become ever more deeply involved in military decisions. The new technology greatly expanded the quantity and timeliness of information available not only to the public but also to the president. Both often first learned of events from the press. On the one hand, the telegraph enhanced the president's ability to command and control his armies. On the other hand, it enabled the president to shut down access to information because those who controlled the telegraph offices controlled the flow of information.

The unprecedented public access to information threatened the secrecy necessary for successful military operations. Access to battlefield information through the press also broke the military's monopoly of that information. Military leaders on both sides were much more hostile to the press than were civil leaders. Civil leaders undoubtedly appreciated the multiple sources of information provided by the press. Moreover, they depended on the press to reach audiences at home and abroad both to cultivate public and diplomatic support and to undermine their political adversaries.

The State of the Art

Americans learned about the progress of the Civil War through newspapers, which became the most popular and sometimes the only public source of information. Newspapers often posted the news on bulletin boards outside their offices because they were so swamped with customers. Some, like the *New York Herald*, placed vendor's carts or tents and wagons in military camps. The format varied from the one-sheet daily papers to illustrated weeklies.[1] Daily newspapers were commonly packaged into weekly or semiweekly editions that were delivered by mail to subscribers outside town, whereas the daily editions were carried to local subscribers or sold on the street. Newspapers could not publish photographs. Rather, photos were typically made available directly to the public. Instead, newspapers published illustrations of battle scenes and soldiers.[2]

The dailies accounted for only about 10 percent of the over thirty-seven hundred America newspapers in circulation at the beginning of the war and produced 1.4 million copies per day. In the year preceding the war over 300,000 people bought a daily newspaper in New York City. Circulation then doubled during the war's first week, with sales spiking thereafter during key battles.[3] New York newspaper correspondents were especially prolific in their attempts to cover the hostilities. They often used telegraph offices in cities like Richmond, Virginia, to file their reports. Three of the era's most powerful newspaper publishers were James Gordon Bennett of the *New York Herald*, which put more journalists in the field than any other newspaper; Henry Raymond of the *New York Times*; and Horace Greeley, who founded the *New York Tribune* in 1841 initially to support the Whig Party and later to support the Republican Party and oppose slavery. Bennett and Greeley became rivals in a no-holds-barred newspaper circulation war. Raymond lived in their shadow after launching the *New York Times* in 1851, but his paper became the leading newspaper in the city. He was a loyal supporter of the Republican Party and held a variety of public offices.[4]

In contrast, the South had about a thousand newspapers on the eve of the war with a total circulation of only a quarter that of the Northern press. With the exception of New Orleans, which fell to Union forces in 1862, the South had no major cities, so there were few newspapers with large circulations. When the Union took control of New Orleans, it clamped down on all its dailies (the *Bee, Bulletin, Crescent, Delta, Picayune,* and *True Delta*). Another paper, the *Vicksburg Whig,* was destroyed by fire in May 1863. A more typical fate for Southern papers, such as the *Arkansas Gazette,* was the severe shortage of paper and other supplies. As the Confederacy's fortunes declined, shortages of newsprint, ink, and staff, as well as advertising revenue, forced many newspapers to cut back or cease publication. Several major Southern newspapers ceased publication entirely, while others dwindled from four to two pages per issue as a result of shortages of both reporters and newsprint.[5]

Illustrations required ten days to two weeks to publish—much faster than ever before. The most extensive illustrations appeared in the weekly newspapers, whose longer production schedule allowed illustrations not available in the dailies.[6] The technology to publish photographs in newspapers did not yet exist, so illustrations took the form of wood engravings based on original drawings or, later, on photographs. Illustrations relating to important news events became available to the public through the new pictorial press, particularly the weekly *Frank Leslie's Illustrated Newspaper,* first published in 1855, and the New York-based *Harper's Weekly: A Journal of Civilization,* which started publication two years later. Both were enormously popular with larger circulations than any of their competitors. *Harper's Weekly* published news items, serials, short fiction, and most important, engraved images. Over the course of the war it produced over three thousand images drawn by its artists, who were present during every major campaign.[7]

Before 1860 virtually no journalists had any military expertise. So smaller newspapers, of which there were thousands, hired local men, often from a local regiment, to report home. Although their stories were usually uncensored, unfiltered, and often poorly written, they had a valued immediacy. There were a few exceptional journalists, such as Whitelaw Reid, Henry Villard, and Charles Coffin, but most war reporting was substandard and often deceptive. Some reported as eyewitnesses at times when no battles took place, such as the false reports of a massive Union defeat at the Battle of Shiloh. Many relied on hearsay.[8]

Press partnerships with politicians produced an unabashedly partisan press and newspaper wars, particularly during elections. The majority of Northern editors and writers supported the relatively new Republican Party, while Southern papers usually supported the Democratic Party, secession, and states' rights. For example, the publisher of the *Chicago Tribune,* Joseph Medill, devoted his newspaper to Republican office seekers in general and to Abraham Lincoln in particular.[9] Another publisher, William Lloyd Garrison, ran one of the most important Civil War–era newspapers, his Boston-based *The Liberator,* on a strictly abolitionist platform as its name suggests.[10] Other papers, such as the *Detroit Free Press,* were staunchly Democrat, antiabolitionist, and racist.[11] Still others supported the Peace Democrats, a minority in the North who opposed the war, advocated negotiation and compromise, sometimes urged Union soldiers to desert, and even conspired with Confederate agents. The Republican press called them Copperheads, declaring their opposition to the war as dangerous as the copperhead snake. All these newspapers inserted their political stance into the reporting and story selection and placement.[12]

Harper's Weekly was perhaps the most politically influential magazine in the Union. It employed the best illustrators available, including German-born Thomas Nast, who created such national icons as the Republican elephant, the Democrat donkey, and Uncle Sam. After the Union defeat at Bull Run in July 1861, *Harper's Weekly* became one of the first publishers to launch a campaign to increase Union Army enlistments by publishing unflattering illustrations of men who did not enlist and heroic portrayals of those who did. Throughout the war, it circulated illustrations of battles and cartoons depicting political events, urging men to enlist in the Union Army and protesting the treatment of African Americans. Lincoln described Nast as the Union's "best recruiting sergeant."[13]

Many newspapers and magazines published propaganda under the guise of art or news. On June 7, 1862, *Harper's Weekly* published numerous sketches of supposed Confederate handiwork made from Union soldiers' body parts: a goblet made from a skull; a jawbone fashioned into a paperweight; a complete skeleton transformed into a reading desk; a necklace and a head wreath made from teeth; and a cake basket created from the ribs. Stories of imaginary or undocumented atrocities circulated, particularly in the North. Such stories also gained credence in the South. For example, the August 3, 1861, issue of *Frank Leslie's Illustrated Newspaper* showed a Confederate shell bursting on a federal artillery train. The accompanying text implied that the choice of target was deliberate.[14]

The Press and Public Relations

Both sides waged propaganda campaigns to influence public opinion at home and abroad. To boost morale, many editors in the Confederacy exaggerated the South's early military successes while minimizing those of the Union.[15] On October 26, 1861, the *Charleston Mercury* exalted, "Ranks of the Northern Army have been broken forever; no trumpet will call them to battle again. However new forces may be mustered and new generals commissioned. . . . Southern independence is assured."[16] On May 10, 1862, the *Missouri Democrat* heralded a document found at Yorktown, Virginia, after the Confederate evacuation, addressed "To the Future Yankee Occupants of This Place." It challenged them: "When you arise as high in the scale of created beings as a Brazilian monkey, we will allow you sometimes to associate with our negroes; but until then Southern soil will be too hot for the sons of the Pilgrims. The only dealings we will have with you is, henceforth, war to the knife."[17]

The telegraph deeply affected public opinion by rapidly bringing news of battle-field defeats and casualties back to the home front. As military fortunes declined and economic hardships increased in the South, many editors became more critical of the government's policies and military leadership. By the last two years of the war, most editors remained loyal to the Confederate cause, but a sense of defeatism and disillusionment began to appear along with a growing minority supporting a peace movement. The Southern press reports of the captures of Petersburg and of Richmond revealed an increasingly defeatist attitude. On April 23, 1865, the *Augusta Constitutional* reported the "Capitulation of Lee's Army."[18]

Lincoln understood the power of the press. His private secretaries included three once and future journalists, beginning in the 1860 campaign with John G. Nicolay, followed by John M. Hay and William O. Stoddard. Lincoln often provided journalists with accurate transcriptions of his speeches so that the newspapers could disseminate them widely. For example, Lincoln's Cooper Union speech helped him secure the presidential nomination, but its influence may have depended less on his oratory than on carefully orchestrated coverage benefiting both the candidate and the press. He apparently provided an advance copy of the speech to the *New York Tribune*, which reached far more voters in print than Lincoln could in person. Similarly, Lincoln made available his speaking notes for the Gettysburg Address of November 19, 1863, to Associated Press (AP) staffer Joseph Ignatius Gilbert, who heard the speech from his front row seat. The transcription allowed Gilbert to report the speech accurately, while the subsequent article publicized the entire speech broadly and in doing so preserved it for all time.[19]

Conversely, Lincoln allegedly trumped editors who criticized his military strategies "by appealing to [the general public] in honest, passionate accessible public letters and speeches."[20] This was often in the form of unsigned letters to the editor that hardly disguised his authorship. In them, he declared that an article about him was incorrect or that the newspaper should stay in the Union, or he might point out what he considered an example of a newspaper's unpatriotic journalism. He also used the press to undermine his political opponents. In 1864, when Gen. George B. McClellan ran for president on a Copperhead platform of compromising with the South, a Congressional Union Committee broadside featured both the Confederate peace conditions and a *Harper's Weekly* illustration by Nast titled "Compromise with the South." It depicted a dejected Union soldier shaking the hand of a haughty Confederate beside a gravestone marked "In memory of the Union Heroes who Fell in a Useless War." The caption below the illustration warned: "A Traitor's Peace . . . That the Northern Copperhead Leaders Would Force upon the Country."[21]

Lincoln also used the press to extend his reach to foreign audiences. In the North, private organizations, such as the Loyal Publication Society and the Union League Board of Publications, began unceasing pamphleteering efforts. The Loyal Publication Society, established 1863, sent publications to Europe to gain Union supporters. One of its major campaigns concerned Lincoln's issuance of his Emancipation Proclamation, which generated an intense propaganda campaign by the North. Secretary of State William H. Seward sent copies to several diplomatic posts abroad while important American newspapers, which normally circulated overseas, published the text. At first the foreign reaction was mixed. On October 7, 1862, the *Times* of London accused Lincoln of attempting to stir up slave revolts. Yet the British working class supported the proclamation and held meetings throughout the country. Those who attended often sent supportive messages to Lincoln, who typically replied. On January 19, 1863, the president sent a moving letter to men working in the cotton mills of Manchester, England, asking them to shun alliance with plantation slaveholders. Lincoln was responding to their address on December 31, 1862, honoring him for the anticipated proclamation.[22] A communications revolution greatly amplified the ability to reach audiences.

The Communications Revolution

Three changes—one organizational and two technological—revolutionized reporting. They were the press pool, the telegraph, and the photograph. In 1846 the publisher of the *New York Sun*, Moses Yale Beach, formed a loose association of newspapers in New York City to pool their resources to collect and disseminate the news. They formed the Associated Press, which today remains one of the most distinguished US news services. Back in the nineteenth century the cooperation meant pool members usually beat the competition to get stories out. As a result, AP soon became the nation's largest news source covering both domestic and international events. When the war broke out, it had over 150 newspaper and magazine reporters in the North covering the conflict, and it soon dispatched reporters to the front. In 1862 the service expanded with the formation of the Western Associated Press. The AP played an important role in recording such historic events as those at Appomattox Courthouse in Virginia on April 9, 1865, when AP reporter William D. McGregor witnessed Confederate general Robert E. Lee's surrender and reported details, which soon circulated nationwide.[23]

The Press Association of the Confederate States of America tried to perform an equivalent function by telegraphing member newspapers throughout the South. But six days after the Union surrender of Fort Sumter in April 1861, the Associated Press of New York severed its ties with the South. This left the newspapers of the Confederacy without any cooperative way to gather or distribute news. Southern editors tried to create their own press pool in Atlanta, when they established the Confederate Press Association (CPA) in March 1863. It had twenty-seven permanent correspondents in the field and six "occasional" journalists who reported on local news for the wire service's forty-plus members. It negotiated agreements with Confederate commanders for access to military information. It also reported on the North with the help of the Confederate Signal Bureau, a branch of the Confederate Secret Service, which regularly received mail from Washington, DC, including newspapers. The CPA received papers directly from the bureau and also paid its own agents to cross the battle line to bring back others. It used its position as combined news-gathering service, wire service, and trade association to improve journalistic standards. Its rules required journalists to be timely, truthful, and accurate, and news stories were not to be scooped.[24]

From the beginning, however, the CPA faced problems. Its members received only a limited amount of copy, usually only thirty-five hundred words of news each week. The Richmond press proved uncooperative, especially in its incredibly sharp criticism of Jefferson Davis, which was the opposite of most Confederate papers, particularly early in the war when the Confederacy tried to adopt a tone of unity or, at least, not public criticism of its leaders. This was important because Richmond was the Confederate capital. The CPA also lost key newspapers over the course of the war, but it remained in operation until the bitter end.

Just as the press pool came into existence, the new technology of the telegraph transformed America. Samuel F. B. Morse developed and patented the electrical telegraph in 1837. It reduced the transmission of messages from days to minutes. But it took time for the United States to build an extensive telegraph network. The first wartime use of the telegraph was during the Mexican-American War (1846–48), but it proved unsatisfactory because of the lack of lines.[25] By the Civil War the country had a much more extensive communications grid so that journalists filed battle reports within the day instead of the week or more required during the Mexican-American War. But only 10 percent of the tens of thousands of miles of telegraph lines were in Confederate states.[26]

After the American Telegraph Company cut the North-South connection upon the fall of Fort Sumter, the Southern assets became the Confederate (or Southern) Telegraph Company. It became the backbone of Confederate communications, but the lack of new telegraph lines and the necessary equipment (battery acid, glass insulators, and wire) undermined communications. As the war progressed, Northern troops cut many of these lines. Thus, the North had a far better communications system than did the South.

The new technology affected both the content and structure of reporting. Reporters, distrustful of the new machine and afraid that their entire dispatch might not go through, put the most important information first, leaving the details and analysis for last. A premium was put on succinctness since longer reports cost more money. This meant an emphasis on facts over verbose editorializing. The sporadic nature of telegraph reports also led newspapers to create "bulletins" that were brief reports containing just the basic facts. The coverage became more objective, focusing on who, what, when, and where. This more disciplined, tighter structure became known as the inverted pyramid. Over a century and a half later, the basis for modern reporting remains the pyramid style of organizing information in order of most to least important.[27]

The invention of the telegraph also marked the beginning of a technologically driven trend of ever more real-time information flowing to civil leaders, who then could become ever more deeply involved in military affairs. Telegraphy made it easier for both Union president Abraham Lincoln and Confederate president Jefferson Davis to communicate with their generals in the field. As Northern troops cut these lines, they undermined communications both between Davis and his generals and between the Confederate home front and those fighting.[28]

Press reports from the front meant that Lincoln was not totally reliant on his generals for battlefield reports but could read a variety of perspectives. The wire became the way he stayed informed and asserted authority. Just four months into the presidency, he relied on telegraphed reports during the First Battle of Manassas (also known as the First Battle of Bull Run). Thirteen months later, when the armies battled again along Bull Run, Lincoln no longer passively awaited information; he actively communicated with the front. During the Second Battle of Manassas the Confederates cut the telegraph connections with Washington. Unable to communicate with his key generals, Lincoln opened a telegraphic dialogue with a subordinate officer, Col. Herman Haupt, who for several days was Lincoln's best source of information.[29]

Thus, the telegraph provided the president with multiple sources of information often within hours of the events reported. It put him in simultaneous contact with his generals in the midst of battle and his advisers in Washington. As a result, the telegraph office of the War Department became the first White House Situation Room. Increasingly Lincoln used the telegraph to exercise command and control. At the start of the Gettysburg campaign in 1863, when Gen. Joseph Hooker intimated his planned move against Richmond, Lincoln telegraphed, "If left to me, I would not go South of the Rappahannock, upon Lee's moving North of it. . . . I think Lee's army, and not Richmond, is your true objective point."[30] Hooker used the telegram to float his prospective military strategies as trial balloons to Lincoln then ignored the president's responses. Hooker's response was usually, "We are [too] busy [to respond]." This use of the telegraph by the commander in chief to communicate with his general in the field only heightened the tension between the two men. Lincoln also relied on the telegraph to communicate with the enemy. In early 1865 his administration conducted secret peace discussions with representatives of the Confederate government by telegram.[31]

If the telegraph brought immediacy through speed, photography brought immediacy through images. Photography brought the war home to Americans with an unprecedented graphic reality. Demand for battlefield photographs, from both civilians and the military, remained high throughout the conflict. Mathew Brady became the war's most celebrated photographer and originator of photojournalism. For this first time in history, he and other talented photographers left a detailed photographic record of a war. Although Brady was not attached to the US Army, he received the Army's cooperation to work on all battlefields. Brady assigned his associates to take photographs, often under his personal supervision; he also distributed Civil War photographs taken by those not in his employ.[32]

Brady and his associates photographed battlefields, camps, towns, and people touched by the war. The photographs show leaders, troops and officers, camp life, routines, war preparations, the moments just before battle, and the aftermath of battle. The images depicted the multiple aspects of the war except one crucial element: battle itself. The technology of the time made war photography difficult, requiring long exposures, heavy cameras, and a wet process that robbed pictures of spontaneity. Subjects had to be still at the moment the camera's shutter snapped.[33]

Censorship

There was little censorship of photographs. Armies moved slowly, and photographers could go where they wanted. The Northern Army of the Potomac alone issued field passes to some three hundred photographers. These battlefield photographers, limited to shooting the aftermath of battle, did not shy away from showing the reality of dead bodies and ruined buildings.[34] A series taken in late 1862 by one of Brady's associates, Alexander Gardner, became known as "The Dead at Antietam." This was the first time that most Americans saw photographs of the true costs of the conflict.[35] Although the Confederacy also had notable war photographers, the Union blockade caused supply shortages that quickly curtailed their production. By 1863 chemicals, cameras, and replacement parts were difficult to acquire. This has resulted in fewer photographs from the South's perspective.[36]

For at least the first two years of the war, there was no organized system of censorship in the North. Throughout the conflict Lincoln endured withering criticism from the press. Copperheads owned the *Chicago Times*, the *New York Journal of Commerce*, and the *La Crosse Daily Union and Democrat* of Wisconsin. The latter captioned a front-page picture of the president: "The Widow-Maker of the 19th Century."

Other articles in the paper referred to him as "fool," "blockhead," "moron," "flat-boat tyrant," "despised depot," and "orphan maker." The editor, the arch-Copperhead Mark "Brick" Pomeroy, openly wished "some bold hand will pierce his heart with dagger point for the public good."[37] Confederate president Davis also suffered unrelenting attacks, in his case, by the *Charleston Mercury* and the *Richmond Examiner*.[38] Although pro-Union voices had been suppressed throughout the Confederacy and its warriors were lionized, Davis found himself under incessant editorial assault for his ineffective direction of the war effort. Maj. Gen. Henry Halleck simply expelled reporters from his area of operations for the duration of the war.[39]

Journalists did not flinch from circulating scurrilous tales about Union commanders—Gen. William T. Sherman was rumored to be insane, while Gen. Ulysses S. Grant was reported to be incapacitated from drinking.[40] The *Chicago Times* referred to Gen. Ambrose Burnside as the "assassin of liberty" and "the butcher of [the Battle of] Fredericksburg," but he "was not the head butcher and assassin; he was only the creature, the mean instrument, the puppet, the jumping-jack of the principle [*sic*] butchers and assassins,"[41] the principal butchers being Lincoln and his administration.

The new organizational structures and technologies allowed not only the rapid transmission and dissemination of information but also its control. "Unofficial" censorship occurred throughout both the North and the South and began immediately. The first known example occurred in Wilmington, South Carolina, in 1861 shortly after the attack on Fort Sumter when a "Vigilance Committee" denied telegraph access to William H. Russell, a British correspondent for the *Times* of London. Russell had originally sympathized with the Confederacy but changed his views about slavery after seeing it in practice. The slave market outside his hotel repelled him, his reporting turned critical, Southerners shut him down, so he departed from the Confederacy.[42] More drastically, less than a month after the surrender of Fort Sumter, Confederate rangers enforced total conformity in Texas by torching the offices of the *San Antonio Alamo Express*. In the North, mobs often stormed Copperhead newspapers to put them out of business. For example, the office of the *North Carolina Standard* was destroyed after it published an article arguing that the war benefited only the wealthy.[43]

Initially there was no censorship of the press, but concerns about military secrecy immediately arose from the near real-time circulation of battle reports and troop deployments. The Civil War became the first conflict in American history in which the government—both governments—censored information that might be militarily useful to the other side, but their systems of control developed gradually. At the initiation of hostilities, the press published official reports before the government received them. For example, the press published verbatim the official report of the surrendering officer at Fort Sumter before Washington received it. So in April 1861

Secretary of State William H. Seward closed Union telegraph lines to press reports on troop movements, and in July he appointed a censor to oversee transmissions emanating from Washington. H. E. Thayer was appointed censor. All Union battlefield reports were routed through Washington, facilitating censorship.[44]

Just before the First Battle of Bull Run in July 1861, Gen. Winfield Scott issued the first official ground rules for reporting in US history. He allowed general battlefield reporting but no discussion of troop numbers of movements. Within days of the Union's rout at Bull Run, he suspended the ground rules and closed the Union telegraph lines to the press. Upon assuming command of the Army of the Potomac, General McClellan also tried to institute a system for voluntary censorship and was equally unsuccessful. Articles critical of Union performance immediately appeared, and McClellan shut down telegraphic communications to the press, but censored reporters simply rode to more distant telegraph offices or sent their reports by mail instead.[45]

On June 21, 1860, Congress established the US Army's Signal Corps to create a system for signal communications on the battlefield.[46] A signal officer on the Army's staff, under the secretary of war, was appointed to have charge of all signal duty and all books, papers, and apparatus connected with the office. In February 1862 Congress transferred control of the telegraph from the State Department to the War Department to deny reporters access to the telegraph lines. Secretary of War Edwin M. Stanton and Undersecretary of State Frederick Seward managed the censorship of the Union telegraph.[47] General Orders No. 67 forbade the dissemination of any information about the military "except with the authorization and with the consent of the commanding officer." Its violation risked execution as a violation of the Articles of War. In response to the public uproar against the restrictions, Secretary of War Stanton authorized an unworkable loyalty-oath system to allow the "loyal" to report. In practice the Union censored on the eve of battles and allowed more information afterward, but not about casualties.[48] It first started on March 17, 1862, when the War Department closed down John Wein Forney's *Washington Sunday Chronicle* for publishing a report on military movements in violation of General Orders No. 67.

President Lincoln imposed the first official US government censorship of news media during wartime as early as July 4, 1861, when he submitted a special message to Congress that effectively suspended the writ of habeas corpus, which briefly defined is a citizen's right to petition for relief from unlawful detention or imprisonment of themselves or another person. Journalists opposed the order, which, among other suspensions, punished journalists for disloyalty, such as reporting unfavorable or inaccurate battle news. He closed down papers that he considered disloyal to the Union and jailed or exiled editors who opposed enlistment or sympathized with secession. Early targets of Union press crackdown were Francis Key Howard, who was imprisoned at Fort McHenry in Baltimore, and Amasa Converse, who was driven from Philadelphia; he relocated to Richmond, the Confederacy's capital. Another publisher, John Hodgson, had his pro-Democratic, antiwar newspaper (*Jeffersonian*) in West Chester, Pennsylvania, seriously damaged. Lincoln's suspension of habeas corpus in order to preserve the Union was one of the most controversial executive decisions in American history.

The Confederate government restricted access to sensitive information, but the low level of press censorship in the South was due to several factors, including the impact of the war on the size and frequency of publication of Southern newspapers, consistent support for the Confederate government by newspaper editors, and a ban on reporters from attending congressional sessions dealing with military matters. In spring 1861 the Confederate Congress passed laws that gave the administration authority to control information over the telegraph and through the mail. In 1862 the Confederate Congress made publication of any news about military movements a crime. Eventually, all reporters had to submit telegraphic dispatches to military authorities, who suppressed material they considered damaging.[49]

Self-censorship was far more effective in the South than in the North because opinion was less divided. The South, like the North, also censored the wires. Southern papers had an informal and voluntary system of self-censorship. Some editors exercised extreme discretion in what they published, while others insisted on the right to publish anything, including scathing attacks on both civil and military officials. Yet the Confederate government, unlike the Union, never shut down a newspaper.[50]

Although the political leaders in both the North and the South tolerated vitriolic criticism, their military leaders were less tolerant. The generals on both sides were far more hostile to the press than were political leaders. The generals feared the circulation of information to the enemy, while the politicians needed the press to communicate with voters and presumably preferred to have multiple sources for battlefield reports over a military monopoly on information. Politicians also reaped voter backlash against censorship. So when the US War Department suspended the publication of *Harper's Weekly* over concerns that two maps published in the April 1862 issue had given "aid and comfort to the enemy," the government rapidly reversed the decision, in recognition of the magazine's key role in aiding recruitments. Secretary of War Stanton publicly thanked the *Weekly* for its service to the Union cause.[51]

The generals found other ways to retaliate against the press. Before General Grant became a successful military commander, he was an early enforcer of Union newspaper suppression.[52] There were other instances of Union generals getting even with reporters who aroused their anger. In 1864 Gen. George G. Meade expelled Edward Cropsey, a correspondent for the *Philadelphia Inquirer*, from his camp, mounted backward on a mule, to the roll of the drums, with a sign labeling him "Libeler of the Press" while the regimental band played the Rogue's March.[53] Perhaps the best known example of the Army's suspicious attitude toward the press is Gen. William T. Sherman's 1863 court-martial of Thomas Knox, a reporter for the *New York Herald*. Knox was exonerated but banned from the front lines for the rest of the war.[54] In January 1862, the Army of the Potomac banished all correspondents, while the Confederate Congress made the publication of any news about disposition, movements, or numbers of army and naval forces a crime.[55] Individual Union military commanders made a series of decisions to ban from their camps newspaper correspondents, whom Sherman termed "the set of dirty newspaper scribblers who have the impudence of Satan."[56] Others held press conferences and relied on press passes to limit unfavorable reporting.

Much like Sherman, Gen. Braxton Bragg of the Confederate Army was notorious for his hostility toward the press. In April 1861, during operations against Fort Pickens, he had L. H. Mathews of the *Pensacola Observer* arrested for publishing information allegedly jeopardizing military security. Bragg frequently had military reports censored and banned any newspapers from his troops. He had another editor, John Linebaugh of the *Memphis Appeal*, arrested for treason allegedly for reporting on troop movement but more likely for criticizing Bragg. Other Confederate generals hostile to correspondents included, most famously, Joseph E. Johnston, Thomas J. (Stonewall) Jackson, and Robert E. Lee. All took strong measures to prevent military reports from being published and to deny correspondents access to their commands.[57]

The most significant acts of Union Army censorship, however, were done by General Burnside. By late 1862 he required all reporters operating in the Army to submit stories with their byline in order to file it, and thus was born the "byline."[58] Many journalists then wrote under pen names to facilitate their behind-the-scenes efforts. AP reports were signed "Dispatched to the Associated Press" in an effort to avoid federal charges under censorship laws.[59] This allowed an AP journalist to publish a story without fear of being caught, thus punished, under the censorship laws. Also, it prevented the Associated Press from being singled out for particular attacks by military officials.

Following Burnside's disastrous command of the Army of the Potomac, in March 1863 he was reassigned to the Department of the Ohio, where he ran afoul of one of the most vocal Copperhead Democratic Party politicians in the North, Clement Vallandigham. To muzzle the Copperheads, Burnside issued General Orders No. 38, which stated, "The habit of declaring sympathy for the enemy will not be allowed in this department. Persons committing such offenses will be at once arrested with a view of being tried . . . or sent beyond our lines into the lines of their friends. It must be understood that treason, expressed or implied, will not be tolerated in this department." Following another inflammatory speech, the Union Army arrested Vallandigham and tried him by court-martial. The following month Burnside took the extraordinary step of closing down the anti-Lincoln *Chicago Times* "on account of the repeated expression of disloyal and incendiary statements." Lincoln bowed to the public outrage over the closure to reopen the paper.[60]

Conclusion

The communications revolution during the US Civil War illustrates the capacity of technology to transform a medium—journalism—and in doing so to greatly increase the ability of messengers to disseminate their messages. Moreover, as this chapter discussed, the advent of telegraphy and photography marked the beginning of technology as the great communications amplifier, a trend that has accelerated ever since. Photography then gave graphic reality to the words the telegraph transmitted. In the US Civil War, the telegraph enhanced the ability of both reporters and presidents to reach diverse and scattered audiences. On the one hand, detailed and timely reporting jeopardized military secrecy and in the process threatened military operations. On the other hand, real-time communications strengthened presidential command and control. Paradoxically, the telegraph facilitated not only the rapid and broad diffusion of information but also its restriction. A watershed political event in the formation of the modern United States, the US Civil War was also a watershed event in the struggle to contain and manage information: this confluence of technologies, media, and messengers ultimately created a capacity to disseminate information that exceeded the capacity to control.

Notes

1. Andrew S. Coopersmith, *Fighting Words: An Illustrated History of Newspaper Account of the Civil War* (New York: New Press, 2004), xv.
2. David A. Copeland, ed., *The Greenwood Library of American War Reporting*, vol. 3, *The Civil War North*, ed. Amy Reynolds (Westport, CT: Greenwood Press, 2005), first page photo insert.
3. Coopersmith, *Fighting Words*, xiv, xv.
4. Harold Holzer, *Lincoln and the Power of the Press: The War for Public Opinion* (New York: Simon & Schuster, 2014), 463. See also Si Sheppard, *The Partisan Press: A History of Media Bias in the United States* (Jefferson, NC: McFarland, 2008), 165.
5. Richard N. Current, ed., *Encyclopedia of the Confederacy* (New York: Simon & Schuster, 1993), 1:273, 3:1141, 1144.

6. Sigrid Kelsey, "Newspapers (Civil War)," in *Encyclopedia of Media and Propaganda in Wartime America*, ed. Martin J. Manning and Clarence R. Wyatt (Santa Barbara, CA: ABC-Clio, 2011), 1:355.

7. Jonathan Heller, ed., *War and Conflict: Selected Images from the National Archives, 1785–1970* (Washington, DC: National Archives and Records Administration, 1990), 4; Wesley Moody, "Frank Leslie's Illustrated Newspaper," in *Encyclopedia of Media*, 1:336; Margaret E. Wagner, Gary W. Gallagher, and Paul Finkelman, eds. *The Library of Congress Civil War Desk Reference* (New York: Simon & Schuster, 2002), 819.

8. Robert Bateman, "Press Coverage," in *Encyclopedia of Media*, 1:364.

9. Holzer, *Lincoln and the Power*, 161.

10. Wagner, Gallagher, and Finkelman, *Library of Congress*, 14.

11. Kelsey, "Newspapers (Civil War)," 1:355–56.

12. Martin Manning, "Copperhead Press," in *Encyclopedia of Media*, 1:320.

13. Sigrid Kelsey, "*Harper's Weekly*," in *Encyclopedia of Media*, 1:342–43; Wagner, Gallagher, and Finkelman, *Library of Congress*, 116.

14. Webb B. Garrison, *Civil War Curiosities: Strange Stories, Oddities, Events, and Coincidences* (Nashville, TN: Rutledge Hill Press, 1994), 242–43.

15. Garrison, *Civil War Curiosities* 186–87; Copeland, *Greenwood Library*, 3:295–316.

16. Garrison, *Civil War Curiosities* 186; Current, *Encyclopedia of the Confederacy*, 3:1144.

17. Garrison, *Civil War Curiosities* 187; see also Copeland, *Greenwood Library*, 3:295–318.

18. Current, *Encyclopedia of the Confederacy*, 3:1144.

19. Holzer, *Lincoln and the Power*, 245, 453.

20. James S. Robbins, "One Way to Deal with Bad Press," *Washington Post*, January 1, 2015.

21. Kelsey, "Harper's Weekly," 1:342. See also Wagner, Gallagher, and Finkelman, *Library of Congress*, 166.

22. Philip V. Stern, *When the Guns Roared: World Aspects of the American Civil War* (Garden City, NY: Doubleday, 1965), 157, 177.

23. Pamela Lee Gray, "Associated Press," in *Encyclopedia of Media*, 1:304.

24. Martin J. Manning, "Press Association," in *Encyclopedia of Media*, 1:361.

25. Martin J. Manning, "Telegraph," in *Encyclopedia of Media*, 1:287.

26. Current, *Encyclopedia of the Confederacy*, 4:1573.

27. Tom Wheeler, "How the Telegraph Helped Lincoln Win the Civil War," History News Network, 2006, http://historynewsnetwork.org/article/30860. See also Tom Wheeler, *Mr. Lincoln's T-Mails: The Untold Story of How Abraham Lincoln Used the Telegraph to Win the Civil War* (New York: HarperCollins, 2006).

28. Current, *Encyclopedia of the Confederacy*, 4:1573.
29. Wheeler, *Mr. Lincoln's T-Mails*, 1–2, 4.
30. Wheeler, 15.
31. These discussions are described more fully in Wheeler, 168–72.
32. Don Nardo, *Civil War Witness: Mathew Brady's Photos Reveal the Horrors of War* (North Mankato, MN: Compass Point Books, 2014), 9–14.
33. Heller, *War and Conflict*, 4.
34. Heller, 5.
35. Robert Bateman, "Photography (Civil War)," in *Encyclopedia of Media*, 1:358.
36. Richard C. Keenan, "Photography: An Overview," in *Gale Library of Daily Life: American Civil War*, ed. Steven E. Woodworth (Detroit: Gale Cengage Learning, 2008), 2:279.
37. Sheppard, *Partisan Press*, 152.
38. Current, *Encyclopedia of the Confederacy*, 1:273.
39. Sheppard, *Partisan Press*, 172.
40. Holzer, *Lincoln and the Power*, 436–38.
41. Robert Bateman, "Censorship of News Media during Wartime (Civil War)," in *Encyclopedia of Media*, 1:313.
42. Bateman, 312.
43. Sheppard, *Partisan Press*, 147.
44. Paul Aswell, "Wartime Press Censorship by the U.S. Armed Forces: A Historical Perspective," MA thesis, US Army Command and General Staff College, Fort Leavenworth, KS, 1990, http://www.dtic.mil/dtic/tr/fulltext/u2/a227383.pdf, 14–15; Current, *Encyclopedia of the Confederacy*, 1:273.
45. Aswell, "Wartime Press Censorship," 15–20.
46. Martin J. Manning, "U.S. Signal Corps," in *Encyclopedia of Media*, 1:368–69.
47. Holzer, *Lincoln and the Power*, 368, Aswell, "Wartime Press Censorship," 18, 22.
48. Aswell, "Wartime Press Censorship," 22–23, 26.
49. Current, *Encyclopedia of the Confederacy*, 1:273; other quotes from Rebecca J. Frey, "Civil Liberties and Censorship," in *Gale Library of Daily Life*, 2:120–25. See also Holzer, *Lincoln and the Power*, 312–13, 340, 343–44.
50. Aswell, "Wartime Press Censorship," 29–31; Current, *Encyclopedia of the Confederacy*, 1:273.
51. Eric Fettmann, "*Harper's Weekly*," in *Encyclopedia of the American Civil War: A Political, Social, and Military History*, ed. David S. Heidler and Jeanne T. Heidler (New York: W. W. Norton, 2000), 932.
52. Holzer, *Lincoln and the Power*, 340.
53. Frey, "Civil Liberties and Censorship," 125.

54. Holzer, *Lincoln and the Power*, 436–38. See also Frey, "Civil Liberties and Censorship," 125.

55. Current, *Encyclopedia of the Confederacy*, 1:273.

56. Frey, "Civil Liberties and Censorship," 124.

57. Current, *Encyclopedia of the Confederacy*, 1:274.

58. Bateman, "Censorship of News," 1:313.

59. Gray, "Associated Press," 1:304.

60. Both quotations in Holzer, *Lincoln and the Power*, 425, 483; Bateman, "Censorship of News," 1:313.

4.

The Cuban Junta in Exile and the Origins of the Spanish-American War

Michelle D. Getchell

The Spanish-American War has become indelibly linked to the phenomenon of "yellow journalism" in both academic scholarship and public perceptions. Yellow journalism is used as a pejorative term to characterize news media outlets devoted more to scandal mongering than to investigative journalism. The notion that yellow journalism deserves the lion's share of the blame for US intervention in Cuba in 1898 is widespread—the war has been referred to as the "*Journal's* war" and "Hearst's war." The most popular historical narrative of the origins of the war reads something like this: the hawkish and jingoistic yellow press, through its constant publication of gruesome and sensationalistic accounts of Spanish depredations in Cuba, whetted the American public's desire to punish Spain, thereby forcing the reluctant administration of Republican William McKinley into declaring war. This narrative maintains, moreover, that the yellow press was motivated not by a sincere attachment to the ideals of freedom and justice but by the circulation wars between Joseph Pulitzer's *New York World* and William Randolph Hearst's *New York Journal*. In a sustained effort to sell copy, each newspaper sought to outdo the other in lurid detail and gross exaggeration of the Spanish atrocities inflicted on the helpless (and hapless) Cubans.

There is some truth to this narrative, but the origins of the Spanish-American War are a bit more complex. The significance of yellow journalism in provoking the war is less that it pushed a reluctant McKinley administration into a military intervention against Spain than that it served as the vehicle through which Cuban rebels in exile shaped the popular narrative and the perceptions of the American public. Cuban exiles in New York City and Washington, DC, strategically employed a variety of media to communicate messages designed to draw the American people and government into supporting Cuban independence. The narrative was crafted as an appeal to the intrinsic values of liberty, justice, and equality and was disseminated not only in newspapers and magazines but through mass meetings and intensive lobbying efforts. Two of the most consistent messages of the Cuban junta in exile—that Spanish colonial control was oppressive, corrupt, and doomed to defeat and that the extension of autonomy was a scheme to deprive the Cuban people of their independence—eventually found favor in the White House. The American public, moreover, enthusiastically supported Cuban independence and signed up in droves to fight the Spanish once war was declared. In the aftermath of the Spanish defeat, however, US political elites and occupation authorities doubted the ability of Cubans to govern themselves and established a measure of control over the island via the Platt Amendment, which placed clear limits on Cuban sovereignty. Ironically, Cuban exiles in New York and Washington drew the United States into a military intervention that ultimately deprived the Cuban people of total independence.

There are considerable grounds for skepticism about the influence of the yellow press on the McKinley administration's decision to declare war. While the *New York Journal* and its rival publications reported extensively and exaggeratedly on Spanish abuses in Cuba, they did not manufacture them. The *Journal*'s editorial line, moreover, was consistently for Cuban independence, not a war between the United States and Spain. Though McKinley formed a close working relationship with journalists, there is little evidence that the sensationalistic copy of the yellow press influenced the political calculations of his administration. Indeed, the *Journal* sometimes complained about the administration's inactivity, suggesting that its copy failed to influence politicians: "The sympathy for the patriots expressed in the Republican national platform was, it appears, campaign sympathy purely, and the pledge to take measures looking to the independence of the island of Cuba was not seriously meant." In the internal deliberations of the McKinley administration, the yellow press was rarely if ever discussed; on the few occasions that it did come up, it was characterized as a mere nuisance.[1]

Perhaps the most famous (or infamous) anecdote regarding the role of yellow journalism in the Spanish-American War is the purported telegram exchange between Hearst and Frederic Remington, one of his journalists, in which Remington cabled that there was unlikely to be a war in Cuba and that he wished to return stateside. Hearst reportedly responded: "Please remain. You furnish the pictures, and I'll furnish the war." Historians have tended to treat the exchange as credible despite a complete lack of corroborating evidence. Journalist James Creelman, who was in Europe when the alleged telegrams were sent, is the sole original source of this anecdote, and his credibility is questionable, given that he had already been investigated by the State Department for his sensationalized and highly exaggerated reporting of the

Japanese massacre at Port Arthur in 1894. Furthermore, the content of Remington's telegram strains credulity given the extent and viciousness of the war raging in Cuba at the time, when Spain had already sent 200,000 soldiers to the island. Creelman himself had already provided copy to the *New York World* describing "the horrors of a barbarous struggle for the extermination of the native population." The editorial view of Hearst's *New York Journal* was that the Cuban rebels were bound to triumph and that Spain was destined for retreat. There is also reason to doubt that such a telegram exchange would have made it past the Spanish censors.[2] In light of these considerations, it seems reasonable to conclude that this exchange never in fact occurred but was fabricated by Creelman.

While it would be difficult to substantiate the claim that yellow journalism played a decisive role in the decision to go to war, it seems to have influenced the perceptions of administration officials and the American public concerning the nature and course of the Cuban independence struggle. The press reported extensively on the conflict between the Cuban rebels and the Spanish colonial authorities, often on the basis of propaganda formulated by the Cuban junta in exile. One of the junta's most influential propaganda messages—that the Spanish Empire was destined for the ash heap of history—animated the arguments of interventionists in and out of government.

The Strategic Communication of the Cuban Junta in Exile

In March 1895 José Martí, the ideological architect of the Cuban independence movement, drafted the Manifesto of Montecristi, elucidating the spirit of the Cuban Revolution. He envisioned two wings of the revolutionary cause acting in tandem to achieve liberation from Spanish colonial rule.[3] The diplomatic wing would be overseen by the Cuban Revolutionary Party (PRC) based in New York, while the armed wing and the fledgling Cuban government would manage affairs on the island. Martí himself headed the New York Council, and Tomás Estrada Palma headed the Cuban legation in Washington.[4] The official order to revolt was issued from New York on January 29, 1895, with Martí "certain that the closely allied and enthusiastic Cuban communities away from the island now have the will and the ability to contribute to making the war short and effective."[5] Though he advocated the use of information and propaganda to lobby the US government in support of Cuban independence, he rejected the desirability of a US armed intervention. Martí spearheaded a filibustering campaign to ship arms and other war matériel to Cuba. Technically, these expeditions, which were organized in the United States, violated international law and US neutrality statutes. Spanish officials understandably sought to hold the US government accountable, invoking international law, issuing complaints, and maintaining a naval patrol to intercept suspicious vessels in Cuban waters.[6]

Martí was perennially suspicious of the United States, describing it as an "avaricious neighbor who admittedly has designs on us."[7] Thus, while working to persuade international public opinion to support the rebel cause, he shunned any prospect of US military intervention in Cuba. After his death in combat, however, PRC representatives in New York launched a propaganda campaign to persuade the United States to intervene on behalf of the rebels, many of whom still shared Martí's fear of US imperial ambitions and his suspicion that US support would endanger rather than facilitate Cuban independence.[8] Máximo Gómez, supreme commander of the Liberating Army, and Antonio Maceo, his second in command, both remained opposed to US military intervention in Cuba. Though they certainly welcomed arms shipments, they too were wary of US imperial ambitions and counseled their fellow revolutionaries not to trust the US government.[9] The Cuban military leadership was far removed from the activities of the PRC in exile, however. These Cuban émigrés sought a direct US military intervention against Spain and served as one of the primary sources of information for the US press and political elite. The Cuban legation in Washington maintained close ties with members of both the House of Representatives and the Senate and had access to a million-dollar lobbying budget. Thus, by the time renewed hostilities between Spanish colonial authorities and Cuban rebels broke out in 1895, the Cuban junta in exile had already begun cultivating US support for Cuban independence, lobbying Congress, organizing demonstrations, and issuing press releases.[10]

From the outset of renewed hostilities, the Spanish expected a US intervention under the auspices of the Monroe Doctrine, which had served essentially to warn the European imperial powers against meddling in the Western Hemisphere. In 1895, moreover, the response of the Grover Cleveland administration to the Anglo-Venezuelan boundary dispute reflected a broad interpretation of the Monroe Doctrine that asserted the US right to intervene in any negotiations between a European power and an American nation. Many European nations had rejected this interpretation, and the Spanish especially feared that the United States would use it to justify interposing itself in relations between Spain and its American colonies.[11]

President Cleveland, a Democrat, was not enthused by the prospect of a war with Spain on behalf of Cuban independence. But the American public had early on decided in favor of the Cuban rebels. In August 1895 Tomás Estrada Palma, the Cuban provisional government's emissary to the United States who had led the Cuban rebels in the Ten Years' War and would go on to serve as the first president of an independent Cuba, declared that despite Cleveland's apparent lack of sympathy for the Cuban rebels, "the United States is with us."[12] The exigencies of partisan politics therefore demanded a Republican response to the president's inaction. It was an opportune moment to portray Cleveland as out of touch with public opinion. Many members of Congress also took a stand in favor of the Cuban insurgency in its war against Spain. Even some Democrats crossed party lines to join the opposition to Cleveland's stance on the issue. Congressional debate centered on the constitutional right of Congress to declare war, and the question of whether Congress was authorized to recognize Cuban independence. In the face of congressional and public demands for action, the Cleveland administration halfheartedly pursued a diplomatic solution to the crisis. Secretary of State Richard Olney met with Spanish foreign minister Enrique Dupuy de Lôme on March 20, 1896, and informed him that the administration would neither recognize Cuban independence nor send an investigatory commission to the island.[13] From early on, therefore, Congress and the Cleveland administration were moving in different directions.

In the 1896 presidential campaigns, Cuba was not prominent. The Republican Party foreign policy platform was more ambitious and expansionist than that of the Democrats, expressing a "deep and abiding interest [in] the heroic battle of the Cuban patriots against cruelty and oppression" and suggesting that the United States "use its influence and good offices to restore peace and give independence to the island." The Democrats, on the other hand, merely offered "sympathy to the people of Cuba in their heroic struggle for liberty and independence" and neglected to call for active US intervention.[14]

Though it can hardly be argued that William McKinley was handed the presidency on the basis of his foreign policy promises, once in office, he took a more active approach to the Cuban crisis. He proved more assertive in his dealings with the Spanish, more responsive to the demands of Congress, and more effusive in his expressions of support for Cuban independence.[15] Though Cleveland and McKinley embodied different approaches to the conflict, they both doubted that Spain had the wherewithal to defeat the Cuban rebels. US policy decisions were grounded in the belief that the complete collapse of Spanish colonial control over Cuba was inevitable.[16] These views were shaped by the efforts of the Cuban junta in exile, which conducted a highly effective propaganda campaign that hit hard on the theme of the inevitability of Spanish defeat.[17]

Cuban exiles in New York and Washington doggedly pursued a strategy aimed at appealing to the ideological inclinations of the American public and the economic interests of US business concerns in Cuba. Cuban representatives traveled across the Eastern seaboard and Midwest, delivering speeches, holding civic events, and giving interviews to reporters in a concerted effort to win the hearts and minds of the American people for Cuban independence. In seeking to appeal to the core convictions of the citizenry, these representatives portrayed the Cuban cause as akin to the American Revolution—devoted to free enterprise, political democracy, and social progress.[18] The yellow press served as a "mouthpiece" for Cuban propaganda, touting every minor victory of the Cuban rebels and giving full vent to the view of the Spanish as a predatory yet fatally weak colonial master.[19] Representatives of the PRC wrote articles for the press, including the yellow journals, that were passed off as the work of American journalists.[20] Spanish officials, moreover, shot themselves in the foot by instituting a press blackout, further compounding the pro-Cuban bias of the US press corps.[21]

One of the major themes of the junta's propaganda line was the repressive brutality of Gen. Valeriano Weyler's *reconcentración* effort, which forced Cuban noncombatants into garrisons where they suffered from disease and malnutrition. General Weyler was sent to Cuba in 1896, before the assassination of the conservative Spanish prime minister Antonio Cánovas del Castillo. He was appointed the governor of Cuba and empowered to do anything necessary to suppress the insurgency. The yellow press highlighted the gruesome details of reconcentration, focusing mainly on Weyler as the architect of the policy. Though in reality Weyler was only one of many advocates of this effort, his physical appearance and personality traits made him remarkably easy to caricature. Estimates of the fatalities associated with the concentration camps were dramatically inflated in US media accounts. It was not at all unusual for the yellow journals to bandy about numbers as high as half a million, even though the casualties resulting from reconcentration were closer to 150,000. These figures were still high relative to Cuba's population, reflecting the vicious and brutal nature of the policy, but well less than half the number of victims yellow journals claimed. At least partly owing to the grisly and sensationalistic reportage surrounding Weyler and reconcentration, the circulation of both the *New York World* and the *New York Journal* had skyrocketed by 1898.[22] Petitions demanding US support for the Cuban insurgents flooded Congress.[23]

In February 1898 the Cuban junta, through unknown means, obtained a letter written by Spanish ambassador in Washington Dupuy de Lôme to Foreign Minister José Canalejas. The letter was political dynamite, and its publication a public relations disaster for Spain. It not only described McKinley in unflattering terms, as "weak" and a "would-be politician," but also implied that the Spanish scheme to extend autonomy to Cuba was a mere smokescreen for delaying political negotiations until the rebellion could be crushed via armed force.[24] Horatio Rubens, the public relations strategist for the Cuban legation in Washington, prepared a translation of the letter into English, emphasizing its insulting tone to maximize the propaganda value. He offered the translated letter to several newspapers for publication, but Hearst's *Journal* got the scoop owing to its comparative laxity of effort in determining the letter's authenticity.[25]

The de Lôme letter ignited the smoldering indignation of the American public, providing seemingly incontrovertible evidence of Spanish duplicity and untrustworthiness. The PRC had already developed a propaganda line asserting that the Spanish scheme to extend autonomy to its colonial possession was merely a plot to keep Cuba enslaved.[26] By implying that autonomy was primarily a dilatory tactic to distract the American government and public and thereby forestall a US military intervention, the de Lôme letter offered concrete proof in service of PRC propaganda. A sense of certainty solidified that the remnants of the Spanish Empire must be destroyed. McKinley was privately irritated with Rubens for bringing the letter to the newspapers rather than to him personally. He continued to seek a diplomatic solution, soliciting an apology from the Spanish and struggling to restrain Congress, where the reaction to the letter included the introduction of three resolutions on US intervention and Cuban independence.[27] After the Spanish sent several notes of formal apology, the McKinley administration considered the matter "close[d] satisfactorily."[28]

It is difficult to quantify the influence of yellow journalism in the US decision to declare war on Spain. The yellow press did not invent the atrocities of the Spanish in Cuba, it merely reported them. Spanish repression was brutal, real, and highly offensive to international public opinion. The *reconcentración* program, which led directly to famine, disease, and death on a massive scale, was especially odious. Nevertheless, it seems safe to conclude that the primary influence of the yellow press was in shaping the prowar sentiment of the US public, which in turn created pressures on the McKinley administration for a direct US military intervention. This pressure was effective only once a string of public relations disasters indicated that the likelihood of securing a diplomatic resolution to the crisis was slim to none. US policy decisions were grounded in the belief that the complete collapse of Spanish colonial control over Cuba was inevitable.[29] McKinley's decision to intervene in the conflict was based on four crucial factors. First was the apparent inability of Spain to quash the rebellion. Second was Spain's unwillingness to grant independence to Cuba. Third was the ongoing political and economic turmoil on the island that threatened US investments and potentially national security. Fourth, and most important, was the sinking of USS *Maine* in February 1898, mere hours after the peaceful resolution of the conflict generated by the de Lôme letter.[30]

Remember the *Maine*! The Path to US Intervention

The McKinley administration's decision to send USS *Maine* to Havana was designed to send different messages to different audiences. Congress, ever clamoring for a more aggressive US intervention on behalf of Cuban independence, would be reassured that the president was doing something to communicate US commitment to the Cuban cause. The administration conveyed a different message to the Spanish—that the *Maine* was making a friendly visit to demonstrate Spanish success in pacifying the Cuban insurgents. The secretary of the Navy declared publicly that "circumstances have become so normal, the situation so quiet, and relations so cordial that our war vessels are to renew their friendly visits to Cuban ports," and the Spanish ambassador in Washington reported the visit as a "mark of friendship."[31] The press in Madrid did not see it this way, however, and portrayed the arrival of the *Maine* in Havana as an effort to encourage the rebels.[32]

On February 15, 1898, USS *Maine* exploded while docked in the Havana harbor, an area nominally under Spanish jurisdiction. The explosion, which claimed the lives of two officers and 264 enlisted men, outraged US political elites and the American public. The yellow press had a field day, splashing papers with headlines that screamed, "Remember the *Maine*—To Hell with Spain!" and an infuriated American public demanded revenge. The Spanish immediately sent their condolences to Washington, expressing "deep sorrow" and offering the assistance of authorities in Havana.[33] They conducted their own investigation of the incident and sought to resolve the crisis through diplomacy, assuring the McKinley administration that they desired peace and were doing everything in their power to quell the rebellion. Spanish diplomats in Washington believed that the Cuban exiles in New York were behind the incendiary press accounts blaming Spain for the *Maine* disaster. They requested the "disbanding [of] the New York junta" but were informed that this was not possible under US law.[34]

McKinley immediately appointed a naval board of inquiry to investigate. On March 21 the board concluded that the disaster could have been caused "only by the explosion of a mine situated under the bottom of the ship."[35] Several circumstances combined to render the report incomplete and even suspicious. Despite evidence that other armored cruisers had experienced internal spontaneous combustion of coal in bunkers, the board's report dismissed that as a possibility, implying foul play on the part of the Spanish. The board of inquiry, moreover, neglected to consult with some of the Navy's foremost experts. The Navy's chief engineer and its leading ordnance expert both suspected that a magazine explosion had caused the disaster on board the *Maine*. As an investigative commission had warned the secretary of the Navy on January 27, 1898—weeks before the explosion in Havana harbor—ships like the *Maine* were vulnerable to spontaneous coal fires that could detonate magazines, as the coal bunkers were located dangerously close to the ammunition on board.[36] Incredibly, four days after the report was issued, the captain of the *Maine* requested leave to destroy the remainder of the ship with dynamite.[37] And though the Spanish investigation concluded that the causes of the explosion were internal, only the US naval board of inquiry's version was discussed in Congress.[38] The yellow press also declined to report on the findings of the Spanish investigation.

The sinking of USS *Maine* galvanized Congress, and in late March five senators and eleven members of the House of Representatives submitted resolutions on Cuba. Even those who doubted that the Spanish had intentionally destroyed the ship still felt that the incident demonstrated Spain's inability to govern the island. In the Senate debate over the various Cuban resolutions, many spoke out for recognizing Cuban independence. Those opposed cited international law and the damage that the Cuban rebels had done to American property and investments on the island. Senator Joseph B. Foraker, a Republican member of the Foreign Relations Committee, submitted the draft that would ultimately provide the basis for Senate action. His resolution demanded the immediate evacuation of the Spanish, US recognition of Cuban independence, and authorization of the use of force to achieve those ends. Spanish diplomats commented on the bloodthirsty mood of Congress, with some believing that "it had arrived at a condition of true insanity." Representative William Sulzer, a Democrat from New York, reflected this mood with his assertion that Spanish actions in Cuba constituted "one long, unending, hideous carnival of crime, of public plunder, of rapine, of official robbery, of cruel, torturing death—a frightful big black blot on the pages of civilization."[39]

Despite the public clamor for revenge, the McKinley administration still sought a diplomatic resolution to the crisis and communicated his aversion to US "possession of the island of Cuba."[40] He also made clear through his ambassador to Spain, Stewart Woodford, that he should in no way be construed as endorsing "the recognition of the independence of the insurgents" but desired merely "the restoration of peace and stable government in Cuba."[41] The Spanish hoped to forestall US intervention through a negotiated settlement that would suspend hostilities in exchange for the withdrawal of US ships from Cuba and McKinley's assistance in convincing the insurgents to lay down their arms. But the McKinley administration desired not only an immediate end to reconcentration but also an actual armistice, which would require the Spanish to recognize the Cuban Republic as a legitimately constituted government.[42] Though the Spanish revoked the reconcentration orders, they remained silent on the armistice issue.[43] No accord based on the Spanish solution could be reached, because it failed to recognize Cuba as an independent political entity.[44] Given the intensity of the furor whipped up by the sinking of USS *Maine*, McKinley's ability to continue seeking a diplomatic solution to the crisis of Spanish colonial control was severely circumscribed.

The day after Easter, McKinley delivered a message to Congress and the American public. He expressly refused to recognize Cuban independence, asserting that to do so "might subject us to embarrassing conditions of international obligation toward the organization so recognized." Citing the "dictates of humanity" and historical precedent, McKinley justified "the forcible intervention of the United States as a neutral to stop the war." The intervention was warranted not only on humanitarian grounds but was necessary to protect the lives, property, and commercial interests of US citizens. Above all, McKinley argued, the situation in Cuba was a "constant menace to our peace," as evidenced by the destruction of the *Maine*, which had "filled the national heart with inexpressible horror." He relayed the findings of the naval court of inquiry, endorsing the view that the explosion could only have been caused by an exterior mine. While acknowledging that responsibility for the sabotage had yet to be determined, he censured the Spanish government for its inability to "assure safety and security to a vessel of the American Navy." McKinley requested congressional authorization for measures, including armed force, to terminate hostilities, establish a stable government, and secure US interests on the island.[45]

Waging War, Securing Peace: The Teller and Platt Amendments

The response to McKinley's speech was mixed. The Spanish were heartened by McKinley's nonrecognition policy but incensed by his assertion of the legality of intervention.[46] Congress, meanwhile, remained divided on the ultimate goal of the intervention—US annexation or Cuban sovereignty? Lobbyists for the PRC urged congressional recognition of Cuban independence—a stance that the faction of Cuba Libre sympathizers in Congress, fully supported. The power of recognition, however, belonged not to Congress but to the executive branch, and McKinley had been nothing if not explicit in his refusal to extend such recognition.

Senator Henry M. Teller, a Republican from Colorado, offered a compromise solution in the form of an amendment that explicitly disavowed "any disposition or intention to exercise jurisdiction or control over said island except for pacification thereof and a determination when that is accomplished to leave the government and control of the island to the people thereof."[47] With the Teller Amendment intact, Congress assented to McKinley's request, issuing a joint resolution demanding that the Spanish evacuate Cuba and authorizing the use of force to achieve that end. The joint resolution sought to placate anti-imperialist sentiment, which was fairly widespread and enjoyed the support of luminaries like Mark Twain, William Jennings Bryan, and David Starr Jordan, president of Stanford University and vice president of the Anti-Imperialist League.[48] The amendment, without usurping the foreign policy prerogatives of the executive branch, assured the American people that they were liberators and that the intervention was aimed at assisting the Cuban rebels in throwing off the yoke of oppressive Spanish control.

Once hostilities were declared, there was a mad rush to volunteer as the American public enthusiastically embraced the war. There were so many volunteers that the Army had to turn away almost five out of six prospective soldiers.[49] Popular songs of the era reflect the conviction of the moral superiority of US intentions. "Cuba Shall Be Free," "Set Cuba Free," and "For the Boys Who Have Gone to Set Cuba Free" are the titles of just a few of such tunes. In the song "Freedom for Cuba," the lyrics "Shouting the battle cry, 'Free Cuba!' / Though it cost our life and blood / We will give her liberty" communicated the message that the American people were selflessly sacrificing their blood and treasure to deliver freedom to Cuba.[50] The war diaries and letters of US volunteers are replete with examples of the effectiveness of the Cuban junta's communication strategies. Poet Carl Sandburg, who volunteered in the Sixth Infantry Regiment of Illinois, recalled that when he read about the struggles of the Cuban rebels, he was "about ready for a war to throw the Spanish government out of Cuba and let the people of Cuba have their republic."[51] The American public was eager to take up this righteous cause, thoroughly convinced of the just purpose of the American armed forces.

Though the Teller Amendment served to obtain the support of influential anti-imperialists for the war effort—or to at least mitigate their hostility—it hindered the peace negotiations and complicated the postwar political settlement. The war itself was relatively brief and painless for American troops, more of whom died from disease than at the hands of the Spanish. The rapid destruction of the Spanish armed forces raised difficult questions about who would govern the island. Few believed that the Cubans were capable of governing themselves, and after the formal termination of hostilities, some who had voted for the Teller Amendment disavowed their support for it. For instance, Senator Albert J. Beveridge, a Republican from Indiana, belatedly lamented that the amendment had been passed "in a moment of impulsive but mistaken generosity" and began to openly advocate for annexation of the island.[52]

During the US occupation of Cuba, which lasted from 1899 to 1902, another narrative arose, this one emphasizing the utter ineptitude of the Cuban people and their total inability to govern themselves effectively. This narrative widened support for the annexationist ambitions of the pro-imperialist political elite and involved a reinterpretation of the joint resolution. The Teller Amendment's emphasis on pacification was now broadened to include much more than the actual termination of hostilities. Pacification was redefined as stability as the Teller Amendment morphed into a justification for US occupation of the island.[53] In practice, stability was defined vaguely enough to satisfy the demands of US political elites for the annexation of Cuba. In effect, it led to the passage of the Platt Amendment, which communicated the intention of the US federal government to continue to exert some measure of control over Cuban politics and foreign policy. The Platt Amendment denied Cubans the ability to enter into any treaty or agreement with any foreign power, and the United States reserved the right to intervene if its national interests were perceived as threatened. Whereas the Cuban belligerents had shaped the narrative that led the United States to war with Spain, US political elites shaped the narrative that justified a substantial measure of quasi-colonial control over Cuba.

To justify the imposition of the rather onerous terms of the Platt Amendment, the construction of a new narrative of the war was necessary. It was no longer sufficient to focus simply on the pure-hearted motives of the US intervention; now, agency needed to be stripped from the Cubans to deny them the ability to govern their affairs. Firsthand and journalistic portrayals of battles complained of Cuban sloth, stupidity, and apathy. In this view the American forces had done the bulk of the fighting, while the worthless Cubans dumbly looked on. If the Cubans could not even bring themselves to fight for their independence, then they were clearly unworthy of it.[54] In this way the popular narrative was recrafted to serve the political purposes of the US occupation.

Conclusion

The Spanish-American War resulted in a transfer of colonial territories from Spain to the United States, effectively establishing the United States as an imperial power while delivering a death blow to the crumbling Spanish Empire. It was described by contemporaries and has been remembered as a "splendid little war" fought by courageous American patriots to save their "little brown brothers" from the tyranny of Spanish misrule and to confer upon them the blessings of freedom and democracy. Many of the works that appeared during and shortly after the war reinforced the portrayal of the US military intervention as an idealistic and righteous campaign on behalf of Cuban independence. One popular account of the war, descriptively titled "America's War for Humanity," was touted as a "Wonderful Record of Human Heroism and Patriotic Devotion."[55] Another contemporary history was titled "The Rescue of Cuba, Marking an Epoch in the Growth of Free Government."[56] The title encapsulated both the presumed purpose of the US intervention and its ostensible outcome—a free Cuba. Reflecting the enthusiasm with which many volunteers enlisted in the war effort, a flood of memoirs, diaries, and autobiographical sketches of military leaders and ordinary soldiers appeared in the years immediately following the termination of hostilities.[57] That so many of these autobiographical accounts appeared in popular magazines, like *Scribner's*, *Century Magazine*, and *McClure's*, suggests that the US public was hungry for war tales of adventure and heroism.[58] Theodore Roosevelt's autobiographical account of his experience with the Rough Riders—as the First US Volunteer Cavalry was known—was so popular that it went through at least seventeen reprints.[59]

But the purpose for which eager American citizens volunteered to fight on Cuba's behalf was not the purpose for which the US political elite authorized a military intervention. The American public fought a war for Cuban independence; the US government waged a war to establish a measure of control over a small island nation struggling to throw off the Spanish colonial yoke. The soldiers fought for ideals; the political elite for interests. The war was for liberation; the occupation for control.

Though US congressional and public opinion was strongly in favor of intervening on behalf of the Cuban rebels, the administrations of Democrat Grover Cleveland and then Republican William McKinley were reluctant to declare war, preferring a diplomatic resolution to the crisis. After the revelation of the de Lôme letter, in which the Spanish foreign minister insulted McKinley's character, and then the sinking of USS *Maine*, the public thirst for vengeance became so intense that it created partisan political pressures to intervene militarily. The exigencies of partisan politics, above all the desire to maintain Republican control in Washington, shaped McKinley's approach to the conflict, which sought to satisfy the American public's demand for war without explicitly guaranteeing support for Cuban independence. McKinley's request for a congressional authorization of war, moreover, was not quite as forceful as proponents would have liked. He refused to recognize the independence of the Cuban rebels and doubted their ability to govern the country.

Thus, during the war and subsequent occupation period, another narrative formed—one that declared the Cuban people unfit for self-government and in dire need of benevolent tutelage. The joint resolution and Teller Amendment were reinterpreted as authorizing a US occupation of indefinite scope and duration for the purpose of securing the stability of Cuba. This interpretation was sufficiently broad and vague to appease the competing interests of pro-imperialists and Cuba Libre sympathizers alike. The Platt Amendment was an awkward compromise that exerted a substantial measure of political control over Cuba while falling short of actual annexation.

There is no small irony in the fact that the PRC in exile was at the forefront of efforts to shape American public opinion of Spanish colonialism and the Cuban struggle for independence. Employing a variety of media, including the yellow press, public meetings and exhibitions, and direct lobbying of Congress, Cuban émigrés in New York and Washington sought to draw the United States into a combat role against Spain, and in doing so popularized a narrative that continues to enjoy currency down to the present day.

Notes

1. W. Joseph Campbell, *Yellow Journalism: Puncturing the Myths, Defining the Legacies* (Westport, CT: Praeger, 2001), 98–99, 111, 119.
2. Campbell, 71, 76, 79, 80–81.
3. José Martí, "Manifesto of Montecristi," March 25, 1895, in *Our America: Writings on Latin America and the Struggle for Cuban Independence*, ed. Philip S. Foner (New York: Monthly Review Press, 1977), 399–400.
4. José Martí, "The Elections of April 10," April 16, 1893, in Foner, *Our America*, 322.

5. José Martí, "The Order to Revolt," January 29, 1895, in Foner, *Our America*, 388.
6. George W. Auxier, "The Propaganda Activities of the Cuban Junta in Precipitating the Spanish-American War, 1895–1898," *Hispanic American Historical Review* 19, no. 3 (August 1939), 289.
7. José Martí to Gonzalo Quesada, October 29, 1889, in Foner, *Our America*, 244.
8. Lillian Guerra, "Contradictory Identities, Conflicted Nations: Cuban Émigrés in the United States and the Last War for Independence (1895–98)," in *Whose America? The War of 1898 and the Battles to Define the Nation*, ed. Virginia M. Bouvier (Westport, CT: Praeger, 2001), 62, 66.
9. Guerra, 78.
10. John Lawrence Tone, *War and Genocide in Cuba, 1895–1898* (Chapel Hill: University of North Carolina Press, 2006), 52, 222.
11. Sylvia L. Hilton, "U.S. Intervention and Monroeism: Spanish Perspectives on the American Role in the Colonial Crisis of 1895–98," in Bonvier, *Whose America?* 42–43.
12. Tone, *War and Genocide*, 83.
13. John L. Offner, *An Unwanted War: The Diplomacy of the United States and Spain over Cuba, 1895–1898* (Chapel Hill: University of North Carolina Press, 1992), 17–18, 25–26.
14. Offner, 31.
15. Offner, 54.
16. Louis A. Pérez Jr., *The War of 1898: The United States and Cuba in History and Historiography* (Chapel Hill: University of North Carolina Press, 1998), 10.
17. Auxier, "Propaganda Activities," 300–301.
18. Guerra, "Contradictory Identities," 70–71.
19. Tone, *War and Genocide*, 166.
20. Guerra, "Contradictory Identities," 75.
21. Paul T. McCartney, *Power and Progress: American National Identity, the War of 1898, and the Rise of American Imperialism* (Baton Rouge: Louisiana State University Press, 2006), 91.
22. Tone, *War and Genocide*, 210, 219, 223.
23. McCartney, *Power and Progress*, 91.
24. Offner, *Unwanted War*, 116.
25. Offner, 117.
26. Tone, *War and Genocide*, 236.
27. Offner, *Unwanted War*, 121–22.
28. Minister Plenipotentiary of the United States to the Minister of State, February 19, 1898, in *Spanish Diplomatic Correspondence and Documents, 1896–1900* (Washington, DC: Government Printing Office, 1905), doc. no. 67, 85.

29. Pérez, *War of 1898*, 10.
30. Campbell, *Yellow Journalism*, 109.
31. Minister Plenipotentiary of His Majesty to the Minister of State, telegram, January 24, 1898, in *Spanish Diplomatic Correspondence*, doc. 49, 68.
32. Offner, *Unwanted War*, 99–100.
33. Minister of State to the Chargé d'Affaires of Spain, telegram, February 16, 1898, in *Spanish Diplomatic Correspondence*, doc. 68, 85; Chargé d'Affaires of Spain to the Minister of State, telegram, February 16, 1898, doc. 69, 86.
34. Minister Plenipotentiary of His Majesty to the Minister of State, telegram, March 16, 1898, *Spanish Diplomatic Correspondence*, doc. 84, 92.
35. *Report of the Naval Court of Inquiry on the Destruction of the Maine* (Washington, DC: Government Printing Office, 1898), 5.
36. H. G. Rickover, *How the Battleship Maine Was Destroyed* (Washington, DC: Government Printing Office, 1976), 46.
37. Minister of State to the Minister Plenipotentiary of the United States, memorandum, March 25, 1898, *Spanish Diplomatic Correspondence*, doc. 93, 96.
38. Minister of State to the representatives of His Majesty abroad, telegram, March 25, 1898, *Spanish Diplomatic Correspondence*, doc. 95, 98.
39. Offner, *Unwanted War*, 128, 156, 169.
40. Minister of State to the representatives of His Majesty Abroad, March 31, 1898, in *Spanish Diplomatic Correspondence*, doc. 111, 108.
41. US Minister to the Minister of State, April 6, 1898, in *Spanish Diplomatic Correspondence*, doc. 118, 111.
42. Minister Plenipotentiary of the United States to the President of the Council of Ministers, memorandum, March 29, 1898, in *Spanish Diplomatic Correspondence*, doc. 108, 106–7.
43. Council of Ministers to the United States Minister, March 31, 1898, in *Spanish Diplomatic Correspondence*, doc. 110, 107.
44. Offner, *Unwanted War*, 174–76.
45. McKinley's speech to Congress, in telegram from the Minister Plenipotentiary of His Majesty to the Minister of State, April 10, 1898, in *Spanish Diplomatic Correspondence*, doc. 129, 117–19.
46. Offner, *Unwanted War*, 182–86.
47. Text of joint resolution, in telegram from the Minister Plenipotentiary of His Majesty to the Minister of State, April 18, 1898, in *Spanish Diplomatic Correspondence*, doc. 143, 133–34.
48. See, for instance, Mark Twain, *A Pen Warmed-Up in Hell: Mark Twain in Protest*, ed. Frederick Anderson (New York: Harper & Row, 1972); William Jennings Bryan, *Republic or Empire? The Philippine Question* (Chicago: Independence, 1899); David

Starr Jordan, *Imperial Democracy: A Study of the Relation of Government by the People, Equality before the Law, and Other Tenets of Democracy, to the Demands of a Vigorous Foreign Policy and Other Demands of Imperial Dominion* (New York: D. Appleton, 1899); Mark Twain, "To the Person Sitting in Darkness," *North American Review* 172 (February 1902): 161–76.

49. McCartney, *Power and Progress*, 144–45.

50. Song titles and lyrics quoted in Pérez, *War of 1898*, 24–25.

51. Pérez, 26–27.

52. Pérez, 28.

53. Pérez, 30.

54. Pérez, 82–86.

55. John J. Ingalls, *America's War for Humanity, Related in Story and Picture, Embracing a Complete History of Cuba's Struggle for Liberty and the Glorious Heroism of America's Soldiers and Sailors. Compiled from the Letters and Personal Experiences of Noted Writers and Correspondents. A Thrilling and Wonderful Record of Human Heroism and Patriotic Devotion* (New York: N. D. Thompson, 1898).

56. Andrew Sloan Draper, *The Rescue of Cuba, Marking an Epoch in the Growth of Free Government* (New York: Silver, Burdett, 1899).

57. A representative sample of such works includes Arthur C. Anderson, *New York Volunteers: A Record of Its Experience and Service during the Spanish-American War, and a Memorial to Its Dead* (New York: C. H. Scott, 1900); John Biglow Jr., *Reminiscences of the Santiago Campaign* (New York: Harper & Brothers, 1899); William H. Carter, *From Yorktown to Santiago with the Sixth US Cavalry* (Baltimore: Lord Baltimore Press, 1900); H. H. Lewis, ed., *A Gunner Aboard the "Yankee," from the Diary of Number Five of the After Port Gun: The Yarn of the Cruise and Fights of the Naval Reserve in the Spanish-American War* (New York: Doubleday McClure, 1898); Edward Marshall, *The Story of the Rough Riders: 1st US Volunteer Cavalry—The Regiment in Camp and on the Battle Field* (New York: G. W. Dillingham, 1899).

58. A representative sample of such articles includes James Francis Jewell Archibald, "The First Engagement of American Troops on Cuban Soil," *Scribner's Magazine* 24, no. 2 (August 1898): 178–82; Richard Harding Davis, "The Landing of the Army," *Scribner's Magazine* 24, no. 2 (August 1898): 184–86; Walter Russell, "Incidents of the Cuban Blockade," *Century Magazine* 56, no. 5 (September 1898): 655–61; William T. Sampson, "The Atlantic Fleet in the Spanish War," *Century Illustrated Monthly* 57 (1898–99): 886–913; William R. Shafter, "The Capture of Santiago de Cuba," *Century Illustrated Magazine* 57 (February 1899): 612–30.

59. Theodore Roosevelt, *The Rough Riders* (New York: Charles Scribner's Sons, 1899).

5.

Narrating the War in the Philippines, 1899–1902

David J. Silbey

With the Philippine-American War (1899–1902) a newly industrialized United States made its debut onto the imperial stage. As an unprecedented foreign war in terms of distance from home and the commitment of resources, it required explanation and narration. To justify the war, the American government had to communicate its vision. It had to make clear to others and even to itself what exactly it was doing in the Philippines and how it would proceed. President William McKinley did so through a newly evolving media; the rise of cheap printing presses, rapid train transportation, and mass literacy were remaking the newspaper industry and exponentially broadening its reach. "You furnish the pictures and I'll furnish the war," as William Randolph Hearst famously said in 1897, was as sincere an expression of yellow journalism as can be found. His words also spoke to the sheer reach of the new media. In a way that was impossible before, Americans could share an unfolding national experience by reading the same news at the same time. The experience was not universal owing to differences in geography and literacy, but it was widespread and broadly national. The story of the Philippine-American War would be told as it happened, at least in first draft form.

Both McKinley and his successor, Theodore Roosevelt, keenly understood the need to communicate their vision of events in the western Pacific, and both strove to develop a communication strategy to do so. The strategies relied on convincing both the American public and the Filipinos themselves that the American presence in the Philippines was beneficial, and in both of those aims, they largely succeeded. Their success depended on a contingent and negotiated communication strategy that both shaped and reflected public opinion. It worked in combination with a generous military settlement that convinced many insurgents to lay down their arms.

Mediating the Message

The Philippines fell to the United States as a side order to the main war against Spain. The triumph of Adm. George Dewey's fleet in Manila Bay broke Spain's hold on the islands, leaving the United States the de facto owner. From the moment of victory, McKinley's administration made this not just a sea battle but also a triumph of American character and virtue. Dewey's telegram home on May 3, 1898, announced the victory in just those tones: "Not one Spanish flag flies in Manila Bay today; not one Spanish warship floats except as our prize." Dewey's biography written in 1899 described it as "the most brilliant naval victory known to history," owing much to American fortitude: "Fertile in resources, quick to take in the situation, brave and resolute in the face of danger, and above all possessed of a patriotism that burns with undying ardor, the defenders of our country have shown themselves to be invincible, and the flag under which they fought has never been struck to a foreign foe." Americans were not a warlike people, the same biographer intoned, but when war came, they, like Dewey, did not flinch. "[He was] a man of peace until the hour came when peace could be maintained no longer, [then] he was suddenly transformed into a warrior of iron mould." It was perhaps a bridge too far to point out, as this biographer did, that Dewey could trace his ancestry to the Norse god Thor.[1]

The triumphalism continued when Dewey returned home. The admiral "was given the full honors of a ceremonial reception on his return. He was paraded on Fifth Avenue under an enormous plaster triumphal arch in the Roman manner; and in front of the Capitol was presented formally by the President with a sword of honor voted to him by Congress."[2] The public celebration of heroism invoked a mythical Roman connection to draw a line of virtue from the ancient republic to the young one. Dewey's face appeared on numerous mementos, including dinnerware sets. Family homes sported his picture above the mantelpiece.

His triumph became a national triumph, one that all Americans owned. As a song put it:

> Dewey! Dewey! Dewey!
> Is the hero of the Day
> And the Maine has been remembered
> In the good old-fashioned way—
> The way of Hull and Perry,
> Decatur and the rest
> When old Europe felt the clutches
> Of the Eagle of the West;

That's how Dewey smashed the Spaniard
In Manila's crooked bay
And the Maine has been remembered
In the good old-fashioned way.[3]

From the beginning, the narrative surrounding the Philippines became a national one inextricably linked with American self-identify. There were great advantages in that, for McKinley no less than anyone else. But if everything did not go as well as Dewey's triumph, Americans might turn against the administration.

The question that followed, however, was more difficult than simply announcing a victory. Should the United States annex the Philippines? They could not be left to the Spanish, Whitelaw Reid, a close friend of McKinley, thought: "It is extremely doubtful whether [Spain] will be allowed to retain the Philippines—not because we want them, but because our people are so convinced of the cruelty and barbarity of Spanish rule over semi-civilized races, that they would consider themselves guilty of any subsequent cruelty if they remanded these islands to the Spaniards."[4]

There was a strong streak of anti-imperialism in American political life at that time. There was also a strong streak of racism. Both militated against acquiring a colony of nonwhites.[5] "Apostles of racial purity warned, more cynically, that peaceful isolation was more likely to improve the native American stock than an imperial conquest that would flood the United States with Cubans, Filipinos, and other 'mezzotints.'" Simultaneously, a jingoistic imperialism, allied to a social Darwinism, demanded the "civilizing" of nonwhites by Westerners. Franklin Giddings, a prominent sociologist at the time, thought that colonial "government should be firmly run by western administrators, the 'socially efficient,' but as a trust on behalf of the world at large and the native inhabitants."[6] The most prominent avatar of the latter was Theodore Roosevelt, then assistant secretary of the Navy in McKinley's administration. Roosevelt saw the Philippines as a continuation of the westward expansion of the United States, with the Filipinos explicitly playing the same role as Native Americans. The same "reasoning which justifies our war against Sitting Bull" also justified the war against the Filipinos, Roosevelt proclaimed.[7]

The sides were fairly evenly balanced. McKinley had declared in 1897 that that American policy did not include "forcible annexation," for that would be "criminal aggression."[8] Congress had voted against annexation of the much smaller Hawaiian islands earlier in the decade.[9] Other empires would have quite willingly taken control of the Philippines if the United States had not. The Germans, in particular, spent much of their time sniffing around Manila Bay after the battle, enough that their actions "began to excite much interest and considerable irritation among the officers and men of the American warships."[10]

McKinley feigned ambivalence. A protocol signed between the United States and Spain on August 12, 1898, freed Cuba from Spanish rule and ceded to the United States the islands of Puerto Rico and Guam but left the status of the Philippines up in the air: "The United States will occupy and hold the city, bay, and harbor of Manila pending the conclusion of a treaty of peace which shall determine the control, disposition, and government of the Philippines."[11] The president had to navigate carefully through the minefield of elite and popular opinion, so he waffled. A commission, McKinley thought, would be an excellent way to decide. Charles Dawes, an administration official, explained, "The Philippines situation is to be subject of consideration by a commission of Americans and Spaniards. . . . [The president] wants the facts to be carefully considered, without the consideration involving the loss of any present advantage."[12] The waffling seems to have been as much strategy as genuine indecisiveness, communicating ambivalence to an American public perhaps feeling the same way. The administration's communication strategies concerning the Philippines remained informal and personal rather than carefully prepared, delineated, and organizational.

As the president dithered, he tried to weigh public opinion. The world before opinion polls required a personal touch, so the president went on a speaking tour of the Midwest in October to test his audiences' reaction to the idea of annexing the Philippines. One notable stop on his tour was the opening of the Trans-Mississippi and International Exposition, which included a model Filipino village illustrating "cannibalistic proclivities." McKinley found that people responded enthusiastically to the idea of taking the Philippines, when it was framed as a spiritual and required part of America's "international responsibilities."[13] Such a religious invocation played well with devout Americans and fit in well with the ongoing organized missionary efforts in Asia. In some sense, taking the Philippines became framed as a religious mission, at a national rather than an individual level. Notably, McKinley built his communication strategy by getting a sense of what Americans felt and then using their own ideas to convince them. McKinley's message was a negotiated one that came as much from Americans as it did from the president.

He pursued this strategy right up to the actual treaty negotiations with Spain. When the peace commissioners left Washington to travel to Paris and meet with the Spanish representatives, McKinley told them to take only Manila and Subic Bay. The rest of the islands would be independent. But he changed his mind after they had left and cabled them, "There is a general feeling in the United States that whatever it might prefer to do, America is in a situation where it cannot let go. The interdependency of the several islands, their proximity to Luzon, the grave problem of what will become of the part we do not take are all being considered by the people. My opinion is that the well considered opinion of the majority believes duty requires we should take the Philippines."[14] Even here, the waffling continued. The "majority," not McKinley, came to this conclusion. The president himself was almost entirely absent in this construction and, at most, simply followed the will of the people. Nonetheless, the decision became final. The United States purchased the Philippines from Spain for $20 million in the Treaty of Paris. When the news broke, the Filipinos reacted with dismay; they had been betrayed by a country they had thought would give them independence. As a result, after a short period of tension, armed conflict broke out between the American Army and the Filipino *insurrectos* (insurrectionists) around Manila in early February 1899.

The Home Audience

The war began in the middle of a completely remade world communications structure. By the end of the nineteenth century, the global communications network had grown dramatically and widely, both in technology and distribution. Telegraph networks—aided by the broadness of the European empires—had almost encircled the world, and mass market newspapers—cheap enough for most to buy—had channeled information to reach to the most distant inhabitant of a particular country. This information distribution system was thus widest at both ends: the gathering and transmission at one end and the distribution at the other. There was more information communicated, and it reached more people. Moreover, the information reached more people more quickly. Events around the world could be transmitted and published within a day of their occurrence. People in one hemisphere could read about events in another that were, with the right timing, only hours old. As a result, people saw themselves as participating in events around the world, not merely hearing of them after they had happened. This was not entirely new. Abraham Lincoln had haunted the telegraph office in Washington, DC, for updates on the Battle of Gettysburg in July 1863. But now the reach had become global, and those reached were no longer as exalted as the president of the United States. Events around the world had nearly become "live."[15]

Public engagement became particularly strong during wars. People at war felt a far stronger urgency about what they were reading than at other times. The Philippine-American War occurred during the age of jingoism, so named for the overwhelming popular reaction to news of military victories, such as the relief of Mafeking in the Anglo-Boer War. But the name remains too condemnatory and too simple.[16] In reality, as people of particular nations read about their unfolding wars, they participated from afar by engaging emotionally.

In this new world of faster communications, militaries had to adjust. Suddenly events on the battlefield became events back home as well, decisions made at war became decisions back home, and controversies at war could well become controversies back home. For example, the sinking of the battleship *Maine* in the Havana harbor, the catastrophic military disaster that began the Spanish-American War, immediately elicited public reaction at home. Although the yellow press then stoked public fervor, it required events to leverage. The press provided immediate public knowledge of events, which then elicited an immediate popular reaction. The militaries, like it or not, were on stage and had to think carefully about the lines they delivered.

McKinley used the start of the war deftly. He portrayed the Battle of Manila as a faithless attack by the inhabitants of an archipelago that America had saved from the Spanish. This narrative played well with both the American public and American Congress. The Senate vote to ratify the Treaty of Paris, which McKinley had seemed to be on the verge of losing, instead squeaked through by a single vote over the two-thirds majority needed. On February 16, 1899, McKinley explained his views in a speech in Boston. How could the United States talk to the Filipinos about their independence when they were attacking Americans? "It was not a good time for the liberator to submit important questions concerning liberty and government to the liberated while they are engaged in shooting down their rescuers."[17] Jingoism won converts, and the Philippines became officially American.

But for what purpose? As the close vote indicated, Americans (and their representatives) were not enamored of the idea of imperialism for imperialism's sake. The rally-round-the-flag effect worked in the immediate moment, but McKinley required an enduring message to explain the purpose of US occupation. Conquest was an inadequate reason, especially given the fraught racial feelings at home. The Filipinos could not become full citizens any more than could African Americans or Native Americans in the United States of 1899.[18]

Those fraught racial feelings, however, provided their own justification. The United States might not wish to bring Filipinos into the national community, but Americans might wish to undertake a civilizing mission there. If the Filipinos were benighted savages, then perhaps Americans could ready them for independence by making them good, educated Christians. The breathtaking and condescending embedded racism fit with US (and global) attitudes. So McKinley pushed the idea of a mission: Americans were in the Philippines as liberators, educators, and saviors. Americans would parent Filipinos and then give them independence when they were ready.[19]

Filipino consent was obviously not required for such a vision. How could they—"half devil and half child" as Rudyard Kipling put it—have such a capacity?[20] As Senator Albert J. Beveridge of Indiana put it, the Filipinos were a "barbarous race, modified by three centuries of contact with a decadent race," thus taking a parting shot at the Spanish.[21] So this would be an imposed mission to bring the Filipinos to full adulthood much against their will. It was a toxic vision, though perhaps less toxic than such other exemplars of imperialism as Germany, which had spent the last decade slaughtering the Herero in East Africa. But toxic it was, and the Filipinos objected vociferously and violently.

The anti-imperialists at home objected violently as well, but here another part of McKinley's messaging concerning the Philippines paid dividends. His comparison with the American West and Native Americans captivated Theodore Roosevelt and provided effective legal framing. The imperialists explicitly invoked the legal status of Native Americans when discussing the Philippines. Henry Cabot Lodge, the Republican senator from Massachusetts, noted, "When our great Chief Justice John Marshall . . . declared to the *Cherokee* case that the United States could have under its control, exercised by treaty or the laws of Congress, a 'domestic and dependent nation,' I think he solved the question of our constitutional relations in the Philippines." This framing hamstrung the anti-imperialists. Arguing against the continued annexation of the Philippines would suggest that the American annexation of the West had been a bad idea as well. Since the West was a critical electoral battleground, most politicians shied away from setting such a precedent.[22]

Thus, McKinley's framing of the issue worked effectively and apparently appealed to the American public. George C. Marshall, the future Army chief of staff in World War II, remembered the debate raging when he was a young cadet at West Point: "McKinley's final decision to demand the whole of the Philippines brought a stirring national debate on the issue of imperialism in which the desire to 'civilize' the Filipinos and to prevent another major power from taking the Islands equaled and perhaps even outweighed our hopes of gaining economic benefits from the Islands."[23] Nor was this simply the imaginings of a soon-to-be officer. Marshall was at home during the summer of 1899, when the local unit of Pennsylvania national guardsmen (Company C of the Tenth Pennsylvania Regiment) returned from fighting in the Philippines. They got, as Marshall put it, "a tumultuous welcome. . . . When their train brought them to Uniontown from Pittsburgh, where every regiment had been received by the President, every whistle and church bell in town blew and rang for five minutes in a pandemonium of local pride. It was a grand American small-town demonstration of pride in its young men and of wholesome enthusiasm over their achievements."[24] At the very least, these observations suggest that the public did not strongly disapprove of the annexation of the Philippines. They also illustrate the way in which any communication strategy that McKinley or the military adopted became both contingent and negotiated. The public (despite William Randolph Hearst's boast that he could deliver a war on command) had its own ideas, and any government message had to take them into account. Americans did not supinely accept government views.

The opinions of volunteer soldiers fighting in the Philippines clearly reflected such independence of mind. Although McKinley (and later Roosevelt) might argue that

America had a duty to take and civilize the Philippines, the ordinary folks—soldiers and otherwise—did not have to agree. As one soldier in a Colorado regiment wrote home, "What Uncle Sam wants with the durned islands I can't see." Nor did soldiers necessarily feel patriotic about their role: "Every volunteer would leave tomorrow if he could. Patriotism leads no man forward any more. Principle has so long been trampled under foot that we have become mere machines, hardly able to distinguish right from wrong."[25] Such cynicism was not universal. Many soldiers felt the opposite, as did Pvt. Harry King Skillman:

> Just as soon as we could pull that Spanish flag down up went the Stars and Stripes, our beloved "Old Glory" and, mother dear, I never felt before like I did at that moment. The tears filled my eyes and I choked up so that I could not shout for a moment, and I knew then what it was that you felt when you told me not to forget for one moment that the most glorious thing in all the world was that same flag, and that it was my first duty to protect it at all hazards. I have not forgotten your glorious words, for the happiest moment in all my life was when I saw that flag on high. You ought to have heard the sailors cheer when it went up—that beautiful banner. . . . The United States is God's country.[26]

Still, the level of skepticism never became outright resistance, even among African American soldiers, who were deeply suspicious of America's civilizing mission.[27] Ultimately most Americans agreed with McKinley's message, and even those with suspicions did not raise much of a protest.

The Filipino Audience

Americans were not the only targets of the US message; so were the Filipinos, who needed convincing that supporting the United States served their interests. The strategy of cooption worked from top to bottom and consisted of amnesty, bribes, and the wholesale provision of benefits. Each insurgent (or civilian) successfully brought over to the American side left one less to fight.

On the ground, communications required numerous languages, as the Philippines had no dominant tongue. The Spanish, despite their long control of the islands, had not imparted their language. The Americans tried to communicate in the many local languages, but they also began educating the Filipinos in English. A national language would enable the message to get through more easily, especially since the United States could propagandize schoolchildren. Marshall, as he made his way to his posting in Mindoro in 1901, passed a "typical" sight: "[I] came upon an American sergeant teaching a group of native children how to speak English and sing English songs."[28]

US strategy included the relatively gentle treatment of the Filipinos, both insurgents and civilians alike, but the treatment was gentle only in comparison to the atrocities of other imperial powers. Gen. Arthur MacArthur, the commanding officer of the islands, had insurgents, even those out of uniform, treated like regular prisoners of war. To bring in insurgents, he often offered amnesties to most and, to insurgent commanders willing to switch sides, positions commensurate with their military experience on the other side. In addition to wooing Filipinos, American commanders tried to keep their own men disciplined and made "strong efforts to punish [even] petty abusers of Filipino civilians."[29] They strove to present Americans as reasonable taskmasters and life under them as generally pleasant. There were exceptions, but for the most part the United States communicated effectively to the Filipinos that they could survive and thrive under American tutelage.

McKinley's and then Roosevelt's communication strategy had two major components. The first aimed at the American public and elites and communicated that the United States had a benevolent role in the Philippines, aimed at uplifting a savage people to become full members of the civilized world. The American aim—in this construction—was not particularly imperial or even permanent. The United States would spend a certain time in the Philippines, educate and ennoble the Filipinos, and then give them their independence. This message targeted the American self-conception of a "city upon the hill," which would provide a model for the rest of the world.[30] The second component focused on the Filipinos. It communicated that the United States was a kindly taskmaster that brought great advantages in education, law, infrastructure, and all the accoutrements of the modern world. This message targeted the wavering Filipino public and elites, as well as active insurgents, whom it tried to convince of the benefits of laying down their arms.

Following through on the strategy was difficult at best. At home the tension between *fighting* a reviled enemy and promising to *civilize* that reviled enemy caused the administration to waffle. In the 1900 presidential election, Theodore Roosevelt, now the Republican nominee for vice president, "waved the bloody shirt" as a way of riling up Americans about the war. This coincided with MacArthur's plans to offer amnesty to insurgents. The Democrats failed to highlight the contradiction. Perhaps the American public was more pleased by 5 percent growth in the gross domestic product over the previous three years than it was frustrated by the war. Despite the contradictions, McKinley won reelection by a substantial margin.[31]

In the islands the difficulties were more severe. The form of the war encouraged atrocities and mistrust on both sides. The Filipino insurgents, quite predictably, used concealment among the civil population and ambush as their primary tactics. This naturally led to grave suspicion on the part of the American troops and continuing identification of *all* Filipinos as the enemy. American soldiers committed a wide number of atrocities and used torture fairly regularly to gather information from captured Filipinos.[32] Such behavior undercut the American message of friendship and caused difficulties when the stories appeared in the press back home. American officers blamed the media. It is "as though the AP were in the pay of the Filipino junta in Hong Kong," General Otis complained in June 1899.

In addition, the Americans, soldiers and civilians alike, brought with them the racial attitudes of home. Americans believed the Filipinos were racially inferior and told them as much: "The Americans, as soon as they saw . . . native troops . . . began to apply home treatment for colored peoples: curse them as damned niggers, steal [from] them and ravish them, rob them on the street of their small change, take from the fruit vendors . . . and kick the poor unfortunate if he complained."[33] Such vocabulary and attitudes reflected not only the vocabulary and attitudes of American southerners but also those of the general population. Americans compared Filipinos not only to African Americans but also to Native Americans, referring to Filipino women as "squaws" and Filipino men as "braves."[34]

Nevertheless, the US communication strategy convinced both Filipinos and Americans alike. In the islands, a large number of Filipino insurgents took advantage of amnesty offers, especially as the war lengthened. In February 1902 Charles Rhodes, an officer in the Sixth Cavalry in Luzon, recounted one such surrender: "Major Jacinto Amoranto, two captains, six lieutenants, and ninety-eight insurgent privates, surrendered to me today at Binan, together with 5 revolvers, 66 rifles, and 1220 rounds of ammunition. Had celebration exercises in the town plaza, with an oration by the town orator, the formal surrender of arms, playing of the 'Star-Spangled Banner,' and a big fiesta afterwards."[35] Note the treatment of surrendering insurgents. The US Army, rather than jailing them or disarming and sending them away, threw them a party in the most public place possible, in front of the townspeople. The message was immediately understandable: come in and the United States will treat you well. The actions showed that the American messaging was not merely propaganda but was backed by actual deeds. Thus, the communication strategy and the military strategy became mutually reinforcing, with success in one encouraging success in the other.

Emilio Aguinaldo, the leader of the insurgent movement, also had a communication strategy, albeit ultimately an unsuccessful one. His message also emphasized ethical issues. He wanted to build a Philippines-wide insurgency. This required winning over widely disparate peoples to fight the Americans. So he tried to convince the Filipinos that the war was winnable and that the American failure to give them independence was a betrayal.

According to Aguinaldo's published account of the Battle of Manila, "The treachery of the American Army . . . received its deserved punishment from our brave soldiers . . . [who] repulsed heroically the heavy and treasonable attack." A few weeks later, discussing another battle, Aguinaldo hammered home the message: "The American traitors received another very hard lesson. . . . Panic reigns in the American Army."[36] However, both battles were substantial American victories, something Aguinaldo glossed over to convince his readers that the Filipinos were winning and could win.

Aguinaldo hoped to convince the American public that the war would be costly. Here, he looked to the election of 1900. If he could get the Americans to vote McKinley out of office, the Philippines might have a chance at independence. Like the North Vietnamese of a later generation, he scheduled his military campaign to coincide with the US electoral cycle. This communication would not be in words but in blood: "In order to help the cause of Philippine Independence in the coming presidential election in the United States of America which will take place early in September [*sic*] of this year, it is very necessary that before that day comes, that is to say, during these months of June, July, and August, we should give the Americans some hard fighting."[37] Aguinaldo was apparently wrong about the month when the election would be held, but his goal was clear. "Hard fighting" might give the Filipinos not only a military but also an electoral victory.

The problem was execution. From the beginning, geographic and demographic disadvantages hampered Aguinaldo. The Philippines comprised thousands of islands, which made it enormously difficult for the insurgents to stay in touch across the entirety of the archipelago. This situation soon worsened as the US Navy (after the somewhat uncooperative George Dewey returned to the United States) developed a "brown water" fleet of small ships that patrolled the water among the islands and severely restricted insurgent communications.[38] The *insurrectos* found themselves fighting separate fights on each island rather than one combined conflict. Communications got through intermittently if at all.

Added to this were Aguinaldo's demographic difficulties. He was Tagalog, the dominant group, but hundreds of other ethnicities were spread across the islands, ethnicities whose members spoke different languages and followed different social norms. Most of the Filipinos, as William Howard Taft observed in 1902, "speak a language that is confined to a narrow part of the territory of the islands [which] prevents their communications with the government, with courts, with people anywhere else."[39] The lack of a common language hindered Aguinaldo. Meanwhile, the Americans instructed Filipinos in English, which helped in the short run, but a population unified by language might resist the United States in the long run. At that moment English instruction worked in America's favor.

Even worse for Aguinaldo, non-Tagalogs were suspicious of the Tagalogs, who had dominated the Philippines economically and politically and not treated other groups particularly well. Thus, the parts of Aguinaldo's messages that did get through were greeted skeptically. The Tagalogs lacked the credibility that native insurgents usually have and so could not make their message more convincing than that of the Americans. As a result, Aguinaldo's messaging strategy largely failed, and the United States filled the vacuum.

Collateral Damage

The war took an ugly turn in the summer of 1901. The Americans had taken to concentrating the Filipino civilian population into large camps to cut off support for the insurgents. The strategy, though effective, disrupted Filipino agriculture and undermined hygiene. One Army surgeon walking through a camp reported seeing "excreta, dead animals, slop, stable manure, and other filth" dumped on the ground and contaminating the water supply.[40] These conditions made the Filipinos vulnerable to disease. In the warm months of 1901, a cholera epidemic broke out throughout the islands. Hundreds of thousands—mostly Filipino civilians—died. The bodies were so numerous that they had to be buried in mass graves, if they were buried at all.

Just as the disease died down as fall arrived, in September 1901, Filipino insurgents on Samar managed to ambush and almost entirely wipe out an American detachment at the town of Balangiga. The brutal setback in a war that had seemed to be going America's way enflamed both national sentiment and rage in the military. The American commander in Samar, Gen. Jacob H. Smith, ordered his men to kill every Filipino male over the age of ten and to turn the island into a "howling wilderness." Though not all of his subordinates obeyed the order, a fair number did, and thousands died, insurgent and civilian alike. The military managed to keep a lid on reports for a while, but in the spring of 1902, stories emerged of horrific American actions in Samar, and Congress ramped up hearings on the Philippines.[41]

The military mishandled the situation. The court-martial of a junior officer, Maj. Littleton Waller, went badly wrong when General Smith perjured himself on the stand, denying that he had ever issued any murderous orders. When Smith was court-martialed, it was for bad conduct, not perjury. His only punishment was an admonishment. In response to the outcry in the United States, Theodore Roosevelt (who became president upon McKinley's assassination in September 1901) forced Smith's retirement. This in combination with a whitewash of the situation in the report by a Senate committee chaired by Henry Lodge of Massachusetts quieted the crisis.[42] The military side of the war was close enough to victory that the darkness did not affect the American effort, but a year earlier it might well have destroyed the credibility of the American message, with potentially awkward consequences.

The grimness of the spring made things ugly back home, but in the Philippines the intensity had subsided. In 1901 Aguinaldo became a prisoner, the insurgency fragmented without leadership, and many of the *insurrectos* switched sides. Teddy Roosevelt welcomed the ebbing. He had inherited the Philippine-American War. Although he approved of America's role, its end allowed him to focus on his own agenda. The controversy over its conduct also ended.

Roosevelt simply declared victory and left it there. Although the fighting had not stopped, on July 4, 1902, Roosevelt pronounced the Philippines pacified.[43] Independence Day was a particularly ironic choice, given the denial of independence to the Philippines. As a communication strategy, simply declaring the war over posed a risk. If the fighting had revived, Roosevelt would have looked foolish, but it did not. The Moro Rebellion (in the southern islands of the archipelago) was distinct enough in geography and motivations not to make the president a liar. To some degree, Roosevelt had ended the war by declaring it over and daring someone to prove him wrong. For an America tired of the war, this turned out to be an acceptable message. The fighting trickled off over the course of the next decade, but even in 1911 US Army analysts thought that a foreign invasion of the islands would see an "insurrection of the native population . . . quite generally."[44]

Even after Roosevelt had declared victory, he found the Philippines a hot political topic in the United States. The Catholic Church expressed concerns about the curricula Filipino schools taught to the (largely Catholic) schoolchildren. Many of the textbooks in American school systems had a strongly anti-Catholic tone, and the Church did not want that attitude exported. As a growing segment of the population, Catholics had political leverage. Roosevelt saw an opportunity to pull Catholic voters into the Republican camp, and so he picked Gen. James Francis Smith, a Catholic Democrat, to be the governor general of the islands in 1903.[45] Such a choice communicated to the Church that Roosevelt understood and supported its concerns, and he did so in a way that did not arouse Protestant voters. This was a final reminder of how contingent, informal, and negotiated the communications over the Philippine-American War were.

Conclusion

The Philippine-American War happened at a particularly chaotic moment for communications, both technologically and socially. The rise of American general education had created a literate mass public, and the new printing presses and telegraph disseminated information globally. The war in the Philippines thus happened under the scrutiny not only of policymakers but also of American voters. The military found itself on a public pedestal, its actions and ideas scrutinized in unprecedented ways. Moreover, this scrutiny became almost immediate, as news from Manila could be sent around the world in hours and days rather than weeks and months. Both the administration and the military had to develop a communication strategy that accounted for this near-real-time situation.

With some exceptions, they did both reasonably effectively. The message that McKinley, Roosevelt, and the military used, the message that the United States had an educational and civilizing mission in the Philippines, resonated with the racial and paternalistic attitudes of the American people and elites. It echoed closely enough the "manifest destiny" of American westward expansion to become a continuation of America's settler ethos. This was perhaps the central factor of the messaging strategy; it acknowledged that communication was a two-way street. The leadership of the United States could not impose its vision on the American public. Rather, it had to find a compelling message that the American public agreed with and would unify around. The failure of the Filipino insurgents came at least partly from their inability to do the same thing. While the US message might not have resonated with the insurgents, they developed no competing unifying message that their diverse population agreed with and would unify around. The US strategy was less about communication and more about a discussion enabling the US government and public to find common ground on annexation; they did, and the islands became American.

Notes

1. Louis Stanley Young, *The Life and Heroic Deeds of Admiral Dewey, including Battles in the Philippines* (Philadelphia: Globe Bible, 1899), vi, 18, 19, 111.
2. William McElwee, *The Art of War from Waterloo to Mons* (London: Weidenfield and Nicholson, 1974), 277.
3. Kenneth Hagan, *This People's Navy: The Making of American Seapower* (New York: Free Press, 1991), 221.
4. Whitelaw Reid to C. Inman Barnard, July 23, 1898, in "Rise to World Power: Selected Letters of Whitelaw Reid, 1895–1912," ed. David R. Conosta and Jessica R. Hawthorne, *Transactions of the American Philosophical Society* 76, no. 2 (1986): 141.
5. Bruce White, "War Preparations and Ethnic and Racial Relations in the United States," in *Anticipating Total War: The German and American Experiences, 1871–1914,* ed. Manfred Boemeke and Roger Chickering (Cambridge: Cambridge University Press, 1999), 97–124.
6. Paul Crook, *Darwinism, War, and History* (Cambridge: Cambridge University Press, 1994), 95, 96.

7. Quoted in Russell Roth, *Muddy Glory: America's 'Indian Wars' in the Philippines, 1899–1935* (W. Hanover, MA: Christopher Publishing House, 1981), 16.
8. Quoted in Robert Asprey, *War in the Shadows: The Guerrilla in History* (New York: William & Morrow, 1994 [1976]), 122.
9. Hagan, *This People's Navy*, 202.
10. Young, *Heroic Deeds*, 94; James K. Eyre Jr., "Russia and the American Acquisition of the Philippines," in *Mississippi Valley Historical Review* 28, no. 4 (March 1942): 539–62.
11. William McKinley, "Second Annual Message to Congress," December 5, 1898, in *The American Presidency Project*, ed. Gerhard Peters and John T. Woolley, http://www.presidency.ucsb.edu/ws/index.php?pid=29539.
12. Charles G. Dawes, *A Journal of the McKinley Years* (Chicago: Lakeside Press, 1950), 166.
13. Robert Rydell, "The Trans-Mississippi and International Exposition: 'To Work Out the Problem of International Civilization,'" in *American Quarterly* 33, no. 5 (Winter 1981): 587–607, 603–4. See also David Silbey, *A War of Frontier and Empire: The Philippine-American War, 1899–1902* (New York: Hill and Wang, 2007), esp. chap. 2.
14. Brian Damiani, *Advocates of Empire: William McKinley, the Senate, and American Expansion, 1898–1899* (New York: Garland, 1987), 98.
15. Roland Wenzlhuemer, *Connecting the Nineteenth-Century World: The Telegraph and Globalization* (Cambridge: Cambridge University Press, 2013).
16. Richard Price, *An Imperial War and the British Working Class: Working-Class Attitudes and Reactions to the Boer War, 1899–1902* (London: Routledge & K. Paul, 1972).
17. Quoted in Mark Joseph Peceny, "The Promotion of Democracy in U.S. Policy during Military Interventions," (PhD diss., Stanford University, 1992), 113.
18. Eric Tyrone Lowery Love, *Race over Empire: Racism and U.S Imperialism, 1865–1900* (Chapel Hill: University of North Carolina Press, 2004), 181–82.
19. Peceny, "Promotion of Democracy," 73.
20. Rudyard Kipling, "The White Man's Burden," 1899, http://www.fordham.edu/halsall/mod/kipling.asp.
21. Quoted in Steffi San Buenaventura, "The Colors of Manifest Destiny: Filipinos and the American Other(s)," *Amerasia Journal* 24, no. 3 (1998): 3.
22. Walter L. Williams, "United States Indian Policy and the Debate over Philippine Annexation: Implications for the Origins of American Imperialism," *Journal of American History* 66, no. 4 (March 1980): 810–31.
23. Forrest Pogue, *George C. Marshall: Education of a General, 1880–1939* (New York: Viking Press, 1963), 51.
24. Pogue, 53.

25. Both quotes from Lewis O. Saum, "The Western Volunteer and 'The New Empire,'" in *Pacific Northwest Quarterly* 57, no. 1 (January 1996): 18–27.

26. Saum.

27. Scot Ngozi-Brown, "African-American Soldiers and Filipinos: Racial Imperialism, Jim Crow and Social Relations," *Journal of Negro History* 82, no. 1 (1997): 42–53.

28. Pogue, *George C. Marshall*, 73.

29. John S. Reed, *External Discipline during Counterinsurgency: A Philippine War Case-Study, 1900–01* (n.p.: Spring, 1995).

30. Susan K. Harris, *God's Arbiters: Americans and the Philippines, 1898–1902* (New York: Oxford University Press, 2011), 142–44.

31. GDP figures from LK, "US Real per Capita GDP from 1870–2001," *Social Democracy for the Twenty-First Century: A Realist Alternative to the Modern Left*, September 24, 2012, http://socialdemocracy21stcentury.blogspot.com/2012/09/us-real-per-capita-gdp-from-18702001.html. For the election of 1900, see Walter LaFeber, "Election of 1900," in *History of American Presidential Elections, 1789–2001*, ed. Arthur M. Schlesinger Jr. (Philadelphia: Chelsea House Publishers, 2002), 5:1875–1962.

32. Richard E. Welch Jr., "American Atrocities in the Philippines: The Indictment and the Response," *Pacific Historical Review* 43, no. 2 (May 1974): 233–52.

33. Anonymous, "From a Colored Soldier in Manila," in *The Public: A Journal of Democracy* 2, no. 80 (October 14, 1899): 13.

34. Willard B. Gatewood, *Black Americans and the White Man's Burden, 1898–1903* (Urbana: University of Illinois Press, 1975), 277.

35. Charles Rhodes Papers, Military History Institute, Carlisle, PA.

36. John R. M. Taylor, *The Philippine Insurrection against the United States: A Compilation of Documents with Notes and Introduction* (Pasay City, Philippines: Eugenio Lopez Foundation, 1971), 4:544, 576.

37. Taylor, 106.

38. Silbey, *War of Frontier and Empire*, 115.

39. Robert D. Ramsey III, *Savage Wars of Peace: Case Studies of Pacification in the Philippines, 1900–1902* (Fort Leavenworth, KS: Combat Studies Institute Press, 2007), 4.

40. Glenn May, "150,000 Missing Filipinos: A Demographic Crisis in Batangas, 1887–1903," *Annales de Demographie Historique* 21 (1985): 215–43.

41. Frank Schumacher, "'Marked Severities': The Debate over Torture during America's Conquest of the Philippines, 1899–1902," *Amerikastudien/American Studies* 51, no. 4 (2006): 475–98.

42. Edmund Morris, *Theodore Rex* (New York: Random House, 2001), 91–107. For a good discussion of Lodge's approach, see Michael J. Hostetler, "Henry Cabot Lodge and the Rhetorical Trajectory," in *The Rhetoric of American Exceptionalism: Critical*

Essays, ed. Jason A. Edwards and David Weiss (Jefferson, NC: McFarland, 2011), 118–29.

43. Morris, *Rex*, 119.
44. Brian McAllister Linn, "The Long Twilight of the Frontier Army," *Western Historical Quarterly* 27, no. 2 (Summer 1996): 158.
45. Judith Raftery, "Textbook Wars: Governor-General James Francis Smith and the Protestant-Catholic Conflict in Public Education in the Philippines, 1904–07," *History of Education Quarterly* 38, no. 2 (Summer 1998): 143–64.

6.

John Reed and US Perceptions of the Russian Revolution

Bruce A. Elleman

There has hardly been a more influential twentieth-century book than *Ten Days That Shook the World*. Journalist John Reed's firsthand account of the 1917 Bolshevik Revolution in Russia was an instant hit in the West upon its first printing in 1919. The manuscript was published in dozens of languages and had innumerable press runs. After 1924, however, the book was banned in the Soviet Union, perhaps because Bolshevik promises to the Russian people were being ignored. On a more personal note, Leon Trotsky's name appeared over fifty times in the text, compared to only two times for Joseph Stalin. This must have upset Stalin mightily, especially since Vladimir Lenin himself, at the end of 1919, wrote a foreword stating that Reed's account was a "truthful and most vivid exposition" of the October Revolution.[1]

After the book had been banned for thirty years, the USSR authorized a new edition of *Ten Days* in 1956. Published right as Nikita Khrushchev was denouncing Stalin in his "secret speech," the new Soviet edition included critical editorial changes. For example, in chapter 11, Stalin's name was no longer listed first in signing the Declaration of the Rights of the Peoples of Russia. Rather, Lenin's name was put first, and Stalin's was listed second.[2] In the "Notes and Explanations" the triumvirate of "Lenin, Trotsky, Lunacharsky" was taken out. A new footnote on Trotsky explained that he was a "concealed liquidator" who was expelled from the party in 1927 for "anti-Party and counter-revolutionary activities" and that in 1929 he was "sent abroad" where he "continued to wage a struggle against the Soviet Union and the Communist Parties."[3] Even as Stalin's historical legacy was being criticized by Khrushchev, Trotsky's contributions to the October Revolution could still not be recognized.

In this essay on Reed and his *Ten Days*, the messenger, medium, and message will each be addressed in two contrasting ways, including Reed's objectivity—or rather lack of objectivity—as a journalist versus his double standard for evaluating America and Russia; *Ten Days* as tragedy versus *Ten Days* as farce; and the origins of the Soviet military dictatorship versus the origins of the Cold War. The conclusions will sum up Reed's role as perhaps the twentieth century's first "super-empowered individual."[4]

Messenger: John Reed as Involved Journalist

John Reed was a modern journalist who wanted to be part of history rather than just reporting on it. He went to Russia without knowing a word of the Russian language—either spoken or written—and did not understand the history or culture of the people he was writing about. He did not care. Since he did not understand Russian, however, Reed's journalistic descriptions all too often attempted to portray events in Petrograd (St. Petersburg) as they might have occurred in the United States. His lack of objectivity appeared early in *Ten Days*, as he presented the Bolsheviks as "the only party in Russia with a constructive program." His failure to remain a detached observer was perhaps best shown when he stood in the back of a truck helping to throw out leaflets "announcing the fall of the Provisional Government."[5]

Unlike Russian journalists, who were frequently denied freedom of the press, Reed was given incredible access to the Bolshevik leaders and to the venues where important decisions were being made. His book includes copies of the many press passes he was given, including to Smolny Institute, the Bolshevik headquarters in Petrograd, and to the Kremlin, which prove that he received special treatment. Reed also had many intimate discussions with the revolution's leaders, including at least an hour-long one-on-one interview with Trotsky, after which the journalist reported their words verbatim. Later, when Trotsky wrote his seminal work, *The History of the Russian Revolution,* he cited Reed's work over a dozen times in volume 3 alone.[6] The considerable time the Bolshevik leaders devoted to Reed proves his value to them.

In hindsight it is easier to see how the Bolshevik leaders used Reed to produce a positive report of the October Revolution. Trotsky, who had lived in New York City, understood quite well the value of having a Western—and in particular American—journalist on their side. Since Reed gave the appearance of being an impartial witness, he was the perfect messenger to publicize the Bolsheviks' views to the outside world. In *Ten Days*'s foreword, Lenin even states, "Here is a book which I should like to see published in millions of copies and translated into all languages."[7] Lenin and Trotsky were using Reed as a messenger to reach a global audience.

Reed was a Soviet mouthpiece who had little choice but to repeat what Russian translators told him. One Russian friend, Angelica Balabanoff, tried to cover this up

by suggesting that it was Reed's "love of Russia that helped him overcome his ignorance of the language when he wrote *Ten Days*."[8] But for anyone who has ever tried
to learn a non-Romance language—and the Russian language's use of the Cyrillic
alphabet makes it one of the most difficult to learn—they know that love alone cannot conquer a foreign language. After Reed had spent almost three years reporting on
events in Russia, a colleague commented that he was only "able to stud his English
with a few words of Russian."[9]

Reed was coached—for example, by English-speaking Bolsheviks, including
Trotsky himself—so that his views corresponded to what the Bolsheviks wanted him
to report. At one point, Trotsky carefully stated that Reed "knew how to see and hear"
but not necessarily how to understand fully what he experienced during the October
Revolution.[10] In other words, Reed was converted into a Bolshevik propagandist, and
Ten Days was the propaganda line that the Bolsheviks wanted him to write. Soviet
director Sergei Eisenstein even made a movie version of the book, described as "a
remarkable synthesis of political propaganda and artistic achievement."[11]

Ten Days That Shook the World was an enormous literary success. Interest in Russia
renewed after World War II, and one author referred back to Reed when he wrote,
"Russia has gone on shaking the world for over a quarter of a century."[12] Even though
the book was published almost a century ago and the Bolsheviks are long dead, *Ten
Days* is still in print and carried by every major bookstore. Rather than being about a
particular revolution, *Ten Days* is a prime example of a type of book—a propaganda
book of the first order. George F. Kennan, author of the "X Article," later wrote of
Reed, "His influence on the course of events was exerted less by his activity in Russia
than by the effect on American liberal opinion of his eloquent literary descriptions
of the Russian political scene."[13] Theodore Draper, historian of the American Communist Party, wrote that Reed's *Ten Days* "converted more people to the Soviet cause
than the combined efforts of all other left-wing propaganda."[14] The reason Reed was
so successful, perhaps, was that he firmly believed every word that he wrote.

Messenger: Reed as a True Believer

Reed's lack of objectivity is shown by his admission that he was a true believer in the
October Revolution, or as one historian called him, "an out-and-out Bolshevik."[15] A
US diplomat who knew Reed well said of him, "Handsome and spoiled, I am afraid
that Jack Reed never quite grew up."[16] To be an effective propagandist, Reed had to
suppress his true feelings on many issues, including middle-class values, the right of
secession, the importance of the secret ballot to democracy, freedom of the press,
and finally, the American cornerstone belief in the freedom of religion. While in his
American writings Reed supported these principles, in *Ten Days* he condemns them.

Reed was a champion of the middle class. His first story, titled "Where the Heart Is" and published in *The Masses* magazine in January 1913, is a highly sympathetic tale of a New York prostitute named Martha. Ignoring how she earned her living, twenty-five-year-old Reed, a recent Harvard graduate, described Martha as a true American, the "Female White Hope." A representative of a newly emerged middle class, Martha returns to New York after a whirlwind tour in Europe and South America, enters the dance hall where she had formerly been a hostess, and only then realized that it was "Home! That's what it was! Home!"[17] In Reed's view, even an American prostitute can be a patriot and love her country.

In his draft manuscript of *Ten Days*, however, Reed was highly critical of Petrograd's middle-class prostitutes: "In the center of the city at night ~~thousands of~~ prostitutes in jewels and expensive furs walked up and down, crowded the cafes."[18] Later, Reed was particularly nasty about women workers at the telephone exchange who refused to work for the Bolsheviks: "The telephone girls were testifying. Girl after girl came to the tribune—over-dressed, fashion-aping little girls, with pinched faces and leaky shoes . . . to narrate her sufferings at the hands of the proletariat, and proclaim her loyalty to all that was old, established and powerful."[19] Reed's critical views of middle-class women in Russia were completely at odds with his highly positive description of American middle-class women just five years before.

To support the Bolsheviks, Reed abandoned his belief in democracy. When hearing the awful truth from a Committee for Salvation opponent, Reed ironically recounted, "The Power of the Soviets is not a democratic power, but a dictatorship—and not the dictatorship of the proletariat, but *against* the proletariat."[20] Yet in an earlier chapter Reed admitted that he witnessed a voting scene in which the Bolsheviks refused to allow secret ballots and demanded unanimity: "It was exactly 10:30 when Kamenev asked all in favor of the proclamation to hold up their cards. One delegate dared to raise his hand against, but the sudden sharp outburst around him brought it swiftly down . . . Unanimous."[21]

Another aspect of democracy was the right of secession. Reed quoted at length the Declaration of the Rights of the Peoples of Russia as including "the right of the peoples of Russia to free self-determination, even to the point of separation and the formation of an independent state."[22] Edited from the typed manuscript, however, was evidence to the contrary: "Poland, White Russia and Siberia manifested nationalist tendencies."[23] Although he died young (at age thirty-three) in 1920, Reed lived through three years of the Russian Civil War, in which the Bolsheviks fought secessionists. During seventy years of Soviet power, many separatist movements—including in the Baltic States and later in Georgia and Chechnya—fought bitter struggles for independence.

Reed forgave the lack of democracy in Russia in a way that he would have never stood for it in America. The best example was the Bolshevik restrictions on freedom of the press. Reed had been arrested and jailed for four days when he refused to heed a policeman's order to move along while he was covering the mill workers' 1913 strike in Paterson, New Jersey. And yet Reed quoted at length—in a clearly critical manner—a protest by the Left Social Revolutionaries: "We protest, moreover, against tyrannical conduct of the Bolsheviki. Our Commissars have been driven from their posts. Our only organ, *Znamia Truda* (Banner of Labor), was forbidden to appear yesterday."[24] Discussing reporters from "the bourgeois and 'moderate' Socialist papers," Reed described how the Bolsheviks "threw us out! . . . They all began to talk at once: 'Insult! Outrage! Freedom of the press!'"[25] While Reed was willing to go to jail in New Jersey to support freedom of the press, he approved the Bolshevik decision to deny this democratic right in Russia.

A final example of Reed's hypocrisy was around the issue of freedom of religion. Baptized in Portland's Trinity Episcopal Church in 1887, Reed graduated in 1910 from Harvard—whose original motto "Veritas Christo et Ecclesiae" means "Truth for Christ and the Church." In America Reed certainly had a healthy Constitution-guaranteed respect for freedom of religion. But in Russia, Reed noted with apparent glee that the Russian Orthodox Church was no longer Russia's state church: "The devout Russian people no longer needed priests to pray them into heaven. On earth they were building a kingdom more bright than any heaven had to offer, and for which it was a glory to die."[26] Of course, as time would show, faith in Communism replaced Christianity, and after the USSR's collapse in 1991, the Russian Orthodox Church revived.

Reed must have found it hard as a Harvard-trained intellectual imbued with a belief in "truth" to reconcile his support for the Bolsheviks with their poor treatment of middle-class women, their failure to uphold democratic principles like the secret ballot, and their denunciation of freedom of the press. As for religion, Reed was perhaps unconsciously writing the "Bible" for his new faith in Communism, yet his version of this religion did not completely satisfy a new set of Soviet leaders. Stalin's later ban on Reed's book lasted for over thirty years. It was fitting, albeit ironic, that within two years of writing *Ten Days*, Reed achieved his own personal "martyrdom" when he died of typhus after a trip to Baku espousing Communism. Moments like these make reading *Ten Days* appear sometimes as a tragedy and other times as a farce.

Medium: Reed's *Ten Days* as Tragedy

Leon Trotsky once described John Reed as the "poet of the insurrection."[27] Reed's failure to be objective makes his book a work of propaganda. Evidence of this appears in the title of the book, *Ten Days*. Was it really ten days? In fact, Reed begins his account with the Bolshevik takeover on November 7 and ends with the decision of the Peasants' Congress on November 18 (Western calendar).[28] Basic math says this is twelve days, not ten. Why is there a simple counting error in the title?

Reed was determined not to call his book *Twelve Days That Shook the World*. Twelve, in Western thinking, can be related to Jesus and his twelve apostles. It is also the number of months in a year, citizens in a trial by jury, and inches in an English and American foot. Reed probably considered twelve to be "old thinking," as compared to the metric system, which was based on tens. Even Marx and Engels in 1848 had shown a preference for scientific thinking when they ended the *Communist Manifesto* with a list of ten goals that had to be accomplished to achieve socialism.

Reed's very choice of title suggests that the Bolsheviks were the wave of the future. He introduced the Bolsheviks in chapter 1: "In this atmosphere of corruption, of monstrous half-truths, one clear note sounded day after day, the deepening chorus of the Boksheviki, 'All Power to the Soviets!'"[29] The Bolsheviks were hardworking revolutionaries, volunteering to enter the revolutionary machine and then being spat out once they are used up: "On the top floor the Military Revolutionary Committee was in full blast, striking and slacking not. Men went in, fresh and vigorous; night and day and night and day they threw themselves into the terrible machine; and came out limp, blind with fatigue, hoarse and filthy, to fall on the floor and sleep." Because of the Bolsheviks' tireless energy, "Smolny thrilled with the boundless vitality of inexhaustible humanity in action."[30]

Reed's heroic description of the Bolsheviks would have been less one-sided if manuscript cuts had been included in the final text. One such cut reads, "In the hall I ran into some of the minor Bolshevik leaders. . . . Said one, nervously, 'You see, it's like this. If the workmen <u>do</u> come out, and it looks good, we'll put ourselves at the head of it. If it doesn't seem to be going, we'll disown the whole business."[31] It is not clear who cut this passage—Reed or some anonymous editor—but its exclusion was certainly intended to cover up Bolshevik opportunism.

By contrast, Reed harshly criticized the Bolsheviks' opponents: "This *Duma* crowd was well-fed, well-dressed; I did not see more than three proletarians among them all."[32] To besmirch them, Reed repeated unsubstantiated rumors: "The speculators took advantage of the universal disorganization to pile up fortunes, and to spend them in fantastic revelry or the corruption of Government officials. Foodstuffs and fuel were hoarded, or secretly sent out of the country to Sweden."[33] This was a bizarre accusation, especially given the German naval blockade of the Baltic Sea. The editor of the 1960 edition of *Ten Days*, the historian Bertram D. Wolfe, noted, "There is no evidence to support this inherently absurd charge that foodstuffs were sent to Sweden.—Ed."[34]

But the damage was done, as Reed depicted the Bolsheviks as wearing white hats and the members of the Duma as wearing black ones. "Constructed like a movie script in which the Bolsheviks figure as the 'good guys' and all their opponents as 'bad guys,' the book was widely perceived as an authentic account, even though it was little more than propaganda by an enthusiastic American in search of romantic excitement."[35] Elsewhere, Reed described the October Revolution as a miracle: "In wide-spreading ripples news of the miracle spread over the face of the land, and in its wake towns, cities and far villages stirred and broke, Soviets and Military Revolutionary Committees against Dumas, Zemstvos and Government Commissars—Red Guards against White—street fighting and passionate speech. . . . The results waited on the word from Petrograd."[36]

Glorifying science, Reed used geological imagery of a volcano to describe the revolution: "A ground-swell of revolt heaved and cracked the crust which had been slowly hardening on the surface of the revolutionary fires dormant all those months."[37] The Bolsheviks were like eagles: "How far they had soared, these Bolsheviki, from a despised and hunted sect less than four months ago, to this supreme place, the helm of great Russia in full tide of insurrection!"[38] Thus, destroying old Russia was like a volcanic eruption: "The Bolsheviki, in one night, had dissipated it, as one blows away smoke. Old Russia was no more; human society flowed molten in primal heat, and from the tossing sea of flame was emerging the class struggle, stark and pitiless—and the fragile, slowly-cooling crust of new planets."[39]

Reed decried any hint of journalistic objectivity in his mistitled *Ten Days*. For example, after his interview with Alexander Kerensky, the leader of the provisional government, Reed edited out Kerensky's timely warning: "The French Revolution, which was the movement of a homogenous people, in a territory not as large as one Russian province, took seven years."[40] Reed did not know it, but seventy years later—ten times longer than the French Revolution—the Russian Revolution finally reached its climax. This knowledge makes what wasn't a tragedy in *Ten Days* often appear as farce.

Medium: *Ten Days* as Farce

To some it might appear sacrilegious to suggest that *Ten Days* can be read as a comedy, but since its first publication in 1919, there have been many bitingly humorous farces about war and politics, from *Catch-22* to *M.A.S.H* to *Primary Colors*. Karl Marx himself said when history repeats itself the first time, it is a tragedy, but the second time it is a farce. The October Revolution is one of history's greatest farces, and Reed's passionately written saga—perhaps unconsciously farcical given his firm belief in Bolshevik goals—can be read as a comedy.

Viewed from almost a century after its first publication, and with the fall of the Berlin Wall in 1989, the dissolution of the Soviet Empire, and the collapse of the USSR in 1991 clearly in mind, Reed's observations about the October Revolution take on a humorous light. For example, at a party meeting one member "asked the comrades not to smoke; then everybody, smokers and all, took up the cry 'Don't smoke, comrades!' and went on smoking."[41] One participant bitterly complained about the difficulty of carrying out politics in Russia: "It is not easy for us Russians, politics. You Americans are born politicians; you have had politics all your lives. But for us—well, it has only been a year, you know!"[42] On a train to Moscow, food was short so each car organized its own food committee: "Before we reached Moscow almost every car had organized a Committee to secure and distribute food, and the Committees became divided into political factions, who wrangled over fundamental principles."[43]

Some of the funniest scenes in the book concern the Bolshevik leaders. For example, Reed recounted Trotsky's undignified reception at the Smolny Institute:

> One day as I came up to the outer gate I saw Trotzky and his wife just ahead of me. They were halted by a soldier. Trotzky searched through his pockets, but could find no pass.
>
> "Never mind," he said finally, "You know me. My name is Trotzky."
>
> "You haven't got a pass," answered the soldier stubbornly, "You cannot go in. Names don't mean anything to me."
>
> "But I am the president of the Petrograd soviet."
>
> "Well," replied the soldier, "if you're as important a fellow as that you must at least have one little paper."
>
> Trotzky was very patient, "Let me see the Commandant," he said. The soldier hesitated, grumbling something about not wanting to disturb the Commandant for every devil that came along. He beckoned finally to the soldier in command of the guard. Trotzky explained matters to him, "My name is Trotzky," he repeated.
>
> "Trotzky?" The other soldier scratched his head. "I've heard the name somewhere," he said at length. "I guess it's all right. You can go on in, comrade."[44]

Reed portrayed Lenin in a manner akin to Ichabod Crane in the *Legend of Sleepy Hollow*: a "short, stocky figure, with a big head . . . Little eyes, a snubbish nose . . . Dressed in shabby clothes . . . Unimpressive, to be the idol of a mob, loved and revered as perhaps few leaders in history have been."[45] Busy with revolution, Lenin granted the delegates a half-hour intermission, urging, "No delay!" But everyone ignored Lenin, and the meeting reconvened only after a two-and-a-half-hour intermission.[46]

Like Mark Twain traveling through Europe as a tourist and reporting on foreign affairs in *Innocents Abroad* a half century earlier, Reed too was fixated on movement.

Most of the book he seems to be going somewhere, on foot, by tram, or in a taxi. While speeding from place to place, Reed described driving at night without lights: "We had no kerosene, so our lights were not burning. . . . We hurtled furiously on, wrenched right and left to avoid collisions that seemed inevitable, scraping wheels, followed by epithets of pedestrians."[47]

Reed also faced personal danger. At one point Red Guards stopped him: "In order not to make any trouble, I got down from the truck, and watched it disappear careening down the road, all the company waving farewell. The soldiers consulted in low tones for a moment, and then led me to a wall, against which they placed me. It flashed upon me suddenly; they were going to shoot me!" Since the soldiers were illiterate, Reed took them to a local farmhouse. There, a "short, stout woman" read the pass to them. Reed was then taken to the Second Tsarskoye Selo Rifles. They confirmed his identity, and he was freed.[48] This story, based on a real event, seems straight out of a Kurt Vonnegut novel like *Slaughterhouse-Five*.

Reed's description of preparation for fighting reads like a Marx brothers script. When the Red Guards needed a machine gun, one Red Guard

> remembered all at once that there was lying in the meeting-room of the *Uprava* a machine-gun which had been captured from the Germans. So he and I and another comrade went there. The Mensheviki and Socialist Revolutionaries [the Bolsheviks' enemies] were having a meeting. Well, we opened the door and walked right in on them, as they sat around the table— twelve or fifteen of them, three of us. When they saw us they stopped talking and just stared. We walked right across the room, uncoupled the machine-gun; Comrade Zalkind picked up one part, I the other, we put them on our shoulders and walked out—and not a single man said a word![49]

Finally, perhaps subconsciously sensing where his beloved revolution would end up seventy years later, Reed at one point remarked that "The Funeral March" fit Russia better than "The Internationale": "The Funeral March seemed the very soul of those dark masses whose delegates sat in this hall, building from their obscure visions a new Russia—and perhaps more."[50] Portraying the Bolshevik revolution as farce, one French officer commented: "Ah, these Russians . . . they are original! What a civil war! Everything except the fighting!"[51]

Reed was perhaps the first person to poke fun—albeit unknowingly—at the Bolsheviks in a published book. He highlighted the total incompetence of the Red Guards and even more so their opponents. Reed was not alone. Within twenty years the peculiar behavior of the Bolsheviks was parodied in such Hollywood films as *Ninotchka*. As a result, *Ten Days* can be read as a political comedy of the first order.

A close reading of Reed's book also reveals a fateful message: it was not the people who took the reins of power in their hands during twelve crucial days in 1917, but the military.

Message: The Russian Revolution as a Military Dictatorship

Readers of *Ten Days* often miss that the October Revolution was really a coup d'etat rather than a true bottom-up revolution. While Lenin was the political leader, Trotsky led the military wing of the revolution. Reed described Trotsky at the podium: "Trotzky mounted the tribune, borne on a wave of roaring applause that burst into cheers and a rising house, thunderous. His thin, pointed face was positively Mephistophelian in its expression of malicious irony."[52] Trotsky knew how to get things done. Reed described an election under Trotsky's ruthless leadership: it took "barely fifteen minutes" because Trotsky "announced its composition: 100 members, of which 70 [were] Bolsheviki."[53]

Trotsky knew what he wanted. Reed gave a vivid description of his interview with Trotsky, in English presumably, since Trotsky had lived in Brooklyn for several years. Trotsky "talked rapidly and steadily, for more than an hour."[54] Under Trotsky worked former czarist officers. Reed described Trotsky's assistant as "a thin-faced, long-haired individual, once an officer in the armies of the Tsar, then revolutionist and exile, a certain Ovseenko, called Antonov, mathematician and chess-player; he [Antonov] was drawing careful plans for the seizure of the capital."[55]

Even though military leaders like Trotsky and Antonov organized the Bolshevik putsch, Reed tried his best to credit the masses: "It was the masses of the people, workers, soldiers and peasants, which forced every change in the course of the Revolution." In another passage average people led the defense against the Cossacks: "Men, women and children, with rifles, picks, spades, rolls of wire, cartridge-belts over their working clothes . . . They rolled along torrent-like, companies of soldiers borne with them, guns, motor-trucks, wagons—the revolutionary proletariat defending with its breast the capital of the Workers' and Peasants' Republic." Yet Reed admitted that military power—such as armored cars, the World War I equivalent of tanks—was crucial: "The *bronoviki* were the Armoured Car troops, the key to the situation; whoever controlled the *bronoviki* controlled the city."[56]

Reed's description of average soldiers listening to political debates revealed that they were incapable of leading the revolution: "Never have I seen men trying so hard to understand, to decide. They never moved, stood staring with a sort of terrible intentness at the speaker, their brows wrinkled with the effort of thought, sweat standing out on their foreheads; great giants of men with the innocent clear eyes of children and the faces of epic warriors." But while describing the impact of the revolutionary ideals on the Army, Reed optimistically wrote, "Such a deluge of high and hot thoughts that surely Russia would never again be dumb!"[57]

In fact, the military, and especially its middle-class leaders, made all the difference to the revolution. Reed described Trotsky as the Bolsheviks' ruthless mastermind: "'For each revolutionist killed,' said Trotsky, 'we shall kill five counter-revolutionists!'"[58] As for Bolshevik violations of prisoners' rights, Reed admitted,

> At half-past two the *yunkers* hoisted a white flag; they would surrender if they were guaranteed protection. This was promised. With a rush and a shout thousands of soldiers and Red Guards poured through the windows, doors and holes in the wall. Before it could be stopped five *yunkers* were beaten and stabbed to death. The rest, about two hundred, were taken to the Peter-Paul under escort, in small groups so as to avoid notice. On the way a mob set upon one party, killing eight more *yunkers*.

As if to excuse this barbaric behavior, Reed noted, "More than a hundred Red Guards and soldiers had fallen." And of another scene, Reed related, "Frenzied by defeat and their heaps of dead, the Soviet troops opened a tornado of steel and flame against the battered building. Their own officers could not stop the terrible bombardment. A Commissar from Smolny named Kirilov tried to halt it; he was threatened with lynching."[59]

If read with a fuller awareness of military strategy, Reed's *Ten Days* clarified that the military, not the people, made the October Revolution a success. An essential precondition to military victory was Trotsky's control of the armored car brigades. Reed also recorded that while Bolshevik propaganda claimed the prime goal was to declare peace and pull Russia out of World War I, the Bolsheviks' actions proved that they were preparing for another—bigger—war, in which the stakes were world domination. This is the true origin of the Cold War.

Message: Cold War Origins

Reed's *Ten Days* included a global message, which largely corresponded with his anti-American sentiments at the time.[60] Reed made much of Bolshevik propaganda: "Land, bread, an end to the senseless war, an end to secret diplomacy, speculation, treachery. . . . The Revolution is in danger, and with it the cause of the people all over the world!"[61] But the Bolshevik promise to end World War I would lead to a new, even larger, global war—the Cold War. The stakes of this global war were high, with the winner taking all: "'There are only two alternatives: either the Russian Revolution will create a revolutionary movement in Europe, or the European powers will destroy the Russian Revolution.'"[62]

Bolshevik propaganda denounced secret diplomacy: "The Government abolishes secret diplomacy . . . and will proceed immediately to the full publication of the secret treaties."[63] The Council of People's Commissars "had promised to publish the Secret Treaties; but Neratov, the functionary in charge, had disappeared, taking the documents with him. They were supposed to be hidden in the British Embassy."[64] But the Bolshevik promise not to resort to secret diplomacy was short-lived. In 1939 the Soviets signed their infamous secret treaty with the Germans—the Molotov-Ribbentrop Pact—which helped to precipitate World War II.

As a first step in declaring war against the rest of the world, Lenin also sought to undermine the world economy: "We shall now proceed to construct the Socialist order!"[65] Since the banks were closed and the Bolsheviks had no money, they in fact stole whatever they needed. Reed recorded, "But Lenin has issued an order to dynamite the State Bank vaults, and there is a Decree just out, ordering the private banks to open to-morrow, or we will open them ourselves!"[66] In addition, Reed recounted how Russia's foreign debts had to be canceled because all records of these debts had been destroyed during the chaos of the revolution. This is a ludicrous claim, considering that copies of all such financial records most certainly were held by foreign creditors.

Even though Reed cheerfully wore blinders to the Bolsheviks' faults, some Russians saw more clearly what was really going on. They understood the menace that Bolshevism might inflict on the world. Reed critically cited Stepan Georgevitch Lianozov's view on revolution: "'Revolution,' he said, 'is a sickness. Sooner or later the foreign powers must intervene here—as one would intervene to cure a sick child, and teach it how to walk. . . . The nations must realize the danger of Bolshevism in their own countries.'" Accurately predicting what would happen over seventy years later, Lianozov said that only "starvation and defeat may bring the Russian people to their senses."[67]

Reed tried to justify the Bolshevik declaration of a worldwide war by blaming foreign countries for opposing the revolution. At one point he argued that the Western countries began the Cold War, stating that "among the dead was a British officer." Elsewhere, he repeated reports of French involvement: "Later the newspapers told of another French officer, captured in a *yunker* armoured car and sent to Peter-Paul." Reed provided no proof, however, and the editor of the 1960 edition of *Ten Days* felt the need to clarify that all of these rumors, including references to German officers leading the Red Guard attacks on the Winter Palace, "presumably" had no truth in them.[68]

Although completely taken in by the propaganda, Reed truthfully recorded the Bolshevik message that the October Revolution would result in global conflict: "Now it would begin. Now there was all great Russia to win—and then the world. . . . Would the peoples answer and rise, a red world-tide?"[69] Rather than pinning the blame on the West, therefore, Reed's *Ten Days* provided convincing proof that the Cold War began with Russia. Reed was present in March 1919 when the

Communist International (Comintern) was created with the goal of spreading Communism worldwide. It is impossible to argue that Reed was biased against the October Revolution, but his own words show that the Bolsheviks started the Cold War. Later authors confirmed that in the midst of this two-camp struggle, Reed "was on the pro-Soviet side of the fence."[70]

Conclusion

John Reed's highly readable history of the October Revolution remains in print and is widely available today. But *Ten Days That Shook the World* is not an accurate history of the October Revolution. In hindsight it is best described as a historical novel, precisely because of all its "mythology and distortions."[71] Books written since the end of the Cold War have been uniformly harsh about Reed, with one describing him as a "radical U.S. journalist, sympathetic to the Communist revolution."[72] But to return to the framework of this edited volume—message, messenger, and media—it is important to see Reed's role not as an unbiased messenger but as a self-proclaimed "enthusiast."[73]

Reed's book has been covered by the media for almost a century, arguably making him the twentieth century's first super-empowered individual for his ability as a private citizen to shape how Americans thought about the Russian Revolution and its revolutionaries. *Ten Days* is the most famous account of any revolution, anywhere, and during all time. Reed "makes us feel as no one else has done what it was like to be there, especially if you happened to be a foreigner and an avid supporter of the Bolsheviks."[74] As the eminent British historian A. J. P. Taylor wrote, *Ten Days* is not only the "best account of the Bolshevik Revolution" but perhaps the "best account of any revolution."[75] For this reason, *Ten Days* continues to have an impact long after the revolution it discussed has not only died away but been buried by successive Russian governments that have criticized the October Revolution's excesses.

Reed's message is also a truthful description of how the Bolsheviks used their success in Russia to declare war on the world, not the other way around. Although Reed was sympathetic to the Bolsheviks and their cause, he provided sufficient documentary evidence to determine who and what the Bolsheviks really were. A careful reading of *Ten Days* proves conclusively that the Bolsheviks created a military dictatorship intent on world domination; later Soviet accusations that the West started the Cold War are simply untrue. This too could be why the book was banned for so long in the Soviet Union, reappearing in print only after Khrushchev had adopted the more reasonable policy of "peaceful coexistence." Indeed, Reed's mastery of the media technology of his time—the newspaper and the book—allowed him to carry the message of the Bolsheviks' true intentions, and *Ten Days* still provides modern readers with a fanciful tale of revolution that shaped American perspectives of Russian revolutionaries.

Notes

1. V. I. Lenin, foreword to *Ten Days That Shook the World*, by John Reed (New York: Modern Library, 1960), xlvi.
2. Dzhon Rid, *10 dnej, kotorye potrjasli mir* (Moskva: Gosudarstvennoe Izdatelstvo Polititsheskoĭ Literatury, 1957).
3. Cited in Bertram D. Wolfe, introduction to Reed, *Ten Days* (1960), xliii.
4. This term was coined by Thomas Friedman in *The Lexus and the Olive Tree* (New York: Farrar, Straus and Giroux, 1999).
5. David C. Duke, *John Reed* (Boston: Twayne Publishers, 1987), 123.
6. Leon Trotsky, *The History of the Russian Revolution: The Triumph of the Soviets* (New York: Simon & Schuster, 1932), see index.
7. V. I. Lenin, foreword to *Ten Days That Shook the World*, by John Reed (New York: Modern Library, 1935).
8. Duke, *John Reed*, 129.
9. Alfred Rosmer, *Lenin's Moscow*, trans. Ian H. Birchall (London: Pluto Press, 1971), 87.
10. Leon Trotsky, *The History of the Russian Revolution: The Attempted Counter-Revolution* (New York: Simon & Schuster, 1932), 187.
11. Michael Kort, *The Soviet Colossus: A History of the USSR* (London: Routledge Press, 1990), 135.
12. George Soloveytchik, *Russia in Perspective* (New York: W. W. Norton, 1947), 43.
13. George F. Kennan, *Russia and the West under Lenin and Stalin* (Boston: Little, Brown, 1960), 53.
14. Duke, *John Reed*, 130.
15. Christopher Lasch, *The American Liberals and the Russian Revolution* (New York: Columbia University Press, 1962), 138.
16. Edgar Sisson, *One Hundred Red Days: A Personal Chronicle of the Bolshevik Revolution* (New Haven, CT: Yale University Press, 1931), 259.
17. John Reed, *John Reed for* The Masses, ed. James C. Wilson (Jefferson, NC: McFarland, 1987), 19.
18. bMS AM 1091 (1245), folder 5, p. 24/57, John Reed Papers (JRP), Houghton Library, Harvard University. Editorial revision in pencil in an unknown hand.
19. John Reed, *Ten Days That Shook the World* (New York: Boni and Liveright, 1919), 204.
20. Reed (1919), 152.

21. bMS AM 1091 (1248), folder 2, p. 19/110, JRP.
22. Reed, *Ten Days* (1919), 260.
23. bMS AM 1091 (1245), folder 3, p. 10/36, JRP.
24. bMS AM 1091 (1248), folder 3, p. 28/119, JRP.
25. Reed, *Ten Days* (1919), 177.
26. Reed (1919), 259.
27. Trotsky, *History of the Russian Revolution*, 327.
28. One of Reed's more recent biographers argues that to get ten days, one must start counting on November 6 and stop counting on November 15, but to do so means ignoring the book's final two chapters. See Daniel W. Lehman, *John Reed and the Writing of Revolution* (Athens: Ohio University Press, 2002), 172.
29. bMS AM 1091 (1244), folder 2, p. 10/18, JRP.
30. Reed, *Ten Days* (1919), 200, 201.
31. bMS AM 1091 (1246), folder 3, p. 18/78, JRP. Underlining in original.
32. Reed, *Ten Days* (1919), 120.
33. bMS AM 1091 (1244), folder 2, pp. 8–9, 16–17, JRP.
34. Reed, *Ten Days* (1960), 9.
35. Richard Pipes, *A Concise History of the Russian Revolution* (New York: Alfred A. Knopf, 1995), 303.
36. Reed, *Ten Days* (1919), 207.
37. bMS AM 1091 (1245), folder 3, p. 13/41, JRP.
38. Reed, *Ten Days* (1919), 88.
39. Reed (1919), 150.
40. bMS AM 1091 (1245), folder 5, p. 21/54, JRP.
41. Reed, *Ten Days* (1919), 87.
42. Reed (1919), 212.
43. Reed (1919), 248.
44. bMS AM 1091 (1246), folder 2, p. 7a/65, JRP.
45. bMS AM 1091 (1248), folder 2, pp. 13–14, 104–5, JRP. Some published accounts mistakenly say "snobbish nose."
46. bMS AM 1091 (1248), folder 3, p. 23/114, JRP.
47. Reed, *Ten Days* (1919), 242.
48. Reed (1919), 236–38.
49. Reed (1919), 169.
50. bMS AM 1091 (1248), folder 2, p. 19/110, JRP.
51. Reed, *Ten Days* (1919), 189.
52. bMS AM 1091 (1246), folder 4, p. 26/88, JRP.
53. bMS AM 1091 (1248), folder 3, p. 31/122, JRP.
54. bMS AM 1091 (1246), folder 2, p. 7a/65, JRP.

55. Reed, *Ten Days* (1919), 56.
56. Reed (1919), 4, 158, 181.
57. Reed (1919), 137, 160.
58. Reed (1919), 204.
59. Reed (1919), 196.
60. Ivar Spector, *An Introduction to Russian History and Culture*, 5th ed. (Princeton, NJ: D. Van Nostrand, 1969), 344.
61. bMS AM 1091 (1244), folder 2, p. 10/18, JRP.
62. bMS AM 1091 (1248), folder 3, p. 30/121, JRP.
63. Reed, *Ten Days* (1919), 128.
64. Reed (1919), 214.
65. Reed (1919), 126.
66. Reed (1919), 214.
67. bMS AM 1091 (1244), folder 1, p. 7/15, JRP.
68. Reed, *Ten Days* (1960), 256.
69. bMS AM 1091 (1247), folder 5, p. 40/63, JRP.
70. Kennan, *Russia and the West*, 52.
71. Paul Dukes, *A History of Russia: Medieval, Modern, Contemporary* (Durham, NC: Duke University Press, 1990), 233.
72. Walter G. Moss, *A History of Russia* (New York: McGraw-Hill, 1997), 2:199.
73. Walter Laqueur, *The Dream That Failed: Reflections on the Soviet Union* (New York: Oxford University Press, 1994), 4.
74. Alan Moorehead, *The Russian Revolution* (New York: Harper and Brothers, 1958), 241.
75. Duke, *John Reed*, 130, citing Taylor's introduction to the 1977 edition of *Ten Days*.

7.

Theodore Roosevelt's Verbal Insurgency against Woodrow Wilson in World War I

J. Lee Thompson

Throughout World War I, former president and recently defeated presidential hopeful Theodore Roosevelt launched a verbal insurgency against Woodrow Wilson, the man whom his third-party candidacy had made president. In newspaper columns Roosevelt castigated Wilson's inadequate preparations for war, his insufficient aid to allies, and his lack of enforcement mechanisms for his peace plan. For a year Wilson tried to ignore Roosevelt's attacks while putting in place wartime censorship laws, but this allowed Roosevelt to dominate the public debate. In 1918 Wilson took actions consonant with many of Roosevelt's criticisms, such as centralizing Army purchases and establishing the War Industries Board. He also took control over the message with his announcement of his Fourteen Points, probably the most consequential presidential policy pronouncement in US history.

The usual narrative of the American media in the First World War traces the patriotic support for the Wilson administration by the mainstream press, despite its merciless suppression of socialist and foreign-language journals.[1] Largely missing from this version of events is the effective wartime criticism by Wilson's most potent political enemy, Theodore Roosevelt, whose voice was decidedly not silenced. By the time the United States joined the war in April 1917, a press and propaganda conflict over neutrality and preparedness had raged between these two preeminent political figures for more than two years. Roosevelt knew only too well that his 1912 Bull Moose rebellion had made Wilson commander in chief. Believing himself supremely qualified, Roosevelt yearned to lead the nation in the greatest war in modern memory.[2]

Both men came to this wartime media battle with long experience as progressive politicians used to courting and manipulating press publicity for their own ends.[3]

111

After the presidency, Roosevelt made a good living with his pen, producing a profusion of articles, essays, and books. During World War I he associated himself particularly with two journals: the monthly eclectic and elite *Metropolitan* magazine and the daily *Kansas City Star*. Though Wilson personally disdained the press, he had at his back numerous pro-Democratic papers, including the *New York Times*, the "independent Democratic" *Baltimore Sun,* the *Washington Times*, and perhaps most notably, the *New York World*, called "Mr. Wilson's organ" during the war years.[4]

Wilson's April 2, 1917, war message proclaimed that American motives were pure and most famously that "the world must be made safe for democracy." He carefully designated the country as an "associated power," not an ally, of Britain, France, and Russia. Though Roosevelt disagreed with these points, there was much in the speech that he supported, such as Wilson's declaration that the "right is more precious than the peace" and his warning that though most German Americans were "true and loyal Americans," disloyalty would be dealt with "with a firm hand of stern repression."[5] The Colonel, as Roosevelt styled himself after the presidency, released a statement to the newspapers that Wilson's message would "rank in history among the great State papers of which Americans in future years will be proud." It now rested with the people to see that "we put in practice the policy" the president had outlined and that "we strike as hard, as soon, and as effectively as possible in aggressive war" against Germany.[6]

In Roosevelt's estimation striking hard meant sending troops to the front as soon as possible. So he traveled to Washington to make his case to Wilson for a volunteer command. Asked by newsmen as he left the White House about his plans, Roosevelt replied they would "depend altogether on the 'course of events.'"[7] In the forlorn hope of gaining a command in France, Roosevelt temporarily curtailed his long-running criticisms of the commander in chief. Once it became clear he would not be allowed to fight and his sons were in the military, Roosevelt again opened his literary guns in a campaign to prod Wilson and his pacifist secretary of war, Newton Baker, to a maximum effort against the enemy.

Censorship: Muting the Message

Through executive orders, new laws, and new committees, the administration put into place mechanisms allowing Wilson to wield the "hand of stern repression" against disloyalty. On April 14, 1917, Wilson used his emergency powers to establish the first of these, the Committee on Public Information, under the leadership of George Creel, a minor muckraker, sycophantic supporter of Wilson, and caustic critic of Roosevelt. To the consternation of many newsmen and advisers, Wilson largely turned his press relations over to Creel. Consequently, before long Roosevelt and the Republican Party he had rejoined saw the committee as a propaganda arm of the Democrats. The Committee on Public Information was officially tasked with controlling war news through voluntary censorship methods and persuading the mass of the American public, which had supported neutrality, to accept Wilson's new moral vision of a crusade to "Make the World Safe for Democracy."[8] Using speakers, pamphlets, press releases, films, and other novel methods, Creel and his organization did their job all too well, helping to incite a wave of patriotic anti-German hysteria, while at the same time also carrying out political propaganda and damage control for the administration.[9]

The Espionage Act, an amalgamation of seventeen proposals much broader in scope than the antispying focus the title implied, also bolstered the government's ability to suppress opposition. Once passed in June 1917, it became the basis for extending federal jurisdiction over speech, the press, and general dissent in the war.[10] Its spying and antisubversive clauses drew little congressional criticism. At first Roosevelt and the Republicans welcomed the prospect of the government moving against aliens, socialists, and others, but a censorship provision against disloyal expression soon provoked fears that it could be used against them. The pro-Wilson *New York Times* led the almost unanimous press criticism, calling the act a "tyrannous measure" that would undermine democracy.[11]

The president appealed to Congress, arguing that the "authority to exercise censorship over the press" was "absolutely necessary to the public safety."[12] After nine weeks of political wrangling, the censorship provision was excised from the Espionage Act of 1917 signed by Wilson. Nevertheless, federal officials soon used two of its remaining provisions concerning interference with the armed services or the war effort to punish "individual casual or impulsive disloyal utterance." Thus began the wartime prosecutions of more than two thousand violations with over a thousand convictions, the most celebrated being the socialist leader Eugene V. Debs, who received the maximum twenty-year sentence.[13] Title III of the act gave the postmaster general, Albert S. Burleson, discretionary power to ban from the mails any published matter "advocating or urging treason, insurrection, or forcible resistance to any law of the United States." Another provision empowered the postmaster general to use his own judgment whether mailing certain kinds of matter constituted "willful obstruction to the progress of the war."[14] If so, this matter could be excluded from the mails without court order, and the burden of proof in any legal action would fall on the person who mailed the allegedly subversive matter. While Wilson announced that such powers would not be used to suppress civil liberties, Burleson directed local postmasters to do just that and to stay alert even for war-related matters that might simply embarrass the administration.[15]

Wilson dubbed Burleson "the Cardinal," in reference to his membership in a small Protestant denomination, the Bible Christian Church. Burleson was a narrow-minded scion of an old Texas political family. He became the self-appointed guardian of the nation, aggressively censuring the "subsidiary press." He particularly targeted socialist and foreign-language newspapers and magazines, fifteen of which were excluded from the mails within a month.[16] Within a year of the Espionage Act's passage, forty-four papers had lost their mailing privileges while thirty others promised to print nothing more about the war. Despite much criticism Wilson refused to rein in Burleson, and before long the Post Office began harassing more mainstream publications such as the *Metropolitan*, which ran Burleson afoul of Roosevelt. Despite these new powers, administration officials continued to demand even more explicit legislation to act against "dangerous utterances."[17]

Roosevelt opened his wartime press battle with the administration in the *Metropolitan*, where he published his lengthy correspondence with Secretary of War Newton Baker concerning the volunteer divisions that Wilson declined to use in favor of a draft Army. Roosevelt made the disclosure to refute scurrilous charges that he, among other things, had demanded command of all the volunteers. His proposed volunteer force would have been ready to sail with John J. Pershing's regular Army division. Agitation led by Roosevelt and "strongly endorsed" by the French envoy Gen. Joseph Joffre had obliged the Wilson administration to reverse its decision not to send troops immediately, and in doing so, the country was "saved the humiliation of taking no military part in the war through 1917 and part of 1918."[18] According to Roosevelt, the greatest danger was the ongoing "Peace Without Victory" promoted by the Anglophobe Hearst press, the German papers, and all the pro-Germans and pacifists.[19]

In July 1917 Roosevelt had already published in the *Metropolitan* his own eleven-part "Peace of Victory" plan, which detailed a complicated global territorial settlement: Italy should acquire territory from Austria-Hungary, the Czechs should receive a new commonwealth, a greater Serbia should unify the South Slavs, Hungary and Romania should become independent states, and a new democratic Russia should gain the Dardanelles and sponsorship over Finland, Poland, and Armenia, with possible independence for Lithuania. Outside Europe, Roosevelt proclaimed that Britain and Japan "must keep the colonies they have conquered."[20]

On September 9, 1917, the newspapers printed Roosevelt's "Children of the Crucible" appeal to "crush sedition in the United States." The American crucible "must melt all who are in it" and turn them out in the "one American mold." He called for "a peace based on the complete overthrow of the Prussianized Germany of the Hohenzollerns."[21] The papers also announced that Roosevelt had formed a related antitreason "Vigilantes" publicity organization staffed by a sympathetic cadre of journalists and writers. Vigilance, he declared, was the best method of fighting the evil of pro-Germanism. He tasked the group to monitor and to report on the seditious speeches of "soap-box" pacifists and pro-Germans.[22]

The Syndicated Column versus the Presidential Speech

Roosevelt's preferred medium was the syndicated column. In September he made a speaking tour west to Illinois, Missouri, and Kansas that allowed him to inspect the offices of the *Kansas City Star*, which he joined at this time as a contributing editor, and he acquired for the rest of the war a daily mass syndicated outlet for his criticisms. At the *Star's* offices Roosevelt joked that he had joined as a "cub" reporter.[23] One of his first editorials lampooned Wilson's "grandiloquent pronunciamentos" without "one single piece of completed achievement"; whereas one day Wilson promised an "infallible remedy against submarine attack," the next day he bemoaned a submarine toll "heavier than any previous month."[24] After giving a speech at Camp Grant, near Chicago, Roosevelt publicly blamed Maj. Gen. William Crozier, the chief of ordnance, along with Secretary of War Baker and Wilson, for the camp's inadequate weapon stocks, which left the draftees to drill with wooden guns.[25]

"Teddy's Ravings" against the administration's handling of the war in the *Kansas City Star* drew the attention of Wilson's cabinet. Treasury Secretary William Gibbs McAdoo denounced Roosevelt's "utter hypocrisy and lack of patriotism in trying to make the rest of the world believe" that America was as "feeble and as weak as he represents her."[26] Secretary of the Navy Josephus Daniels noted in his October 5, 1917, diary, "T.R. at large, writing and speaking in disparagement of America's preparation for war" was "helping Germany more than the little fellows" who were being arrested for giving seditious "aid and comfort" to the enemy. He wondered if the *Star*, which printed Roosevelt's "allusions to soldiers training with broomsticks," could be excluded from the mails (as authorized by the Espionage Act) along with the other papers, which spread what was "construed as seditious." Postmaster General Burleson told Roosevelt that the *Star* was being watched and that he would "not hesitate to act."[27] Although a postal inspector did visit the newspaper offices, no further action was taken.[28]

Rather than syndicated columns, Wilson relied on a dignified presidential medium. In his December 4, 1917, annual message to Congress, he reaffirmed his faith in the sanctity of the cause and in the adequacy of the war measures. He dismissed as of no consequence Roosevelt and the other "noisily thoughtless and troublesome" voices that spread doubts among the people. Wilson denounced Germany but stated that the United States had no desire to interfere with the internal affairs of Austria-Hungary. Nevertheless, he called for a declaration of war on the dual monarchy, as Roosevelt had for months demanded, and this occurred three days later.[29]

The declaration of war on Austria-Hungary did not soothe Roosevelt for long. He soon returned to the attack in the *Star*, pointing out that the country was not at war with all Germany's allies. Wilson recommended declaring war against Austria but not Bulgaria and Turkey. In Roosevelt's view, there was "no use in making four bites of a cherry" and no use in "going to war a little, but not much." The Austro-Hungarian and Turkish Empires must be broken up "if we intend to make the world even moderately safe for democracy." Only in this way "can we remove the menace of German aggression" that had become "a haunting nightmare for all civilizations, especially in the case of small, well-behaved, liberty-loving peoples."[30]

General Crozier's admission of deficiencies in testimony before the Senate Military Affairs Committee, while laying the blame on funding, labor, and contract problems, led Roosevelt to attack again in the *Star*. Because the administration continued its policies of unpreparedness, it therefore assumed "complete responsibility for every blunder and delay, and for all the misconduct." After eleven months of war, the United States still lacked modern military aircraft, artillery, small arms, and warm clothing but apparently had ample coffins. All this was due, "solely and entirely," to the administration's policy of unpreparedness for the last two and half years "when even the blind ought to have read the lesson of the Great War."[31]

Hearst's editor in chief, Arthur Brisbane, who himself owned the *Washington Times*, complained to Wilson that Roosevelt should not be permitted "in all the newspapers of the United States to say unrebuked that which would put in jail some little socialist editor, and cause his newspaper to be suppressed." He recommended that Wilson "remind Mr. Roosevelt" that the "United States at war" was not a "playground for ex-presidents to display their foolish egotism." Brisbane also pointed out that Roosevelt's attacks were printed abroad and belittled the United States in the eyes of the European nations, particularly England, where the attacks would be passed "BY THE CENSOR THERE AND PRINTED EVERYWHERE." The British did not allow Hearst's reply to be sent abroad via the cables they controlled because, said Brisbane, Hearst's newspapers "had not been edited to suit England."[32] Wilson replied that the best way to treat "Mr. Roosevelt" was to "take no notice of him. That breaks his heart and is the best punishment that can be delivered." While what Roosevelt said was "outrageous in every particular," he did "keep within the limits of the law," for he was "as careful" as he was "unscrupulous."[33] Although Wilson took no action against Roosevelt, Wilson's administration did see to it that England dropped its prohibitions against the Hearst publications.

In the Senate on January 21, 1918, Roosevelt's old enemy, William Stone of Missouri, labeled Roosevelt the "most seditious man of consequence in America." The

Republicans, Stone charged, had instigated the congressional investigations underway, most prominently in the Senate Military Affairs Committee chaired by Democratic senator George E. Chamberlain, simply to make political capital. Roosevelt had
been a "menace and obstruction to the successful prosecution of the war." He spoke
daily in "bitter and contemptuous disparagement of the President and of the Majority members of this Congress." He was publishing under contract "for money—think
of it for money—villainous screeds in the *Kansas City Star.*"[34] Far from being cowed
by the attack, Roosevelt challenged his critics to point out any untruths in his statements and declined to subscribe to the "servile doctrine that we dare not tell the truth
about our public servants." As Wilson had clamored for "pitiless publicity," he would
receive as Roosevelt thought proper, "not merely as much as he thinks proper."[35]

As all this played out in January 1918, Roosevelt arrived at Washington to take
the fight directly to Wilson, discuss party matters with congressional Republicans,
and further war supply reforms. Roosevelt told the press that he had come "to help
every man who sincerely desires to speed up and make effective our preparations in
this war." When the newsmen asked for comment on Stone's attack, Roosevelt replied
that he found it amusing to be accused of aiding the kaiser by a man who had in his
opinion "done everything to help Germany before the United States entered the war
and since then had done everything that would help America to be inefficient in the
war."[36] "I am here," he also told reporters, "if they wish to arrest me."[37]

Roosevelt used the medium of the press conference when in Washington, where
he stayed with his daughter, Alice Longworth, whose residence became a rallying
place for those critical of Wilson. As always, Roosevelt attracted a horde of reporters.
At one point Longworth recalled counting "thirty-three newspaper correspondents,
fairly stacked in the small hall." A representative front-page headline from the *Cleveland Plain Dealer* blared, "Wilson Ready to Battle Roosevelt, President in Hot Fight
for War Control."[38]

At the same time, Brisbane commented in his paper, the *Washington Times*, that
the "spectacle of a former President coming to the capital to organize war against the
Government" when the nation was at war with Germany was "something new" and
the "most original of Theodore Roosevelt's many original ideas." Roosevelt came to
Washington "as the spokesman of high finance" and acted as the "agent of the very
rich, organizing a political fight to give the corporations control of the United States
Government at the next Congressional election." Further, Roosevelt's attacks on the
president had "encouraged Germany and prolonged German resistance."[39] This editorial, Wilson wrote Brisbane, was "a corker."[40]

Roosevelt's only public appearance in Washington came before the National Press
Club, where he had been the first president to speak nine years before. He attacked
the administration for "shielding incompetence," called for an acceleration of the war

effort, and supported congressional calls for a British-styled ministry of munitions and a war cabinet. All good Americans regardless of party had the duty to provide constructive criticism. The only mention Roosevelt made of Wilson was to quote a passage from his 1885 *Congressional Government* that called for Congress to "scrutinize" and "sift" the "acts and the disposition" of the "administrative agents of the government." Otherwise the country "must remain in embarrassing, crippling ignorance" of the very affairs it was "most important that it should understand and direct."[41]

Secretary of the Navy Daniels noted in his diary on January 25, "TR came to town to set up a rump gov. but failed."[42] However, that same day the J. P. Morgan partner Edward R. Stettinius, who had coordinated Allied purchasing for the firm, became surveyor general of all Army purchases. Roosevelt admitted in the *Star* that the appointment of the "trained and capable" Stettinius represented "a certain advance" but it did not represent "even half a step toward bringing order out of the administrative chaos at Washington."[43]

All this relentless pressure had some effect, although not as much as Roosevelt desired. In February Wilson began weekly meetings of what became known as the War Cabinet. The next month Wilson appointed the aloof "Lone Eagle" of Wall Street, Bernard Baruch, to chair and invigorate the War Industries Board, which coordinated the national industrial effort.[44] On the Army front, Baker recalled an able officer from France, Maj. Gen. Peyton March, as chief of staff in place of Tasker Bliss, who was sent to Paris as American military representative to the Supreme War Council, created the previous year to coordinate the Allied war effort.

Wilson on the Offensive

Wilson also began to take control over the message concerning the public understanding of the war's purpose. After the overthrow of the czarist and then provisional governments in 1917, the victorious Bolsheviks had begun publishing the secret treaties concluded with Czar Nicholas II in which the Allies had agreed to carve up the Middle East, cede Austrian territory to Italy, and turn over the Rhineland to French domination.[45] On December 22, 1917, a week after they had concluded an armistice, representatives of the Central Powers sat down at Brest-Litovsk with Bolshevik representatives who demanded a general peace conference on liberal terms, including national self-determination, and invited the Allies to send representatives.[46] The British and French had no intention of doing so, but Wilson decided to answer by stating his terms.

Consequently, before a joint session of Congress on January 8, 1918, Wilson offered "the only possible" program for world peace, his famous Fourteen Points, including open diplomacy, freedom of the seas, and a league of nations. He also made clear for the first time his views on territorial questions, supporting France's claim to Alsace-Lorraine and the creation of an independent Poland, while rejecting Italy's claims as revealed in the secret treaties. His plan, Wilson declared, responded both to the "voice of the Russian people," reflected in the Bolshevik demand for a general liberal settlement, and to the aims of the Central Powers to dismember Russia. The treatment of Russia, Wilson declared, would be the "acid test" of the good-will of nations. Point fourteen, the most dear to Wilson's heart, called for a "general association of nations," including postwar Germany, to be formed for the "purpose of affording mutual guarantees of political independence and territorial integrity to great and small nations alike."[47] Although the speech received almost unanimous American press acclaim, Roosevelt dismissed the Fourteen Points, crowned with a "league of peace," as "fourteen scraps of paper" aimed not at the unconditional surrender of Germany but a "peace without victory" of conditional surrender of US sovereignty to an international league.[48]

On March 3, 1918, the Russian delegates signed the Treaty of Brest-Litovsk imposed at gunpoint by the Central Powers to cede huge swathes of territory to Germany, Austria-Hungary, and Turkey. The vindictive terms led Roosevelt to comment in the *Star* that the Bolshevik negotiating experience "ought to be illuminating to our own people." The country should "quit talking peace" with a foe who, if we entered into negotiations, would seek only to "trick us as he has already tricked the Bolsheviki." Every "peace utterance" pleased the Germans, rendered allies uneasy, strengthened the "pacifists, pro-Germans, and the various seditious elements in our own country," and disheartened "our honest citizens."[49]

Victory in the east allowed German troops to redeploy to the west to try to knock the French out of the war before the Americans arrived in force. On March 21, 1918, Germany began a series of five major drives over the next four months on the Allied trench lines.[50] In the *Kansas City Star* Roosevelt blamed the "shameful betrayal" of the Bolsheviks and the "delay and incompetence of the American Government" for giving the Germans a "free hand for their drive against the British Army." Owing to the "folly and the procrastination of our Government and its inveterate tendency to substitute rhetoric for action," the American Army was smaller than the Belgian and was not holding more of the line than "little Portugal," which had joined the Allies in March 1916.[51]

Wilson responded both to Roosevelt's criticisms and to Germany's onslaught on April 6, the anniversary of America's joining the war. Before a crowd of fifteen thousand, the president denounced Germany for seeking "mastery of the world" and for imposing the Treaty of Brest-Litovsk. This left but one response: "Force, Force to the utmost, Force without stint or limit, the righteous and triumphant force which shall make Right the law of the world, and cast every selfish dominion down in the dust." Although this statement appeared to repudiate his moderate peace policy, a few days later, he hedged, telling a group of foreign newspaper reporters that he had no desire to "march triumphantly into Berlin" and that he eschewed the "language of braggadocio."[52]

The Wilson administration went on the offensive not only verbally but also legally. In March the New York postmaster threatened to ban the *Metropolitan* from the mails under the Espionage Act. The *Metropolitan* requested an explanation, none was forthcoming, and on March 11, the postmaster general reversed his action without comment. Meanwhile, advertisers in the *Metropolitan* began receiving letters suggesting they withdraw their support for the magazine. At least one agent of the Justice Department made a personal visit along the same lines.[53]

Apparently, the administration considered current laws inadequate. Warned that pending sedition legislation would make slurring the president illegal, Roosevelt responded in a *Kansas City Star* editorial, "Sedition, a Free Press, and Personal Rule." Although Roosevelt believed that the pending amendments to the Espionage Act should "deal drastically with sedition," they should also guarantee the right to "speak the truth freely of all their public servants, including the President." Criminalizing criticism of the president was not only unpatriotic and servile but "morally treasonable to the American public." Throughout 1917 the administration had "shown itself anxious to punish" newspapers that criticized its inefficient conducting of the war but not those "which opposed the war or attacked our allies or directly or indirectly aided Germany against this country," because these papers "upheld the administration and defended its inefficiency." The administration deserved no additional powers to silence papers that criticized it. Roosevelt called on Congress to "scrutinize" the actions of Postmaster General Burleson and Attorney General Thomas Gregory, who had "already exercised discrimination between the papers they prosecuted and the papers they failed to prosecute."[54]

In response Burleson issued an official Post Office statement dated May 8, 1918, inviting Roosevelt to demonstrate the "truth or falsity" of his charges by naming names.[55] Two days later Roosevelt released a "preliminary" response, listing the *Metropolitan*, *Collier's Weekly*, and the *New York Tribune* as victims of official "unfair discrimination" carried out by George Creel. Meanwhile the administration had failed "to proceed against really hostile and damaging utterances," most notably the dozen newspapers and half dozen magazines owned by the wealthy William R. Hearst. Quoting as evidence several anti-Allies and antiwar editorials from Hearst's *New York American*, Roosevelt declared that it was "absolutely impossible to reconcile" the government's "failure to proceed against Mr. Hearst's papers on any theory that justice was to be done alike to the strong and to the weak." As a final bit of evidence, Roosevelt offered the tribute of the former German correspondent of the *Koeinische Zeitung* (*Cologne Newspaper*) praising Hearst and his editor in chief, Brisbane, for being "auxiliaries of valued influence" to Germany, especially through the editorials of the Hearst papers. He promised to deliver further evidence by letter to the Senate.[56]

A week later the postmaster general issued another statement that pointed out his department had not acted against either *Collier's Weekly* or the *New York Tribune*. Further, the aborted ban in March of the *Metropolitan* from the mails had not stopped any copies; rather, the publicity had increased circulation. All but two of the Hearst articles quoted by Roosevelt had been published before the Espionage Act was passed. In fact, the government had received more public complaints that Roosevelt's articles violated the Espionage Act than those of Hearst.[57]

Meanwhile, Congress had made explicit the implicit powers in the Espionage Act by passing an amended version as a new Sedition Act, which substantially increased the administration's war powers and has been called the "most repressive legislation in American history."[58] It made illegal

> uttering, printing, writing or publishing any disloyal, profane, scurrilous, or abusive language intended to cause contempt, scorn, contumely or disrepute as regards the form of government of the United States, or the Constitution, or the flag, or the uniform of the Army or Navy, or any language intended to incite resistance to the United States or to promote the cause of its enemies; urging any curtailment of production of anything necessary to the prosecution of the war with intent to hinder its prosecution; advocating, teaching, defending or suggesting the doing of any of these acts; and words or acts supporting or favoring the cause of any country at war with the United States, or opposing the cause of the United States therein.

The penalty was a $10,000 fine, or not more than twenty years in prison, or both. The 1918 Sedition Act also gave the postmaster general the power to refuse to deliver mail to individuals or businesses that employed the mails to break the statute. Any such mail would be returned to the sender stamped with the damning message: "Mail to this address undeliverable under the Espionage Act."[59]

Roosevelt's promised letter to the Senate raised more fears about the administration's "firm hand of stern repression." The *New York World* charged that the "bureaucrats of the Post-Office Department" seemed determined to "set up an intellectual reign of terror in the United States." In practice, the terror, which reigned over socialists and other radicals, as Creel later pointed out, silenced some voices that might have supported Wilson's brand of peace.[60]

War Termination

Success in war then turned Roosevelt's thoughts to war termination and the nature of the postwar peace. He warned against the "internationalists" who would "bid us promise to abandon the idea of keeping America permanently ready to defend her right by her strength" but would rely instead on written agreements to form a league of all nations that agreed to disarm and to treat each other, large or small, "on an exact equality."[61] The *New York World* responded that there was "no salvation in the old formula of preparedness." This was now "pre-eminently a war to end wars," and a league of nations was "the only way out of the Golgotha of militarism."[62]

Mid-September 1918 peace feelers from Austria-Hungary met a cold response in the American press, which in the heated wartime mood followed Roosevelt's lead, called for unconditional surrender, and pilloried the *New York Times* when it became the first and only major daily to hold out for acceptance of terms.[63] Most of the press, in America and Europe, dismissed the subsequent German proposal for peace talks based on the Fourteen Points as an obvious sham to gain time for the German Army to regroup. Absolute surrender, the *Baltimore Sun* demanded in a representative article, was the "sine qua non for peace."[64]

In an October 12 *Kansas City Star* editorial, Roosevelt noted the "greedy eagerness" with which the Central Powers had accepted Wilson's Fourteen Points. He recommended, if a league of nations meant that Germany, Austria, Turkey, and Russia "as presently constituted" would "have the say-so about America's future destiny, we ought to be against it." He preferred the de facto league made up of the United States and the Allies. In his view the country should not consider any peace proposal until unconditional surrender "has been accomplished by the victorious arms of our allies and ourselves."[65]

Meanwhile, Wilson's envoy, Col. Edward M. House, arrived in Paris to attend the meeting of the Supreme War Council that would hash out the armistice terms. House, according to Roosevelt, was not in the public service of the nation, but in the "private service of Mr. Wilson." He asked why House's instructions and purpose were "shrouded in profound mystery" instead of discussed "frankly in the public view" as the first of his Fourteen Points mandated.[66]

Roosevelt's unceasing attacks on Wilson led the *Nation* to inquire, "Why Is Roosevelt Unjailed?" Earlier that year New York postal authorities had held up an issue over an editorial titled "Civil Liberty Dead." This time the periodical suggested that any soapbox orator other than Roosevelt would have been given twenty years in jail for "interfering with the draft" with his repeated public accusations that "in the cloak rooms of Congress it is a bitter jest to speak of the President thus: 'Here's to our Czar, last in war, first toward peace, long may he waver.'"[67]

When Turkey followed Bulgaria and left the war at the end of October, Roosevelt lamented that since the country had taken no hand in freeing Palestine, Syria, and Armenia, the British and French would determine the fate of Turkey. Roosevelt desired the expulsion of Turks from Europe and the independence of Armenia but lamented that "we have lost the right to insist on these points." Roosevelt criticized Wilson's recent and premature peace initiatives to enter negotiations with Germany, writing that had they continued "along the line he started, might have caused disaster." Fortunately, the Allied commander Gen. Ferdinand Foch would be the real master of the situation, for the "men with the guns and not the men with fountain pens" would "dictate the terms."[68] Roosevelt was correct that Foch and the generals in Europe set the punitive terms of the November 11, 1918, armistice that ended the fighting, disarmed the enemy, and ensured that Germany could not carry on further hostilities. These terms contained many of the Allied war aims, so Roosevelt could declare with some truth that peace came, "not on Mr. Wilson's fourteen points, but on General Foch's twenty-odd points," which had "all the directness, the straightforwardness, and the unequivocal clearness" that the Fourteen Points "strikingly lacked."[69]

After Wilson announced that he would break precedent and go in person to Paris to join the Allied leaders at the peace conference, Roosevelt declared in the *Metropolitan* that no "public end of any kind" would be served by the president going to Paris with "Mr. Creel, Mr. House, and his other personal friends." Roosevelt reminded his readers that in the 1918 congressional elections that had just cost the Democrats control of both houses, Wilson had "abandoned the position of President of the whole people" and appealed to the people as a "party dictator." In any other "free country in the world today," this defeat would have forced Wilson to resign, so he had "no authority whatever to speak for the American people at this moment." His Fourteen Points, four supplementary points, and five complementary points had "ceased to have any shadow of right to be accepted as expressive of the will of the American people." The newly elected Congress came far nearer to having that right. Yet Wilson had sent Creel and sixteen Committee on Public Information employees as "the United States official press mission to the Peace Conference" to disseminate "world-wide propaganda" playing up "American accomplishments and American ideals." Further, Postmaster General Burleson had seized the cables after the fighting had ended, when there could be "no possible object except to control the news in the interest of President Wilson."[70]

Roosevelt did not live to see peace made. Less than two months after the armistice was signed, he died in his sleep at Sagamore Hill. His friend Henry Cabot Lodge took up the fight against the ratification of the Versailles Treaty and its embedded League of Nations, the internationalism that Roosevelt railed against in his last contribution to the *Kansas City Star*, published posthumously on January 13, 1919. America, he preached, should not become an international "Meddlesome Matty." The country should not send its "gallant young men to die in obscure fights in the Balkans" or in a "war we do not approve of." Moreover, America did not intend to give up the Monroe Doctrine. Let "civilized Europe and Asia" introduce police systems for the "weak and disorderly countries at their thresholds." The United States would treat Mexico as "our Balkan peninsula" and refuse to allow other powers to interfere on this continent. Americans had no desire to fight abroad except "for a very great cause." Fittingly, in a Senate tribute a month after Roosevelt's death, Lodge pointed out that the importance of Roosevelt's work mobilizing the country for war "was proven by the confession of his country's enemies, for when he died the only discordant note, the only harsh words, came from the German press. Germany knew whose voice it was that had more powerfully than any other called America to the battle on behalf of freedom and civilization."[71] Wilson's own health soon collapsed, and with it his dreams of US leadership in the League of Nations when Congress refused to ratify the Treaty of Versailles. There was a huge price for Wilson's failure to commandeer the message on foreign policy from the get-go. Roosevelt had mastered the art during the Philippine-American War.

Conclusion

Roosevelt, as former president and recently defeated presidential candidate, became a potent messenger with his diatribes against Wilson's conduct and termination of the war. His preferred medium was the syndicated column that allowed him to launch an uninterrupted barrage of attacks. Although Wilson took advantage of the centralized postal system to impose censorship of foreign-language and socialist journals, he could not stifle a former president. Initially, Wilson tried to ignore the messenger and the barrage, while responding to the message, for instance, by improving arms acquisitions through the establishment of the War Industries Board. This left Roosevelt in control of the message and the terms and tempo of the debate. Wilson did not effectively respond until the fall of Russia threatened a Germany victory and he went public with his Fourteen Points, which permanently overshadowed all Roosevelt's many columns to become an artifact of US foreign policy. Wilson's key mistake may have been his failure to allow Roosevelt to resume active military service, as Roosevelt desired. This would have kept the messenger out of town and out of time to keep up the barrage.

Notes

1. Michael Emery, Edwin Emery, and Nancy Roberts, *The Press in America*, 9th ed. (Boston: Allyn and Bacon, 2000), 254–58; Troy R. E. Paddock, ed., *A Call to Arms: Propaganda, Public Opinion and Newspapers in the Great War* (London: Praeger, 2004).

2. For this see J. Lee Thompson, *Never Call Retreat: Theodore Roosevelt and the Great War* (New York: Palgrave Macmillan, 2013).

3. For this see Stephen Ponder, *Managing the Press: Origins of the Media Presidency, 1897–1933* (New York: St. Martin's Press, 1998); George Juergens, *News from the White House: The Presidential-Press Relationship in the Progressive Era* (Chicago: University of Chicago Press, 1981); Doris Kearns Goodwin, *The Bully Pulpit: Theodore Roosevelt and the Golden Age of Journalism* (London: Penguin, 2013).

4. John L. Heaton, ed., *Cobb of the World: A Leader in Liberalism* (New York: E. P. Dutton, 1924), xvi; James D. Startt, *Woodrow Wilson and the Press: Prelude to the Presidency* (New York: Palgrave Macmillan, 2004); James D. Startt, "Prophet and Politician: Woodrow Wilson, the Great War, and the Fourth Estate" (unpublished manuscript, n.d.).

5. John Milton Cooper Jr., *Woodrow Wilson: A Biography* (New York: Vintage Books, 2009), 384.

6. *New York Times*, April 4, 1917.

7. *New York Times*, April 4, 1917.

8. Stephen Vaughn, *Holding Fast the Inner Lines: Democracy, Nationalism and the Committee on Public Information* (Chapel Hill: University of North Carolina Press, 1980).

9. Jörg Nagler, "Pandora's Box: Propaganda and War Hysteria in the United States during World War I," in *Facing Armageddon: The First World War Experienced*, ed. Hugh Cecil and Peter Liddle (London: Leo Cooper, 1996).

10. Paul L. Murphy, *World War I and the Origin of Civil Liberties in the United States* (New York: W. W. Norton, 1979), 74–77.

11. Seward W. Livermore, *Politics Is Adjourned: Woodrow Wilson and the War Congress, 1916–1918* (Middletown, CT: Wesleyan University Press, 1966), 33; John Byrne Cook, *Reporting the War: Freedom of the Press from the American Revolution to the War on Terrorism* (New York: Palgrave Macmillan, 2007), 87–103.

12. Quoted in Geoffrey R. Stone, "Mr. Wilson's First Amendment," in *Reconsidering Woodrow Wilson: Progressivism, Internationalism, and Peace*, ed. John Milton Cooper Jr. (Washington, DC: Woodrow Wilson Center Press, 2008), 194.

13. Murphy, *World War I*, 79–80.

14. Espionage Act of 1917.

15. As postmaster general, Burleson already had the power to act against obscene and other matter in the mail.

16. Murphy, *World War I*, 79–80, 98–99; David Kennedy, *Over Here: The First World War and American Society* (Oxford: Oxford University Press, 1980), 75.

17. Harry N. Scheiber, *The Wilson Administration and Civil Liberties, 1917–1921* (Ithaca, NY: Cornell University Press, 1960), 22.

18. "Correspondence of Theodore Roosevelt and the Secretary of War," *Metropolitan*, August 1917.

19. Roosevelt to Lee, August 17, 1917, in *The Letters of Theodore Roosevelt*, ed. Elting Morison (Cambridge, MA: Harvard University Press, 1954), 8:1224–25 (hereafter cited as *TRL*); Cook, *Reporting the War*, 87–103.
20. "The Peace of Victory for Which We Strive," *Metropolitan*, July 1917.
21. For the manuscript of the appeal, see fMS Am 1454.17, Theodore Roosevelt Collection (TRC), Harvard University.
22. *New York Times*, August 18, 1917, and September 21, 1917.
23. Theodore Roosevelt to Archibald Roosevelt, September 28, 1917, MS Am 1541.4, TRC.
24. Theodore Roosevelt, "Sam Weller and Mr. Snodgrass," October 2, 1917, in *Roosevelt in the* Kansas City Star*: War-Time Editorials by Theodore Roosevelt* (Boston: Houghton Mifflin, 1921), 9.
25. Theodore Roosevelt to Archibald Roosevelt, September 28, 1917, MS Am 1541.4, TRC.
26. Quoted in Livermore, *Politics Is Adjourned*, 64.
27. Josephus Daniels, October 5, 1917, entry, in *The Cabinet Diaries of Josephus Daniels, 1913–1921*, ed. E. David Cronon (Lincoln: University of Nebraska Press, 1963), 216.
28. Ralph Stout, introduction to *Roosevelt in the* Kansas City Star, xli.
29. Livermore, *Politics Is Adjourned*, 66–67.
30. Theodore Roosevelt, "Four Bites of a Cherry," December 7, 1917, in *Roosevelt in the* Kansas City Star, 64–66.
31. Theodore Roosevelt, "Being Brayed in a Mortar," December 18, 1917, in *Roosevelt in the* Kansas City Star, 69–71.
32. Brisbane to Wilson, December 18, 1917, in *The Papers of Woodrow Wilson*, ed. Arthur Link (Princeton, NJ: Princeton University Press, 1980), 45:320–21. Hereafter cited as *PWW*.
33. Wilson to Tumulty, ca. December 18, 1917, in *PWW*, 45:320.
34. *New York Times*, January 22, 1918.
35. Roosevelt to Johnson, January 18, 1918, in A. Lincoln, "My Friend and Champion: Letters between Theodore Roosevelt and Hiram Johnson in 1918," *California Historical Society Quarterly* 48, no. 1 (1969): 20.
36. *New York Times*, January 23, 1918.
37. Lincoln, "My Friend and Champion," 21.
38. Alice Roosevelt Longworth, *Crowded Years: Reminiscences of Alice Roosevelt Longworth* (London: Charles Scribner's Sons, 1934): 268–69; *Cleveland Plain Dealer*, January 23, 1918, quoted in Livermore, *Politics Is Adjourned*, 266n7.
39. *Washington Times*, January 24, 1918, quoted in *PWW*, 46:102n1.

40. Wilson to Brisbane, January 26, 1918, in *PWW*, 46:102.

41. *New York Times*, January 25, 1918.

42. Josephus Daniels, January 25, 1918, entry, in *Cabinet Diaries*, 272.

43. Theodore Roosevelt, "Justification of Constructive Criticism," January 28, 1918, in *Roosevelt in the* Kansas City Star, 93–95.

44. Kennedy, *Over Here*, 129–30.

45. David Stevenson, *With Our Backs to the Wall: Victory and Defeat in 1918* (Cambridge, MA: Belknap Press, 2011), 25; Keith Neilson, *Strategy and Supply: The Anglo-Russian Alliance, 1914–1917* (London: Allen & Unwin, 1984), 296.

46. John W. Wheeler-Bennett, *Brest-Litovsk: The Forgotten Peace, March 1918* (New York: Macmillan, 1956).

47. Cooper, *Wilson*, 422–23.

48. Edward J. Renehan, *The Lion's Pride: Theodore Roosevelt and His Family in Peace and War* (New York: Oxford University Press, 1988), 171–72.

49. Theodore Roosevelt, "Quit Talking Peace," March 5, 1918, in *Roosevelt in the* Kansas City Star, 111–13.

50. For "Michael" and the following attacks, see Stevenson, *With Our Backs*, 53–68.

51. Theodore Roosevelt, "The Fruits of Our Delay," March 26, 1918, in *Roosevelt in the* Kansas City Star, 120–22.

52. Cooper, *Wilson*, 431; David F. Trask, *United States in the Supreme War Council: American War Aims and Inter-Allied Strategy, 1917–1918* (Middleton, CT: Wesleyan University Press, 1961), 51–52.

53. Roosevelt to Poindexter, May 22, 1918, in *TRL*, 8:1322–23.

54. *Kansas City Star*, May 7, 1918.

55. *New York Times*, May 9, 1918.

56. *New York Times*, May 11, 1918.

57. *New York Times*, May 20, 1918.

58. Stone, "Mr. Wilson's First Amendment," 205.

59. Scheiber, *Wilson and Civil Liberties*, 22–25.

60. Scheiber, 27–30, 40.

61. Theodore Roosevelt, "Sound Nationalism and Sound Internationalism," August 4, 1918, in *Roosevelt in the* Kansas City Star, 188–95.

62. *New York World*, August 28, 1918.

63. Livermore, *Politics Is Adjourned*, 212.

64. Thomas Fleming, *The Illusion of Victory: America in World War I* (New York: Basic Books, 2003), 288.

65. Theodore Roosevelt, "War Aims and Peace Proposals," October 12, 1918, in *Roosevelt in the* Kansas City Star, 226–29.

66. Theodore Roosevelt, "What Are the Fourteen Points?" October 30, 1918, in *Roosevelt in the* Kansas City Star, 241–43.
67. *Nation*, November 9, 1918, in *Censorship 1917*, by James R. Mock (Princeton, NJ: Princeton University Press, 1941), 193–94.
68. Theodore Roosevelt, "The Turks Surrender Unconditionally," November 3, 1918, in *Roosevelt in the* Kansas City Star, 251–53.
69. Theodore Roosevelt, "The League of Nations," November 17, 1918, in *Roosevelt in the* Kansas City Star, 261.
70. Theodore Roosevelt, "President Wilson and the Peace Conference," November 26, 1918, in *Roosevelt in the* Kansas City Star, 272–75.
71. *New York Times*, February 10, 1919.

PART III. Introduction

Early Mass Media: Print and Radio

Marc A. Genest

The early mass media era covers the rise of broadcast news from the 1930s through the 1950s. While papers and magazines continued their prominent role in supplying news to millions of readers, this section also examines how radio transformed the delivery and consumption of news. Americans began to rely on new, faster, and more dramatic media to deliver information about the world in which they lived. Just as important, politicians, journalists, and entertainers learned how to use these new broadcast technologies to reach directly into the living rooms of the American people.

Yet the traditional print media remained immensely popular, profitable, and powerful throughout this period and beyond. Indeed, the first chapter in this section, by S. C. M. Paine, examines Edgar Snow, an influential author and print journalist. Snow's books and magazine features on Mao Zedong and the Chinese Revolution written in the 1930s and early 1940s "captured the imagination" of many Americans and "influenced US policy toward China at the highest levels."

Although radio technology had been around for over a decade, radio stations began proliferating in the early 1920s as broadcasters finally attracted enough advertising revenue to expand their media outlets. The "radio craze" was soon in full swing. In 1924, 2.5 million radios were operating in the United States. In 1926 the National Broadcasting Company (NBC) began regular radio broadcasting, followed quickly by the Columbia Broadcasting System (CBS) one year later. By 1930 almost half of all American homes had receivers, and by World War II radios were in over 90 percent of households. Americans were entranced by the variety of news and entertainment provided by this new medium.

Many journalists embraced radio as an opportunity to reach an even larger audience by delivering breaking news in real time to listeners sitting in the comfort of their homes or even driving in their cars. Radio provided live audio coverage of events happening around the country and the world. Radio news covered everything from sports to presidential campaigns to the dramatic crash of the German passenger airship *Hindenburg*. Radio also turned some reporters into media stars. Journalists like William Shirer and Edward R. Murrow reported on the rise of Nazism and the beginning of World War II live from Europe to an American audience that increasingly trusted radio reporters to deliver accurate news instantly.

It did not take long for politicians to realize that radio was an ideal tool to inform and persuade the American people. Calvin Coolidge was the first president to use the radio to deliver speeches directly to the public. Herbert Hoover also delivered frequent radio addresses during his time in office. Franklin Roosevelt, however, was the first president to master the medium and exploit it as an effective tool to enhance his political power and prestige. Roosevelt used prime-time evening "fireside chats" as an opportunity to inform, persuade, and charm the public with his wit, folksy manner, and warm personality.

In chapter 9 Mike Carew studies how the Roosevelt administration's communication strategy evolved throughout World War II. Carew concludes that Franklin Roosevelt's communication strategy helped him accomplish his three main goals of building an electoral coalition to support American intervention in the war, mobilizing American industry, and formulating a strategy to achieve victory.

The final chapter in this section, by Steven Casey, looks at the communication strategy implemented by Harry Truman to attract and maintain public support for a limited war in Korea. Casey points out it became increasingly difficult for Truman to sell the war after the fighting stalemated in the summer of 1951 because many Americans disliked the limitations placed on how it was fought. Meanwhile, Truman had to contend with the volatile Gen. Douglas MacArthur, who courted the press, demanded to expand the war to China, and advocated the use of nuclear weapons.

8.

Edgar Snow and Shaping US Perceptions of the Chinese Civil War

S. C. M. Paine

In this book about how the message, messenger, and media have been used in America to communicate war and revolution, Edgar Snow is the second messenger who could be termed a "super-empowered individual."[1] Journalist Thomas L. Friedman coined the term to indicate someone, like Snow, far more influential than position or circumstances would suggest possible. Indeed, Snow possessed no electoral mandate, nor expertise beyond being an eyewitness, yet he made it his life's work to influence US China policy at the highest political levels. In 1936 his reporting on Mao Zedong, previously an unknown figure in the West as well as in much of China, written in page-turning prose, captured imaginations back home and shaped both the development of Chinese studies abroad and US perceptions for generations to come. The Mao interviews formed a central part of Snow's best-seller *Red Star over China*, which gained the author instant and enduring fame and amplified his message.[2]

The Message

Snow's journalistic legacy would have been marginal without Mao, his literary muse. Snow alone provided the world with biographical details about a man who was about to rule a continent. Snow presented the Chinese Communists as idealists intent on creating a socialistic but still democratic future and the Nationalist Party and its leader Chiang Kai-shek as hopelessly corrupt and brutal.[3] It sounded nice. If only it were true.

Snow presented the Communists as agrarian reformers. The famous journalist and author John Gunther echoed this message in his book *Inside Asia*, published

131

just after *Red Star Over China* and republished dozens of times thereafter.[4] This story line persisted until the late 1980s. For instance, Harvard professor Roderick MacFarquhar's exhausting trilogy on the origins of the Cultural Revolution, which won the prestigious Levenson Prize, missed entirely the Great Famine, which killed forty million Chinese from 1958 to 1962, the central period covered in the trilogy. "Famine" does not even appear in the index.[5] This oversight is impossible to understand without appreciating how many internalized Snow's positive views of the Communists and therefore failed to perceive obvious and gross human abuses. It took photographs of the Tiananmen Massacre in 1989, publicized more than two generations after *Red Star over China*, to puncture the myths spread globally through Snow's beguiling prose.

The book's publication just after two of the most notorious events in modern Chinese history (the Xi'an incident and the Marco Polo Bridge incident) made sales soar. Less than two months after Snow's return from four months in the main Communist base area (later known as Yan'an) in Shaanxi, Chiang's generals allegedly kidnapped the Chinese leader in Xi'an, making international headlines. Chiang's release yielded a cease-fire in the Chinese Civil War and a Communist-Nationalist Second United Front to fight Japan. Japan retaliated in late July 1937 at the Marco Polo Bridge near Beijing, where full-scale, conventional fighting erupted and rapidly spread down the coast and up the Yangzi River.[6] Snow finished the book in Beijing during the Marco Polo Bridge incident, and it came out in London in October.[7] The Nationalists' sinking of USS *Panay* in mid-December on the Yangzi River near their capital in Nanjing attracted further Western attention.[8] In the United States and Europe, these events were hazy yet portentous. Snow filled the information void.

In December 1936 the *London Daily Herald* cofeatured the Mao interviews with news of Chiang's kidnapping, promoted Snow to its chief Far Eastern correspondent, and serialized the book. Meanwhile, in November 1936 *China Weekly Review*, a magazine widely read by China's business, professional, and intellectual elite, published transcripts of the Mao interviews. Then, in early 1937, *Life* magazine featured many of Snow's photos, and the *Saturday Evening Post* followed suit. The American edition of *Red Star over China* appeared in June 1938. In the first month it went through three printings in London, selling 100,000 copies. It was soon translated into half a dozen languages, and a seventh printing was ordered in August 1942. The US Random House edition initially sold just 23,500 copies, but still a US record for a nonfiction work on China, and an additional 27,000 copies sold in 1944.[9]

A London reviewer raved, "This is the most exciting, rare, timely and important book published this year; and it will probably remain so for a long time to come."[10] Of the more than a hundred reviews, virtually all were positive, using such adjectives as "dazzling," "indispensable," "outstanding," "prophetic," and "magnificent."[11]

Over three-quarters of a century later, *Red Star over China* remains influential and in print. The famous sinologist Owen Lattimore described it as "the biggest journalistic scoop in years" because Snow "broke the blockade" of Communist territory and "interviewed almost every important leader."[12] Another famous sinologist, John K. Fairbank, much later described Snow as "the top interpreter of Mao to Americans" and "special foreign friend of the [Chinese] revolution." According to Fairbank, the book "did indeed make Mao a world figure in 1937."[13] Snow's ex-wife, Helen Foster Snow, claimed that "Snow introduced Mao to the Chinese, as well as to the West."[14] Pearl S. Buck, winner of the 1938 Nobel Prize in literature, described Snow as "an eyewitness historian" who "established a new kind of writing about China."[15] Others considered Snow "one of the greatest foreign correspondents of all time," "Mao's 'American Boswell.'"[16] In 1938 Zhou Enlai, China's de facto foreign minister for the Maoist period, told a foreign journalist, "To us Snow is the greatest of foreign authors and our best friend abroad."[17]

Snow had earned Zhou's praise; he spread the Communist interpretation of events far and wide. In the 1930s Snow knew all the State Department China experts as well as US ambassadors to China, and he apparently influenced the ideas of Britain's wartime minister to China, Sir Archibald Clark Kerr.[18] In 1941 US ambassador to China Nelson T. Johnson wrote Stanley K. Hornbeck, special adviser to Secretary of State Cordell Hull, that Snow seemed "to have completely hypnotized the British in Hongkong." He continued, "I am fond of the Snows but think that Snow's accounts of what he has seen in China have been one sided and most biased."[19] When Snow sent Johnson a copy of his 1936 Mao interviews, Johnson forwarded them to Washington. In a February 1942 meeting, President Franklin Roosevelt requested Snow write him "now and again" about China, an arrangement they maintained until the president's death.[20] In May 1942 Zhou Enlai requested Snow deliver a message to Lauchlin Currie, Roosevelt's economic adviser, inviting a military mission to the Communist base area at Yan'an, which the United States sent two years later.[21] In October 1944 Snow spoke at length in Moscow with Maxim Litvinov, the recently discharged Soviet ambassador to the United States. Snow, by his own account, wrote up his notes, "about a dozen pages, single spaced . . . and sent them to President Roosevelt (as Max had asked me to do) and he [Franklin Roosevelt] received them just before he left for Yalta" to meet with Winston Churchill and Joseph Stalin.[22]

Before the book's publication, Chiang Kai-shek did not have powerful detractors in the United States. Afterward, Snow's morality tale gradually persuaded American voters, public servants, and military officers that China's future lay not with Chiang but with Mao.[23] The United States sent the official mission, the so-called Dixie Mission, to the Communist base area in the 1940s over Chiang's strenuous objections. After World War II, while the civil war was still raging, the United States cut all aid to Chiang, until his imminent demise frightened lawmakers into resuming aid when it was too late.

Snow was thirty-two at his book's publication but became an entry in the next edition of *Who's Who in America*.[24] Over a generation later, when Secretary of State Henry Kissinger was preparing for his secret trip to China in July 1971 to begin the process of diplomatic normalization, his staff pored over Snow's most recent interview of Mao, published that April.[25] Zhou Enlai brought up Snow at the beginning of his first meeting with Kissinger.[26]

Snow changed both the political debate in the West and also politics in China. Mao used Snow to enhance his own standing in Communist Party infighting by making himself appear to be an international figure at a time when he was hiding in exile after a devastating military defeat known as the Long March.[27] Having a well-known foreign reporter extol Mao's virtues enhanced Mao's credibility as a "world leader." Mao's fascinating story brought Snow into the limelight with him.

Numerous short books and pamphlets in Chinese under Snow's authorship highlighted the Mao interviews.[28] Other Chinese pamphlets by Snow focused not on Mao but on life in the Communist base area in Yan'an or on the fight against Japan.[29] Snow took the iconic photo of Mao sporting Snow's cap, which adorns Jung Chang's anything-but-iconic biography of Mao.[30] Snow later recounted that the pirated edition of *Red Star over China* inspired many Chinese youths to made the trip to Yan'an.[31] Indians, Burmese, Malayans, and Russians told him that they used the book as a guerrilla manual in their respective countries.[32]

Edgar Snow: Mao's Messenger to the World

Snow's first wife described him as a "left-wing journalist" who "was the most anti-Japanese of the foreign correspondents and had the most influence."[33] His biographers have called him a romantic socialist.[34] Yet Snow had a quintessentially American background. He was born in Kansas City, Missouri, where he sang in the church choir and became a boy scout. After he had attended the University of Missouri School of Journalism for one year, adventure called.[35] He explained to his parents that he had set off for China in 1928 to find "travel!! Adventure! Experience!" and "to know perils and danger" rather than submitting to "the consistent drabness of the days through which I have been wearily dragging myself"—the nine-to-five routine that he abhorred.[36] He started out in Shanghai as the assistant advertising manager of *China Weekly Review*, owned by fellow Missourian John Benjamin Powell, but quit the job at the end of 1929 to work as a correspondent for Consolidated Press. Eventually he became a stringer for the *Chicago Tribune*, the *New York Sun*, the *New York Herald Tribune*, and the *London Daily Herald*, the latter a socialist paper, before he joined the conservative magazine the *Saturday Evening Post*, where he remained from 1941 to 1951. In the 1930s the *Saturday Evening Post* had the second-largest circulation of any US magazine.[37]

Snow did not have a quintessentially American ending. The Nationalists detested him for his accurate criticism of their sins and undue praise of the Communists. Since the Nationalists could not curb Snow's message, they eventually curbed Snow. In January 1941 in the New Fourth Army incident, the Communists and the Nationalists turned their guns on each other, resuming the civil war and ending the Second United Front. The Communists gave Snow their detailed version of events, which the Nationalists feared might jeopardize US aid to fight Japan. When the *Herald Tribune* printed Snow's story on December 26, 1940, and January 22, 1941, the Nationalists canceled his press privileges. In 1942 Madame Chiang had him expelled and banned from China. The Nationalists blamed him for their bad image in the West. So Snow returned home for the first time in thirteen years and soon tried to report on another Communist country, but by 1945 the Soviet Union denied him further visas, and neither Nationalist nor Communist China welcomed him back.[38]

When he became caught up in Senator Joseph McCarthy's anticommunist witch hunt in the 1950s, Snow published hardly any articles any more.[39] Instead, he supported himself writing a series of popular but redundant books that kept returning to his months with the Communists in Shaanxi.[40] He ended his days in exile in Switzerland, where he died of pancreatic cancer, attended by Mao's physician, who hoped in vain to patch him up to report on President Richard Nixon's impending China trip.

Snow never asked why a busy leader like Mao had so much time for a young journalist. Apparently, he did not consider that he could become a pawn in a global game of strategic communication or that Mao, one of the greatest communicators of all time, could deftly manipulate him for purposes antithetical to Snow's Fabian socialist values. To his dying day, Snow remained Mao's apologist, denying the existence of the Great Famine and ignoring the disappearance of many of his original contacts, whom Mao had imprisoned if not murdered.[41]

Instead, Snow portrayed himself as "an unofficial envoy, the eyes and ears of average Americans."[42] He had his role backward; he was Mao's American envoy, serving at Mao's pleasure and perhaps at Stalin's instigation.[43] With the rise of virulently anticommunist leaders in Germany and Japan in the 1930s, Stalin had apparently wished to foreclose the growing possibility of a two-front war by redirecting Japanese ambitions away from Russia to China. At the time Mao needed a national and international reputation to gain legitimacy and international funding to wrest power from the Nationalists. In 1936 Mao and Stalin may have envisioned Snow playing the role that the left-wing US journalist John Reed had assumed for the Bolsheviks in Russia. Reed's *Ten Days That Shook the World*, published in 1919, glorified the Bolshevik Revolution, gaining sympathizers worldwide. By 1958 some made the comparison: "As John Reed reported the birth of socialism, and as Lincoln Steffens became the prophet of its permanence, now Edgar Snow . . . [has become] the militant chronicler of the role of socialism in overthrowing colonialism through the world."[44] A biographer of Snow concurred: *Red Star over China* "shared with Reed's *Ten Days* the distinction of being a primary historical source."[45] Snow became Mao's messenger to the world.

Snow as Mao's Pawn: Translating and Editing

The symbiotic relationship between muse and pawn began as early as 1930, when Snow expressed an interest in visiting Communist territory.[46] Probably in the spring of 1932, he met Madame Sun Yat-sen, who had connections with the Communist International (Comintern), which Russia used to orchestrate Communist movements worldwide. In May 1936 he approached her about interviewing Communist leaders. Meanwhile, Mao had been looking for his own John Reed. Snow fit the bill for three reasons. First, he had numerous contacts in the mainstream Western press. Second, as a Westerner, extraterritoriality protected him from the very capable Nationalist secret police. Finally, to Western readers he gave the appearance of an objective observer since he was neither a citizen of a colonial power (an imperialist) nor of the Soviet Union (a Communist).[47]

Mao's instructions to Snow's handlers were "security, secrecy, warmth and red carpet."[48] By the end of May, Snow had received an invitation authorized by Liu Shaoqi (eventually Mao's second in command). Zhou Enlai soon drew up an itinerary for a tour of the Communist base area at Bao'an (later moved to the more famous Yan'an), along with hours set aside for the Mao interviews.[49] Snow remained in episodic contact with Madame Sun and Chairman Mao for the rest of his life. Given the number of VIPs attending to all aspects of his trip, clearly Snow's position was not that of a typical journalist.

Snow's sympathies and contacts with Chinese leftists made clear to the Communists that he was no neutral observer. Indeed, he was an active participant, horrified by Nationalist abuses and smitten by Communist ideals.[50] During the December 1935 student demonstrations in Beijing, Snow helped translate their broadsides into English.[51] His wife took the pseudonym Nym Wales to promote the student cause, while allowing her husband to retain the appearance of journalistic objectivity.[52] In 1937, when the Japanese invaded full bore, Snow hid student books, kept a short-wave radio station in his home for Manchurians, and helped others leave Beijing in disguise—most notably, Zhou Enlai's wife.[53] Snow and his wife were also the founders of Indusco, an industrial cooperative movement attempting to use foreign financial support to replace industry lost to Japan.[54] This activism gave passion to Snow's writing.

In July 1969, when Snow was angling for another invitation to visit China, he wrote Mao, "I hope that you will not forget that I have been for many years a firm supporter of your great leadership. . . . I feel rarely fortunate to have, by chance, been privileged to know you and talk to you, and for that reason to have been able to help make known to the world the life and work of a revolutionary fully the peer of Lenin. I hope that my work has not been useless."[55] Snow composed this letter after the Anti-Rightist Campaign, the Great Leap Forward, the Great Famine, and in the midst of the Cultural Revolution—events that took the lives of millions. Upon Snow's death, Mao's obituary to him was the first such tribute to a foreigner in the Great Hall of the People.[56]

For someone who jealously guarded his independence and excoriated the Nationalists for their manipulation of information, Snow was remarkably obliging to Mao on the translation and editing process for *Red Star over China*. At Bao'an, Mao's secretary, Long March veteran Wu Liangping, served as the interpreter who translated Snow's English questions into Chinese and Mao's Chinese answers into English. Snow's own interpreter, the student leader Huang Hua, arrived later. Huang subsequently became the PRC's first UN ambassador. Thus, he was no ordinary translator. Snow based his notes on Wu's oral translations of Mao's comments. Huang then translated Snow's notes back into Chinese so that Mao could read and correct them before Huang translated them back into English.[57] This was hardly the normal translation process for interviews.

Even these editorial controls proved insufficient for the Communists. When Helen Foster Snow visited Bao'an on her own the following year, she noted that Zhou Enlai was "irked" that her husband had revealed "information about radio stations" and Communist success breaking "all" the Nationalists' codes.[58] Zhou requested the deletion of his comments that Chiang was "an inept horseman who did his troops the greatest disservice by going to the front with them."[59] Snow told her to reassure the Communists that he had cut the chapter describing the role of a high-ranking Communist officer, Chen Geng, in Chiang's kidnapping in Xi'an and another chapter describing Zhou.[60] The deleted sections on Chen Geng were never published, and it is unknown whether those about Zhou were ever published in their entirety.[61]

On a second trip Snow spent another ten days in September 1939, including two days of formal interviews with Mao. Huang again interpreted. These interviews appeared in January 1940 in *China Weekly Review*. The Nationalists responded by blockading the Communist base area so that no other foreign journalists made it until 1944.[62] As a result, Snow became both the first (1936) and last (1939) foreign correspondent to Bao'an until the summer of 1944. In the interim the Nationalists unwittingly assured his "authority" on the Chinese Communists.[63] This allowed Snow to become the founding footnote for modern Chinese studies' understanding of the Communists. Sinologists writing about the Communists all read Snow because his was virtually the only source on Mao. Thereafter they quoted each other so that over the years there were numerous secondary sources with interpretations similar to Snow's—small wonder since he was the source of their information.

Not only did Snow submit to Mao's intrusive translation process, but he continued to alter the story line in subsequent editions of *Red Star over China* in a manner suiting Mao's purposes. The initial 1938 US edition included photographs with the original text, but a revised edition, printed that year, modified passages on the Soviet Union and added a final chapter covering the ongoing Japanese escalation of the war.[64] The book received positive reviews from virtually everyone save US Communists. Apparently, Stalin did not appreciate the story line that he, not Leon Trotsky, had nearly destroyed the Chinese Communist Party in 1927 by insisting it remain in the First United Front with the Nationalists, who then annihilated the Communists.[65]

Major changes appeared in the 1942 London edition, with cuts minimizing the Soviet role in China. Deleted passages included, "It appears that in 1927 the Comintern was not giving 'advice' but flat orders, to the Chinese Communist Party, which was apparently not even empowered to reject them."[66] Eliminated from the conclusion was that "the victory of the revolution in China may hinge on the ability of the U.S.S.R. . . . to make the transition from a programme of Socialism in one country to Socialism in all countries, to world revolution, without undergoing a self-immolative counter-revolution within its present boundaries."[67] Deletions in 1968 included descriptions of the Comintern as "virtually a bureau of the Russian Communist Party," of the subordination of Communist Parties worldwide to "the broad strategic requirements of Soviet Russia, under the dictatorship of Stalin,"[68] and of Stalin's "tightened . . . grasp" on both the Comintern and Communist Party of the Soviet Union.[69]

Other deletions from the 1968 edition focused on sections pertaining to purged cadres. Gone were pictures of Commissar for Finance Lin Baichu and Commissar for the Interior Cai Qian, who no longer even appeared in the index.[70] Cut passages included the following: "Li [Lisan] was one of the most brilliant (if also erratic) of Chinese Communists, and perhaps the nearest to a Trotsky that China produced. He dominated the Party from 1929 to 1931, when he was . . . sent to Moscow for 'study,' where he still remains."[71] Li had been a strong supporter of the Soviet Union.

Cuts also focused on leaders of the ill-fated original Fourth Route Army, which some have accused Mao of destroying and whose commander, Zhang Guotao, was a key rival.[72] Gone was the passage that Zhang was "one of the great leaders of the Chinese cultural renaissance of 1917."[73] Gone was a positive reference to another leader, Xu Haidong: With one exception, Xu "was probably the only 'pure proletarian' among the Army commanders. . . . He was fighting to get rid of the vices."[74]

Snow also sanitized the record of those who remained in favor. The 1968 edition downplayed the opium addiction of Mao's close associate, Zhu De. It no longer referred to him as a "scion of a family of landlords, rising to power and luxury and dissipation while still young" or as a "fiend in human form" because of his brutality.[75] It no longer referred to Zhou Enlai as an "honours student in missionary school," a "scholar turned insurrectionist," or as the "son of a great Mandarin family."[76] Missing was "Do not suppose . . . that Mao . . . could be the 'saviour' of China. Nonsense."[77] Gone too was the reference to Mao's second wife, Yang Kaihui: "She was from all accounts a brilliant woman. . . . They were evidently very devoted."[78] Likewise cut was the role of foreigners: "The nucleus of a Red cavalry had been trained by the German adviser, Li Te [Li De, Otto Braun], an expert horseman who was once in the Red Army cavalry."[79]

Snow also altered his record of the Red Army's military performance. Deleted passages showing that the Communists had rarely fought the Japanese included the following: "Like the Arabs, the Reds have given but mediocre performances in their few big ventures at positional warfare."[80] "With the exception of the sabotaged struggle at Shanghai [where the Nationalists, not the Communists, fought the Japanese in 1932], no serious resistance has thus far been attempted."[81] "For pure military strategy and tactical handling of a great army in retreat nothing has been seen in China to compare with Chu Teh's [Zhu De's] splendid generalship of the Long March."[82] Also cut were two pages extoling Zhu De's generalship, giving him, not Mao, pride of place in the hagiography of the Long March.[83]

Snow as Mao's Medium

Once the first edition of *Red Star over China*, colored by Mao's intrusive translation process and initial amendments, was released in 1937, Snow had served his primary purpose of making Mao a national and international figure. The writer had far less quality time with Mao on his second trip to Shaanxi in 1939. Similarly, when he traveled to China in 1960, 1965, and 1970, he spent his days touring model plants and communes, not with Mao. In 1960, although Mao gave him nine hours (not weeks as in 1936), most of his talks were off the record.[84]

In these years Mao reached out to Snow episodically when he wanted to make contact with the West. Snow was Mao's medium. By 1960 the Sino-Soviet split had become public, leaving Mao diplomatically isolated and benefactorless. His Great Leap Forward was killing millions of primarily rural Chinese in the Great Famine. A renewed Taiwan Strait crisis at this juncture would have been dangerous. So Zhou Enlai arranged for Snow to visit for several months. Snow was eager to become the first US reporter to interview Mao since 1949. This time around Mao used Snow as his messenger to confirm what Zhou Enlai had told British field marshal Bernard

Law Montgomery in May: Mao wished to trade a US troop withdrawal from Taiwan for a Chinese promise to resolve the two-China problem peacefully. In October Mao told Snow he would not attack Quemoy (Jinmen) and Matsu (Mazu).[85] Snow self-importantly concluded that Chinese leaders "were obviously hopeful that my visit might help to rebuild a bridge or two."[86]

Whereas the timing of the release of *Red Star over China* was good, Snow's post-trip book, *The Other Side of the River: China Today*, coincided with the disastrous years of Mao's rule. In the 1930s Snow was the critic of the incumbent government; after the Communists came to power, he became the government's apologist.[87] Snow did not question the purge of Peng Dehuai, who had figured prominently in *Red Star over China* but eventually lost his life for criticizing Mao's famine-inducing policies.[88] When Michael Lindsay, an early supporter of the Chinese Communist Party, reviewed *The Other Side of the River*, he wrote that Snow's "intellectual development . . . seems to have stopped in the 1930s when it was plausible to identify the conflict of the political left and right with a conflict of good and evil." Snow never publicly questioned the harsh treatment his friends from the 1930s meted out during Mao's subsequent political campaigns.[89]

Snow's October 1964 to January 1965 trip made him the last reporter to visit China before the Cultural Revolution. Again, Mao used Snow as his messenger. Snow sent a copy of his latest four-hour interview with Mao to Undersecretary of State Averell Harriman. The major US newspapers had declined to print the uninformative interview. If Mao hoped to improve Sino-US relations to offset the widening Sino-Soviet rift, he offered nothing in return for US friendship and seemed to prefer a protracted war in Vietnam.[90] When Snow learned that during the Cultural Revolution he had come under attack, accused of being a spy, this in no way diminished his enthusiasm for the red star over China.[91]

In 1969, the year that Liu Shaoqi was tortured to death, Snow wrote, "Whereas in Stalin's Russia such contradictions [policy disagreements] could have been quickly settled by the physical liquidation of the obstinate comrade who refused to resign, that has not happened in the case of Liu Shaoqi." Snow knew that Liu had been imprisoned the preceding year; he failed to draw the obvious conclusions as to the deadly consequences for Liu.[92] Liu had been the one to authorize Snow's career-making trip to Bao'an in 1936.[93]

In 1970 Mao again summoned Snow to Beijing. In June Snow received a telephone call from the Chinese embassy in Paris, in July he and his second wife received their visas, and by mid-August they were in Guangzhou.[94] Front-page pictures on newspapers throughout China showed the couple side by side with Mao at Tiananmen during the National Day Parade.[95] On Christmas a photo of Mao and Snow on the balcony at Tiananmen Gate graced the front pages of *People's Daily*.[96] The symbolism indicated that the United States was no longer China's primary enemy. By process of elimination, Russia now was.

According to Kissinger, the United States (the target audience) missed the message because "the Chinese had vastly overrated the importance of Edgar Snow in America." While Mao thought Snow was a CIA agent, Kissinger and other US officials considered him "a communist tool."[97] Kissinger also missed the message from Mao's December 1970 interview with Snow inviting Nixon to China.[98] Mao then worked through the Pakistani president, who successfully delivered the invitation.[99] Nixon soon accepted, and Sino-American cooperation to undermine Russia began.

Conclusion

To return to the framework of message, messenger, and media, Snow's message of Nationalist villainy and Communist virtue contained powerful partial truths. He accurately portrayed Nationalist villainy and assumed that surely the Communists must be better. Chiang's actions then seemed to substantiate Snow's interpretation. He was reporting during a civil war overlaid by a regional war with Japan, so there was much villainy in evidence, and his medium of expression—newspaper journalism—ensured his ideas were read far and wide. Snow's own frame of reference limited his analysis: when Communists talked about "the elimination of classes," Snow envisioned the elimination of social divisions, not the imprisonment and execution of entire social classes that Mao actually implemented.[100] Snow studiously shied away from the negatives because, as his biographer explained, "a positive picture of China validated his past reporting."[101] Unbeknownst to Snow, once the Communists took power, *Red Star over China* became virtually unattainable in China from the 1950s through 1979, when a complete Chinese translation of the 1968 edition was issued eight years after Snow's death.[102]

As a messenger—a communicator of revolution to American audiences—Snow was as flawed as he was influential. In Nationalist China he was free to go where he pleased. In Communist country he was always on an official itinerary and usually with official handlers. He never put the pieces together, perhaps because he did not want to. Recognition that Mao at least equaled, if not surpassed, Chiang's villainy would have made Snow the messenger of a mass murderer. Among other things, Snow's story and his impact highlight the power of messengers with messages that appeal to their audiences' biases. The quintessentially American assumption that if one side is evil, surely the other is good, did not apply to Asia in the 1930s. Americans had no idea how fortunate they were or how unfortunate others could be. Snow's card file of favorite quotations included one by George Bernard Shaw: "Of course that was an overstatement—as all statements must be if they are to receive attention."[103] Snow's many marketable overstatements distorted sinology for generations.

Notes

1. Thomas L. Friedman, prologue to *Longitudes and Attitudes* (New York: Farrar, Straus & Giroux, 2002), http://www.thomaslfriedman.com/bookshelf/longitudes-and-attitudes-prologue.

2. S. Bernard Thomas, *Season of High Adventure: Edgar Snow in China* (Berkeley: University of California Press, 1996), 138; Robert M. Farnsworth, *From Vagabond to Journalist: Edgar Snow in Asia, 1928–1941* (Columbia: University of Missouri Press, 1996), 194.

3. Edgar Snow, *Battle for Asia* (New York: Random House, 1941), 287; also published as *Scorched Earth* (London: Victor Gollancz, 1941).

4. John Maxwell Hamilton, *Journalism's Roving Eye* (Baton Rouge: Louisiana State University Press, 2009), 357; John Gunther, *Inside Asia*, 31st ed. (New York: Harper & Brothers, 1939).

5. Roderick MacFarquhar, *The Origins of the Cultural Revolution*, 3 vols. (New York: Columbia University Press, 1974–97).

6. John S. Service, "Edgar Snow: Some Personal Reminiscences by John S. Service," *China Quarterly*, no. 50 (April–June 1972): 211, available in Box 230, Subject File: Edgar Snow, Karl A. Wittfogel Papers, Hoover Institution Archives (HIA), Stanford, CA.

7. John Maxwell Hamilton, *Edgar Snow: A Biography* (Bloomington: Indiana University Press, 1988), 84–85.

8. Hamilton, *Journalism's Roving Eye*, 357.

9. Peter Rand, *China Hands* (New York: Simon & Schuster, 1995), 170; Thomas, *Season of High Adventure*, 151, 170, 360, 389; Hamilton, *Edgar Snow*, 85, 89; Edgar Snow, *Red Star over China* (London: Victor Gollancz, 1942).

10. Philip Jordan, "The Story behind China's Heroism," *News Chronicle* (London), 1937[?], in Box 15, Folder 503, Edgar Snow Papers (ESP), University of Missouri–Kansas City.

11. Hamilton, *Edgar Snow*, 84–85; Hamilton, *Journalism's Roving Eye*, 357; Thomas, *Season of High Adventure*, 172–73.

12. Owen Lattimore, "The Chinese Communists," *Yale Review*, n.d., 813–14, Box 15, Folder 504, ESP.

13. John K. Fairbank, "To China and Back," *New York Review of Books* 19, no. 6 (October 19, 1972), Box 15, Folder 500, ESP.

14. Nym Wales (Helen Foster Snow), "My China Years," 1976 manuscript, p. 2, Box 38, Nym Wales Papers, HIA.

15. Pearl S. Buck, "American Winters in the Orient," *Asian Bookshelf*, ca. 1941, p. 205, Box 16, Folder 506, ESP.

16. Frank Gervasi, "Edgar Snow," *Book Find News*, April 1947, p. 4, Box 16, Folder 509, ESP; Leo Huberman, "Mao's 'American Boswell,'" *Monthly Review*, December 1958, 323–29, Box 16, Folder 510, ESP.

17. Quoted in Hamilton, *Edgar Snow*, 225.

18. Rand, *China Hands*, 185.

19. Nelson T. Johnson to Stanley K. Hornbeck, March 13, 1941, Box 262, Nelson T. Johnson 1941, Stanley K. Hornbeck Papers, HIA.

20. Thomas, *Season of High Adventure*, 152, 256; Farnsworth, *From Vagabond to Journalist*, 396; Hamilton, *Edgar Snow*, 128.

21. Michael M. Sheng, *Battling Western Imperialism* (Princeton, NJ: Princeton University Press, 1997), 76.

22. Edgar Snow to Bertram Wolfe, May 6, 1956, Box 13, Correspondence, Edgar Snow, Bertram D. Wolfe Papers, HIA; Hamilton, *Edgar Snow*, 148–49.

23. Rand, *China Hands*, 185, 187; Richard Bernstein, *China 1945* (New York: Alfred A. Knopf, 2014), 106, 218; Hamilton, *Journalism's Roving Eye*, 353.

24. Hamilton, *Edgar Snow*, 91.

25. Edgar Snow, "A Conversation with Mao Tse-tung," *Life*, April 30, 1971, 46–48; Edgar Snow, "What China Wants from Nixon's Visit," *Life*, July 30, 1971, 22–26; Hamilton, *Journalism's Roving Eye*, 374; Thomas, *Season of High Adventure*, 391.

26. NSC Box 846, File Book I, HAK's 1971 visit by subject matter [Part I], p. 1, Richard Nixon Presidential Library, Yorba Linda, CA.

27. Thomas, *Season of High Adventure*, 137.

28. Edgar Snow, 中國新的西北 [*China's New Northwest*], trans. 恩三 (En San) (N.p.: 平凡書店, May 1937); Edgar Snow, 毛澤東訪問記 [*Collection of Interviews of Mao Zedong*] (Shanghai: 無名出版社, November 11, 1937); Edgar Snow, 外國記者西北印象記 [*Account by a Foreign Reporter of the Influence of the Northwest*] (Shanghai: 丁丑編譯社出版, 1937); Edgar Snow, 紅軍四傑 [*Four Heroes of the Red Army*], trans. 郭文彬 (Guo Wenbin) (Shanghai: 上海一心書店, April 1938).

29. Pamphlets on the Communist base include Edgar Snow, 中國新的西北 [*China's New Northwest*], ed. 張劍萍 (Zhang Jianping) (Shanghai: 戰時讀物社, December 1937); Edgar Snow, 共黨與西北 [*The Communist Party and the Northwest*], trans. and ed. 庸夫 (Yung Fu) (Shanghai: 大眾出版社, January 20, 1938); Edgar Snow, 紅軍四講 [*Four Talks on the Red Army*] (Guangzhou: 新生出版社, January 30, 1938). Pamphlets on the fight against Japan include Edgar Snow, 太陽旗上的暗影

[*Dark Shadow on the Flag with the Rising Sun*], trans. 克明 (Ke Ming) (N.p.: 中華出版社, October 1938).

30. Hamilton, *Edgar Snow*, photo caption between 145–46, 225; Jung Chang and Jon Halliday, *Mao: The Unknown Story* (New York: Alfred A. Knopf, 2005), dust jacket.

31. Snow, *Battle for Asia*, 259.

32. Hamilton, *Edgar Snow*, 94, 161; Christopher Bayly and Tim Harper, *Forgotten Armies: The Fall of British Asia, 1941–1945* (Cambridge, MA: Harvard University Press, 2005), 24.

33. Nym Wales, "My China Years," 1976 manuscript, 1–2, Box 38, Nym Wales Papers, HIA.

34. Hamilton, *Edgar Snow*, 147; Rand, *China Hands*, 146.

35. Farnsworth, *From Vagabond to Journalist*, 10; Hamilton, *Edgar Snow*, 9.

36. Hamilton, *Edgar Snow*, 14–15; Thomas, *Season of High Adventure*, 33.

37. Rand, *China Hands*, 144, 312; Farnsworth, *From Vagabond to Journalist*, 22, 49, 402.

38. Thomas, *Season of High Adventure*, 390; Hamilton, *Edgar Snow*, 122, 170–71, 180.

39. Service, "Edgar Snow," 214; Rand, *China Hands*, 144; Hamilton, *Edgar Snow*, 206; Farnsworth, *From Vagabond to Journalist*, 402.

40. Edgar Snow wrote *Random Notes on Red China, 1936–1945*, Harvard East Asian Monographs, no. 5 (Cambridge, MA: Harvard University Press, 1957); *Journey to the Beginning* (New York: Random House, 1958); *The Other Side of the River: Red China Today* (New York: Random House, 1962); *China, Russia and the U.S.A.: Changing Relations in a Changing World* (New York: Marzani & Munsell, 1963); *Red Star over China*, rev. ed. (New York: Grove Press, 1968); *Red China Today: The Other Side of the River*, rev. ed. (New York: Random House, 1970); *The Long Revolution* (New York: Random House, 1972).

41. Yang Jisheng, *Tombstone: The Great Chinese Famine, 1958–1962*, trans. Stacy Mosher and Guo Jian (New York: Farrar, Straus & Giroux, 2008), 15.

42. Quoted in Hamilton, *Edgar Snow*, 147.

43. Rand, *China Hands*, 156–57.

44. Angus Cameron and Carl Marzani, eds., *Liberty Book Club News*, December 15, 1958, Box 16, Folder 510, ESP.

45. Hamilton, *Journalism's Roving Eye*, 354.

46. Rand, *China Hands*, 154.

47. Rand, 154–58; S. C. M. Paine, *The Wars for Asia 1911 to 1949* (Cambridge: Cambridge University Press, 2012), 92–93; Hamilton, *Edgar Snow*, 42, 60, 63, 67–69; Thomas, *Season of High Adventure*, 131–32; Farnsworth, *From Vagabond to Journalist*, 130, 202.

48. Chang and Halliday, *Mao*, 191–92.

49. Hamilton, *Edgar Snow*, 68, 71.

50. Edgar Snow to O. Edmund Clubb, April 7, 1969, Box 7 Correspondence, Edgar and Lois Snow, O. Edmund Clubb Papers, HIA; Rand, *China Hands*, 154–58; Hamilton, *Edgar Snow*, 42, 60, 63, 67–69, 71; Thomas, *Season of High Adventure*, 131–32; Farnsworth, *From Vagabond to Journalist*, 130, 202.

51. Hamilton, *Edgar Snow*, 57; Rand, *China Hands*, 148–49.

52. Farnsworth, *From Vagabond to Journalist*, 195.

53. Hamilton, *Edgar Snow*, 98, 225; Rand, *China Hands*, 181; Service, "Edgar Snow," 213.

54. Hamilton, *Edgar Snow*, 120–21; Farnsworth, *From Vagabond to Journalist*, 5, 309, 318, 330.

55. Quoted in Thomas, *Season of High Adventure*, 333–34.

56. Hamilton, *Edgar Snow*, 282.

57. Thomas, *Season of High Adventure*, 138; Farnsworth, *From Vagabond to Journalist*, 194; Service, "Edgar Snow," 217.

58. Nym Wales, "My Yenan Notebooks," 1937, 164, Box 19, Folder 1, Nym Wales Papers, HIA.

59. Hamilton, *Edgar Snow*, 94.

60. Farnsworth, *From Vagabond to Journalist*, 293–94.

61. In 1957 Snow published information on Zhou, impugning Chiang's military abilities, but nothing connecting Chen Geng with the Xi'an incident. Whether the section on Zhou coincided with the deleted chapter is unclear (Snow, *Random Notes*, 56–63).

62. Hamilton, *Edgar Snow*, 115–17; Thomas, *Season of High Adventure*, 159, 389; Service, "Edgar Snow," 214.

63. Hamilton, *Edgar Snow*, 117–18; Hamilton, *Journalism's Roving Eye*, 358.

64. Edgar Snow, *Red Star over China*, rev. ed. (New York: Random House, 1938), 448–96; Thomas, *Season of High Adventure*, 176, 180.

65. Hamilton, *Edgar Snow*, 85–86; Thomas, *Season of High Adventure*, 174–76, 178–79, 182.

66. Edgar Snow, *Red Star over China* (London: Victor Gollancz, 1937), 162; cut from Snow (1942), 162; and Snow (1968), 164.

67. Snow (1937), 455; cut from Snow (1942), 451; and Snow (1968), 408.

68. Snow (1937), 382; Snow (1942), 382; cut from Edgar Snow, *Red Star over China* (New York: Random House Modern Library, 1944), 410; and Snow (1968), 355–56.

69. Snow (1937), 384; Snow (1942), 384; Snow (1944), 412; cut from Snow (1968), 358.

70. Snow (1938), pictures between pp. 66–67. Illustrations were more lavish in the original US edition than in the UK edition.

71. Snow (1937), 174–75; Snow (1942), 174–75; Snow (1944), 181; cut from Snow (1968), 176.

72. Chang and Halliday, *Mao*, 210–11.

73. Snow, *Red Star* (1937), 311; Snow (1942), 311; Snow (1944), 330; cut from Snow (1968), 298.

74. Snow (1937), 307; Snow (1942), 307; Snow (1944), 326; cut from Snow (1968), 295.

75. Snow (1937), 354, 363; Snow (1942), 354, 363; cut from Snow (1968), 333–34, 339.

76. Snow (1937), 55, 59; Snow (1942), 55, 59; Snow (1944), 46, 51; cut from Snow (1968), 90.

77. Snow (1937), 80; Snow (1942), 80; Snow (1944), 71; cut from Snow (1968), 90.

78. Snow (1937), 153; Snow (1942), 153; Snow (1944), 156; cut from Snow (1968), 155.

79. Snow (1937), 337; Snow (1942), 337; Snow (1944), 360; cut from Snow (1968), 321.

80. Snow (1937), 285; Snow (1942), 285; Snow (1944), 300; cut from Snow (1968), 274.

81. Snow (1937), 290; Snow (1942), 290; cut from Snow (1944), 305; Snow (1968), 278.

82. Snow (1937), 361; Snow (1942), 361; Snow (1944), 389; cut from Snow (1968), 339.

83. Snow (1937), 361–62; Snow (1942), 361–62; Snow (1944), 389–90; cut from Snow (1968), 339.

84. Philip Kuhn, "Some Current Books on China," *Harper's Monthly*, November 1962, 114–18, in Box 15, Folder 488, ESP.

85. Hamilton, *Edgar Snow*, 226; Mingjiang Li, *Mao's China and the Sino-Soviet Split* (London: Routledge, 2012), 71; Thomas, *Season of High Adventure*, 294, 298.

86. Quoted in Thomas, *Season of High Adventure*, 185.

87. Thomas, 304–5; Edgar Snow, *The Other Side of the River: China Today* (New York: Random House, 1962).

88. Hamilton, *Edgar Snow*, 233–34.

89. Thomas, *Season of High Adventure*, 303, 317, 321, 323.

90. Edgar Snow to Averell Harriman, February 6, 1965, Box 92 Increment, 1998, Subject File: China-Mao Tse-tung—Interview with Edgar Snow, Charles Hill Papers, HIA; Sergey Radchenko, *Two Suns in the Heavens: The Sino-Soviet Struggle for Supremacy, 1962–1967* (Stanford, CA: Stanford University Press, 2009), 143–44.

91. Hamilton, *Edgar Snow*, 260.

92. Edgar Snow, "Mao and the New Mandate," *New Republic*, May 10, 1969, 19, in Box 9, Folder 377, ESP.

93. Nym Wales, "How Edgar Snow Arranged to Make His Trip to the Northwest, 1936," May 26, 1983, Box 34, Folder 927, Nym Wales Papers, HIA.

94. Thomas, *Season of High Adventure*, 320.

95. Ang Sheng Guan, *Ending the Vietnam War* (London: RoutledgeCurzon, 2004), 61.

96. Hamilton, *Edgar Snow*, 267–68.

97. Henry Kissinger, *Diplomacy* (New York: Simon & Schuster, 1994), 725.

98. Kissinger, 725–26; Radchenko, *Two Suns in the Heavens*, 13.

99. Thomas, *Season of High Adventure*, 330; Hamilton, *Edgar Snow*, 269, 275.

100. Snow, *Battle for Asia*, 294–95.

101. Hamilton, *Edgar Snow*, 228.

102. Thomas, *Season of High Adventure*, 185–86.

103. Box 23, Folder 715, ESP.

9.

Franklin D. Roosevelt and World War II

Michael G. Carew

The iconic news commentator Edward R. Murrow described the public reaction to the attack on Pearl Harbor as "angry, frightened and confused."[1] He had spent the evening of December 7, 1941, at the White House, having a late supper with President Franklin Delano Roosevelt. The following day Roosevelt, recognizing the popular mood, delivered his request to Congress for a declaration of war. He concluded the request with a definitive message: "With confidence in our armed forces, and the unbounded determination of our people, we will gain the inevitable triumph, so help us God."[2] By crystalizing the confidence of the people to overcome this defeat and to pursue its redemption, Roosevelt set the country on a course toward victory.

In this early era of the mass media, the government's communication strategy for World War II evolved over a five-year period from late 1937 through early 1943. The messaging, the technologies, the reach of the mass media, and the mass audience all changed. While the war continued through 1945, by 1943 the message of total war and the unconditional defeat of the Axis enemies had already been absorbed and become doctrinal. The success of the strategy depended on the skills of the lead messenger, President Roosevelt, and the communication resources he assembled.

Roosevelt used a communication campaign to rally Americans behind him. His approach was informed in significant part by negative lessons learned from the failures of the Woodrow Wilson administration in World War I and enabled by his own great personal gift for using words to touch the hearts of Americans. Professional journalists also played a central role in the fulfillment of their responsibility to criticize the message and the messenger.

Roosevelt's efforts began even before US belligerency, when, by communicating his ideas in step with the public's growing receptivity to them, he led without seeming to lead one of the most successful communication campaigns in US history. The effectiveness of the government's communication is still evident in such enduring terms as the "Good War," in reference to World War II, and the "Greatest Genera-tion," in reference to those who fought it.[3]

The Message and the New National Media

The 1930s were a transition period not only in the central crisis facing Americans but also in the news media that helped them make sense of the crisis. In the early and mid-1930s the American political arena fixated on the economic collapse from the Great Depression. Inaugurated on March 4, 1933, President Roosevelt pursued his program of economic recovery, social reform, and political innovation known col-lectively as the New Deal. His 1936 reelection and the subsequent "court-packing" conflict with the Supreme Court kept the focus of government and the electorate on domestic matters. Congressional investigations of international finance and the arms trade as "merchants of death" amplified domestic concerns. These congressional initiatives congealed into the Neutrality Acts of 1935, 1936, and 1937, designed to insulate the United States from war. Congress mirrored the public mood, which gave little attention to foreign affairs and the rise of fascism.

Yet the president, fulfilling his role as the constitutional maker of foreign policy and commander in chief, could not ignore the threat posed by Germany and Japan to vital American national security interests. In October 1937, in a speech to the Team-sters Union in Chicago, Roosevelt warned of the dangers and suggested a policy to "Quarantine the Aggressors."[4] The subsequent editorial outrage at the implied mili-tary role of the United States in foreign affairs chastened the president concerning any such policy innovation. The American people rejected a replay of an American Army sent to Europe or elsewhere to make the world "safe for democracy" as had been done at great sacrifice in World War I.[5]

The new social science of popular opinion polling confirmed the electorate's firm rejection of any American military intervention. The three different national polling organizations—the Office of Public Opinion Research, which Nelson Rockefeller funded at Princeton; the Roper organization, which conducted polls for Time Inc.; and the Gallup organization—all tracked the emerging public consensus. Only after perfervid reporting on the Battle of Britain did a marked increase in support for bel-ligerence against Germany occur in the gap in polling from September to December 1940. Data in table 9.1 cover the twenty months from the Nazi attack on Scandina-via in April 1940 through the month before Pearl Harbor.

From 1937 to 1941 President Roosevelt's message stressed the maintenance of peace, the avoidance of involvement in the emerging military conflicts, and the sepa-ration of the Western Hemisphere from "the age old struggles amongst the European

Table 9.1. Electoral preferences for and against US intervention (%)

	April 1940	June 1940	September 1940	December 1940	July 1941	November 1941
Stay out	96.4	84	83	41	38	18
Defeat Axis	2.4	16	17	55	57	68
No response	1	2	0	4	5	14

Source: Data from Hadley Cantril, ed., *Public Opinion, 1935–1946* (Princeton, NJ: Princeton University Press, 1951).

family of nations."[6] This required a substantial dissimulation in the government's communication strategy as it had already committed to a program of rearmament at home and alliance building abroad in response to the rapid Axis advance in the European and Asian theaters. The preparations, the alliance building, the messages of "total war" and "unconditional surrender," and the plans for a better postwar world all transcended the time frame of the war. In his budget message of January 1941, Roosevelt began to articulate his vision in what came to be known as the Four Freedoms speech: "In the future days which we seek to make secure, we look forward to a world founded upon four essential human freedoms." These were freedom of speech, freedom of worship, freedom from want, and freedom from fear.[7]

From the eighteenth century to the mid-twentieth century, American newspapers were of local origin and focus. The national media evolved from technological developments only from about 1940. Henry Luce, the creator of *Time*, which first appeared in 1926, and *Newsweek* magazine, which first appeared in 1933, pioneered national media coverage.[8] By the late 1930s the development of coated paper and handheld 35-milimeter cameras using film rather than glass plates permitted the publication of large-format newsmagazines, such as *Life*, *Look*, and *Collier's*. Their popularity and circulation burgeoned so that by 1940 nearly half of American households received one or more of them.

This aggregate readership of almost 40 million approximated 47 percent of the adult population during the 1939 to 1941 period. The readership of the four newsmagazines roughly equaled that of the total US newspaper circulation of 41.5 million. The size and social standing of the educated readership and the regularity of the magazines' appearance each week (or ever other week in the case of *Look*) amplified their influence. Their excellent photo content transformed them into the original national news media. Although some newspapers, such as the *New York Times*, the *Washington Post*, and the *Chicago Tribune*, retained substantial regional influence, they could not compete with the newsmagazines for national reach and increasingly concentrated on local news and issues of local significance. As a result, publishers such as Garner Cowles of *Look*, Averell Harriman of *Newsweek*, and Henry Luce of

Table 9.2. Readership of the major newsmagazines

Magazine	Pass-along rate	Paid circulation	Estimated readership
Life	7	2,800,000	19,600,000
Look	6	1,800,000	10,800,000
Newsweek	6	420,000	2,520,000
Time	7	820,000	5,740,000
Totals	26	5,840,000	38,660,000

Source: Carew, *Power to Persuade*, 35.

Time-Life became extraordinarily influential in shaping the national popular appreciation of events in this period (see table 9.2).[9]

The second transformation of media in this period was the newsreel. "Talking" films became widely available in the late 1920s, and color film arrived in the late 1930s. By then Hollywood produced almost three hundred "feature" films annually. By 1939, 91 percent of American adults went to the movies at least once a week.[10] Unlike today, the typical "movie show" included a main feature, a second feature film, a cartoon, and a newsreel. Typically, the newsreels provided moving images of broad national events, such as presidential activities, speeches, visits, and ship launches. War photographers provided battle images. Sports events, such as boxing championships, baseball series, and auto races, were also featured. Generally a new newsreel arrived each week. While typically of no particular political orientation, this media amplified the more partisan coverage in newspapers and newsmagazines.[11]

The third new media of this period was radio. Initially radio stations broadcast local content locally. The rare national radio broadcast required arrangements to transmit the radio signal over telephone lines to local radio stations. In October 1939 the NBC network broadcast nationally the first regular radio program, the Metropolitan Opera, to an audience of less than 1 percent of the population. Until 1941 the news content on radio remained quite small, even though by then 84 percent of American households owned a radio receiver.[12] With the outbreak of war Americans turned to the new radio media for news. The proportion of daily news content rose dramatically from less than 2 percent in 1938 to over 15 percent in 1944. With certain notable exceptions, such as WGN in Chicago, the editorial content of radio news tended toward objectivity rather than partisanship.[13]

The national newsmagazines were early users of public-opinion polling. *Look* hired George Gallup from Iowa State University as a graduate student to conduct polling for the *Des Moines Register*. Luce's *Fortune* retained Elmo Roper to track the dynamics of American political opinion for the magazine's Round Table section.[14] The Roosevelt administration was equally adept at applying this new science to measure the popular response to its policies. It employed Hadley Cantril, founder of the

Office of Public Opinion Research at Princeton University, and assigned him to track changes in the American electorate's perception of the Axis threat and support for the administration's initiatives.[15] At each step to expand America's military capability, the magazines and the administration measured the breadth and depth of support for rearmament and belligerency.

The fine-tuning of public-opinion measurement became ever more sophisticated during the war. The newsmagazines used polling techniques to gauge the responses of their readership. Luce commissioned public-opinion polling for *Fortune* that also provided useful insights for the management of *Life* and *Time*. Cowles periodically employed Gallup to conduct surveys for both his newspapers and for *Look*. Hadley Cantril's compendium of public-opinion polls from 1935 through 1946 comprises a mass of data on several of these polls and their measurement of the American electorate's view of rearmament and belligerency. These polls reflect a substantial growth of support for the administration's wartime initiatives.

Two polls in particular documented the evolving opinion of the electorate regarding the Axis threat and the administration's foreign policy. Support for withdrawal from Asia rather than a confrontation with Japan declined from 82 percent in 1937 to 2 percent in November 1941, while the number "favoring all aid to Britain short of war" rose from 21 percent in 1939 to over 80 percent in 1941. The newsmagazines adjusted their editorial presentation accordingly.[16] The covers of *Time* magazine illustrated the changes graphically (see table 9.3).

The polls from 1939 to 1941 revealed a persistent opposition to any declaration of war or deployment of the Army overseas. So both the newsmagazines and the administration presented their advocacy of increasing belligerency in accordance with the public aversion to foreign entanglements.[17]

In this period the newsmagazines led portrayal of the Axis threat to the United States. Only after readers accepted this reality did other components of the media reinforce the message. Newspaper and radio professionals closely followed the leading

Table 9.3 Changing composition of *Time* cover stories

	1939	1940	1941
Beautiful women	3	2	1
US politicians (nonmilitary)	8	9	4
Business and economic officials	4	1	3
Arts, science, education	13	6	4
US military leaders	0	3	4
US politicians (military)	7	5	5
Foreign Allied leaders	11	18	17
Foreign Axis leaders	5	9	10
Miscellaneous (sports, etc.)	1	0	1

newsmagazines. When the electorate gradually accepted the existence of a serious military threat to the United States, advocates for initiatives to confront the threat materialized in the political arena. The Roosevelt administration responded by proposing ever more determined military efforts against the Axis powers. This transition in attitudes resulted from what Henry L. Stimson called the "education" of America. A primary instrument of this education was the national newsmagazine media. The Roosevelt administration, starting with the president, sought to use this novel media to move public opinion toward belligerency.

Roosevelt as Messenger and the Lessons of World War I

As the United States and its government moved through the approach and the arrival of the war, President Roosevelt served as the national spokesman. By the time of the attacks on Pearl Harbor, he had been president for almost nine years and was a nationally recognizable image and voice. His focus on the emergent Axis threat lent credence to the perception of his prescience and leadership. As the war progressed, Roosevelt prioritized the articulation through the changing media world of the purpose, the concerns, and the prospects of the American war effort. To this responsibility he brought an especially broad and deep set of communication skills.

When an undergraduate at Harvard, Roosevelt had been president of the student daily newspaper, the *Harvard Crimson*. In subsequent years he regularly contributed articles and reviews to newspapers and journals. On his income tax returns he identified his profession as "journalist." Thereafter, his many political campaigns (including five presidential campaigns) made him appreciate the needs and schedules of the working press, an appreciation he quickly demonstrated. After his election in 1933, he transformed the government's relationship with the press in two ways: first, through his own press conferences and, second, by his insistence that the government departments and agencies establish press offices. Prior presidents had held rare press conferences, usually limited to selected journalists and to responses to previously submitted questions. Unlike any previous president, Roosevelt held scheduled, twice-weekly press conferences, open to all accredited journalists, in which he bantered with the journalists. This regular access to his thinking and planning influenced his audience's thinking.

Roosevelt was also the first president to regularly exploit the radio media with his formal addresses and in his informal "fireside chats." The latter were usually twice annual, thirty-minute informal presentations delivered in open conversational style as if he were in a discussion among friends about the fireside and as if he were speaking to both the political arena and to voters in the intimacy of their homes. To this day his historic statements define the US role in World War II: "the Arsenal of Democracy" to arm democracies; "the Four Freedoms" or inalienable liberties belonging to all; "a day that will live in infamy" at Pearl Harbor; "our sons, the pride of our nation," called to arms; and "my little dog Fala," the innocent object of the slander of others. The president's radio program became the most effective means of amplifying the messages of national sacrifice, the unity of the Grand Alliance, the liberation of the conquered, and a postwar world free of fear. In effect, Roosevelt addressed not only the American people but also the peoples of the alliance and ultimately those of the emerging United Nations.

As the president formulated and communicated his message during the war, he was in many ways seeking to avoid the failures of the American war effort twenty-five years earlier. From 1938 to 1942 the American electorate felt real disappointment and chagrin over the US role in World War I. With the passage of time President Wilson's early efforts to "make the world safe for democracy" and his crusade for the League of Nations today seem to have presaged success in World War II and the coming of the United Nations. Likewise, American reluctance to enter the European conflict from 1914 to 1917 now seems to mirror American reluctance from 1938 to 1941, as do American military unpreparedness and ultimate military victory. In Roosevelt's day no positive pattern was yet evident.

The political and governmental leadership from 1938 to 1942 emerged from the ranks of the four million American veterans who had served in World War I. One needs only to recall the domination of American politics by veterans of the American Civil War in the thirty years after that conflict or of the veterans of the Vietnam War a century later to appreciate the influence of a war on the political inclinations of its veterans. They might have taken quiet pride in the intense combat they experienced, while lamenting the losses of comrades and celebrating American victory, but they also remembered the war's failures and defeats.

In April 1917 Wilson had sought a declaration of war against Germany in direct contravention of his just completed close reelection on the platform of "He kept us out of war." The consternation of the electorate required a special communication effort and message to justify belligerency. Wilson's message was the war was needed to "make the world safe for democracy."[18] He picked George Creel, a radical journalist from Missouri, to head a special presidential agency, the Committee on Public Information (CPI), to pursue the communication campaign. Under Creel's leadership the CPI carried out activities to stir America's fervor for war. The Four-Minute Men, one of his most successful creations, was a group of thousands of volunteers who visited meetings and movie theaters across the country to make prowar speeches. Both a federal Films Division and a News Division helped get out the war message. Creel then created the Division of Pictorial Publicity to reach those Americans who might not read newspapers, attend meetings, or watch movies. These divisions were not reluctant to use "persuasion" to ensure journalists, photographers, and publishers understood their patriotic duties.[19]

Perhaps for domestic political reasons or for reasons of future diplomacy at a postwar peace conference, Wilson avoided direct contact with the political leaders of Britain, France, or Italy during the war. Rather than employ the facilities and personnel of the State Department, including Secretary of State Robert Lansing, Wilson preferred to use his friend "Colonel" Edward M. House in communication and negotiations with these foreign "associates." By holding himself aloof from the policy formulation and decision-making attendant to the war effort, perhaps the president sought to preserve his role as the appellate jurisdiction, rendering judgment and decision only to settle disputes among his appointed officers and officials. Yet by doing so, he allowed the leadership of the war effort to slip into confusion of other hands, among them the British, the French, and assertive Americans.

His withdrawal of leadership had substantial consequences. While Wilson could avoid direct political responsibility for the policies and decisions of the war effort, the Democratic Party suffered a stunning defeat in the midterm congressional elections of 1918, despite the then-apparent American victory in the war. Further, the president was unable to persuade either the American people or the US Senate of the rectitude of his Treaty of Versailles and the cherished League of Nations covenant. Finally, as the country reviewed Wilson's conduct in the calm of postwar analyses, it perceived the war effort as grievously flawed.

Wilson's intense communication campaign had transmuted into war bond drives and "patriotism rallies" to censure the inadequately patriotic. These in turn had led to political dissent among the Progressives and the American Socialist Party leadership; 1912 presidential candidate Eugene V. Debs was even jailed for preaching "sedition." This in combination with the postwar Red Scare arising from the Russian Revolution and the Palmer raids on political "radicals" left a miasma of rancor. (In 1919 and 1920 Attorney General A. Mitchell Palmer, with the approval of the White House, had sent officers of the newly formed Federal Bureau of Investigation [FBI] to raid the homes and offices of prominent socialists.) Collectively, the tortured entry, confused prosecution, failed victory, and postwar turmoil matured to an electoral commitment to isolation and neutrality for the subsequent twenty years.

In advocating the moral high ground of "making the world safe for democracy," Wilson had tapped into an American idealism of long-standing and resilient persistence. While the League of Nations was not ratified, the new Republican leadership had its own proposal for a league to enforce peace. American "exceptionalism" and the avoidance of "entangling alliances" with exploitive European imperialists have deep traction in the American political arena. The balance between limiting

American foreign interests and maintaining traditional ideals remained at the center of foreign and defense policy formulation.

The basis for the electorate's aversion to foreign involvement was as complex as it was firmly held. From pulpits and the religious press came a constant invocation that America, unlike other nations, was historically and morally an "exceptional" and pacific nation. From the beginning of the American Republic in 1787, the former colonists sought to avoid any "standing" military, instead relying on the militias of citizen soldiers. Any permanent military establishment was seen as the source of government abuse of authority. That tradition persisted well into the twentieth century. In foreign policy the founding fathers advised the avoidance of "entangling alliances" with other nations and the maintenance of democracy in a world of imperial powers. The Monroe Doctrine, the foundation of American foreign policy, extended this advice to the protection of the republics of Latin America from imperialist ambitions. "Realist" arguments highlighting American foreign interests received little enthusiasm in the years before World War II.

In the interwar years the American electorate came to see the compromise of Wilson's devotion to neutrality as a fundamental error. A compendium of postwar disclosures cast American involvement in the Great War as an odious mistake. Starting with the failure of the Versailles Treaty, reinforced by revelations of Allied duplicity in portraying German brutalities, British condescension of America, the manipulation of American news media, and the revelations of attempts to subordinate the American Expeditionary Force, the conviction that the war had been an error grew to a certainty. The Allies' failure to pay their war debts to the United States became the signal confirmation of this belief, and American candidates for office competed as to who would be tougher on the defaulting former Allies. The complaint that fifty-five thousand Americans had given their lives in France merely to maintain the British Empire was difficult to refute. Finally, from 1933 to 1934 Senator Gerald Nye of North Dakota held a series of investigative public hearings to expose the role of American banks and "Wall Street"—the "merchants of death"—in conspiring to seduce the United States into that war.[20] In this atmosphere of revulsion, President Roosevelt's message concerning the Axis threat and requisite military preparation needed patient timing and careful delivery.

Starting in 1937 the president tried to condition his political audience by invoking the concept of collective security as embodied in the League of Nations Covenant. Few were willing to die for such an abstraction. As the Axis rose, its victims Austria, China, Czechoslovakia, and Spain became the victims of the delusion of collective security. When Britain rejected Roosevelt's invocation of the ideal in January 1938 to pursue "appeasement," a new message was needed.[21]

The communication of the president's evolving foreign and defense policy required confirmation of the Axis threat, which Axis aggression over the next three years provided. The parlous state of the American military in the years immediately before American entry in World War II forced the president to gain time to permit rearmament. Fortunately, such needed time gave him the opportunity to carefully communicate to the electorate to prepare them for war. Initially, in response to Neville Chamberlain's appeasement at Munich and Hitler's persecution of Jews during Kristallnacht in the fall of 1938, Roosevelt made a request to Congress for twenty-five thousand aircraft per year. The invasion of Poland and outbreak of war permitted changes to the Neutrality Act to allow the United States to provide munitions to those fighting the Axis. In response to the fall of France, Roosevelt obtained such big-ticket items from Congress as authorization to build a two-ocean Navy, to establish a draft for a large-scale Army, and to double the size of the Air Forces. The president proceeded opportunistically to achieve his foreign and defense policies with the constant message of mobilizing for the defense, avoiding intervention, and aiding those fighting the ascendant Axis powers.

The essence of the president's communication strategy was appearing to respond to the concerns of the electorate about inadequate defense capabilities while promising to avoid another foreign "adventure." Through the summer of 1941, he refrained from any implication of American intervention and limited policy to the provision of "lend-lease assistance," which was far more militarily significant than voters imagined. Ultimately the Lend Lease Act provided over $50 billion in aid and over 17 percent of the total war expenditures.[22] The president effectively led American defense preparation by appearing to be following the voter preferences. By waiting on events and carefully couching his message in terms of limited involvement and hopes for peace, he allowed the electorate to mature in its resolution.

Roosevelt also rallied Republicans. He shifted away from contentious New Deal social reforms, disappointing liberal Democrats but attracting "progressive" Republicans. Henry Stimson, a prominent former Republican secretary of state, became the secretary of war. The Republican vice presidential candidate in 1936, Frank Knox, became secretary of the Navy. Wendell Willkie, Roosevelt's Republican opponent in 1940, became his special ambassador, and there were to be many others. Roosevelt emphasized the "hemispheric" nature of defense policy by sending his former boss at the Navy Department, Josephus Daniels, to Mexico as ambassador. In August 1940 the Ogdensburg Agreement of mutual military support strengthened Canadian defense. These actions signaled to the American electorate a message concerning the administration's prioritization on national defense and to the Axis a message concerning the electorate's receptivity to the prioritization.

The German invasion of Soviet Russia on Sunday, June 22, 1941, affected US strategy in three ways. First, the American political arena was distinctly unsympathetic toward Communist Russia, causing problems of perception for the president's policies. Second, it was unclear whether and how the United States could assist the struggling Soviets. Third, the United States had limited arms production and numerous potential claimants. The American armed services and now Soviet Russia claimed strategic priority. So the president portrayed the Soviets as important Allies, essential for the defeat of Germany, to justify the huge lend-lease aid that he soon provided.

The Axis victories in 1940 and again in 1941 brought the threat of war ever closer to America. Even after the Axis domination of continental Europe and invasion of the Soviet Union, the electorate remained suspicious of the president's policies. In August 1941 the House of Representatives extended the draft by the narrowest of votes—203 ayes to 202 nays. Since the beginning of the war, the president had reiterated a three-part message in response to Axis success. First, the United States would rebuild its defense capabilities through military and industrial mobilization. Second, barring direct attack, the United States would not intervene in the war. Finally, the United States would pursue opportunities for peaceful resolutions, despite their fading probability. Unlike Wilson, Roosevelt would not ask the electorate to be "neutral in thought and deed." From 1917 to 1919 Roosevelt had experienced the political trauma of pursuing a policy without electoral support and was determined to maintain a consistent message in building electoral support for his defense policies.

From Neutrality to Alliance Leadership

The attack on Pearl Harbor eliminated domestic political acrimony as Americans unified in their own defense. The previously suspicious Republican opposition in Congress joined in the unanimous declarations of war against Japan and, four days later, Germany and Italy. The doubts as to the cause and failures of the Pearl Harbor disaster were postponed to some postwar congressional investigation. War scares imagining enemy attacks on the West Coast and the visible sinking of American ships off the East Coast lent poignancy to the unification of national determination.

The president, in a series of personal appearances and speeches, provided a voice for this determination: first in his terse but definitive request for a declaration of war in the "day of infamy" speech; then in a fireside chat to the nation on December 19, 1941, promising that "we will gain the inevitable triumph, so help us God"; and finally in his State of the Union address of January 6, 1942, declaring "it must be done."[23] President Roosevelt calmed, inspired, and rallied the nation to mobilize and win the war. The patient assembling of a more national administration in the prior two years, the careful transformation of public ambivalence toward another world war into a commitment to victory, and the formulation of defense strategy and an attendant foreign policy now provided a sound and supportive political basis for the American conduct of the war.

The real uncertainty among the American leadership in the winter of 1941–42 was the probable prospects of a war against the Axis. The president had confronted that uncertainty the prior July when he had requested that the armed services formulate their victory plans. He transmitted these plans to the industrial mobilization authority on the Supply Priorities Allocation Board. Although the industrial mobilization had been faltering before Pearl Harbor, there had been no suggestion that the victory plan requirements for armaments could not be fulfilled. The question was whether the armaments would become available in time to save vital Allies and whether Germany and especially Japan would be able to use the resources of conquered areas to their advantage.

In his State of the Union address on January 6, 1942, President Roosevelt spoke about economic mobilization to his largest radio audience to date, an estimated 80 million people:

> The superiority of the United States in munitions and ships must be overwhelming. . . . The United States must build planes and tanks and guns and ships to the utmost of our national capacity. We have the ability and capacity to produce arms not only for our own armed forces, but also for the armies, navies, and air forces fighting at our side. . . .
>
> This production of ours in the United States must be raised far above present levels, even though it will mean the dislocation of the lives and occupations of millions of our own people. We must raise our sights all along the production line. Let no man say it cannot be done. It must be done—and we have undertaken to do it. . . .
>
> To increase our production rate of airplanes so rapidly that in this year, 1942, we shall produce sixty thousand planes, ten thousand more than the goal we set a year and a half ago. . . .
>
> Only this all-out scale of production will hasten the ultimate all-out victory. Speed will count. Lost ground can always be regained—lost time, never.[24]

Thus, within a month of US belligerency, the president set forth to the nation and its armed forces his strategy to win the war: armaments production, industrial mobilization, conscription, aid to allies, and Americans in combat—all on a massive scale. America was committed to the destruction of the Axis in total warfare.

In the immediate aftermath of Pearl Harbor, Roosevelt's cabinet officers, specifically Secretaries Harold Ickes, Frank Knox, and Henry Morgenthau, recommended the establishment of an education effort to help the media provide positive war information to the electorate. They recommended as a model the Wilson administration's notorious CPI under George Creel. The president demurred recalling the negative political and morale consequences. Instead he emphasized the maintenance of normal American political and media communication practices and the avoidance of infringements on freedom of speech and the press at home other than voluntary commonsense self-censorship left to the press.

However, he immediately began controlling the flow of information across US borders. On December 19, 1941, he established the Office of Censorship to monitor international communication, and the military censored letters home from its expeditionary forces. On June 13, 1942, Roosevelt created the Office of War Information (OWI) to coordinate the dissemination of wartime information, but he put it under the directorship of the popular radioman Elmer Davis and in control of professional journalists. The OWI soon established the Voice of America to reach foreign audiences and the Bureau of Motion Pictures to work with Hollywood. Increasing pressure from the military to tighten censorship led to resistance from those working at the OWI, the controversy emboldened Roosevelt's domestic critics, and Congress curtailed its funding in 1943. As the president understood, the infringement of individual freedom was unwarranted and counterproductive.[25] Normal life, albeit with rationing, should go on.

The president became the national spokesman to the general public for the realities, necessities, and objectives of the war. This was especially true in the transitional year of 1942, when the quantity and prominence of his public addresses increased. Roosevelt was a master of the twice-weekly news conference, the radio address, informal speeches, fireside chats, and formal addresses to Congress. From the State of the Union message to Congress on January 6 to the Christmas holiday fireside chat on December 23, the president made nineteen radio broadcast speeches in 1942, heard both in the United States and abroad. Previously he had limited his chats to twice a year, lest he exhaust his precious political capital. The urgency of the war effort in 1942 demanded more frequent exposure. The subject matter ran the gamut of the tasks at hand: the consequences of early setbacks, the pride in early successes, the nature of worldwide war and Allied strategy, and the need for increased armaments production, reductions in consumption, rationing of consumer goods, sharply higher taxation, and price restraints in both the agricultural and the labor markets.[26]

Roosevelt appreciated the necessity of a special effort to mobilize Americans to support the war effort. The experience of World War I, with President Wilson's focus on the achievement of a postwar world made "safe for democracy," rather than on the wartime mobilization of the nation, provided a cautionary lesson. Roosevelt urged the building of a national purpose in support of the war effort so as to permit a better postwar world. He was determined to be not only the leader of the Allied coalition but also the national wartime leader at home.[27] His oratory skills fit the task.

At the beginning of 1943 the president again met with Churchill in North Africa at Casablanca. Roosevelt viewed this meeting as an opportunity to recast his role to the American electorate and to the Allies. President Wilson had refrained from traveling to the battlefront in World War I, in an effort to remain above the battle and thus impeccable when he joined the postwar peace negotiations. Roosevelt understood the rancid political consequences of ignoring the American armed services after their sacrifices in battle and the success of their exertions. As Lincoln was in his visits to the Union Army during the Civil War, Roosevelt wished to be seen as the commander in chief of the American armed services, fully cognizant of their sacrifices. This connection to the nation's soldiers and sailors was vital to the success of his leadership at home and abroad as he became the physical embodiment of Allied coalition.

At Casablanca, Roosevelt presented himself to the Allied coalition, the American electorate, and the incipient United Nations as the architect of the destruction of the Axis ascendancy and the creation of the world defined in the Atlantic Charter. The conference resulted in a military-naval agenda that guided the evolving military and naval campaigns in both the Atlantic and the Pacific for the balance of the war. On January 24, at the conclusion of the conference, President Roosevelt presented his overarching objective at a press conference. In a departure from both the chiefs' and Churchill's expectations, Roosevelt pronounced the goal of the war to be the "unconditional surrender" of the Axis, recalling the byword of the American Civil War and General Ulysses Grant's relentless pursuit of victory. The goal was simple and easily understood by all audiences, although its realization would be complex.

His prayer on D-Day, June 6, 1944, effectively served as the peroration of his administration's World War II communication program:

> Almighty God: our sons, pride of our nation, this day have set upon a mighty endeavor, a struggle to preserve our Republic, our religion, and our civilization, and to set free a suffering humanity.
>
> Lead them straight and true. Give strength to their arms, stoutness to their hearts, steadfastness in their faith.
>
> They will need Thy blessings. Their road will be long and hard. . . .
>
> They will be sore tried, by night and day, without rest—until victory is won. The darkness will be rent by noise and flame. Men's souls will be shaken with the violences of war. . . .
>
> Some will never return. Embrace these, father, and receive them, Thy heroic servants into thy kingdom. . . .

Give us strength too—strength in our daily tasks to redouble the contributions we make in the physical and the material support of our armed
forces.

And let our hearts be stout, to wait out the long travail, to bear sor-
rows that may come, to impart our courage to our sons wheresoever they
may be.[28]

Roosevelt faced his fourth presidential election campaign in the fall of 1944. To
consolidate national support, he traveled to the Pacific to conciliate the MacArthur-
Halsey feuding, he campaigned throughout the Northeast, and he traveled twenty-
three thousand miles to Yalta and back for his final conference with Stalin and
Churchill. The crucial years of 1938 to 1943 had seen the president successfully deal
with the three major tasks he defined for himself: building an electoral coalition that
would support American intervention and prosecution of the war, managing the
mobilization of American industry, and formulating the strategy and foreign policies
that would permit the achievement of victory.

Conclusion

Three new media platforms—the radio, the newsreels shown with every movie, and
the national, large-format, illustrated newsmagazine—for the first time in US history created a truly national audience that Roosevelt, the messenger, mobilized for
war. Previously the press had been local and at best regional. Henceforth it would
be national. Roosevelt pioneered the biweekly presidential press conference, open
to all members of the accredited press, as well as the biannual, half-hour fireside
chat by radio, allowing for more complicated messages. The ubiquitous illustrated
newsmagazines pioneered polling so that the president and everyone else could
compare messages to the receptivity of the audience and could tailor future messages accordingly. Roosevelt used these mechanisms to transform ever so gradually
an isolationist country thoroughly disillusioned with US participation in the last
world war into a people prepared for total war in the pursuit of unconditional surrender, his ultimate message.

He profited from Wilson's negative example: Wilson's failure to prepare public
opinion in advance of his political objectives or to launch a communication campaign in the first place hamstrung Wilson politically. Roosevelt's communication
campaign began before hostilities and allowed him to coordinate with both the Allies
and US citizens to wage a far more effective war effort and termination of hostilities,
which took place after Roosevelt's death but which he had thought about deeply and
set in motion.

Notes

1. Edward R. Murrow, *I Can Hear It Now*, vol. 3 (New York: Columbia Records, 1949).

2. Terry Golway, *Together We Cannot Fail: FDR and the American Presidency in Years of Crisis* (Napersville, IL: Sourcebooks, 2009).

3. See Studs Terkel, *The Good War: An Oral History of World War II* (New York: New Press, 1997); Tom Brokaw, *The Greatest Generation* (New York: Random House, 1997).

4. Jean E. Smith, *FDR* (New York: Random House, 2007), 418–19.

5. William L. Langer and S. Everett Gleason, *The Challenge to Isolation: The World Crisis of 1937–1940 and American Foreign Policy* (New York: Harper and Row, 1952), 11–13.

6. Charles A. Lindbergh, *The Wartime Journals of Charles Lindbergh* (New York: Harper Bros., 1971).

7. Golway, *Together We Cannot Fail.*

8. Rob Verger, "Newsweek's First Issue Debuted Today in 1933," *Newsweek*, February 17, 2014, http://www.newsweek.com/newsweeks-first-issue-debuted-today-1933-229355.

9. Michael G. Carew, *The Power to Persuade: FDR, the Newsmagazines, and Going to War, 1939–1941* (Lanham, MD: Rowman & Littlefield, 2005), 30–74.

10. Carew, 40–42.

11. Association of National Advertisers, "Magazine Circulation and Rate Trends," 1940; Audit Bureau of Circulation, "Magazine Trend Report, 2000," December 2000, in Carew, 36–38.

12. Matthew Chappell and C. E. N. Cooper, *Radio Audience Measurement* (New York: Smith Daye, 1944), chap. 5.

13. Chappell and Cooper, 205, 207, 217.

14. Box 40, "The Time Inc. Round Table," R. W. Davenport Collection, Library of Congress.

15. Hadley Cantril, *Gauging Public Opinion* (Princeton, NJ: Princeton University Press, 1944), 84.

16. Vox 40, "The Time Inc. Round Table," R. W. Davenport Collection, Library of Congress.

17. Hadley Cantril, ed., *Public Opinion, 1935–1946* (Princeton, NJ: Princeton University Press, 1951), 967–78, 1171–85.

18. Arthur Link, *Wilson*, vol. 5, *Campaign for Progressivism and Peace* (Princeton, NJ: Princeton University Press, 1963), 108–24.

19. Herbert C. Hoover, *The Ordeal of Woodrow Wilson* (New York: McGraw-Hill, 1958).

20. W. I. Langer, "Political Problems of a Coalition," in "Turning Points of the War," *Foreign Affairs* 26 (October 1947): 76.
21. W. S. Churchill, *The Second World War*, vol. 1, *The Gathering Storm* (Boston: Houghton Mifflin, 1948), 478.
22. Warren F. Kimball, *The Most Unsordid Act, Lend Lease, 1939–45* (Baltimore: Johns Hopkins University Press, 1969), 252.
23. Leighton and Coakley, *Global Logistics and Strategy, 1940–1943* (Washington, DC: Center for Military History, 1955), 197–202; Donald Nelson, *Arsenal of Democracy* (New York: Harcourt-Brace, 1946), 186; R. Elberton Smith, *The Army and Economic Mobilization* (Washington, DC: Center for Military History, 1985), 141–42.
24. Franklin D. Roosevelt, State of the Union Address, January 6, 1942, in *The American Presidency Project*, ed. Gerhard Peters and John T. Woolley, http://www.presidency.ucsb.edu/ws/index.php?pid=16253.
25. Box 35, "Office of Information File," Lowell Mellett Collection, FDR Presidential Library, Hyde Park, NY.
26. Golway, *Together We Cannot Fail*, 195–224.
27. Samuel Irving Rosenman, *Working with Roosevelt* (New York: Harper & Brothers, 1952), 266–67.
28. Franklin D. Roosevelt, "Prayer on D-Day," June 6, 1944, in *American Presidency Project*, https://www.presidency.ucsb.edu/node/210815.

10.

Selling a Limited War in Korea, 1950–53

Steven Casey

A mood of frustrated concern gripped the White House on February 2, 1951, not over the latest developments on the Korean battlefield but over the state of American public opinion. Republicans in Congress, emboldened by their recent gains in the midterm elections, had launched a sustained attack on the administration's foreign policy, including the wisdom of intervening in Korea. Then came a Gallup poll in the middle of January recording that 66 percent of the public wanted the US to "pull out" of Korea altogether.[1] President Harry S. Truman began the inquest at a weekly cabinet meeting. "Why are we in Korea?" Truman stressed, "is a pertinent question," but no one at the meeting had a ready answer, which raised a deeper question: Why, after seven months of war, had officials been unable to make the public case for their government's foreign policy?

Korea did not become unpopular because the American people were repelled by limitations placed on how it was fought.[2] Nor did Korea become increasingly difficult to sell when the fighting bogged down in stalemate beginning in the summer of 1951. Instead, Truman's problems stemmed from the constraints placed on what administration officials could say and how they could say it. This chapter examines why these constraints were in place and how Truman's administration managed to overcome the challenge of communicating America's Korean War.

Fears of Military Escalation and Opposition Domination of the Media

On the first Monday of the Korean crisis, Harry Truman latched onto a seemingly appropriate analogy. "Korea is the Greece of the Far East," he declared to an aide. "If we are tough enough now, if we stand up to them like we did in Greece three years ago, they [the Communists] won't take any next steps."[3] Yet when it came to public rhetoric, this analogy had surprisingly little relevance. After all, in 1947 the president had responded to the Greek crisis with the rousing Truman Doctrine, attempting to "scare the hell out of America" by issuing an ideological call to arms. Now, he adopted a decidedly low-key public posture, summed up by his injunction to journalists on June 25, 1950: "Don't make it alarmist," he instructed. "Don't exaggerate the seriousness of the attack."[4] During the first weeks of the Korean War, this became something of a motif for the administration's entire information campaign. Despite deploying four US divisions, the president delivered no ringing public addresses, preferring instead to explain his actions in three short and factual press statements, a number of relatively uninformative press conferences, and a series of private meetings with congressional leaders.[5]

The content of these utterances was particularly cautious, as demonstrated by the government's depiction of the enemy. In private the president and his key advisers had no doubt that the Soviet Union had masterminded the whole invasion. But in public they were not ready to make this link explicit—as Edward W. Barrett, the assistant secretary of state for public affairs, found out to his cost. On June 25 Barrett unguardedly told a reporter that the North Koreans had no autonomy and were utterly dependent on Moscow; their relationship, in his vivid phrase, was like that between "Walt Disney and Donald Duck." Very quickly Barrett received an urgent telegram from the State Department to "pipe down."[6]

Over the next week Truman and Secretary of State Dean Acheson then went out of their way to tell reporters that there had been no move "from a 'cold war' to a 'hot war' with communism." "We are not at war," the president stressed in a press conference on June 29. This was only a "police action." Two days later, having briefly and simply announced that "General MacArthur has been authorized to use certain supporting ground units" in Korea, Truman pointedly sought to exude an air of calm confidence by heading off on a preplanned cruise in keeping with his normal routine.[7]

Truman's preference for a subdued public posture stemmed from a variety of concerns. For a start he deemed it prudent to avoid overtly taunting Stalin. A presidential statement publicly blaming the Soviets for the Korean invasion could become a serious provocation.[8] Instead, the administration moved rapidly to exploit the brazen nature of the North Korean invasion to foster a broad international coalition behind its policy. This placed the new United Nations (UN) organization at the center of American policy, which in turn meant that officials worked hard to ensure that their pronouncements conformed to the whole ethos of a collective-security campaign. On June 27 US delegates explicitly rejected extending the bipolar, confrontational message in the Truman Doctrine to Korea on the revealing grounds that it was "not consistent with principle of keeping Korean matter a *UN* rather than a *U.S.* affair."[9]

At the same time, officials had one eye firmly fixed on domestic public opinion. In the current Cold War environment, ratcheted up in recent months by the Soviet A-bomb test and the Chinese Revolution, few Americans doubted that the Soviet Union lurked behind the North Korean attack. And almost everyone agreed that this aggression had to be countered. Indeed, there was bipartisan support for sending GIs to Korea, letters to the White House ran ten to one in favor of the president, a Gallup poll recorded that 81 percent approved of Truman's action, and the State Department's Office of Public Affairs found that virtually all the media viewed America's intervention in Korea "as the best means of preventing World War III."[10]

Although gratified by these signs of support, Truman worried that the public might panic. In May, 40 percent of respondents in one poll had singled out war as their chief concern—"the highest . . . at any time since the end of World War II"— while 22 percent had expected war with the Soviets in one year and a further 57 percent thought it would come within five years. Cities like New York were already publicly laying plans for a mass evacuation in case of such a war.[11] Against this backdrop, Truman was determined not to go before Congress to ask for a joint resolution supporting his Korean decision, for as one White House official told reporters, this might "contribute to a war hysteria." Instead, a limited war required a low-key public response. As the *U.S. News and World Report* shrewdly noted, "The real idea was to fix in the public eye a picture of the Government in a calm mood . . . to keep Korea in its place: a pint-sized incident, not a full-scale war. . . . Official Washington was doing everything it could to keep a firm line against the communists, and keep the home front cool at the same time."[12]

Yet this strategy had one distinct drawback: the government rapidly lost control over the news agenda. In theory, officials were now in a tremendously powerful position to develop their own interpretation of the Korean conflict and the way it related to the broader Cold War struggle. Not only does the media naturally tend to rally behind the president during periods of crisis, but this was also the era of so-called objective journalism, when the mainstream press engaged in little editorializing in its news pages and tended to rely instead on "official facts" when developing a story. In practice, however, with the government making available few "official facts," reporters soon resorted to speculation.[13]

The lack of forceful presidential leadership also enabled the Republican opposition to develop its interpretation of the Korean crisis. For over a year the Republican right had savaged Truman and Acheson for pursuing an "appeasement" policy in Asia that had "lost" China and would pave the way for a Communist takeover of Taiwan. The outbreak of the Korean War, far from silencing the likes of Kenneth S. Wherry, Robert Taft, and (most notoriously) Joseph McCarthy, provided them with ammunition. As well as attacking the constitutionality of going to war without congressional authorization, they charged that Truman's recent "hands off" policy in Asia had invited the North Korean attack.[14] To the administration's dismay, these allegations found much support in the press. Numerous newspapers hastened to point out that Truman's strong stand in Korea "marks an almost complete reversal" in government policy. "It almost amounts to 'vindication' of the attitude taken" by senior Republicans, the *New York Herald Tribune* editorialized on June 28. By overturning our old do-nothing Asian policy, agreed the *New York Times*, we have finally regained "our national self-respect. . . . Our good conscience has been restored."[15]

In the absence of sustained official cues, Why Korea? was quickly becoming a contested question. Far from just another case of unprovoked Communist aggression, the Korean crisis was being portrayed by some as part and parcel of the Democrats' neglect of Asia. As a result, the strategy of keeping the home front cool had confused the rationale for America's involvement in the Korean War.

The Administration's Belated Media Campaign

Truman finally took to the airwaves on July 19. Significantly, the president still refused to go up to Capitol Hill in person, lest this create the impression that he was asking for a declaration of war. Instead, he agreed to an awkward compromise, whereby legislators received a long, detailed message at noon, before Truman directly addressed nearly 130 million Americans in a fireside chat that evening.[16]

The speech itself began by stressing exactly why GIs had been sent to this "small country, thousands of miles away." The reason was simple. The North Koreans had launched a brazen and premeditated act of aggression against a small, independent country that was sponsored by the UN and supported by the United States. Speaking in a slow, measured manner, his anger barely concealed, the president insisted that this assault was a "direct challenge to the efforts of the free nations to build the kind of world in which men can live in freedom and peace." Placing the current crisis in its global perspective, Truman explained that Korea was likely to be only the first in a series of "sneak" attacks. America had to increase its strength and war preparedness to meet the new challenges that were bound to emerge. This meant making a "considerable adjustment" to the country's economy, both to ensure that defense industries had access to the necessary raw materials and to "prevent inflation and to keep our government in a sound financial condition." It also meant raising taxes to pay for the $10 billion increase in defense spending.[17]

In the next few weeks, the administration's information efforts went into high gear. In late July the State Department issued a white paper on Korea, which expanded on the reasons for fighting the war.[18] The State Department also provided briefing papers for Democrats standing in November's midterm elections and distributed 200,000 copies of a pamphlet titled "Our Foreign Policy" to newspapers, pressure groups, schools, and public libraries. In August, attempting to exploit the new medium of television, the White House began a series of weekly broadcasts on NBC titled *Battle Report, Washington*. Hosted by John Steelman, a senior White House aide, this was a chance for officials to brief the 20 million or so Americans who now owned television sets.[19]

As the administration's information efforts finally took off, however, an even more damaging problem emerged: the difficulty of coordinating these official utterances. The outbreak of war transformed the normal demand for, and supply of, official news. Suddenly, foreign policy was no longer the preserve of just the White House, State Department, and Pentagon. Quickly, officials at, say, the Commerce Department and the Labor Department were easily drawn into statements (sometimes controversial and contradictory) on America's productive capabilities, which now had a direct bearing on the war effort.

Bureaucratic and personal rivalries only compounded the situation. The Army and Navy had already been engaged in something approaching open warfare for the dwindling resources resulting from stringent budget cuts. The huge mobilization plan announced by Truman on July 19, which increased the military budget by $10 billion, did not eliminate the problem. The Marine Corps continued to lobby tirelessly for their own cause—much to the annoyance of Truman, who angrily commented in September that the Marine Corps had "a propaganda machine that is almost equal to Stalin's."[20] In the Pentagon the Office of Public Information (OPI), established in 1950 to coordinate Army-Navy pronouncements, was clearly failing at this task, leading reporters to condemn it for being "clumsily ineffective in the face of crisis."[21]

Secretary of Defense Louis Johnson's antics worsened the situation. Truman had become increasingly impatient with Johnson's scheming against the State Department, his connections with leading Republicans, and his constant leaks to the press. "If this keeps up," an exasperated president remarked early in the war, "we're going to need a new secretary of defense." Equally voluble but more difficult to sack was Gen. Douglas MacArthur. At the start of the conflict, John Foster Dulles had recommended that, rather than giving MacArthur the command of US forces in Korea, he should be "hauled back to the United States immediately." The president disagreed. He explained that "the general was involved politically in this country—where he has from time to time been mentioned as a possible Republican candidate—and that he could not recall MacArthur without causing a tremendous reaction in the country where he has been built up, to heroic stature." UN command gave MacArthur even more visibility to snipe at the administration's "defeatist" Asian policies.[22]

The limited political goals of the Korean conflict greatly exacerbated these tensions. With top officials acutely aware that "if each department guns for itself we can bring about a general panic and a bad result," there was much talk of reviving the

Office of War Information (OWI), the agency that had led the propaganda battle in World War II.[23] White House officials even consulted the former head of OWI, Elmer Davis, but ultimately they decided that a limited conflict did not warrant its own separate propaganda agency.[24] Instead, the White House simply tightened existing procedures. It reactivated an informal interagency committee under the State Department. Meeting twice a month, this committee distributed background materials, instructions, and guidance to other departments. If anyone still doubted what to say, they were instructed to approach the White House Press Office for clearance.[25]

In Truman's eyes these lesser solutions not only befitted a limited war; they also had the merit of concentrating power in the White House. Still, they came with very real costs. For one thing they placed an almost unbearable strain on the White House Press Office—an area soon known as the "homicidal center" because of the killer levels of stress suffered by incumbents.[26] For another they failed to stop certain senior figures from issuing deeply discordant statements. In August the commerce and labor secretaries got into a very public spat about the nation's personnel problems. Far more disturbingly, later that month Francis Mathews, the secretary of the Navy, declared that the US ought to be willing to pay "even the price of instituting a war to compel cooperation for peace." Although swiftly condemned by a State Department spokesman, who likened it to a proposal for "preventive war," this episode generated the impression of a government at war with itself. Even mainstream media organs like the *New York Times* called on the president to take "more active charge of our foreign policy."[27]

Truman duly obliged with a series of speeches at the start of September emphasizing the government's major goals in Asia and his efforts to prevent an escalation into a general war. Yet his overall tone remained defensive. In July and August the government had tried to reestablish control over a debate that Republicans had helped to define in the early days of the war. Now, Truman's speeches focused on clarifying government policy after all the damage done by Mathews, MacArthur, and others.[28]

During the fall these efforts seemed sufficient, largely because they coincided with the major battlefield success sparked by the Inchon landings on September 15, 1950. In November, however, China's massive intervention resulted in even more vicious public infighting, with MacArthur again in the vanguard. In a series of interviews, the general defended his drive deep into North Korea and claimed that "Washington's restrictions prevented a short, successful end to the war." Truman was furious, privately raging against MacArthur for "shooting off his mouth." The president responded with two decrees: one reiterated that all government statements must be cleared by senior officials in Washington; the other ordered all officials abroad "to exercise extreme caution in public statements, to clear all but the most routine statements with their departments, and to refrain from direct communications on military or foreign policy with newspapers, magazines, or other publicity material in the U.S."[29]

This silenced MacArthur—for a time. But it also silenced virtually everyone else in the administration, preventing them from speaking out on Korea at a time when battlefield fortunes were taking a disastrous turn and opinion polls revealed growing public confusion about America's whole involvement in Korea.

In the first days after the Chinese intervention, the president and secretary of state moved quickly to explain the new dangers to the American public. At a press conference on November 30, Truman even created a flurry of panic when he inadvertently suggested that the US might use nuclear weapons. The White House Press Office soon clarified and toned down his statement, but in the next few weeks the president and secretary of state often made far from restrained pronouncements.[30] Chinese aggression, declared Acheson, had created "a situation of unparalleled danger. . . . No one can guarantee that a [general] war will not come." A declaration of a state of national emergency was vital, emphasized Truman toward the middle of December, largely because it would "have great psychological effects on the American people." Such a declaration, he explained to congressional leaders, "would be good for the country. It would help create a united front to enable us to 'meet the situation with which we are faced.'"[31]

Despite the danger, leading Republican politicians remained unwilling to rally behind their president, largely owing to political self-interest. Many Republicans believed that the "me too" bipartisanship practiced by Thomas Dewey in 1948 had only reaped electoral defeat, while tough anticommunist crusading, charging the Democrats with softness toward Reds at home and in Asia, had won votes in the recent midterm elections. As the Chinese offensive threatened to force all US troops off the peninsula during December and January, the whole Republican Party seemed ready to unite around this tough new position.[32]

In response, the White House summoned leaders from both parties, including Taft, who had been excluded from such meetings in June, to consultations, while rank-and-file legislators received invitations to cocktail parties and luncheons. The president hoped to give congressmen the impression that their views were being taken into account at a moment of grave peril.[33]

Yet Truman refused to follow Franklin Roosevelt's example from the big international crisis ten years earlier and appoint two prominent Republicans (in FDR's case, Henry Stimson and Frank Knox) to key positions in his cabinet. Back then, Stimson and Knox had become formidable spokesmen, publicly making the case for controversial measures just months before the 1940 presidential election.[34] Truman had recently had the perfect opportunity to follow this precedent when he fired Louis Johnson. But the president had turned instead to the tried-and-tested figure of Gen.

George C. Marshall, even though Marshall had become the object of fierce right-wing attacks for his failure to end the Chinese Civil War back in 1946. Dean Acheson was even more of a hated figure for those on the right, and soon after the 1950 election Republicans in Congress began a sustained attempt to force his resignation. Truman refused to budge, however, defiantly telling reporters on more than one occasion that Acheson would definitely stay.[35]

The intensely partisan president never felt comfortable with the thought of even moderate opposition politicians holding prominent positions inside his government. He had only reluctantly agreed to appoint John Foster Dulles to work on a Japanese peace treaty the previous spring, and he now balked at the idea of promoting another Republican whose ego might be just as "monumental."[36] Back in the summer, when Senator William Knowland had urged the president "to establish 'a government of national unity for as long as the crisis lasts' by inviting Republicans into his cabinet," Truman had demurred for a revealing reason. As a White House spokesman told reporters, "for the president to appoint a 'coalition cabinet' . . . might imply that we are going into a global war, whereas the Korean conflict might not lead to one."[37] In other words, fighting a limited war once more imposed an important constraint on what could be done.

It was a constraint that became especially important during the winter of 1950–51, as Republicans continued their attacks against the secretary of state. By now Acheson—and to a lesser extent Marshall—were deeply polarizing figures. Their public appearances, far from providing a chance for them to make their case, became the perfect opportunity for Republicans to assault the administration. In January the situation became so acute that the State Department limited Acheson's speech schedule. He must not become "the principle [*sic*] antagonist of opposition spokesmen in the 'great debate,'" the department's Working Group on Public Relations concluded. "The Secretary should not take so prominent a place in the current public discussions as to revive antagonism to him as a personality."[38] As a result, during January and February Acheson often dropped out of the public eye, thereby creating another information vacuum that Taft and Wherry gleefully filled with accusatory press releases.[39]

Unable to make their case directly to the public, Acheson and his colleagues tried to do so indirectly. Throughout the winter crisis, senior decision-makers held off-the-record meetings with numerous reporters, columnists, and broadcasters. The administration also forged a close relationship with the Committee for Present Danger, a pressure group consisting of leading academics and ex-officials whose aim was to foster public support for a large arms buildup and to coordinate with the Advertising Council to develop radio and television commercials.[40]

The Great Debate

With the battlefield still looking bleak at the start of 1951, a group of Republicans led by Taft, and vocally supported by Herbert Hoover, called for the reexamination of the entire basis of US foreign policy. Their quest centered on whether to send American forces to Europe rather than reinforce MacArthur in Korea. The administration, viewing Korea as only a small part of the global Communist challenge, deemed it vital to bolster Europe's defense. Right-wing Republicans were skeptical, however, partly because of cost, partly because of the delegation of congressional authority it entailed, and partly because of fears that even more American boys would die in far-away places. As this "great debate" unfolded, Marshall, Acheson, and the Joint Chiefs went before Congress to make the administration's case. But the setting was far from ideal. Their testimony tended to focus on the details of just one aspect of policy rather than on the administration's overall mobilization strategy or the relationship between the European and Korean theaters.

Developments in the UN added to the fragmented nature of official rhetoric in early 1951. Initially, UN involvement had bolstered the Truman administration's information efforts, especially since officials could point to the international legitimacy that their action enjoyed. In the aftermath of the Chinese intervention, however, the UN suddenly posed a major problem. Under intense congressional pressure, the administration pressed for a UN resolution branding China as an aggressor. Many UN allies, however, feared that this would pave the way for retaliatory measures against China, and so they focused on passing a cease-fire resolution. Weeks of diplomatic wrangling ensued, which sparked intense domestic criticism of supposed UN weakness. The delay, declared Taft, was tantamount to "surrender" and a disaster for the "whole moral basis of the UN." The organization, raged Senator William Jenner, had become "a debating society death trap for American GIs."[41]

With US troops still struggling against the Chinese onslaught, the maneuvering in the UN, as Acheson recognized, "completely confused the American people."[42] Small wonder that on February 2—the day after the UN General Assembly finally adopted an aggressor resolution—Truman's cabinet fretted about its failure to get its message across. Soon after, one White House aide circulated a plan of action. "What needs to be said at this time," he informed the president, were answers to the questions "why we are fighting in Korea, why we are building up the military establishment, why we have to pay high taxes, and why boys have to be drafted." "One or two statements or speeches will not be enough; what is needed is a hard-hitting, carefully-thought-out program."[43]

The administration finally implemented this program in the spring, but in circumstances that, at first glance, appeared even less favorable than those of February.

On April 11 Truman finally fired MacArthur, partly for another insubordinate out-burst, although in the clumsiest fashion imaginable. Worried that the *Chicago Tribune* had gotten hold of the story, the White House Press Office summoned reporters to an impromptu 1:00 a.m. conference to announce the news. Truman's critics were appalled. They attacked "the hasty and vindictive" manner in which MacArthur was removed and the administration's failure to answer the central question: "How and when can a conclusive decision be reached in the Korean War?"[44] When MacArthur returned to a tumultuous reception a couple of weeks later, he seemed to have the perfect answer: escalation including a blockade of China, aerial reconnaissance of the mainland, and the use of Nationalist Chinese troops. Sticking with the current policy of limiting troop levels and enemy targets, he added, would "mean a long, indecisive war and the needless sacrifice of many American boys."[45]

Although MacArthur's emotional homecoming both dented popular support for Truman's limited-war strategy and precipitated a major congressional inquiry into the administration's whole Asia strategy, it did provide officials with an opportunity to develop a more aggressive public information strategy. In March, Truman had invited his leading public relations advisers to the Oval Office. As well as discussing "a nation-wide speaking campaign in which cabinet officers and sub-cabinet officers would carry the message of the administration's policies and objectives to the 48 states," they also considered the appointment of a new administrative assistant "to supervise and carry out a coordinated program of speeches and similar PR [public relations] activities."[46] When MacArthur's relief sparked public outrage, the president's aides rapidly put these ideas into operation. The White House Press Office collated material on foreign and defense policies for distribution to officials at all levels of the administration as a way of encouraging them to speak out more frequently. Truman also appointed former congressman John A. Carroll to liaise with Congress, work on speeches, and reach out to potential supporters outside the capital.[47]

As the MacArthur hearings got under way before a joint committee of the Senate Armed Services and Foreign Relations Committees, the administration enjoyed additional strengths. One was the joint committee's comprehensive remit, which allowed officials to discuss the full range of their Cold War policies. Another was the government's impressive new unity, so different from the public spats of the previous summer, as senior military officials paraded up to Capitol Hill to demolish MacArthur's call for escalation.[48]

By June 1951 the Truman administration was enjoying the better of the debate. Although opinion polls still showed major public support for MacArthur, the popular mood had started to cool, and elite opinion solidly backed the White House. One tabulation of press reaction estimated that 60–70 percent "was now favorable to the administration on both foreign policy and the broader issues involved."[49]

By the time that the MacArthur hearings had come to an end, the fighting had stalemated along a front that remained almost static for the next two years. American military negotiators had also started to discuss armistice terms with the Chinese and North Koreans, in talks that would also show little progress for the next two years, as both sides haggled over the cease-fire line, the enforcement of an armistice, and the fate of the prisoners of war.

This deadlock greatly complicated the administration's selling efforts. What had briefly been a war to unite Korea and turn the whole peninsula into a beacon of democracy now threatened to become a war waged for the details of the truce-talk agenda. Worse, although US goals contracted, casualties mounted, with America sustaining 45 percent of its 142,000 casualties during in this period.[50]

In an attempt to remobilize popular support for this stalemated war, the administration latched on to its prisoner-of-war policy. During lengthy meetings in the first months of 1952, officials decided to base their minimum truce-talk negotiating position on voluntary repatriation: no US-held prisoner would be forcibly returned to the Communists. Principally humanitarian and psychological warfare considerations motivated senior officials, who did not want to force prisoners back to a Communist state where they would face torture and even execution as had prisoners of war returned to the Soviet Union after World War II.[51]

On the American home front, such a policy came with both a danger and an opportunity. The danger derived from the likelihood that the enemy would oppose America's unorthodox new demand, which would in turn extend the war into the 1952 presidential campaign. The opportunity stemmed from the prospect of using voluntary repatriation to portray the war in more appealing ideological terms. If China and North Korea rejected the principle, the US government could depict the war as a moral crusade fought on behalf of America's traditional respect for human rights. It could also emphasize the appeal of the Western system over Communist oppression. As one State Department official noted, "This issue gets to the heart of the contention between communism and the tradition we live by. It bears on the rights of men to make choices and to claim protection." The riots that erupted in the UN prison compounds in May 1952 dented this argument. Senior officials immediately launched a coordinated campaign to emphasize that, as Truman put it, "We will not buy an armistice by turning over human beings for slaughter or slavery." To do so, he insisted, "would be repugnant to the fundamental moral and humanitarian principles which underlie our action in Korea."[52]

Crucially, this argument played well on the home front. A wide range of media chains, major newspapers, and influential commentators warmly endorsed it. So did legislators on both sides of the aisle, from powerful Democrats, such as Paul Douglas and Richard Russell, to nationalist Republicans, like Jenner and Knowland.

Given this rare elite consensus, it was scarcely surprising that most Americans also supported voluntary repatriation. Just before leading officials began their publicity drive, one poll found the public skeptical of the policy, with no less than 81 percent willing to "accept *in*voluntary repatriation either to hasten an armistice (38 percent) or if necessary in order to secure the return of captured Americans (43 percent)." Within weeks, however, the public mood had changed completely so that, by July, 58 percent now supported the administration's stance on voluntary repatriation, whatever the cost.[53]

The Advent of Eisenhower

This elite consensus was not an isolated instance. During 1951, to be sure, the Republican right sought to foster and exploit the controversy surrounding MacArthur's recall, McCarthy continued to launch savage attacks on Communists in government, and Taft stepped up his claims that the Korean War was a "useless and expensive waste."[54] Yet in the aftermath of the MacArthur hearings, those internationalist Republicans who had been tempted to endorse Taft during the worst moments after China's intervention, gravitated back toward the bipartisan center. This was a momentous development. It not only helped to mute the overall potency of the Republican Party's attacks but also enabled the government's own enhanced efforts to gain greater visibility.

Eisenhower's emergence as the Republican nominee was an even more pivotal event. It meant that election-year rhetoric, although as vicious as ever, would not be based on fundamental foreign policy differences. As one analyst of Eisenhower's speeches has concluded, during the summer of 1952 Eisenhower remained firmly "within the rhetorical range of the Truman-Acheson policy." In his first press conference he even stressed that it was vital "to stand firm" in Korea and work for a "decent armistice." As the campaign progressed and Republicans fretted about a repeat of the Democrats' surprise 1948 victory, Eisenhower toughened his speeches. He focused on Korea as the main issue. He charged that administration mistakes were responsible for the war. And he famously announced that he would personally visit Korea in an effort to bring about an end to the fighting.[55]

Even so, Eisenhower never delivered the massive verbal assaults that had characterized Taft's campaign. While concentrating on the broader "mistakes" the administration had committed before Korea, he rejected the twin alternatives to Truman's current strategy—namely, massive escalation or total withdrawal. Nor did he ever question the basic need to send US troops to defend Korea. Instead, Eisenhower declared that the US intervention "was inescapable."[56]

Unlike in June and July 1950, when a rally-round-the-flag effect produced massive support for intervention, Americans had become increasingly war weary by 1951 and 1952. Yet Korea did not become a detested war. Despite the mounting casualties and contracting objectives, there were no powerful antiwar movements and no popular protest meetings. Available opinion poll data also suggest that the government created a relatively stable floor, beyond which popular disapproval never plunged.

In fact, by early 1952 a majority of Americans apparently endorsed the reasons for fighting. Back in January 1951, when the war had been going badly, a Gallup poll had suggested that 66 percent of Americans wanted to withdraw, and other surveys revealed that those thinking the US had "made a mistake going into Korea in the first place" had shot up from 20 percent to 50 percent. A year later, in January 1952, the situation had reversed with 56 percent of those polled believing the US was right to have intervened in Korea, while only 16 percent favored "pulling our troops out of Korea."[57]

As the 1952 election campaign got under way, the public's attitude toward Korea remained relatively favorable. Although support for withdrawal gradually crept up to the 30 percent mark, those who thought an armistice based on the division of Korea would be a success for the US jumped up from 30 percent to 54 percent between July 1951 and June 1952. The one exception to such figures came at the very end of the campaign. In the aftermath of Eisenhower's concerted attack on the administration's bungling, one poll found that 56 percent had suddenly concluded that "the war in Korea was *not* worth fighting," while another survey recorded that 40 percent felt that the government had not done "all it should have done" to keep the Communists from invading South Korea in the first place.[58]

Conclusion

When Eisenhower concluded an armistice six months into his presidency, the public remained ambivalent about the Korean War. Polls demonstrated that a plurality of 48 percent considered a truce along the present battle line to be a success, while 69 percent now approved of an armistice that left Korea divided. A majority of media opinion also considered the last round of negotiations a victory for the US because "just about all the concessions" had been made by the enemy. But there was little jubilation. The armistice only halted the fighting in Korea; it was not a peace treaty that ended wider struggle against Communism. People felt relief that the fighting had ended after more than three years and 140,000 American casualties but little exultation given this was the first time the US had fought a conflict with no clear-cut decision.[59]

Still, the situation could have been far worse. Two and a half years earlier, Truman had rightly worried that his administration had failed to provide a plausible public answer to the crucial question, Why are we in Korea? Since then, he had found not just a method and a message that resonated, but crucially willing partners on the other side of the political divide. As a result, the Korean War never became as unpopular as it had threatened to become, largely because the combination of message, messenger, and media had served its purpose in communicating the war in Korea to American audiences.

Notes

1. State Department, Office of Public Affairs, "Monthly Survey of American Opinion on International Affairs," Survey No. 117, January 1951, Entry 568L, box 12, RG 59, National Archives at College Park, MD (NARA II); "Public Favors Withdrawing from Korea by Nearly 3 to 1," *Washington Post*, January 21, 1951.
2. State Department, Office of Public Affairs, "Monthly Survey," July 1950.
3. "Truman's Conversation with Elsey," June 26, 1950, box 71, Elsey Papers, Truman Library, Independence, MO.
4. Leviero, "Don't Make It Alarmist, Truman Bids Press," *New York Times*, June 26, 1950; Ayers diary, June 25, 1950, box 20, Ayers Papers, Truman Library; State Department, *Foreign Relations of the United States, 1950* (Washington, DC: Government Printing Office), 7:956–57 (hereafter cited as *FRUS, 1950*).
5. Truman, "Statement by the President on the Situation in Korea," June 27, 1950, Public Papers, https://www.trumanlibrary.org/publicpapers/index.php?pid=800&st=&st1=; Glenn D. Paige, *The Korean Decision, June 24–30, 1950* (New York: Free Press, 1968), 202, 212.
6. Edward R. Barrett, *Truth Is Our Weapon* (New York: Funk and Wagnalls, 1953), 157.
7. Acheson, "Press Conference," June 28, 1950, box 82, Acheson Papers, Truman Library; Truman, "The President's News Conference," June 29, 1950, Public Papers, https://www.trumanlibrary.org/publicpapers/index.php?pid=806&st=&st1=; Ross, "Press Conference," June 29, 1950, box 17, Ayers Papers.
8. *FRUS, 1950*, 7:158, 169–70, 186–87; Antony Farrar-Hockley, *British Part in the Korean War* (London: HMSO, 1990), 1:31–32.
9. Gross to Austin, June 27, 1950, UN: Korea, Secret Reports, box 5, Austin Papers, University of Vermont, Burlington, VT. Emphasis in original.
10. Hassett, "Memo for Ross," June 29, 1950, OF 471-B, box 1305, Truman Papers, Truman Library; State Department, Office of Public Affairs, "Monthly Survey," June 1950; Harold B. Hinton, "Legislators Hail Action by Truman," *New York Times*, June 28, 1950.

11. Ayers diary, July 11, 1950; Paige, *Korean Decision*, 47.

12. "March of the News," *U.S. News and World Report* 29 (July 14, 1950): 2, ellipses in original. See also James Reston, "U.S. Acts to Avert Fighting's Spread," *New York Times*, July 6, 1950; *FRUS, 1950*, 7:286–91; "Preparation of President's Message to Congress on Korea," July 19, 1950, box 71, Elsey Papers; "Notes on Cabinet Meetings," July 8, 1950, box 1, Connelly Papers, Truman Library.

13. Montague Kern, Patricia W. Levering, and Ralph B. Levering, *The Kennedy Crises: The Press, the Presidency, and Foreign Policy* (Chapel Hill: University of North Carolina Press, 1983), 7–9; Daniel C. Hallin, *The "Uncensored War": The Media and Vietnam* (Berkeley: University of California Press, 1986), 25, 83, 169, 186; William M. Hammond, *Reporting Vietnam: Media and Military at War* (Lawrence: University Press of Kansas, 1998), 38, 53, 121, 199, 285; Anthony Leviero, "President Asks 260 Millions to Expedite Hydrogen Bomb," *New York Times*, July 8, 1950.

14. Taft, "The Korean Crisis Caused by Wavering Foreign Policies of Administration," June 28, 1950, box 628, Taft Papers, Library of Congress; James T. Patterson, *Mr. Republican: A Biography of Robert A. Taft* (Boston: Houghton Mifflin, 1972), 453–55; Ronald J. Caridi, *The Korean War and American Politics* (Philadelphia: University of Pennsylvania Press, 1968), 36–37.

15. "Truman Act Given Support by U.S. Press," *Washington Post*, June 28, 1950; "Political Hay in Korea," *Cleveland Plain Dealer*, July 3, 1950; "The Story of America's Policy Shift," *Wall Street Journal*, June 28, 1950.

16. "Preparation of President's Message to Congress on Korea, July 19, 1950," box 71, Elsey Papers; Ayers, July 20, 1950, PSF (Speech File), box 42, Truman Papers.

17. Truman, "Radio and Television Address to the American People on the Situation in Korea," July 19, 1950, Public Papers, https://www.trumanlibrary.org/publicpapers/index.php?pid=823&st=&st1=.

18. Jessup to Rusk, July 10, 1950, Entry 1530, RG 59, box 11, NARA II; "White Paper," *New York Times*, July 22, 1950.

19. Transcripts, *Battle Report—Washington*, SMOF: Jackson, box 18, Truman Papers; Nancy Bernhard, *U.S. Television News and Cold War Propaganda, 1947–1960* (Cambridge: Cambridge University Press, 1999), chap. 5.

20. William S. White, "Truman Likens 'Propaganda' of Marines to Stalin Set-Up," *New York Times*, September 6, 1950.

21. OPI, "Activity Reports: In the Magazines," July 19, 1950, Entry 134, box 152, RG 330, NARA II. See also Doris M. Condit, *History of the Office of the Secretary of Defense*, vol. 2, *The Test of War, 1950–1953* (Washington, DC: Government Printing Office, 1988), 26–27, 497–98.

22. Ayers diary, July 1, 1950; Clayton D. James, *Triumph and Disaster, 1945–1964*, vol. 3 of *The Years of Douglas MacArthur* (Boston: Houghton Mifflin, 1985), 437.

23. Acheson to Webb, undated [August 1950?], box 67, Acheson Papers.

24. Elsey, Memo for Information, n.d.; Davis to the Chairman, NSRB, August 18, 1950; and Elsey to Ross, August 28, 1950, all in box 54, Elsey Papers. Hassett to Ross, September 21, 1950, box 2, Ross Papers, Truman Library.

25. Oechsner to Barrett, July 21, 1950, entry 1530, box 7, RG 59, NARA II; Barrett to Elsey, September 22, 1950, PSF (General), box 119, Truman Papers; Sargeant to Elsey, October 4, 1950, box 54, Elsey Papers.

26. Francis H. Heller, *The Truman White House: The Administration of the Presidency, 1945–1953* (Lawrence: Regents Press of Kansas, 1980), 145.

27. Walter Waggoner, "U.S. Disowns Mathews Talk of Waging War to Get Peace," *New York Times*, August 27, 1950; "Preventive War Talk—Why? Fear of A-Bombs on U.S. Cities," *U.S. News and World Report* 29 (September 8, 1950): 11–12; "The MacArthur Incident," *New York Times*, August 29, 1950; "Confusion in a Crisis: Why?" *U.S. News and World Report* 29 (August 18, 1950): 25–26.

28. Murphy to Truman, September 13, 1950, PSF (General): Murphy, box 131, Truman Papers; Neustadt, "President's Fireside Speech Scheduled for Friday, September 1," August 30, 1950, SMOF: Murphy, box 7, Truman Papers; Truman, "Radio and Television Report to the American People on the Situation in Korea, September 1, 1950, Public Papers, https://www.trumanlibrary.org/publicpapers/index.php?pid=861&st=&st1=.

29. "MacArthur's Own Story," *U.S. News and World Report* 29 (December 8, 1950): 16–17; James, *Triumph and Disaster*, 540–41. Lovett called these efforts MacArthur's "posterity papers." See Memo of Conversation with Lovett, December 2, 1950, box 67, Acheson Papers.

30. Truman, "The President's News Conference," November 30, 1950, Public Papers, https://www.trumanlibrary.org/publicpapers/index.php?pid=985&st=&st1=.

31. "Notes for the Secretary," December 2, 1950, box 67, Acheson Papers; "Meeting of the President with Congressional Leaders," December 13, 1950, Subject File, box 73, Elsey Papers; Rosemary Foot, *The Wrong War: American Policy and the Dimensions of the Korean Conflict, 1950–1953* (Ithaca, NY: Cornell University Press, 1985), 108.

32. "Row over Acheson—Why," *U.S. News and World Report*, 29 (December 29, 1950): 14–15; David R. Kepley, *The Collapse of the Middle Way: Senate Republicans and the Bipartisan Foreign Policy, 1948–1952* (New York: Greenwood Press, 1988), 89, 131; Nancy Bernkopf Tucker, *Patterns in the Dust: Chinese-American Relations and the Recognition Controversy, 1949–1950* (New York: Columbia University Press, 1983), 161–64.

33. Lanigan to Harriman, "Congressional Liaison," November 30, 1950, box 282, Harriman Papers, Library of Congress; Murphy to Truman, "Bipartisan Meetings on Defense and Foreign Policy," December 9, 1950, PSF (General): Murphy, box 131,

Truman Papers; Acheson-Hickenlooper meeting, December 27, 1950; "Congressional Attitudes concerning Our Legislative Program," January 9, 1951; Acheson-
Anderson meeting, January 12, 1951, all in box 67, Acheson Papers; "Proposal for
departmental Saturday morning briefings for members of Congress," January 19,
1951, Entry 1530, box 2, RG 59, NARA II.

34. "Notes of Cabinet Meetings," July 21, 1950, box 1, Connelly Papers.

35. Truman, "The President's News Conference," December 19, 1950, Public Papers,
https://www.trumanlibrary.org/publicpapers/index.php?pid=999&st=&st1=.

36. Harry S. Truman, *Memoirs: Years of Trial and Hope, 1946–1952* (New York: Sig-
net, 1965), 487; Acheson, "Princeton Seminar," March 14, 1954, box 90, Acheson
Papers; Kepley, *Collapse of the Middle Way*, 79–80; Dean Acheson, *Present at the
Creation: My Years in the State Department* (New York: W. W. Norton, 1969), 368.

37. Robert C. Albright, "Truman Calls Senate Leaders to 4th 2-Party Meeting Today,"
Washington Post, July 11, 1950.

38. Working Group on Public Relations, "Summary of Meeting," January 18, 1951,
Entry 1531, box 1, RG 59, NARA II.

39. This conclusion is derived from a content analysis of page-one coverage in the *New
York Times* and *Washington Post*, January–March 1951.

40. "Off-the Record Briefing on America," January 15, 1951, SMOF: Jackson, box 17,
Truman Papers. See also Barrett to Acheson, "Your meeting with the National Associa-
tion of Broadcasters Group," December 13, 1950, Entry 1530, box 8, RG 59, NARA
II; Tannenwald, diary, February 21, 1951, Tannenwald Papers, Truman Library;
Samuel F. Wells, "Sounding the Tocsin: NSC 68 and the Soviet Threat," *International
Security* 4 (1979): 116–58; Russell to Lehrbas, "Examination of Comment by Selected
Radio Correspondents," March 30, 1951, Entry 1530, box 8, RG 59, NARA II.

41. *Congressional Record*, December 13, 1950, 16675, and January 8, 1951, 101–2;
"Why UN Is Breaking Down," *U.S. News and World Report* 30 (January 19, 1951):
13–15; Caridi, *Korean War*, 114; William W. Stueck, *The Korean War: An International History* (Princeton, NJ: Princeton University Press, 1995), 151–57.

42. Acheson, Memo of Conversation, January 23, 1951, box 67, Acheson Papers.

43. Elsey to Truman, "Cabinet Discussion on Korea," February 2, 1951; Elsey, memorandum for the president, February 9, 1951, both in PSF (General): Elsey, box 119,
Truman Papers.

44. "Views of Nation's Newspapers on General MacArthur's Removal," *Baltimore Sun*,
April 12, 1951; "U.S. Press Comment on Removal of MacArthur," *New York Times*,
April 12, 1951.

45. Robert J. Donovan, *Tumultuous Years: The Presidency of Harry S. Truman, 1949–
1953* (Columbia: University of Missouri Press, 1982), 359–60; James, *Triumph and
Disaster*, 611–18.

46. Memcon, March 30, 1951, Elsey Speech File (Speech Clearance), box 54, Elsey Papers.

47. Elsey, Memo for the File, April 19, 1951, Speech File: Speech Clearance, box 54, Elsey Papers; Murphy, Memo for Truman, April 16, 1951, PSF (General): Murphy, box 131, Truman Papers; Tannenwald, Memo for Carroll, April 16, 1951, MacArthur Hearings: Background, box 304, Harriman Papers; Kenneth W. Hechler, *Working with Truman: A Personal Memoir of the White House Years* (New York: G. P. Putnam's Sons, 1982), 168–70.

48. US Senate, *Military Situation in the Far East: Hearings before the Committee on Armed Services and the Committee on Foreign Relations* (Washington, DC: Government Printing Office, 1951), 324–25, 501, 736–37, 730–32, 1379, 1492–93, 1503.

49. "Poll of Newsmen Backs Truman, 6–1," *Washington Post*, June 9, 1951; Working Group on Public Relations, Summary of Meeting, May 9, 1951, Office of Public Affairs, Assistant Secretary of State, PRWG File, box 1, RG 59, NARA II; Gallup, "U.S. Public Reveals Lack of Interest in Senate Inquiry on Policy concerning Korea," June 9, 1951, Newspaper Clipping File, DNC Papers, Truman Library.

50. Walter Hermes, *Truce Tent and Fighting Front* (Washington, DC: Center for Military History, 1992), 500–501.

51. Rosemary Foot, *A Substitute for Victory: The Politics of Peacemaking at the Korean Armistice Talks* (Ithaca, NY: Cornell University Press, 1990), 96; Charles S. Young, *Name, Rank, and Serial Number: Exploiting Korean POWs at Home and Abroad* (New York: Oxford University Press, 2014), 61–65.

52. Marshall to Nitze, January 28, 1952, PPS Files, Subject: Korea, box 20, RG 59, NARA II; Truman, "Statement by the President on General Ridgway's Korean Armistice Proposal," May 7, 1952, Public Papers, https://www.trumanlibrary.org /publicpapers/index.php?pid=1288&st=&st1=.

53. State Department, Office of Public Affairs, "Articulate and Popular Opinion on Issue of Involuntary Repatriations and POWs," April 16, 1952, Entry 1530, box 5, RG 59, NARA II; State Department, Office of Public Affairs, "Monthly Survey," July 1952; Barton J. Bernstein, "The Struggle over the Korean Armistice: Prisoners or Repatriation?" in *Child of Conflict: The Korean-American Relationship, 1943–1953*, ed. Bruce Cumings (Seattle: University of Washington Press, 1983), 280n53; Foot, *Substitute for Victory*, 221.

54. Trumbull Higgins, *Korea and the Fall of MacArthur: A Precis in Limited War* (New York: Oxford University Press, 1960), 183; Caridi, *Korean War*, 173; Thomas C. Reeves, *The Life and Times of Joe McCarthy* (New York: Stein and Day, 1982), 371–72; Kepley, *Collapse of the Middle Way*, 117–21; Foot, *Substitute for Victory*, 8, 38.

55. Martin J. Medhurst, "Text and Context in the 1952 Presidential Campaign," *Presidential Studies Quarterly* (2000): 464–82; John Robert Greene, *The Crusade: The Presidential Election of 1952* (New York: Lanham, 1985), 215–20.

56. "Text of Eisenhower's Speech," *New York Times*, October 25, 1952.

57. Russell, "Comparison of American Popular Opinion on Foreign Policy a Year Ago and Today," January 2, 1952; Foster to Sargeant, "Late March Opinion Survey," April 3, 1952, both in Entry 568N, box 20, RG 59, NARA II; State Department, Office of Public Affairs, "Monthly Survey," February 1952.

58. Polls taken from State Department, Office of Public Affairs, "Monthly Survey," May–November 1952.

59. Memo on Recent Polls, June 2, 1953, Korea Folder, box 4, Jackson Records, Eisenhower Library, Abilene, KS; State Department, Office of Public Affairs, "Monthly Survey," July 1953.

PART IV. Introduction

Mass Media: Print, Radio, Television, and Cable

Marc A. Genest

Commercial television broadcasting began in the late 1940s, and by 1955 half of all US households had televisions. The early years of TV were dominated by entertainment programming with nightly news relegated to only fifteen minutes. The election of the young, telegenic John Kennedy as president in 1960 stimulated greater interest in news coverage of the White House. In September 1963 CBS and, soon after that, NBC evening news broadcasts expanded to thirty minutes. Only a few months later John Kennedy was assassinated, and Americans turned to television in unprecedented numbers desperate for news about the horrific event. The demand for TV news and entertainment continued to grow, and by the mid-1960s over 90 percent of American households had a television, many of which provided color pictures. The expansion to three major television networks along with extended nightly news broadcasts set the stage for more intense coverage of the escalating Vietnam War. In chapter 11 David Kaiser offers a cautionary assessment of the political impact of media coverage during the Vietnam War. Kaiser contends that neither news coverage of the conflict nor the various communication strategies used by five presidents could alter the fact that the United States was unable to implement an effective military or political strategy to defeat the enemy.

By the 1980s cable and direct-satellite systems dramatically increased the number of television networks available to viewers around the world. This vast expansion of channels created a new market for stations that served the needs and tastes of relatively narrow audiences. One of those new networks was Ted Turner's Cable News Network (CNN), which introduced twenty-four-hour television news. Judith Baroody's chapter on the 1991 Gulf War provides ample evidence of the growing reach and influence of cable news. Both President Bush and Iraqi leader Saddam Hussein monitored the network to follow breaking events in the war. US military leaders, Chairman of the Joint Chief of Staff Colin Powell and Gen. Norman Schwarzkopf, used the lessons they learned in Vietnam to limit reporters' access to the battlefield. Instead, the US military fed the press a steady diet of carefully selected film clips of "smart bombs" deftly hitting all their targets. Coverage of America's first "cable TV war" was carefully orchestrated by the victor.

11.

How Presidents Explained Vietnam, 1954–75

David Kaiser

For twenty-one years, from 1954 through 1975, five different presidents sought to preserve an independent, non-Communist South Vietnam. They failed to do so not primarily because of faulty strategic communication but rather as a result of the political and military balance of forces within Vietnam itself. From Eisenhower through Nixon, every president argued that the defense of South Vietnam was at least an important element of the US policy of containing Communism. Public opinion initially supported that position, but by the end of the Johnson administration, a large part of the public was no longer willing to make an endless effort to achieve it. While Nixon promised he could simultaneously reduce the scale and nature of American involvement and keep South Vietnam out of Communist hands, it soon became clear that getting out of the war had become more important than winning.

A brief history of presidential statements on Vietnam from Eisenhower through Ford tells a great deal not only about the emerging nature of that conflict but also about the Cold War foreign policies of these presidents more generally and about the ways in which the war changed American thinking about the US role in the world. From 1954 through 1963 South Vietnam generally stayed on the back burner of American foreign policy, not least because presidents wanted to keep it there. From 1964 through 1972 it took center stage and became the most controversial foreign war in US history. American participation came to an end in 1973, and South Vietnam fell in 1975. Presidential statements on Vietnam show not only how presidents hoped to prevail but also how they hoped to keep the American people behind them.

Dwight D. Eisenhower

In the wake of the 1954 Geneva Accords, the Eisenhower administration promulgated the strategies that led the United States into the Vietnam War. While the Southeast Asia Treaty Organization (SEATO) committed its signatories, including the United States, Britain, France, Australia, New Zealand, and the Philippines, to consult in the event of a threat to the security of South Vietnam, Laos, or Cambodia, it did not commit them to action. The administration had fewer than a thousand military advisers in South Vietnam, purportedly permitted by the 1954 cease-fire agreement. But in a series of policy statements approved by the National Security Council, the Eisenhower administration promised to come to the armed defense of any of those nations if they were attacked by Communist aggression, and other policy statements made clear that nuclear weapons would be used, if necessary.[1] The administration also used aid and covert action both to try to set up pro-Western governments in South Vietnam and Laos and to overturn the neutralist Sihanouk government in Cambodia (this latter project was abandoned in the late 1950s). All these moves were parts of a larger worldwide strategy, largely conceived and executed by Secretary of State John Foster Dulles and his brother, CIA director Allen Dulles, to organize as much of the globe as possible into pro-Western blocs. Until a civil war broke out in Laos in 1960, these policies seemed to be working reasonably well.

Yet while taking these fateful steps, Eisenhower had almost nothing to say in public about either Vietnam or Laos. He made numerous major addresses about Berlin, the Middle East, Taiwan, and the Soviet nuclear threat, but not once did he make an address devoted mainly to the problems of Southeast Asia in general or Vietnam in particular. His longest statement on Vietnam by far came at the end of President Ngo Dinh Diem's visit to Washington in May 1957. He lauded Diem's progress in building up South Vietnam, advocated its admission to the UN (which the Soviet Union had vetoed), and reaffirmed the SEATO treaty.[2] South Vietnam figured regularly in Eisenhower's statements on foreign aid as one of the nations most threatened by Communism and most in need of assistance. Eisenhower also made this point in an address at Gettysburg College on April 4, 1959, stating that "free Vietnam" was under threat and that its fall to Communism would be a serious defeat with broader consequences.[3] He spoke similarly in one of his periodic and brief exchanges of letters with Diem on October 26, 1960, but also assigned the main responsibility for the defense of South Vietnam to "the Vietnamese people."[4] Meanwhile, the president made a goodwill tour of Asia in June 1960 but did not include Vietnam or Laos on the itinerary.

The contradictions between Eisenhower's public calm and his administration's policies emerged quite dramatically in his last months in office as a result of a crisis in

Laos. By the end of 1960 neutralist Souvanna Phouma, with military support from both North Vietnam and the Soviet Union, overthrew the pro-Western government that the United States had maneuvered into power in 1958. At least since 1954 Eisenhower had allowed his national security bureaucracy to assume commitments and plan campaigns with the same freedom enjoyed by his military staffs during the Second World War. In neither case did the American public have much idea of what was happening. Joint Chiefs of Staff chairman Gen. Lyman Lemnitzer briefed Eisenhower on a deteriorating military situation on December 31, 1960, and the president stated that the United States would have to go to war in Laos, even without allies, to prevent a Communist victory. In a later meeting he indicated that the United States would not undertake another limited war, as in Korea, but would have to "clear up the problem completely." He reiterated these views in a meeting with President-elect John F. Kennedy on January 19, identifying Laos as the most important crisis facing the nation.[5] Commander in Chief of Pacific Command Adm. Harry D. Felt was preparing for a war that might easily involve nuclear strikes against China, but the American people had virtually no idea of what might lie in store for them. It fell to Eisenhower's successor to devise a workable strategy and communicate it to the American people.

John F. Kennedy

Having promised in his inaugural address to "bear any burden and pay any price to assure the survival of liberty," Kennedy in the first three months of his administration faced continual pressure from all his leading civilian and military advisers to go to war in Laos. He reacted skeptically, however, and quickly adopted the views of the British and French governments, which had found the Eisenhower policies in Laos unwise and proposed a return to a neutral Laotian government. Kennedy began a press conference on March 23, 1961, with a long statement on Laos.[6] He implicitly threatened to act under the SEATO treaty if Communist aggression continued but also reversed Eisenhower administration policy and endorsed a truly neutral Laos. In fact, this statement started him down a diplomatic path that led to the reconvening of the Geneva Conference on Indochina and the negotiation of a cease-fire and a new coalition government in Laos that concluded in September 1962. This was a major departure from his predecessor. Kennedy imposed this solution on his own team and sold it privately to bipartisan congressional leaders, but he did not make any speeches about it.[7]

In this respect, Kennedy closely resembled Eisenhower. Both were probably more oriented toward foreign than domestic affairs, but neither one ever gave a major speech devoted to the problems of Laos and Vietnam. From the spring of 1961 through the fall of 1963, Vietnam figured in presidential speeches as one of many trouble spots where the United States was attempting to contain Communism. His critical foreign policy speeches related to the crisis in Berlin, Cuba, Soviet relations, and the Test Ban Treaty—the great problems that Kennedy wanted to solve.

Behind the scenes, however, Vietnam and Laos caused much internal debate during 1961 that eventually precipitated far-reaching decisions. Regarding South Vietnam, as in Laos, all the president's senior advisers, military and civilian, called for the immediate introduction of combat troops to counter the growing Communist insurgency, and once again, as in Laos, Kennedy rejected that recommendation. In October 1961 he sent Gen. Maxwell Taylor, now his special military representative in the White House, and Walt Rostow, deputy national security adviser, to Vietnam to report on the situation. Kennedy gave Taylor instructions clearly designed to avoid a recommendation for American combat troops, but that failed to stop Taylor and Rostow from asking for just that. In November he rejected their recommendation, as well as a much larger one from the Pentagon. Kennedy did agree, however, to an expanded advisory effort, including pilots to fly ground support missions while posing as trainers for the South Vietnamese. But he decided *not* to make a speech or even a major public announcement of these new steps, trying to keep South Vietnam on the back burner, where clearly he thought it should remain.[8]

The decision not to present the new decisions to the American people ceded the initiative to the press and to the Republican Party. In a January 15, 1962, press conference a reporter asked whether American troops were "now in combat in Vietnam"; the president replied, "No," and took the next question.[9] But new press stories, Republican attacks, and further questions induced him in another press conference on February 14 to make a prepared statement. Stressing that the war in South Vietnam had heated up, he referred to US obligations under the SEATO treaty, acknowledged that US assistance had increased, but insisted that "we have not sent combat troops in the generally accepted sense of the term."[10] This remained the administration line for at least the next year and a half, although the size of the American presence grew steadily until it reached 3,000 advisers and 14,500 support personnel by the fall of 1963.

Vietnam rated only the briefest of mentions in Kennedy's famous year-end interview on December 17, 1962, which focused on the Cuban crisis, the desegregation of the University of Mississippi, the crisis over steel prices, and relations with Moscow generally.[11] By that time the president had apparently conveyed to Secretary of Defense Robert McNamara that he wanted to reduce, rather than increase, the American commitment, and McNamara had told Gen. Paul Harkins, the senior American military commander, to prepare a plan to finish the job by 1965.[12]

In the spring of 1963 McNamara was insisting that the war was going well when South Vietnamese troops fired into a Buddhist demonstration on May 8, precipitating nationwide Buddhist protests against the Catholic-led Diem government. This transformed the situation, forcing Kennedy to say much more on the subject during the last six months of his life. On July 17 he reaffirmed that the war was going well and hoped for a solution to the "religious dispute" that had brought thousands of Buddhists into the streets. Kennedy also warned that the loss of South Vietnam would have wider consequences for Southeast Asia.[13] He largely remained quiet for the next six weeks, while the press became increasingly critical of Diem, his brother Nhu, and the photogenic and outspoken Madame Nhu, who gave inflammatory interviews to the press. Finally, on Labor Day, Kennedy made an important policy statement in an interview with Walter Cronkite, the most widely respected anchorman of his generation, inaugurating the expansion to thirty minutes of the *CBS Evening News*. The South Vietnamese government, he said, could succeed only with "a greater effort . . . to win popular support." He called the repressions against the Buddhists "very unwise" and recommended that the Saigon government could regain support "with certain changes in policy and perhaps with personnel"—presumably the retirement of Nhu. He rejected withdrawal but stated tellingly, "In the final analysis, it is their war. They are the ones who have to win it or lose it. We can help them, we can give them equipment, we can send our men out there as advisers, but they have to win it, the people of Vietnam, against the Communists."[14] A week later, in a parallel interview with two nationally known anchormen, Chet Huntley and David Brinkley on NBC, he affirmed a belief in the domino theory as it applied to South Vietnam.[15] Yet South Vietnam remained off the itinerary for his planned trip to Southeast Asia in the spring of 1964.

McNamara traveled to South Vietnam in late September with chairman of the Joint Chiefs of Staff General Taylor. He returned with an important strategic communication of his own, insisting that the war was still going well and that most American troops could be withdrawn by the spring of 1965. Kennedy, despite some skepticism, agreed to release this statement. For the second time, however, he changed the proposed public language referring to the security of South Vietnam as "vital to United States" to "a major interest of the United States, as of other free nations."[16] He confirmed that a thousand-troop withdrawal was beginning on October 31, 1963, the day before Diem and Nhu were murdered.[17] On November 14, in his last formal press conference, Kennedy referred to a forthcoming high-level meeting in Honolulu designed to work toward US objectives: "to bring Americans home, permit the South Vietnamese to maintain themselves as a free and independent country, and permit democratic forces within the country to operate—which they can, of course, much more freely when the assault from the inside, and which is manipulated from the north, is ended."[18] The speech Kennedy never delivered at the Trade Mart in Dallas on November 22 discussed his administration's buildup of strategic nuclear forces at length; referred briefly to holding off the Communists in Berlin, Laos, and Cuba; but mentioned South Vietnam only within a long list of aid recipients.[19] Kennedy evidently died without learning that the military situation in South Vietnam had actually been deteriorating for most of 1963 and had become critical. We shall never know how he would have reacted to that news, but he had refused to go to war there in 1961, and he had never given the American people any indication that he would be willing to do so.

Lyndon B. Johnson

On December 11, 1963, the new president gave senior civilian and military officials at the Pentagon a clue to his thinking, citing "the spread of Communist subversion into Vietnam" and "the spread of Communist subversion in the Caribbean" as their two most urgent pieces of business.[20] Privately, Johnson was doing exactly what Kennedy had refused to do: making Vietnam his most critical foreign policy problem. In December McNamara returned from another trip to Vietnam with a devastating report on the situation, and by the end of March 1964 Johnson had privately made clear his willingness to begin a full-scale war to save South Vietnam—but only after he had been elected in his own right. Three nights after North Vietnamese patrol torpedo (PT) boats made an unauthorized, unsuccessful attack on American destroyers patrolling the North Vietnamese coast on August 1, mistaken reports from another patrol convinced McNamara and the Pentagon that the North Vietnamese had attacked again. Johnson took advantage of the second reported attack—which had not in fact occurred—to make the first bombing raids against North Vietnam and secure a congressional authorization (the Gulf of Tonkin Resolution) for the use of force to defend Southeast Asia. The speech Johnson made on that occasion described both torpedo attacks on American ships and North Vietnamese losses that never occurred, but he insisted he was responding appropriately and nothing more. Congress—frightened by the nuclear saber rattling of his opponent, Barry Goldwater—almost unanimously gave him what he wanted.[21]

Johnson campaigned as a liberal, running against an extreme conservative. He defended increased assistance to the South Vietnamese, while rejecting either a withdrawal or "a wider war" or getting "bogged down in Asia," much less the use of nuclear weapons.[22] Yet in his most explicit discussion of the issue, on September 28, 1964, he carefully left himself an escape hatch:

As far as I am concerned, I want to be very cautious and careful, and use it only as a last resort, when I start dropping bombs around that are likely to involve American boys in a war in Asia with 700 million Chinese. . . . So just *for the moment* I have not thought that we were ready for American boys to do the fighting for Asian boys. What I have been trying to do, with the situation that I found, was to get the boys in Viet-Nam to do their own fighting with our advice and with our equipment. That is the course we *are following*.[23]

Buoyed by his reassuring stance in foreign affairs, his already impressive legislative achievements, and unprecedented prosperity, Johnson won one of the greatest landslide victories in American history.

Days later an interdepartmental committee chaired by Assistant Secretary of State William Bundy began preparing courses of action in Southeast Asia. In the first week of December Johnson approved a two-stage plan. Phase II, to be implemented in February, would include both sustained bombing of North Vietnam and the progressive deployment of large numbers of ground troops.[24] But Johnson refused to admit that there had been any change in policy, fearing that he would distract Congress from the passage of his extraordinary Great Society program, including the Voting Rights Act, Medicare, and a huge education bill. Then, two speeches, on April 7 and July 28, 1965, laid out his view of the Vietnam War and his strategy to the American people.

South Vietnam, Johnson explained on April 7 at Johns Hopkins University, was an independent nation (a status that it did not enjoy under the 1954 Geneva Accords) under attack from North Vietnam. The United States would always "oppose the effort of one nation to conquer another nation . . . because our own security is at stake." But looking forward with the optimism of his generation, Johnson offered to develop Southeast Asia. Peace on American terms in Vietnam, he argued, could be a step toward the end of war, death in battle, and hunger.

He also tried to give the impression that the war might end the moment the North Vietnamese saw reason. He expressed a readiness for "unconditional *discussions*"— not negotiations—with any North Vietnamese representatives, anywhere, any time. As Johnson spoke, South Vietnam hardly had a government worthy of the name, and he could not possibly *negotiate* based on the military status quo, but he was willing to have American and North Vietnamese officials exchange views. Since Hanoi was already demanding a halt to US bombing, the withdrawal of troops, and agreement to a coalition government in Saigon as a precondition to talks, this was unlikely to take place.[25]

On July 28, after seven weeks of deliberations over Gen. William Westmoreland's request for 175,000 ground troops at once, with more to follow in 1966, Johnson introduced the technique he would use to minimize the impact of escalation on the public. After he had reiterated that he was the third president to pledge the United States to defend South Vietnam, he announced only the dispatch of the additional 50,000 men who could leave at once, for a total of 125,000, deferring the announcement of the following 50,000 for some months more and adding merely that "additional forces will be needed later, and they will be sent as requested." While announcing a doubling of draft calls to 35,000 men a month, he reassured the public that it was unnecessary to call up the Reserves, as the Pentagon had in fact requested.[26] The process that increased American forces to half a million men in Vietnam within the next two years had begun. For the rest of the Johnson administration, the war would command the attention of both the government and the American people.

In sharp contrast to both his predecessor and his successor, Johnson rarely spoke directly to the American people via network television. He had to take questions about Vietnam in virtually every press conference, and he made major speeches before friendly audiences away from Washington, but his longest televised address on the subject was on March 31, 1968, when he announced that he would not run for reelection. Perhaps because he believed he was following the conventional wisdom about the war, he was content to allow newspapers and news shows to filter his message. That strategy opened a gulf between him and the American people on the defining topic of his presidency.

Again and again in major speeches, Johnson argued in all sincerity that he was acting in the tradition of the last four presidents, backing the united will of the US Congress, and following the best traditions of the American people. He repeatedly praised the bravery of America's fighting men and lauded the supposed brilliance of their leadership. He reinforced this message with a steady stream of presidential unit citations, awards of individual medals, and summits with the few small powers willing to join the fight. He paid relatively little attention to the growth of dissent. Even in November 1968, when his agreement to a full bombing halt paved the way for peace talks, he continued to argue that he had never altered his view of the struggle and that the United States was achieving its objectives. But by that time—with more than 30,000 Americans dead in the war, the Democratic Party rent asunder, and much of the younger generation alienated from many mainstream values for all time—the United States for which he claimed to speak no longer existed. And while it might eventually have died anyway, the war he chose to fight accelerated its demise.

For two and a half years, while casualties rose steadily, the war was punctuated by two periodic events: force increases and bombing halts. The latter, as Secretary McNamara admitted privately, were designed to secure the support of the American people by demonstrating that their government wanted peace. Johnson on January 31, 1966, announced the end of the longest such pause—thirty-seven days—to the American people, claiming that more than a month of ceaseless efforts to start negotiations had failed.[27]

He frankly described his strategy on many occasions: to inflict enough pain to convince the enemy to quit. After meeting with Westmoreland on August 14, 1966, he reported their agreement that "the single most important factor now is our will to prosecute the war until the Communists, recognizing the futility of their ambitions, either end the fighting or seek a peaceful settlement." He added that "no one can say when this will be or how many men will be needed, or how long we must persevere."[28] "We have chosen to fight a limited war in Vietnam," he told the Congress in his January 1967 State of the Union address, "in an attempt to prevent a larger war—a war almost certain to follow, I believe, if the Communists succeed in overrunning and taking over South Vietnam by aggression and by force. I believe, and I am supported by some authority, that if they are not checked now the world can expect to pay a greater price to check them later." That, he thought, was the clear lesson of history, and the American people, he thought, agreed.[29]

The Democrats suffered a major defeat in the congressional elections of 1966, losing forty-seven seats, and Johnson's own looming reelection campaign increased the pressure to show progress. Addressing the Tennessee state legislature on March 15, 1967, he referred frequently to the heroic example of Andrew Jackson and argued that the "strengthening of allied forces in 1966, under the brilliant leadership of General Westmoreland, was instrumental in reversing the whole course of this war," inflicting a four-to-one casualty on the enemy.[30] That spring McNamara, who had developed grave doubts about the war, convinced Johnson to reject Westmoreland's request for yet another 200,000 troops to bring the total number to about 750,000 by 1969, but no word of this leaked into the press. An ugly controversy did break out during the summer, when McNamara and the Joint Chiefs aired their differences over bombing strategy before a Senate committee, but Johnson tried to reassure the American people that 300 of 350 recommended targets in North Vietnam had been approved. In his thirty-six years in Washington, he said, "I have never known a period during that time when I thought there was more harmony, more general agreement, and a more cooperative attitude, or when there were more able men in control" of military affairs.[31]

In San Antonio, on September 29, 1967, Johnson began a major speech by repeating that he was following the policies of Eisenhower and Kennedy, although the strongest quote he could find from Kennedy was that "withdrawal in the case of Vietnam and the case of Thailand might mean a collapse of the entire area." He quoted various leaders from Southeast Asia warning of similar consequences but could not cite any comforting words from allies in Europe. Then he boasted that South Vietnam now had an elected government, even though President Nguyen Van Thieu had won a very disappointing plurality of the vote. He declared that the United States "is willing to stop all aerial and naval bombardment of North Vietnam when this will lead promptly to productive discussions. We, of course, assume that while discussions proceed, North Vietnam would not take advantage of the bombing cessation or limitation." The reference to "prompt and productive discussions," a phrase he owed to Secretary of State Dean Rusk and National Security Adviser Walt Rostow, was designed to ensure against lengthy, indecisive, Korean-style talks. The North Vietnamese, he said, were still convinced that Americans would not tolerate a "long, inconclusive war"—but he was sure that they were wrong. Totalitarian regimes, he said, mistook "dissent for disloyalty," "restlessness for a rejection of policy," "a few committees for a country," and "individual speeches for public policy." Americans had not failed in the past and would not fail this time.[32] In November Westmoreland told the National Press Club that "the enemy's hopes are bankrupt," that the enemy could mount large operations only on the borders of South Vietnam, and that the South Vietnamese would take a much larger share of the war in 1968.[33] In December, in a year-end conversation with TV correspondents, Johnson made clear that the Viet Cong would have to accept the new government and constitution of South Vietnam and insisted that disaffected youth, who had mounted a massive demonstration in front of the Pentagon that fall, were only a tiny minority.[34]

Westmoreland's and Johnson's words came back to haunt them in January and February 1968, when the North Vietnamese and Viet Cong combined an offensive against the Marine base at Khe Sanh, with surprise attacks on almost every major South Vietnamese city, known as the Tet Offensive. Although Johnson spoke optimistically about the results of the Tet Offensive in a late January 1968 press conference, he made no major speech about it for two months. The scale of the offensive, however, rightly convinced many leading opinion makers, including Walter Cronkite of CBS, that the United States had not managed to reduce enemy capabilities in almost three years of war and that military victory was probably impossible. The Tet Offensive also had major political effects. Dissident Democratic candidate Eugene McCarthy nearly beat Johnson in the New Hampshire primary, and Senator Robert F. Kennedy entered the race for the nomination. Westmoreland, arguing that his military situation was suddenly precarious, asked for the same 205,000 additional troops that McNamara had rejected in 1967. This time the request reached the newspapers and set off a Washington firestorm. McNamara's replacement, Clark Clifford, persuaded Johnson to reject the request. Instead, on March 31 Johnson announced a partial bombing halt of North Vietnam in an effort to start negotiations and withdrew from the presidential race.[35]

Johnson stuck with the same strategy. The number of American troops in Vietnam increased marginally after Tet and, thanks to the North Vietnamese Army offensives, the level of fighting for the rest of 1968 and the first half of 1969 was the highest of the entire conflict.[36] More important, Clifford completely failed to convince the triumvirate of Dean Rusk, Walt Rostow, and Johnson himself that military victory was impossible and that the objectives had to change.[37] In the presidential campaign both Republican Richard Nixon and Democratic candidate Vice President Hubert Humphrey initially continued to support the president's policy, although Humphrey eventually called for a halt to the bombing of North Vietnam. Johnson in the first week of November announced a full bombing halt and the planned beginning of peace talks in Paris because Rusk and Rostow had persuaded him that the enemy was in fact beaten and ready to meet American terms.[38] The problem of rallying the American people behind continuing the war fell to Johnson's successor.

Richard M. Nixon

Nixon avoided any significant strategic communication about Vietnam during his 1968 campaign. On March 5, 1968, he declared that Johnson had a responsibility to end the war by November and suggested that Johnson mobilize more diplomatic support, including the Soviet Union.[39] Nixon declared in his August 8 acceptance speech at the Republican Convention "that the first priority foreign policy objective of our next Administration will be to bring an honorable end to the war in Vietnam,"[40] but he did not mention the war in his inaugural address. For the next four years, however, direct strategic communication to the American people became perhaps the single most critical element of his Vietnam strategy. He made thirteen direct televised addresses on the subject: on May 14, November 3, and December 15, 1969; on April 20, April 30, June 3, and October 7, 1970; on April 7, 1971; on January 13, January 26, April 26, and May 8, 1972; and finally on January 23, 1973, when he announced the conclusion of the Paris Peace Accords. Nixon made these statements for two reasons: First, by the fall of 1969 he needed to reassure the American people that he was in fact winding down the war. By 1971 he had succeeded in doing so. Second, as protests escalated and became more violent on campuses and elsewhere from 1969 to 1970, Nixon concluded that he was more popular among the electorate than the protesters and that Vietnam had therefore become a good political issue for him, particularly as American casualties began to drop. The election of 1972 vindicated that insight.

During the first four months of the Nixon administration, the North Vietnamese launched new offensives and fighting continued at a high level. In his first televised address, Nixon renounced a purely military solution but also rejected withdrawal.

He was now a moderate within the spectrum of American politics. He repeated that the loss of South Vietnam would be internationally disastrous, but he abandoned Johnson's strategy of basing his policy on statements by previous presidents. He assured the American people that "Vietnamization," the strengthening of the South Vietnamese armed forces, would soon allow them to take on more of the fighting. He proposed a settlement based on mutual withdrawal of US and North Vietnamese forces and offered the Viet Cong participation in the constitutional processes of the Thieu government. The North Vietnamese, meanwhile, were insisting that a coalition government replace it.[41] In June, Nixon met with Thieu and announced a 25,000-troop American withdrawal, accomplished by randomly canceling the orders of troops scheduled to deploy.[42] On the same trip he informally promulgated what became known as the Nixon Doctrine, which *in the future* would confine US assistance to naval and air support for threatened nations like South Vietnam.

Nixon had not in fact given up on a military solution. When tough talking to the North Vietnamese and the Soviets failed to move Hanoi toward peace on his terms, he and his national security adviser, Henry Kissinger, commissioned a study of military escalation code-named Duck Hook, involving the mining of North Vietnamese harbors, sustained bombing on an unprecedented scale, and possibly the use of nuclear weapons, until Hanoi acceded to Nixon's terms.[43] Nixon, however, rejected these plans in early October, ordering a worldwide nuclear alert to demonstrate his resolve. He was influenced in part by the prospect of massive demonstrations in Washington, DC, on November 15 and December 15, which would have coincided with the Duck Hook operation. Instead, he developed his strategic communication further in another speech on November 3.

Playing for high stakes, this time he quoted his three immediate predecessors, as Johnson had done, and argued repeatedly that withdrawal would have been disastrous. He announced, without giving any numbers, a plan to replace US forces progressively with South Vietnamese ones. He could now report for the first time that casualties had fallen significantly in recent months. He spoke directly to dissenting young people, as Johnson had never done, assuring them that he wanted peace as much as they did, so that their energy, "now too often directed into bitter hatred against those responsible for the war, can be turned to the great challenges of peace." He asked "the great silent majority of my fellow Americans" for their support.[44] Meanwhile, privately, he and his senior aides believed that the increasingly violent demonstrators would shock the conscience of that great silent majority, as indeed they did. Just six weeks later, on December 15, Nixon reported that although the North Vietnamese still insisted on the end of the Thieu government, he would reduce American forces by another 50,000 men by April 15, 1970, making a total reduction of 115,500 since he came into office.[45]

Nixon had in fact found a winning formula for communicating with the American people: a combination of apparently reasonable peace proposals with reports of stronger Vietnamese forces and a continually updated timetable for troop withdrawals—a brilliant contrast to Johnson's endless, but unspecified, timetable for troop increases. Nixon continued in the same vein on April 16, 1970, announcing more South Vietnamese progress, wider pacification in South Vietnam, and lower casualties and promising the withdrawal of another 150,000 Americans during the next twelve months. But he warned of North Vietnamese offensives in Laos and Cambodia and complained bitterly about their insistence on peace terms aiming at a Communist takeover in South Vietnam. "The decision I have announced tonight," he said, "means that we finally have in sight the just peace that we are seeking."[46] The country did not know, however, that Nixon still regarded dramatic new military initiatives as necessary both to prevent a South Vietnamese defeat and to compel North Vietnam to make peace on his terms.

On April 30 Nixon told an astonished nation, "I have concluded that the actions of the enemy in the last 10 days clearly endanger the lives of Americans who are in Vietnam now and would constitute an unacceptable risk to those who will be there after withdrawal of another 150,000." He announced that US forces were at that moment crossing into Cambodia to capture Viet Cong headquarters and clear out enemy sanctuaries. "This is not an invasion of Cambodia," he assured the nation, promising a quick withdrawal.[47] The reaction on college campuses was immediate and ferocious, and Congress began moving to pass legislation outlawing any further US military action on the ground in Cambodia or Laos. The National Guard killed four students at a demonstration in Kent State, and Nixon himself was clearly shaken when he had to meet the press eight days later. On June 3 he addressed the nation, calling the Cambodian "incursion" "the most successful operation of this long and very difficult war."[48] Nixon now knew that any further ground escalation was out of the question. In any case, two years of high-intensity combat had forced the North Vietnamese Army to retreat and regroup, and the rest of 1970 and all of 1971 were relatively quiet. On October 7, 1970, Nixon tried to take advantage of the relatively favorable military position by proposing a cease-fire in place and an international conference as steps toward peace. Nixon also asked for the immediate release of all prisoners of war (POWs) on both sides.[49] The North Vietnamese, however, were still looking at a long timetable and insisting on a coalition government in Saigon, so the proposal went nowhere.

Exactly six months later, on April 7, 1971, Nixon gave another progress report, noting that combat troops in South Vietnam had risen from zero in January 1961 to 540,000 in January 1969 but had now fallen to about half of that figure. A further 100,000-troop withdrawal, he told his listeners, would reduce the total to 175,000.

Commenting on a recent operation undertaken by South Vietnamese forces with American air support against the Ho Chi Minh trail in Laos, he pronounced it a success and added, "Consequently, tonight I can report that Vietnamization has succeeded." He repeated his proposal of October 7 and again called for the immediate release of American POWs. But he took great pains to promise that American involvement in Vietnam would indeed come to an end.[50] Because the situation remained relatively quiet, he did not make another televised address on Vietnam until January 1972—the beginning of another presidential election year.

The American ground combat role had nearly ended in South Vietnam, and casualties had fallen so far that Nixon would probably have been willing to continue the war at that level indefinitely. On January 13, 1972, he announced that US troops would drop to 69,000 by May 1.[51] Then on January 25, in a long address, he evidently attempted to preempt Democratic criticism that he had not negotiated seriously enough. Detailing for the first time Kissinger's numerous meetings with the North Vietnamese in Paris, he insisted that the enemy had turned down reasonable proposals again and again. Buried within the speech was a critical detail: the United States had offered in May 1971 to set a timetable for the withdrawal of all American forces in return for a standstill cease-fire throughout Indochina and the return of all POWs. The North had rejected it. He repeated this offer that night, but his only political concession was a promise of a new presidential election in South Vietnam, coupled with a promise by Thieu to resign from office one month before the election. The North Vietnamese still insisted on a new government. Nixon also hinted, accurately, at the possibility of an imminent North Vietnamese offensive.[52]

In April 1972 the North Vietnamese launched a massive multifront offensive against South Vietnam, rapidly taking Quang Tri Province and threatening other key positions. Nixon on May 8 announced an unprecedented escalation in response: the heaviest bombing campaign of the North of the whole war and the mining of its harbors. "We shall do whatever is required," he said, "to safeguard American lives and American honor." He insisted that the North Vietnamese were demanding the imposition of a Communist government on South Vietnam. But despite the presence of much larger North Vietnamese forces in South Vietnam, he again offered a peace based on a return of prisoners and a cease-fire in place.[53] While Democratic candidates and much of the press reacted bitterly to the escalation, most Americans, satisfied with the virtual elimination of American casualties, accepted these steps. The North Vietnamese offensive eventually halted, and Nixon defeated George McGovern in a landslide, carrying forty-nine states.

In September and October Kissinger and the North Vietnamese reached an agreement. The North dropped its demand for a coalition government in return for an agreement that recognized the authority of the Viet Cong over much of

South Vietnam and left the determination of South Vietnam's future up to tripartite talks among Thieu's government, the Viet Cong, and neutralists. The United States pledged a full withdrawal and the end of military action in Indochina once cease-fires in Laos and Cambodia were negotiated as well. About 150,000 North Vietnamese troops would remain in South Vietnam. Agreement proved elusive when the Saigon government refused these terms. Hanoi made them public on October 25, and the next day Kissinger, in his first public press conference in four years in office, did some strategic communication of his own, announcing his belief that "peace is at hand." During November and early December, the talks had stalled. Then Nixon, without making any public statement or television address at all, accepted Kissinger's proposal for the Christmas bombing. After a week of heavy bombing and heavy losses, the talks resumed and quickly reached agreement on terms almost identical to those of September.

In his last major address on the subject, Nixon reported that the United States had secured "peace with honor." He never referred to the more troublesome parts of the agreement—those allowing North Vietnamese troops to remain in the South and putting the Viet Cong on an equal political footing with Thieu—and he evidently encouraged surrogates to claim that the Christmas bombing had allowed him to end the war on his terms. He did publicly warn the North Vietnamese of serious consequences should they violate the agreement. Within a couple more months the Watergate scandal had broken out in full force, and Nixon never spoke to the nation on Southeast Asia again. In the late summer of 1973 he finally yielded to congressional pressure to end the bombing of Laos and Cambodia. Tapes show that he and Kissinger had discussed the problem of explaining a possible South Vietnamese collapse within a couple of years to the American people, but as it turned out, he had left the White House before it occurred.[54] Nixon's careful, patient strategy had allowed him to keep the American people behind him, score political points at the expense of the antiwar movement, and claim victory in January 1973. It did not, however, allow the South Vietnamese to win the war.

Gerald R. Ford

Watergate absorbed the attentions of the American people from 1973 to 1974, while the South Vietnamese government steadily weakened.[55] Ford replaced Nixon as president in August 1974, and the Democrats swept the congressional elections three months later. Congress had already refused to grant the full appropriation for South Vietnamese military aid. Then, in the spring of 1975, the North Vietnamese launched a new major cross-border offensive. Thieu ordered a precipitous withdrawal from the Central Highlands, and the South Vietnamese Army began to disintegrate.

By early April the situation was desperate. The Saigon government released letters written by Nixon to Thieu in January 1973 promising American military action if North Vietnam violated the peace agreement.

On April 10 Ford went before a joint session of Congress and made a televised address pleading for $722 million in military aid and $250 million in humanitarian assistance for South Vietnam, the whole sum to be made available by April 19. He also called on the North Vietnamese to halt their offensive. He did not ask for authority to undertake new military operations, which Congress had prohibited almost two years earlier. Like Johnson and Nixon before him, he asked Congress to think of "the free nations of Asia. These nations must not think for a minute that the United States is pulling out on them or intends to abandon them to aggression."[56] It was much too late for effective aid to have reached South Vietnam, and Congress declined to act on Ford's request.

On April 23 Ford spoke to a large crowd at Tulane University in New Orleans. The complete collapse of South Vietnam was obviously only days away, and he realized that it was time to take a new tack. "Today," he said, "America can regain the sense of pride that existed before Vietnam. But it cannot be achieved by refighting a war that is finished as far as America is concerned. As I see it, the time has come to look forward to an agenda for the future, to unify, to bind up the Nation's wounds, and to restore its health and its optimistic self-confidence."[57] Ford and his speechwriters crafted these words on their own. The next morning a furious Kissinger made Ford call speechwriter Robert Hartmann into his office, where Kissinger berated Hartmann for bypassing him and embarrassing him all over the world.[58] But Ford sat calmly smoking his pipe and said nothing. This much-underrated president, who was destined to lose a close election in another eighteen months, knew that he had caught the mood of the American people. Kissinger—who had explained to Nixon in the fall of 1972 that the United States could survive the eventual fall of South Vietnam if the South Vietnamese could clearly be held responsible—immediately began blaming the Soviet Union and Congress for the debacle. But Ford gave the American people permission to feel that they had given far more than anyone could ever have expected to this hopeless cause and that, contrary to so many statements by Johnson and Nixon, the nation and the world could both survive and prosper despite the fall of South Vietnam.

From Eisenhower through Nixon, every president argued that saving South Vietnam from Communism was at least important to prevent the further spread of Communism in Asia and around the world. Eisenhower and Kennedy never faced a serious problem explaining their policies in Southeast Asia because they asked relatively little of the American people. Johnson drew on widely accepted Cold War principles to justify the enormous war he undertook but could not achieve the success that would have vindicated his optimistic predictions. Nixon cleverly persuaded Americans that he was bringing the war to a successful conclusion while steadily reducing its scale and reached a peace agreement that allowed him to claim victory. It fell to Ford to face up to the failure of American policy, and in his own way, he did. Strategic communication allowed these presidents to carry out their policies—but not, as it turned out, to save South Vietnam. Fortunately, it turned out that all these presidents overestimated the consequences of its fall.

Notes

1. David Kaiser, *American Tragedy: Kennedy, Johnson, and the Origins of the Vietnam War* (Cambridge, MA: Belknap Press, 2000), 13–21.
2. Dwight Eisenhower, "Joint Statement Following Discussions with President Diem of Viet-Nam," May 12, 1957, in *The American Presidency Project*, ed. Gerhard Peters and John T. Woolley, https://www.presidency.ucsb.edu/node/233272.
3. Eisenhower, "Address at the Gettysburg College Convocation: The Importance of Understanding," April 4, 1959, in *American Presidency Project*, https://www.presidency.ucsb.edu/node/235390.
4. Eisenhower, "Message to President Diem on the Fifth Anniversary of the Independence of Viet-Nam," October 26, 1960, in *American Presidency Project*, https://www.presidency.ucsb.edu/node/234283.
5. Kaiser, *American Tragedy*, 30–33.
6. Press conference, March 23, 1961, http://www.presidency.ucsb.edu.
7. Kaiser, *American Tragedy*, 56–37.
8. Kaiser, *American Tragedy*, 91–121.
9. John F. Kennedy, News Conference 20, January 15, 1962, John F. Kennedy Presidential Library, https://www.jfklibrary.org/Research/Research-Aids/Ready-Reference/Press-Conferences/News-Conference-20.aspx.
10. Kennedy, "The President's News Conference," February 14, 1962, in *American Presidency Project*, https://www.presidency.ucsb.edu/node/236482.
11. Kennedy, "Television and Radio Interview: After Two Years—A Conversation with the President," December 17, 1962, in *American Presidency Project*, https://www.presidency.ucsb.edu/node/236799.
12. Kaiser, *American Tragedy*, 139.
13. Kennedy, "The President's News Conference," July 17, 1963, in *American Presidency Project*, https://www.presidency.ucsb.edu/node/237214.
14. Kennedy, "Transcript of Broadcast with Walter Cronkite Inaugurating CBS Television News Program," September 2, 1963, in *American Presidency Project*, https://www.presidency.ucsb.edu/node/237355.

15. Kennedy, "Transcript of Broadcast on NBC's *Huntley-Brinkley Report*," September 9, 1963, in *American Presidency Project*, https://www.presidency.ucsb.edu/node/237406.

16. Kaiser, *American Tragedy*, 260–63.

17. Kennedy, "The President's News Conference," October 31, 1963, in *American Presidency Project*, https://www.presidency.ucsb.edu/node/236627.

18. Kennedy, "The President's News Conference," November 14, 1963, in *American Presidency Project*, https://www.presidency.ucsb.edu/node/236680.

19. Kennedy, "Remarks Prepared for Delivery at the Trade Mark in Dallas," November 22, 1963, in *American Presidency Project*, https://www.presidency.ucsb.edu/node/236838.

20. Lyndon B. Johnson, "Remarks to the Joint Chiefs of Staff and to Officials of the Department of Defense," December 11, 1963, in *American Presidency Project*, https://www.presidency.ucsb.edu/node/239580.

21. Johnson, "Radio and Television Report to the American People following Renewed Aggression in the Gulf of Tonkin," August 4, 1964, in *American Presidency Project*, https://www.presidency.ucsb.edu/node/238730.

22. Johnson, "Remarks in Memorial Hall, Akron University," October 21, 1964, in *American Presidency Project*, https://www.presidency.ucsb.edu/node/242136.

23. Johnson, "Remarks in Manchester to the Members of the New Hampshire Weekly Newspaper Editors Association," September 28, 1964, in *American Presidency Project*, https://www.presidency.ucsb.edu/node/242645; emphasis added.

24. Kaiser, *American Tragedy*, 341–81.

25. Johnson, "Address at Johns Hopkins University: Peace without Conquest," April 7, 1965, in *American Presidency Project*, https://www.presidency.ucsb.edu/node/241950.

26. Johnson, "The President's News Conference," July 28, 1965, in *American Presidency Project*, https://www.presidency.ucsb.edu/node/241349.

27. Johnson, "Statement by the President Announcing Resumption of Air Strikes on North Vietnam," January 31, 1966, in *American Presidency Project*, https://www.presidency.ucsb.edu/node/239134.

28. Johnson, "Remarks to the Press at the LBJ Ranch Following a Report on Vietnam by General Westmoreland," August 14, 1966, in *American Presidency Project*, https://www.presidency.ucsb.edu/node/239188.

29. Johnson, "Annual Message to the Congress on the State of the Union," January 10, 1967, in *American Presidency Project*, https://www.presidency.ucsb.edu/node/238176.

30. Johnson, "Address on U.S. Policy in Vietnam Delivered before a Joint Session of the Tennessee State Legislature," March 15, 1967, in *American Presidency Project*, https://www.presidency.ucsb.edu/node/237953.

31. Johnson, "The President's News Conference," September 1, 1967, in *American Presidency Project*, https://www.presidency.ucsb.edu/node/237787.

32. Johnson, "Address on Vietnam before the National Legislative Conference, San Antonio, Texas," September 29, 1967, in *American Presidency Project*, https://www .presidency.ucsb.edu/node/237536.

33. "War's End in View—Westmoreland," *Washington Post*, November 22, 1967.

34. Johnson, "'A Conversation with the President,' Joint Interview for Use by Television Networks," December 19, 1967, in *American Presidency Project*, https://www .presidency.ucsb.edu/node/237864.

35. Johnson, "The President's Address to the Nation Announcing Steps to Limit the War in Vietnam and Reporting His Decision Not to Seek Reelection," March 31, 1968, in *American Presidency Project*, https://www.presidency.ucsb.edu/node /238065.

36. See Ronald H. Spector, *After Tet: The Bloodiest Year in Vietnam* (New York: Free Press, 1993).

37. Clark Clifford with Richard Holbrooke, *Counsel to the President* (New York: Random House, 1991), 527–53, 567–84.

38. George Herring, *LBJ and Vietnam: A Different Kind of War* (Austin: University of Texas Press, 1994).

39. *New York Times*, March 31, 1968, p. 1.

40. Richard Nixon, "Address Accepting the Presidential Nomination at the Republican National Convention in Miami Beach, Florida," August 8, 1968, in *American Presidency Project*, https://www.presidency.ucsb.edu/node/256650.

41. Nixon, "Address to the Nation on Vietnam," May 14, 1969, in *American Presidency Project*, https://www.presidency.ucsb.edu/node/239084.

42. Nixon, "Remarks on Return from Meeting with President Thieu at Midway Island," June 10, 1969, in *American Presidency Project*, https://www.presidency.ucsb.edu /node/239404.

43. Documents on these plans were declassified in 2006. See William Burr and Jeffrey Kimball, eds., "Nixon White House Considered Nuclear Options against North Vietnam, Declassified Documents Reveal," in *National Security Archive Electronic Briefing Book No. 195*, July 31, 2006, http://www2.gwu.edu/~nsarchiv/NSAEBB /NSAEBB195/.

44. Burr and Kimball.

45. Burr and Kimball.

46. Nixon, "Address to the Nation on Progress toward Peace in Vietnam," April 20, 1970, in *American Presidency Project*, https://www.presidency.ucsb.edu/node/241144.

47. Nixon, "Address to the Nation on the Situation in Southeast Asia," April 30, 1970, in *American Presidency Project*, https://www.presidency.ucsb.edu/node/239701.

48. Nixon, "Address to the Nation on the Cambodian Sanctuary Operation," June 3, 1970, in *American Presidency Project*, https://www.presidency.ucsb.edu/node /239816.

49. Nixon, "Address to the Nation about a New Initiative for Peace in Southeast Asia," October 7, 1970, in *American Presidency Project*, https://www.presidency.ucsb.edu /node/240926.

50. Nixon, "Address to the Nation on the Situation in Southeast Asia," April 7, 1971, in *American Presidency Project*, https://www.presidency.ucsb.edu/node/241224.

51. Nixon, "Remarks Announcing Withdrawal of Additional United States Troops from Vietnam," January 13, 1972, in *American Presidency Project*, https://www.presidency .ucsb.edu/node/254608.

52. Nixon, "Address to the Nation Making Public a Plan for Peace in Vietnam," January 25, 1972, in *American Presidency Project*, https://www.presidency.ucsb.edu/node /254597.

53. Nixon, "Address to the Nation on the Situation in Southeast Asia," May 8, 1972, in *American Presidency Project*, https://www.presidency.ucsb.edu/node/254759.

54. http://millercenter.org/presidentialrecordings/rmn-e760-06.

55. See Robert Brigham, *Guerrilla Diplomacy: The NLF's Foreign Relations and the Vietnam War* (Ithaca, NY: Cornell University Press, 1999), 113–26.

56. Gerald R. Ford, "Address before a Joint Session of the Congress Reporting on United States Foreign Policy," April 10, 1975, in *American Presidency Project*, https://www .presidency.ucsb.edu/node/255982.

57. Ford, "Address at a Tulane University Convocation," April 23, 1975, in *American Presidency Project*, https://www.presidency.ucsb.edu/node/256234.

58. Robert L. Hartmann, *Palace Politics: An Inside Account of the Ford Years* (New York: McGraw-Hill, 1980), 321–23.

12.

American Wartime Communication Strategies during the Gulf War

Judith Baroody

American wartime communication strategy shifted profoundly during Desert Storm, the world's first live, 24-7 satellite television war. For the first time, the military and the press negotiated information policy during active combat. It was a watershed moment for how, when, by whom, and to what audiences the war was reported. The Pentagon's Desert Storm public affairs strategy met with resistance from the moment the first reporters touched down in Saudi Arabia, and the debate continues to the present day.[1]

Three factors shaped the communications environment of the Gulf War. First, to inform the public and protect operational security, the Pentagon created a system of press pools, ground rules, and security reviews. Media organizations resisted the constraints through protests and litigation, charging that the military was restricting the freedom of the press to report and verify information independently. Some journalists opted out of the Department of Defense's oversight and protection, choosing to cover the war independently and to accept the dangers of following a fast-moving battle, often fought at night, in a vast desert. The military services reacted in diverse ways to the challenges of dealing with the press, the Marines with considerable success and the Army with difficulty.

Second, for the first time in US history, military officials briefed audiences worldwide from the Pentagon and Saudi Arabia by direct satellite in real time. The news media chose to broadcast the briefings live, thus removing the filter of media interpretation and redefining the way people learned about the war. Defense Department briefers shaped public perception by selecting words, maps, and pictures that portrayed their view of Desert Storm.

Finally, while government and military officials were largely successful in managing the information environment, the intense media coverage strongly influenced policymakers. The George H. W. Bush administration was sensitive to public perceptions and by some accounts was prepared to cease hostilities after footage of the "Highway of Death" showed what appeared to be US targeting of masses of fleeing Iraqis. Media reluctance to include graphic images that might shock viewers gave rise to charges of self-censorship.

Media–US government negotiations constantly transformed public affairs policy throughout Desert Shield and Desert Storm, with such tangible results as an increase in the number of pools and a relaxation of security reviews. The result was a carefully considered evolution of the US military doctrine for dealing with the press during war.

Operation Desert Shield: With Troops Come Reporters

Thousands of Iraqi troops moved across the border into Kuwait two hours after midnight on August 2, 1990, overwhelming Kuwaiti forces in intense combat and forcing half of the small kingdom's population to flee. Saddam Hussein's Iraqi forces established control over the entire country within five hours. The UN Security Council condemned the invasion (UNSC Resolutions 660 and 662) and demanded that Iraq withdraw.

President Bush ordered economic sanctions against Iraq while the Pentagon quietly began to ramp up for war. On August 5 Defense Secretary Richard Cheney, Chairman of the Joint Chiefs of Staff Colin Powell, and Commander in Chief of US Central Command (CENTCOM) Gen. Norman Schwarzkopf flew to Saudi Arabia to ask for King Fahd's permission to deploy US forces to defend his country. President Bush called for the immediate and unconditional withdrawal of all Iraqi forces from Kuwait and the restoration of Kuwait's government. The operation to prepare for war, Desert Shield, was underway.

The United States began pulling together an international coalition, placing warships in the Persian Gulf on alert, and sending allied air and ground forces. The president issued an executive order authorizing the call-up of selected reservists to active duty, and the first troops departed August 7. F-15 Eagle fighter jets from Langley Air Force Base arrived in Saudi Arabia the same day.

No Western reporters were in Saudi Arabia when the first troops arrived. Planning of press coverage began as soon as Defense Secretary Cheney, General Powell, General Schwarzkopf, and Assistant Secretary of Defense for Public Affairs Pete Williams returned from Saudi Arabia.[2] Assistant Secretary Williams prepared what to say about the presidential reserve call-up, the start of maritime intercept operations, and the buildup of forces. The era of 24-7 live communications confronted the Defense

Department with new problems concerning how to release casualty information while also avoiding relatives' learning about deaths through the media. The department also had to time announcements about search-and-rescue missions to avoid giving the enemy a head start.

The Saudis did not want journalists and their satellite transmitters in the country, but Secretary Cheney persuaded them that reporters came with the troops.[3] The Department of Defense called up its national media pool, created after the firestorm of protests over media exclusion during the US invasion of Granada in 1983. The pool consisted of reporters, photographers, and technicians from preselected organizations who could be called on short notice to cover the first phases of military operations.[4] On the night of August 10, Assistant Secretary Williams notified the news organizations included in the pool. The reporters and camera operators brought their passports to the Pentagon the next morning, a Saturday, and that afternoon Williams personally took them to the Saudi embassy, which processed their documents. The pool departed the US for Saudi Arabia two days later.

When the journalists arrived in Dhahran, after stopping at MacDill Air Force Base for a briefing by General Schwarzkopf, there was little to report other than the arrival of troops. The initial group included seventeen journalists representing the Associated Press (AP), United Press International (UPI), Reuters, Cable News Network (CNN), National Public Radio, *Time*, the *Los Angeles Times*, Scripps-Howard, and the *Milwaukee Journal*, accompanied by six Pentagon press officers supervised by Navy captain Mike Sherman. The military ordered the reporters not to tell anyone the pool had been activated or to file stories until the information had been pooled. They were also instructed to stay with military escort officers until they were released.[5]

The Defense Department Public Affairs Office set up press operations, hotel accommodations, and transportation. Principal Deputy Assistant Secretary of Defense for Public Affairs Bob Taylor asked CNN to supply a satellite uplink so broadcast journalists could air their stories. The Defense Department transported it to Saudi Arabia, and CNN set up an earth station outside the Dhahran International Hotel to serve as the primary means for the electronic transfer of most news stories during Desert Shield. Later, during Desert Storm, a second earth station was erected on top of the Hyatt Regency Hotel in Riyadh to transmit news from military briefings.

The Pentagon set up joint information bureaus (JIBs) for press needs, the first and biggest at the Dhahran International Hotel and the second in Riyadh. It established smaller bureaus in Bahrain to handle the press covering the Navy and in Dubai for journalists who could not get visas to enter Saudi Arabia. The Dhahran hotel was soon filled with the paraphernalia of news gathering: laptops, satellite phones, faxes, and the CNN satellite dish.

The Pentagon disbanded the national media pool, which operated from August 13 to 26, when the Saudi government began to issue visas to independent media. Navy public affairs officer Dave Barron assessed that "the DOD [Department of Defense] Media Pool which deployed in the beginning was the most successful exercise of its type to date. Members developed unit integrity. With no Western news media in Saudi Arabia, the pool allowed for the earliest possible coverage."[6]

Even as the short-lived national media pool was dissolving, military public affairs planners were developing a new system of combat pools for the hundreds of reporters arriving in Saudi Arabia. The idea was to embed pools with combat units for a week to ten days, then rotate a new group of reporters to the field. The goal was to make sure that some journalists were in the battle zones when combat began.

By November there were nearly eight hundred media representatives in the region—far outnumbering the military public affairs officers equipped to work with them—but reporters could go only where the military permitted. This prompted many protests of the restrictions of the pool system, saying they constituted prior restraint. Former White House press secretary Ron Nessen argued that the restrictions allowed the Pentagon to win "the last battle of the Vietnam War" by controlling what the world would see.[7]

The Pentagon argued that pool coverage was the only practical way to operate given the size of the area of combat, the anticipated speed of the US advance, the possible Iraqi use of chemical weapons, and the violence of armored battle.[8] In return for ceding control over where reporters went, the media would be assured of access, protection, transportation, and basic needs. Each pool would consist of eighteen news representatives drawn from those already in Saudi Arabia. The Joint International Bureau in Dhahran immediately began to form the first two pools and to familiarize the reporters with troops, equipment, and filing procedures from the field. By early January, sixty journalists began reporting from the field in seven pools.

Some reporters abandoned the confines of the pool system and covered the war on their own. The *Washington Post* obtained all-terrain vehicles, chemical protective gear, and a satellite phone that functioned when other forms of communications were down so that its staff could work independently. *New York Times* reporter Malcolm Browne observed that it was easy for reporters to get a jeep and drive around in Saudi Arabia, where they would meet troops who could choose to arrest or accommodate them. Browne regretted not breaking out of the pool system but acknowledged that the desert was a dangerous place to navigate, with few roads, constant winds, great distances, minefields, and no filling stations.[9]

Among those who paid a price for breaking from the pool system was CBS's Bob Simon and his three-person crew. Iraqi forces captured them at the town of Al Ruqi while they were driving their four-wheel-drive vehicle to the Kuwait-Saudi border.

Held for forty days, they were released through high-level intervention and considerable cost in time and labor to the US government.[10]

Technology Revolution: The First Real-Time Satellite War

The Gulf War marked a milestone in wartime communications planning because of a revolutionary change in technology: the advent of satellite broadcasting. Vietnam was considered the first TV war, but the technology of that time meant reporters and their crews dragged around heavy broadcast equipment and shot images on film that had to be developed, spliced by hand, and flown to broadcast facilities. During the Vietnam War the big three networks—CBS, NBC, and ABC—had controlled the flow of broadcast information to the American public. Desert Storm ushered in the era of real-time round-the-clock transmission.

Desert Storm showcased CNN's advantages in covering rapidly developing events and transformed the cable channel into a major news outlet. CNN correspondent Peter Arnett went to Baghdad before the January 15 UN deadline for an Iraqi withdrawal from Kuwait and remained to cover the war from Baghdad's al-Rashid Hotel with colleagues John Holliman and Bernard Shaw. They reported live as the air war began, first from cell phones and then on camera, a dramatic game changer in the way TV news did business.

Military planners worried about the impact of live satellite coverage on operational security. When a CNN correspondent reported live that there had been a major artillery battle between the Eighty-Second Airborne Division and the Iraqis, General Schwarzkopf believed the report would tip off the Iraqis that the Eighty-Second was positioned for a flank attack, a plan the US had tried to keep secret. A Defense Department public affairs escort was standing next to the reporter when she made the statement but could not prevent her from divulging the information on live broadcast.[11] As Lt. Gen. Charles Horner described the challenge of real-time news transmission, "The effect of a military decision is not only felt on the battlefield, it is felt immediately back home. And the impact of that can find its way back to the battlefield within hours."[12]

The Pentagon adapted to direct broadcasting and initiated briefings that television news organizations transmitted live. This allowed the administration to bypass media filters to tell the story of the war in its chosen words and images. Less than a week after he had arrived in Saudi Arabia, General Schwarzkopf held a press conference at the Dhahran International Hotel, vowing "not to repeat the mistake we'd made in Grenada, where the military had stonewalled."[13] When he stepped into the ballroom, he faced about two hundred reporters and cameras broadcasting live worldwide and knew that "Saddam and his bully boys were watching me on CNN in their headquarters." Allies also listened intently. When General Schwarzkopf told the media that the Scud was not a militarily significant weapon, he reassured the coalition troops, but Israel felt a lack of US concern about Iraqi Scuds falling on Tel Aviv.[14]

In Washington, General Powell advocated ratcheting up the level of briefer from staffers to senior administration officials. He saw the air strikes broadcast on television live from Baghdad. Concerned that initial reports of success created an unrealistic expectation of quick victory, he persuaded Secretary Cheney to conduct a press conference with him to explain the battle plan: using airpower to take out the Iraq's air defense system, neutralizing its logistics support, and then attacking its forces in Kuwait. Lt. Gen. Tom Kelly and Rear Adm. Mike McConnell briefed the media in Washington as did Brig. Gen. Richard Neal in Riyadh.[15] Lieutenant General Horner would also speak to the press as events proceeded.

Desert Storm was the first time viewers and listeners worldwide learned about a war through daily briefings—as many as five per day—directly from the US military. In Riyadh, General Neal gave half-hour live updates at 10 a.m. EST, with General Schwarzkopf occasionally at the podium. In Washington the Pentagon began hourlong televised press briefings at 3 p.m. EST. Assistant Secretary Williams introduced the sessions, and General Kelly and Admiral McConnell outlined the day's developments. Secretary Cheney and General Powell briefed major events.

The sessions became more elaborate as the fighting wore on, progressing from verbal recitations to high-tech presentations with maps and videos, including grainy images of military operations that one analyst concluded transformed Desert Storm into "a deadly video game."[16] In addition to the televised, on-the-record briefings, General Schwarzkopf initiated background briefings about halfway through Desert Storm. Military briefings about the conflict in Vietnam—the Five O'Clock Follies— were later shown to be laced with misinformation on the US role in the air war and in Laos. In Iraq, reporters questioned whether the information they were hearing and seeing was similarly selected to win support for the war by highlighting precision accuracy and coalition Air Force success while suppressing videos showing the bombing of noncombatants or damage to unintended targets.[17]

Pentagon briefers emphasized that the coalition was doing everything possible to avoid "collateral damage," but Tomahawk Land Attack Missiles were not as precise as President Bush suggested when he called the bombing "fantastically accurate." Coalition bombers avoided hitting mosques, hospitals, and schools, but Baghdad credibly reported to the United Nations after the cessation of fighting that the air strikes killed almost 2,300 and injured 6,000 Iraqi noncombatants.[18] The *Washington Post* quoted a Pentagon source that 70 percent of the 88,500 tons of bombs dropped on Iraq missed their target.[19]

The briefings enabled the military to talk directly to worldwide audiences without the intervening filter of media interpretation. It also made household names of some of the top officers, such as General Schwarzkopf. The Commander of Allied Forces came across as calm and confident, "a one-man performer before a rapt audience."[20] The Pentagon could point out that never before had so much information about war fighting been available to such large audiences so quickly. Whether this resulted in better-informed audiences, given the complexity of the information and the selectivity of what was presented, remains a matter for study.

Journalists who accompanied troops in the field were required to sign ground rule agreements when combat began. The Pentagon Public Affairs Office examined all ground rules back to World War II to devise guidelines to protect operational security while respecting press freedom.[21] The new rules included Department of Defense prepublication "security reviews" of articles to ensure the reports did not contain information that would aid the enemy.

The ground rules prohibited journalists from covering religious services or filming severely injured personnel. They required the media to work in pools for the duration of the war and included twelve categories of information that could not be reported, including specific numbers of troops and weapons systems, intelligence-collection activities, and specific locations of forces. Reporters were not to give numerical descriptions of troop strength but could describe units as "company-size," "multibattalion," or "carrier battle group." Equipment and supplies could be described as "large."

Reports were not to identify locations of military forces—Navy embark stories could give only the ship name with the dateline "Persian Gulf" or "Red Sea"—and articles written in Saudi Arabia could be datelined only in terms such as "near the Kuwaiti border." Damage and casualties were to be described as light, moderate, or heavy.[22] Only journalists assigned to pools would be allowed in forward areas. Reporters were expected to stay with military escorts while on Saudi bases and in forward areas and to follow the instructions of medical officials in reporting casualty information.

The presidents of ABC News, CBS News, NBC News, and CNN objected jointly in writing to the ground rules, particularly to the security review provisions and the requirement to remain with military escorts. Thirteen other journalists and media organizations filed a lawsuit against the Department of Defense in protest of the regulations, contending that the pool system, military escorts, and security reviews were more restrictive than those regulated during Vietnam.

Assistant Secretary Williams briefed Department of Defense public affairs officers in Riyadh and Dhahran on the ground rules on January 12, the same day Congress authorized President Bush to use military force to eject Iraq from Kuwait. Assistant Secretary Williams said that if reporters threatened to take off into the desert alone, the Department of Defense escorts should warn them of the dangers but not try to stop them. If journalists showed up at a military unit uninvited, commanders should send them back to Dhahran in fairness to those who followed the pool rules.

Desert Storm: Covering the Air War

Iraq had until January 15 to comply with demands to withdraw from Kuwait, after which coalition forces would use all necessary means to force withdrawal. When the US-led coalition began air attacks on January 16, nearly fourteen hundred reporters were in the Gulf.

American wartime communication strategy continued to evolve—with well-publicized, daily negotiations between the military and media. The pool system was in place to cover the launch of the air war. A handful of journalists coordinated the print pool, among them John Fialka of the *Wall Street Journal*. Five photographers cochaired the photo pool. Tom Giusto of ABC News led the television pool, and the general manager of news operations for ABC radio ran the radio pool.

A public affairs officer awakened AP correspondent Edith Lederer so she could cover the first air strike for the Air Force pool. After witnessing the first wave of F-15E jets fly north from the desert air base toward Iraq and Kuwait, she dictated the story to colleagues in Dhahran on a phone in a construction trailer. The pool report was hand-carried to the JIB and posted. With that, AP ran the first bulletin that the air war had begun.[23]

CNN's Carl Rochelle and team were on board *USS Wisconsin* the first night of the war. Navy public affairs officers told him there would be a Tomahawk Land Attack Missile strike from the ship. CNN did not have the technical capability at that time to broadcast live from the ship. If it had, the Iraqis could have seen the launch at 1:31 a.m. and prepared for the Tomahawks falling on downtown Baghdad an hour and a half later.

News organizations protested restrictions on coverage of the start of the air war almost as soon as the first missiles hit the ground. The *Chicago Tribune* charged that the military delayed reporters in the pools from filing reports of air launchings or interviews with soldiers for thirty-six to forty-eight hours. The AP complained that the press missed reporting on combat on the Saudi-Kuwaiti border because no pool reporters were with forward units. ABC's George Watson observed, "It was only after the air war started that the full meaning of what the Pentagon had done suddenly dawned on our rather none too quick reactions. There was a tremendous unhappiness and the pool system was in the process of falling apart."[24]

Independently verifying information about the air war became a journalistic challenge. "With the war being waged mainly from the skies," one reporter observed, "it is not clear whether unfettered press access to the troops would help reporters understand whether Pentagon assessments are overly optimistic or merely provide them with better quotes and pictures."[25] Given the nature of the air war, the Pentagon gave the press the best access possible, according to Assistant Secretary Williams:

> The difficulty in covering an air war is that a plane takes off and lands from where you are, and drops its bomb from where you're not. I can't control the fact that the Iraqis wouldn't allow reporters into the battle zone. They wouldn't allow them into occupied Kuwait or Iraq. That was, in the air war, where the action was. We did allow them to go onto the air bases, interview pilots, watch planes take off and land, go out on aircraft carriers and do the same thing—naval planes were taking off and landing.[26]

Just after the start of the air war, a C-141 cargo plane with 126 more journalists landed in Dhahran. Charles Lewis, Washington bureau chief for Hearst newspapers, was among the new arrivals. He had fought for a pool slot in Dhahran for four weeks before he was assigned to the Second Armored Division of the VII Corps, along with a Reuters photographer. The division was part of the "left hook" that crossed the berm into Iraq, turned northeast, and ended up in Kuwait.[27]

UPI reporter Thomas Ferraro was also on the C-141. The Pentagon had notified him that once the air war started, reporters would leave for Saudi Arabia within twenty-four hours, but he was skeptical that he would ever cover the conflict. "I always thought Saddam Hussein would back down, so I bought everything but I didn't really think I was going. I saved all the receipts, thinking I'd be returning the equipment. Then when the assault began, the next morning we got to the Pentagon at 4:00, the plane left at 09:00 and we took off."[28]

The security review system complicated coverage of the air war. Just as the strikes were about to begin, *Wall Street Journal* reporter John Fialka wrote a piece about destroying the enemy's airpower. He filed it on Tuesday and was assured it would be cleared by Thursday for the Friday paper. "They censored the hell out of it," he wrote, "because they insisted I had their plan. I didn't have any plan. I could just see what was going to happen." By the time it got to Dhahran and was released for pool use, someone had intervened to "uncensor" the piece. All the other media organizations used the report, but it was too late for publication in the *Wall Street Journal*, which does not publish on weekends.[29] Disgruntled reporters found a champion in Representative Barbara Boxer, who submitted a resolution, drafted with the help of the American Society of Newspaper Editors, calling on the Pentagon to make the security review voluntary.[30]

The Iraqi invasion of the Saudi Arabian town of Khafji on January 30 gave some journalists their first chance to see ground combat. Pool and independent reporters covered the battle, which resulted in the deaths of eleven Marines, fifteen Saudi soldiers, and thirty Iraqis. Thomas Ferraro found being at the site of combat a transformative experience: "We were on the outskirts of Khafji. We saw the helicopters go in and come back. . . . We were told we were within range of fire. . . . Just from human terms it changed the way you viewed the story, because it was like getting into the water for the first time."[31] The next day the Pentagon held a briefing on the Battle of Khafji that the media charged was incomplete, inaccurate, and delayed.

General Schwarzkopf invited a group of reporters to his office to talk about it. Afterward he replaced the briefing officer and changed the way the military responded to media inquiries. The Defense Department set up a hotline between the hotel where the reporters were based and the Public Affairs Office (which was in communication with the Command Center) and promised to respond to urgent questions within an hour and a half.[32] CENTCOM committed to transporting reporters to the scene of military action and back, communicating their reports to the JIB in Dhahran for filing, and permitting unilateral coverage of combat as soon as possible.[33] By February 4 there were over a thousand reporters in Saudi Arabia, but only seventy-five out in pools at any time. CENTCOM announced it would double the number of pools assigned to ground forces.

Desert Storm: Covering the Ground War

A week later the Pentagon issued contingency guidance for the ground war and distributed protective gear to reporters. When the ground offensive began, 27 pool reporters witnessed it from ships and air bases, and 132 were embedded with ground forces. Secretary Cheney announced that the military was suspending press briefings in Washington and Riyadh, a decision several news organizations labeled a blackout.

The Office of the Secretary of Defense cabled public affairs officers instructing that all sensitive media pool reports, videotapes, photos, and audiotapes would be held at forward-staging locations to protect operational security at the start of the ground war. That order was rescinded within hours, but public affairs officers informed reporters that pool reports must not reveal information helpful to the enemy.

The JIB in Dhahran did not release the first dispatches until ten hours after they had been filed. The delay privileged nonpool reporters: British reporters shot the first footage broadcast after the start of the ground offensive; French journalists gave hourly updates of the progress of their division. American reporters operating independently beat pool reporters to Kuwait by an entire day. A CBS crew followed a Saudi tank column into Kuwait and then broadcast by generator from the desert.

Few combat pool reporters embedded with ground forces in Kuwait, Iraq, and Saudi Arabia were able to file reports that got into US papers or on the evening news the day the war began. Part of the problem was that journalists had to either go to fil-ing centers in person or have someone else carry their reports to the centers to transmit them. Eventually, the tactical communications network overloaded, and reporters had to rely on fax machines and other low-tech methods to file. The Pentagon determined that in the future, the press would need its own dedicated communications systems.

Some commanders gave more priority than others to transporting reporters and helping them file their reports. Differences among the services gave the public a distorted picture of the war. There were 295,000 Army troops and 80,000 Marines, but coverage of the ground war as reported in the four largest newspapers and four networks mentioned the Marines 293 times and the Army 271 times. Marine battles were reported in detail; Army combat was not.[34]

Marine pools were successful because the reporters were in the right places and had good access to troops. Senior US Marine commander general Walter Boomer had been a public affairs officer and encouraged the incorporation of the media into the operational planning.[35] The Marines avoided grouping TV crews, with their special media needs, with print reporters. Once the pools began operation in January, some reporters placed with specific Marine units chose to stay with them until the end of the ground war, having built relationships and trust. Other services pulled reporters away from combat units after a week or two and brought in others. The Marines also had the best record for helping reporters file their stories by the deadline.

The Army was considered the least media friendly. Some speculate that this reflected beliefs that the press had turned the American public against the Vietnam War. Coverage of the Army VII Corps was especially problematic. Fighting deep in the desert, its First and Third Armored Divisions conducted fierce combat with Iraqi tank forces, but media coverage was limited because of the speed of the advance and distance from filing points.[36]

According to Hearst's Charles Lewis, when he arrived at the Second Armored Division, officers did not know he was coming, did not know what a pool was and did not know what to do with a reporter. "They had a responsibility at that point to provide me with transportation, lodging, food, communications, and they had nothing like that."[37] Some commanders later regretted they had not worked out transportation and communications logistics for their press embeds in advance.[38] A few reporters did get access. Joseph Galloway, senior writer for *U.S. News and World Report*, was allowed an uninterrupted, unescorted ten days living with the Army's Twenty-Fourth Mechanized Infantry Division thanks to his reporting in Vietnam and his personal connection with General Schwarzkopf.[39]

The Navy faced unique problems in accommodating reporters, who had to reach ships by helicopter. The Navy had only four helicopters to serve the entire Gulf at the beginning of Desert Storm, and two were down at any one time. Only five or six reporters could fit into a chopper. Navy Public Affairs Officer Mark Walker complained that "some weeks we were only able to do one ship embark, which was not satisfactory from our point of view or from the media's point of view."[40]

The administration placed a priority on public perceptions of the war. Concern about image played a role in the decision by President Bush and senior officers to end the land war at a hundred hours. On February 25 allied warplanes destroyed fourteen hundred vehicles and twenty-eight tanks fleeing Kuwait City along a six-lane road to the Iraqi border town of Safwan. The press labeled it "the Highway of Death"; later, two hundred to three hundred Iraqis were found dead at the scene. The press inflated the number of casualties, referring to the mission as a "turkey shoot" of retreating Iraqi forces. Concern about fallout from the Highway of Death prompted General Powell to approach General Schwarzkopf about ending the war: "The television coverage . . . was starting to make it look as if we were engaged in slaughter for slaughter's sake."[41]

At a meeting the president and others also expressed concern that a planned air attack on Iraqi forces fleeing across the Euphrates would be seen as another "turkey shoot" and the coalition would be accused of slaughtering fleeing Iraqis. The second attack was called off, and according to one participant, President Bush then made the decision to suspend offensive ground combat operations at a hundred hours. The president later said it was not the White House but General Schwarzkopf who asked for a few more hours to clean up loose ends, making it an even hundred-hour ground war.[42]

Impact of Gulf War Communication Strategies

Desert Storm was a remarkable military achievement. The US and its coalition of 37 other countries sent almost 800,000 combatants into battle with 225 naval vessels and 2,800 aircraft. They overcame 42 Iraqi divisions, sank the entire Iraqi Navy, and captured 82,000 Iraqi soldiers—all within 43 days of combat. For the first time since World War II, the United States decisively won a major land war.

It succeeded in winning American public support, an important factor in boosting morale at home and among allies. Approval of the president's handling of the war following Iraq's invasion of Kuwait declined from 76 percent in August 1990 to 54 percent in October 1990. As preparations for military intervention began, public support climbed. The president's popularity rose to 89 percent through March 1991. Whether press coverage of Desert Storm influenced public opinion is a matter of debate; most research indicates that the media reflects, but does not lead, public thinking.[43] But Vietnam-era fears that media coverage would turn Americans against war were largely dispelled.

Media representatives offered mixed opinions about Desert Storm. The pool system, ground rules, and other restrictions resulted in open disgruntlement and lawsuits by those in the media who believed the public had been ill-served and who wanted to improve future combat coverage. The Society of Professional Journalists argued that the pool system produced homogeneity of coverage because of the limited sources the reporters were allowed to question.[44] Former US government press spokesman Barry Zorthian concluded at a National Press Club forum on March 19, 1991, that "the war is over and the press lost."[45]

Some took their disgruntlement to court. Agence France Presse, which had been excluded from the press pools, argued that this posed an unconstitutional interference with the media's ability to gather news. The case was dismissed after active hostilities had ended. The American Civil Liberties Union also filed suit, alleging that the Pentagon decision to deny access to the base where the remains of those killed in war returned to the United States violated First Amendment protections of free speech and free press. US District Court Judge Royce C. Lambert denied the request for a temporary restraining order against the military.

More than a dozen Washington editors and bureau chiefs met at ABC to discuss press policy during Desert Storm and followed up by writing to Secretary Cheney. They argued that the Pentagon blocked the flow of information to the public, the pools did not work, reports and photos were late or lost, and the system of military escorts and copy review denied the media adequate access. Seventeen other news executives sent a second letter to Secretary Cheney protesting the public affairs policy during Desert Storm and recommending that the public affairs system created for that war should not serve as a model for the future. Secretary Cheney met with major media organizations and reached consensus on a statement of principles that led to new doctrine on war coverage.

During Desert Shield and Desert Storm, US government policy on press coverage of military operations rapidly evolved. The changes in Pentagon communication strategies included the deployment of the Department of Defense national media pool to cover the arrival of troops; the creation of officially sanctioned, escorted press pools; the embedding of reporters with military units during battle; and frequent, in-depth briefings by top US military officials broadcast directly to international audiences, bypassing media filters and interpretation.

Pentagon officials saw the wartime communication strategy as a success. Assistant Secretary Williams cited polls showing that the American public had greater respect for both the military and the media after Desert Storm and that press arrangements— including the imposition of pools, ground rules, and copy review—got reporters to the battle sites and gave Americans at home a view of the action without compromising military operations. He admitted that the Department of Defense could have done more to help journalists in the field but noted that the number of media representatives in the war zone was excessive and the US government was ultimately responsible for their security. The press arrangements constituted "a good faith effort to allow as much freedom in reporting as possible while still preventing the enemy from knowing what we were up to."[46]

Conclusions

Criticism of the Gulf War communication strategy has been long lasting and ultimately led to institutional change. Much of it came from reporters such as Patrick Sloyan of *Newsday*. His series of articles after the war, detailing "friendly fire" deaths, unreported battles, and allegations of American atrocities, won the Pulitzer Prize in 1992. Sloyan alleged that military commanders deliberately delayed or lost film footage and reports so they would arrive too late for deadlines and that Pentagon briefers provided most of the video and news content to create lasting impressions of what had occurred.[47]

Books published after the war, including John R. MacArthur's *Second Front: Censorship and Propaganda in the Gulf War* and Douglas Kellner's *The Persian Gulf TV War*, accused the Pentagon of media orchestration and the press of quiet collusion with its own loss of rights to observe, question, and report. Historian Clarence Wyatt was among those who concluded that media policies enabled the administration to shape coverage, charging that "the portrayal of a high-tech U.S. military . . . gave the U.S. public a picture of a war that was inflicting very few civilian casualties."[48]

The Pentagon criticized some of its own public affairs officers for being undertrained and outclassed by the media. One Army media specialist concluded, "I will be the first to tell you the Army does not do very well in training our public affairs officers to deal with crisis communications in joint public affairs activities."[49] The Department of Defense subsequently created advanced courses for dealing with the media at its Defense Information School.

The press shared the blame for incomplete coverage. At the end of the war, the pools were promptly abandoned, and reporters had the choice of remaining in Saudi Arabia to interview US combatants for a deeper examination of what had actually happened. Almost all left to cover the liberation of Kuwait. Some journalists were less than impressed by their media colleagues. Joseph Galloway warned General Schwarzkopf about correspondents ignorant of anything military. David Bartlett observed reporters who did not even try to gain access to the battlefields but would "just take the handouts."[50] Eric Schmitt concluded, "You didn't have a cadre of trained people over there asking the kind of questions that the American people should have been hearing the answers to."[51]

Self-censorship played a role in what readers and viewers learned. Peter Turnley took grim photos along the Highway of Death and posted them on a website, the Digital Journalist, but they never appeared in traditional media. Ken Jarecke, a photographer under contract for *Time* magazine whose images were available to all members of the press pool, took a picture of the charred corpse of an Iraqi soldier at the wheel of his vehicle. The AP did not transmit the graphic image, and it was not published until after the war.[52] Jarecke was with a military public affairs officer, Patrick Hermanson, when they came across the scene: "He could have stopped me because it was technically not allowed under the rules of the pool. But he didn't stop me and I walked over there."[53] The military did not prevent photographers from taking or transmitting the photos; publishers chose not to run them.

Media-military relations might have improved if the war had gone on longer. The brevity of the conflict did not allow relationships and trust between the two groups to develop. Likewise, journalists who lacked war-reporting experience never had a chance to acquire a feel for combat or an understanding of military culture. On a more practical level, the hundred-hour ground war was so short that many print reports, videos, and still photos were not filed in time to be disseminated.

Department of Defense public affairs policy changed after the Gulf War. On May 21, 1992, the Pentagon announced a new policy for press coverage of military operations, limiting the use of pools to the early stages of an operation, when space is limited or the location remote. The updated guidelines required journalists to be credentialed by the military and to follow ground rules to ensure operational security. Military public affairs officers would act as liaisons but not impede reporting, provide transportation for media representatives when engaged in open coverage and always when in pools, and assist them to file reports if needed.[54] The principal means of coverage of military operations was to be through open and independent reporting.

Thus, the conflict between the press and the Pentagon during Desert Storm led to permanent changes in joint doctrine and a sharpened understanding that whether the media is viewed as a force multiplier or a watchdog for American interests, its impact must be factored into war planning before the first missile is launched.

Notes

1. A portion of this chapter is drawn from Judith Baroody's previously published book *Media Access and the Military: The Case of the Gulf War* (Lanham, MD: University Press of America, 1998). Georgetown University Press acknowledges and accepts such prior publication.

2. Assistant Secretary of Defense for Public Affairs Pete Williams, interview by the author, July 6, 1992.

3. Deputy Assistant Secretary of Defense for Public Affairs Robert B. Hall, interview by the author, April 30, 1992. In his autobiography General Schwarzkopf wrote that at one point after the journalists arrived, the Saudis decided to expel them, but CENTCOM interceded to prevent it. H. Norman Schwarzkopf, *The Autobiography: It Doesn't Take a Hero* (New York: Bantam Books, 1992).

4. John William Vessey and Winant Sidle, *CJCS Media and Military Relations Panel Report (Sidle Panel Report)* (Washington, DC: Joint Chiefs of Staff, 1984), sec. II, recommendation 2.

5. DOD National Media Pool Ground Rules, August 1990. Reissuance of April 13, 1990, rules, reprinted in *Pentagon Rules on Media Access to the Persian Gulf War: Hearings before the Senate Committee on Governmental Affairs*, 102nd Cong. 349 (1991).

6. Cdr. William Davis Barron, interview by author, 1992.

7. Ron Nessen, "The Pentagon's Censors," *Washington Post*, January 12, 1991.

8. "Conduct of the Persian Gulf Conflict: An Interim Report to Congress," AD-A249 445, July 1991, Department of Defense, https://apps.dtic.mil/dtic/tr/fulltext/u2/a249445.pdf.

9. Malcolm W. Browne, "The Military vs. the Press," *New York Times Magazine*, March 3, 1991, 45.

10. Bob Simon, *Forty Days* (New York: G. P. Putnam's Sons, 1992).

11. Schwarzkopf, *Autobiography*, 440.

12. Tom Clancy, *Every Man a Tiger*, with Chuck Horner (New York: G. P. Putnam's Sons, 1999), 217.

13. Schwarzkopf, *Autobiography*, 343.

14. See Michael R. Gordon and Bernard E. Trainor, *The General's War: The Inside Story of the Conflict in the Gulf* (Boston: Little, Brown, 1995), 234.

15. Colin Powell, *My American Journey*, with Joseph Persico (New York: Random House, 1995), 529–30.

16. Phillip Knightly, *The First Casualty* (Baltimore: Johns Hopkins University Press, 2004), 483.

17. John Balzar, "Daily Military Briefings: A Mixture of Substance and Smoke," *Los Angeles Times*, February 12, 1991.

18. For more discussion, see Rick Atkinson, *Crusade: The Untold Story of the Persian Gulf War* (New York: Houghton Mifflin, 1993), 223–28.

19. Barton Gellman, "U.S. Bombs Missed 70% of Time," March 16, 1991, *Washington Post*.

20. David Lamb, "Schwarzkopf Takes Center Stage and Stars in a Low-Key Assessment of Conflict," *Los Angeles Times*, January 31, 1991.

21. Williams interview.

22. Operation Desert Shield Ground Rules, January 14, 1991, *Pentagon Rules on Media Access to the Persian Gulf War*, 756.

23. Edith Lederer, "Getting the Word Out the First Night," *Editor and Publisher* 124, no. 5 (February 2, 1991): 9.

24. ABC's George Watson, interview by the author, 1992.

25. Howard Kurtz, "Journalists Say Pools Don't Work," *Washington Post*, February 11, 1991.

26. Williams interview.

27. Charles Lewis, Hearst Newspapers, interview by the author, 1992.

28. Thomas Ferraro, United Press International reporter, interview by the author, 1992.

29. John J. Fialka, staff reporter, *Wall Street Journal*, interview by author, 1992.

30. H.R. 37, 102nd Cong. (1991).

31. Ferraro interview.

32. Capt. Michael Doubleday, Navy Public Affairs, interview by the author, 1991.

33. CENTCOM Pool Membership and Operating Procedures, January 30, 1991, in *Pentagon Rules on Media Access*, 331.

34. John Fialka, *The Hotel Warriors: Covering the Gulf War* (Washington, DC: Woodrow Wilson Center Press, 1991), 6.

35. Marine Colonel John M. Shotwell, Marine Public Affairs, interview by author, 1992.

36. Jay Sharbutt, "Most Media Pools Disband as Reporters Flock to Kuwait," Associated Press, March 1, 1991.

37. Lewis interview.

38. Doubleday interview.

39. Joseph Galloway, interview by the author, 1992.

40. Lt. Mark Walker, Navy Public Affairs, interview by the author, 1992.

41. Powell, *My American Journey*, 520.

42. Gordon and Trainor, *General's War*, 512–13.

43. John Mueller, *Policy and Opinion in the Gulf War* (Chicago: University of Chicago Press, 1994), 70.

44. Paul McMasters, Deputy Editorial Director, *USA Today* and Chairman, Freedom of Information Committee, Society of Professional Journalists, Feb. 20, 1991, cited in *Pentagon Rules on Media Access*, 45.

45. Barry Zorthian was director of the Joint Public Affairs Office in Saigon during the Vietnam War and conducted the briefings that became known as the "Five O'Clock Follies."

46. Pete Williams, "The Press and the Persian Gulf War," *Parameters*, Autumn 1991, 2–9.

47. Patrick Sloyan, "What I Saw Was a Bunch of Filled-in Trenches with People's Arms and Legs Sticking out of Them. For All I Know, We Could Have Killed Thousands," *Guardian*, February 13, 2003.

48. Clarence R. Wyatt, *Encyclopedia of Media and Propaganda in Wartime America* (Santa Barbara, CA: ABC-CLIO, 2011), 2:825.

49. Col. Donald Kirchoffner, US Army Chief, Media Relations Division, Office of the Chief of Public Affairs, interview by the author, 1992.

50. David Bartlett, president of the Radio-Television News Director Association, interview by the author, 1992.

51. Eric Schmitt, Pentagon correspondent, *New York Times* Washington Bureau, interview by the author, 1992.

52. Lori Robertson, "Images of War," *American Journalism Review*, October/November 2004, ajrarchive.org.

53. Torie Rose DeGhett, "The War Photo No One Would Publish," *The Atlantic*, August 8, 2014.

54. Office of Assistant Secretary of Defense (Public Affairs), News Release No. 241-92, May 21, 1992.

PART V. Introduction

The Twenty-First Century Information Age: Print, Radio, Cable TV, Internet, and Social Media

Andrea J. Dew and Marc A. Genest

The internet age began in the twentieth century with the earliest forms of email becoming available by the late 1960s, but the technology was unwieldy and inaccessible to many until the 1980s, when the home computer became widespread. After Tim Burnes-Lee at the European Organization for Nuclear Research (CERN) proposed a networked nonhierarchical architecture to access files (what became the World Wide Web) in 1989, however, the ability of individuals to communicate with people whom they did not know and who did not know them blossomed. This combination of electronic communications, searchable communities of interest, and global access transformed the media to expand its audiences yet again. By the late 1990s the first blogging sites began multiplying on the internet, and social media grew exponentially in the first decade of the twenty-first century as sites like YouTube, Facebook, Twitter, Tumblr, and Pinterest rushed to fill a vast assortment of communications niches. Moreover, the popularity of smartphones, tablets, and computer technology, together with the placing of advanced telecommunications and fiber-optic undersea cables, physically connected the world to the internet. Today, almost half of the world's population has access to the internet, bringing a deluge of information to over three billion people and dramatically increasing the audiences for media.

The rapid spread of communications technology, the emergence of social media, and the Global War on Terror are all intimately intertwined. The information revolution introduced a vast multiplicity of voices and images onto the world stage, blurring the lines between those who create messages and those who receive them. In 2001 the cutting-edge social media website was Myspace; the site allowed individuals to post their thoughts, their photos, and their friendships to the world. Those first

Myspace pages seem quaint compared to its social media successors. Facebook, You-Tube, Instagram, Twitter, Snapchat, and Telegram provide slick forums and voices to all regardless of their intent. As the brutal videos of the Islamic State in Iraq and Syria (ISIS) executing its prisoners demonstrated in 2014, a wave of even more sophisticated new technologies—smartphones, Skype, Google maps, editing apps, high-resolution cameras, and video compression—has empowered presidents, citizens, soldiers, and terrorists alike.[1]

This section explores how the communications revolution leveled the playing field among powerful states, terrorist groups, and even individuals. This increasingly egalitarian information environment has shaped, facilitated, and constrained the actions of all sides in the war on terrorism that has been raging since 2001. All three chapters share an alarming theme—that despite enormous military, economic, and technological advantages, the United States and its allies have failed to implement successful communication strategies to combat the spread of violent extremism. In chapter 13, Thomas Johnson and Matthew DuPée compare the communication strategies used by the Taliban and the United States in Afghanistan. The authors conclude that the Taliban was remarkably adept at strategic communication for two reasons: First, it developed simple, explicit messages that resonated with the rural population. Second, the Taliban learned how to exploit a wide array of modern communications technology to spread its ideas. For its part, the United States and its allies relied on a "poorly formulated leaflet program, billboards, and radio messages that in most instances have little resonance with the Afghan population."

The next chapter by Haroro J. Ingram and Craig Whiteside examines the communication strategies used by the United States and the Islamic State. Like the authors of the previous chapter, Ingram and Whiteside argue that the US failed to implement a successful strategic communication plan to combat the enemy's propaganda campaign. On the other hand, the Islamic State developed a "resilient infrastructure based on semi-autonomous regional and local cells" led by competent individuals. The Islamic State's decentralized operations allow the organization to survive despite devastating physical attacks and cyberattacks by the United States and its allies.

Chapter 15 by Andrea Dew explores how three successive presidents, George W. Bush, Barack Obama, and Donald Trump struggled to define and articulate clear policy goals and clear strategies to achieve those aims. The cumulative result of this eighteen-year failure has eroded American prestige and influence around the globe, weakened support for the war against violent terrorism, and threatened US civil liberties within the United States.

Note

1. On ISIS violence, see START, "Patterns of Islamic-State Related Terrorism," August 2016, https://www.start.umd.edu/pubs/START_IslamicStateTerrorismPatterns_Back groundReport_Aug2016.pdf; "The Islamic State," Mapping Militant Organizations, accessed April 12, 2019, http://web.stanford.edu/group/mappingmilitants/cgi-bin /groups/view/1; and Brian Oakes, *Jim: The James Foley Story*, HBO, 2016, http:// www.hbo.com/documentaries/jim-the-james-foley-story.

13.

Struggling to Overcome the Afghan Taliban's Master Narratives

Thomas H. Johnson and Matthew C. DuPée

Despite the overthrow of the Taliban government, which, to the surprise of many, took only eight to ten weeks in late 2001, the US and its North Atlantic Treaty Organization (NATO) allies have struggled to define the parameters of the war ever since. Many have condemned the United States for failing to set feasible strategies for Afghanistan, Pakistan, and Central Asia.[1] It tried to leverage strategic communication to gain the support of the Afghan people. From the beginning, it emphasized information operations (IO) and psychological operations (PSYOP), but these strategic communication strategies have remained controversial. The Afghan Taliban has countered with its own information campaign designed to delegitimize the Afghan government and garner local support by exploiting US and NATO missteps. Although the United States has poured money into Afghanistan and tried to communicate the benefits of the aid, its message of help and hope has not resonated among Afghans and is not likely ever to do so.[2]

The US Message and Foreign Forces as Messengers

Following the terrorist attacks in New York City and Washington, DC, on September 11, 2001, a US-led coalition attacked Afghanistan on October 7, 2001, to remove the Afghan Taliban regime, which had refused to hand over Osama bin Laden, the mastermind of the September 11 attacks.[3] The US-led coalition sought to target and destroy al Qaeda, a global terror network based in Afghanistan. During the onset of the war, the US employed conventional PSYOP, such as dropping hundreds of thousands of crude leaflets with messages intended to gain local support to overthrow the Taliban government and prepare the local population for the presence of foreign troops.[4] The September 11 terror attacks heavily influenced the leaflets, which included images of the burning World Trade Center—visuals lost on many rural Afghans who had never seen modern Western infrastructure.[5]

The battle space became more complicated in December 2001, when the US-led coalition became the International Security Assistance Force (ISAF)—a NATO-led security mission established by the United Nations Security Council. Although the main purpose of ISAF was to maintain security in Kabul, train the Afghan National Security Forces, and assist Afghanistan in rebuilding key government institutions, ISAF elements also engaged in armed conflict with the myriad Afghan insurgents and employed a wide range of strategic communication efforts often in parallel with US efforts.[6]

The diversion of funds to support the US-led invasion of Iraq in March 2003 then degraded the capability of the US PSYOP Task Force in Afghanistan.[7] The task force significantly struggled to compete with the Afghan Taliban messaging, which expertly played on religious and cultural values and historical aversion to the presence of foreign forces.[8] Nevertheless, groups like the Taliban lacked the labor and matériel to impose the large-scale occupation of territory inside. In 2008 the International Crisis Group suggested that the Taliban "still puts out contradictory messages that indicate internal rifts and the diffuse nature of the insurgency."[9] Then in 2009 the US adopted counterinsurgency (COIN) tactics. One way to conceptualize COIN is as an information war supported by military kinetics.

From 2001 to 2006 the US relied on a fairly consistent set of strategic communication messages: (1) the war on terror is right and just; (2) coalition forces come in peace; (3) al Qaeda and the Taliban are enemies of the people of Afghanistan; (4) US forces are technologically superior (a difficult sell when it comes with collateral damage); (5) there are monetary rewards for information about Taliban and al Qaeda leaders; (6) there are monetary rewards for turning in weapons; (7) the Afghan government is legitimate; (8) Afghan National Security Forces serve the people of Afghanistan; and (9) democracy benefits the people of Afghanistan.[10]

These messages targeted the general Afghan population, but they often did not resonate with the target audience. By contrast, senior insurgent leaders and rank-and-file insurgents ranked seventh and eighth, respectively, in terms of importance as target audiences.[11] These target audiences ranked as follows: (1) the Afghan population, (2) the Afghan government, (3) the Pakistani government and military, (4) the Pakistani population, (5) the governments of ISAF troop-contributing nations, (6) populations of ISAF troop-contributing nations, (7) the enemy leadership (al Qaeda, Taliban, criminal networks), (8) the Taliban rank and file, (9) Central Asian governments, (10) Central Asian populations, (11) intergovernmental and nongovernmental organizations, and (12) the US domestic audience.

In 2007 the US in conjunction with NATO-ISAF revamped and complicated its strategic messages:

1. The Government of the Islamic Republic of Afghanistan, NATO-ISAF, and the U.S. are committed to ensure a democratic, stable, and peaceful Afghanistan that is inhospitable to terrorism. The Afghan people can rely on their allies, including the U.S. government and NATO, to stay the course.
2. Success in Afghanistan over insurgency, terrorism, violent extremism, and trafficking in narcotics is critical to the security of the Afghan people, the United States, the NATO allies, Central Asian countries, and the international community.
3. Afghanistan's security, reconstruction, and development needs remain large but progress has been significant and remains ongoing.
4. Success requires a comprehensive approach that includes security and stability as well as reconstruction and development.
5. The Taliban targets innocent Afghan civilians, engages in criminal activity, and employs brutal tactics. It cannot provide long-term security, stability, or development for the people of Afghanistan.[12]

These narratives and US strategy were problematic on multiple levels. The United States failed to present the narratives to the Afghan population in a coherent manner. Most of the time it tailored messages to the urban, the educated, or the elite and so failed to resonate with the 75-80 percent of the population living in rural areas. Ignorance of Pashtun culture and cultural dynamics undermined US IO efforts.[13] For example, the United States never came to grips with what the term "jihad" meant to average Afghans, especially those in the south.[14] To the average southern Afghan, jihad meant broadly any effort to protect Islam from invaders and negative influences. While historically this often entailed armed actions, in many instances it merely meant following the faith and personal Islamic virtues ("greater" jihad in Islamic teachings) and supporting those battling for Islamic righteousness. Americans never understood these nuances. According to *Joint Forces Quarterly*, in 2009 Chairman of the Joint Chiefs of Staff Adm. Mike Mullen said "that U.S. efforts in Afghanistan and elsewhere [needed] to send a positive message about U.S. military action and development efforts hurt U.S. credibility when they do not coincide with what the populace sees on the ground."[15]

In recognition of these failures, the NATO-ISAF Strategic Communication Framework for 2011 reset the key communication themes as the US and NATO prepared to transition to a long-term partnership with Afghanistan. First, they again tried to communicate that stability in Afghanistan was crucial to global security and that NATO-ISAF would never again allow Afghanistan to become a launching pad for international terrorism. Instability and civilian deaths had become a major issue for President Hamid Karzai and an important source of US-Afghan tensions. In 2009 US general Stanley McChrystal had implemented the US-ISAF directives limiting the use of airpower to curtail the perception that coalition airstrikes were responsible for civilian casualties. Shortly after the directives' implementation, US Army colonel Francis Scott Main wrote that the "inability of PSYOP and strategic communications to address this perception of excessive [casualties] had restricted one of the most effective kinetic tools available to the coalition."[16]

Second, the United States and NATO planned to coordinate with the Afghan government (the Islamic Republic of Afghanistan) to explain and gain support for the transition to independent rule. Ten years into Operation Enduring Freedom and after the December 2001 Bonn Accords, which established the international effort in Afghanistan, the Afghan government still faced charges of flagrant corruption and a lack of democracy and transparency. The rural population had become extremely antagonistic to Kabul, and this in turn had significant implications for US COIN efforts throughout the country. US night raids, for example, became a rallying point not only for the rural population but also for Karzai, the recipient of so much US aid.

Third, the United States and ISAF intended to generate active support for their mission from the Afghan people and government, the people of those countries contributing troops, and the international community generally. The death of Afghan innocents as a result of US, ISAF, and Afghan security forces had become a major recruiting tool for the Taliban and associated groups, which exploited collateral damage to delegitimize the government and its foreign allies.

Fourth, the information campaign tried to promote NATO's long-term commitment to and close coordination with the Afghan government. However, after a decade with little apparent progress, the populations of many NATO countries questioned the wisdom of their continuing combat presence in Afghanistan. In any case, the message did not resonate among Afghans. This in turn undermined a fifth objective to communicate ISAF progress. Attempts to employ theater-defined measures of effectiveness for IO and PSYOP failed. A basic lack of knowledge of Afghanistan and the Pashtuns undermined the effort. The United States and its NATO-ISAF partners focused on discussions with elites and technocrats at the expense of understanding the needs and desires of rural Afghans. This omission was especially problematic given the rural nature of the insurgency. From this arose the sixth goal to diminish support for the insurgents and criminal patronage networks that undermined the ISAF mission and effective governance. Criminals and drug mafias quickly became associated with the Taliban. Groups such as the Haqqani Network were as much criminal as insurgent.[17] They preyed on the Afghan population and subverted development efforts.[18]

The repackaged strategic communication goals redefined the messages as follows:

a. *Resolve*—We are realistic about the challenges we face and our goals. At the Lisbon summit NATO/ISAF reaffirmed a resolve that has been demonstrated over the last year by increased forces, resilience in the face of casualties and a high and effective pace of operations.

b. *Maintain momentum*—The effective implementation of our strategy has enabled ISAF and its Afghan partners to increasingly recapture the initiative creating momentum towards success that we will sustain.

c. *Partnership*—NATO's support for Afghanistan will continue beyond the end of the current mission through an enduring partnership. The Afghan people can have confidence in the long-term support of their international partners. NATO/ISAF will work closely with Afghan and international stakeholders, both civilian and military to achieve a stable Afghanistan within a stable region.

d. *Afghan Lead*—The clear and sustained strategy of NATO-ISAF and its partners will enable an irreversible transition to Afghan lead. As transition is implemented, the Afghan Government must take increasing responsibility in all areas, including being responsive and accountable to its public.

Focus Topics: Focus topics provide further guidance on the scope of communication activities, products and programs at the strategic level. During 2011, the focus of communication efforts was on the following topics which provide opportunities to promote and/or reinforce the themes:

a. *Communicate ISAF Progress* to maintain Afghan and international support for the continuation of the mission. Progress must be communicated credibly, making appropriate use of campaign objectives, priorities and theatre-defined measures of effect. In particular, progress will need to reflect what has happened in the ten years since 9/11.

b. *ANSF growth and development* as both an enabler for and part of transition to Afghan lead, with an emphasis on highlighting qualitative improvements, an increasing Afghan lead in the planning and execution of operations, and that the structures and resources are in place to enable progress to be sustained.

c. *Transition implementation* as a conditions-based, irreversible and sustainable process led by the Afghans with ISAF support. Successful transition will require the Afghan Government to take responsibility and be accountable to the public. Alliance communication activities must reflect the Afghan lead, and not detract from it.

d. *An Enduring NATO/Afghanistan Partnership.* NATO demonstrates its evolving commitment to Afghanistan through a mutually-agreed action programme which will endure beyond the completion of the ISAF mission.

e. *Mission evolution* underpinned by reinvestment of resources, measured troop drawdown, evolution of PRTs to Provincial Support Teams and Alliance solidarity.

f. *Delivery of civilian effect* to consolidate security gains and ensure outcome of campaign no longer in doubt. Promote, in partnership with the Afghan Government, the delivery of government services and the enduring and stable political settlement necessary for success.

g. *Regional Dimension.* Use multilateral fora to highlight the key importance of a regional dimension in stabilizing Afghanistan and the broader region.[19]

The core strategic message at this time emphasized the partnership among the United States, NATO-ISAF, and Afghanistan: "This mission is essential for our shared security. Our strategy is sound, our long-term commitment is solid and with our Afghan partners we will succeed."[20] The facts on the ground suggested otherwise.

Following the conclusion of the NATO-ISAF mission mandate in late 2014, the NATO-led Resolute Support Mission–Afghanistan (RSMA) began on January 1, 2015. It sought to "build on the achievements made by the now completed ISAF mission while officially and formally recognizing Afghan Security Forces' growing capabilities and their assumption of full security responsibility for the future of Afghanistan."[21] It operated under a training and advising directive that supported four lines of effort: to posture the force, to protect the force, to complete the building of Afghan security institutions and of Afghan national defense and security forces, and to support the ongoing political transition. These four lines of effort then focused on eight essential functions: (1) multiyear budgeting and the execution of programs; (2) transparency, accountability, and oversight; (3) civilian governance; (4) force generation; (5) sustainment; (6) strategy and policy planning, resourcing, and execution; (7) intelligence; and (8) strategic communication.

The eighth essential function—strategic communication—relied on a train, advise, and assist framework to create a consistent message among Afghan institutions, such as the Ministry of Interior and Ministry of Defense. It combined two components: one focused on potential friends and the other focused on foes.

The effort focused on friends combined government relations, media communication, issue management, and information dissemination and fell under the management of the Government Media Information Center and the Cross Ministry News Desk. The Afghan government and general population were the most likely intended audiences for these efforts. The Government Media Information Center coordinated, produced, and distributed accurate and timely information; trained Afghan communicators; and provided a venue for press briefings. The Cross Ministry News Desk was an information nerve center comprising representatives from the Ministries of Defense and Interior, the National Directorate of Security, and the Independent Directorate of Local Governance. The desk allowed these representatives to coordinate and disseminate press releases and official statements about Afghan security operations and activities.

The second component of the strategic communication effort focused on countering and disrupting insurgent communication through messaging at the national level. This included standard message-dissemination techniques such as billboards, leaflets, and radio and TV spots. The most likely intended audiences were the insurgent leadership, the insurgent rank and file, and the local Afghan population.[22] At the tactical and operational level, communication efforts targeting insurgents and their leadership sought to undermine their morale, counter their propaganda, exploit their fissures, and disrupt their wider support and supply network. But most of these efforts proved ineffective. Strategic communication requires understanding not only the intended audiences but also the IO efforts of the enemy. IO strategies and tactics cannot be viewed in isolation.

The Taliban Choice of Message and Medium

The Afghan Taliban identifies itself as the "Islamic Emirate of Afghanistan (IEA)," the protector of Islam, and the only legitimate authority able to implement social justice through the implementation of Shar'iah law. Undoubtedly the name is meant to confer authority and legitimacy. It must always be remembered that 99 percent of Afghans are Muslims, and Islam plays a critical role in Afghan life.[23] Religious narratives have remained a foundation of the Afghan Taliban movement since its earliest inception during the civil war period between 1991 and 1996. Even during the anti-Soviet jihad in the late 1970s and the 1980s, mujahidin effectively used IO and narratives to counter the Soviet occupation.[24]

The Taliban continues to use Islamic piety, based on the strict dogmatic Deobandi interpretation of Islam, to construct a righteous jihadist image to justify its violent antigovernment military campaign.[25] Deobandi Islam is an egalitarian model that seeks to emulate the life and times of the Prophet Mohammed. The Taliban uses Islam, with its terminology of jihad, *shaheed* (martyrdom), and Shar'iah (Islamic canonical law), as the primary vehicle to target a wide variety of audiences, including the local, regional, and global Islamic communities as well as international audiences. The United States cannot counter these religious narratives with any authority. The Afghan population has met all US attempts with disdain for the messenger and message.[26] As a result, the United States and NATO-ISAF have conceded 90 percent of the IO-narrative battle space in Afghanistan. This, in turn, has undermined US missions, strategies, and tactics.

According to the Taliban, jihad is an obligatory war for *all* Muslims, particularly Afghans, and must be undertaken against all enemies of Islam, including infidels, apostates, and their supporters, both civil and military. The Taliban appears to pick with care the topics for such media as their *Taranas* (musical chants), an effective Afghan IO method, so that the message expresses in local dialects deeply held Afghan and particularly Pashtun values. Taliban chants use symbolism and iconic portraits to evoke sorrow, pride, desperation, hope, and complaint within an overarching narrative often delivered in familiar poetic forms designed to resonate with local audiences.[27]

Every Muslim's duty to protect Islam is a central theme, designed to gain recruits and allegiance; this theme remains a powerful motivator among rural Afghans. The Taliban effectively used Islamic rhetoric to legitimize its actions and fuel anger against the foreign forces. Most Afghans accept Allah's divine will and believe that Allah will punish the oppressor (i.e., foreign invaders) because Allah is fair and just. In rural and even in some urban areas, mullahs hold a near monopoly on religious authority; they define what is right or wrong. In rural areas the mullahs have developed a powerful patron-client relationship with the local population, allowing the Taliban to deliver a coordinated narrative, which the United States cannot counter.

The Taliban has ascribed *shaheed*, or "martyr," to its fighters killed in combat, not just those who commit suicide bombings. The belief that *shaheed* will be rewarded in heaven facilitates popular mobilization and the recruitment of suicide bombers from the madrassa (Islamic religious school) networks in Pakistan, including many in North and South Waziristan. By 2007 over 80 percent of all suicide bombers in Afghanistan had first traversed one or both of these tribal areas.[28] Nearly all Taliban and Afghan insurgent literature features obituaries of Taliban *shaheed*. Recently, music and poetry has also venerated *shaheed*, especially suicide bombers and well-known Taliban commanders killed in battle. During the Soviet-Afghan War, many mujahidin fighters were eulogized as *shaheed*. In 2011 US forces had the Taliban-produced book *Convoy of Martyrs* translated. It offers Quran-based advice for jihad, eulogizes fifteen Taliban fighters killed in combat, and concludes with warrior poetry. Similar propaganda appears throughout Taliban periodicals, websites, newsletters, and interviews.

The Taliban strategic communication campaign also emphasizes the Shar'iah. To resolve disputes, Afghan villagers do not typically rely on the Kabul government (viewed as inefficient and corrupt at best and as a US puppet generally). Some communities view the Taliban as able and willing to resolve disputes quickly and without bribery.[29] By contrast, Afghans paid an estimated $3 billion in bribes to the government in 2015, an almost 50 percent increase compared to 2014, according to a survey conducted by Afghan Integrity Watch. The survey also reported that respondents who dealt with Afghan government courts were asked for bribes 55 percent of the time.[30] Taliban leaders conveyed their intentions regarding Shar'iah during an interview in late June 2011 in a district of Nuristan Province in the northeast that had been under Taliban control since March. According to Mullah Omar's Eid festival message of September 8, 2010:

> Hamdullah [Praise be to Allah], the *mujahideen* are now in charge of this area, and the people's problems are solved under Shari'ah law. The tribe(s) welcomed us, and now they bring us their problems and we deal with them. They understand implementing Shar'iah is one of their duties. . . . Smoking is forbidden here; our religious department will punish those who intoxicate themselves. Schools and hospitals are open; under Shar'iah law . . . we will respect the Islamic rights of all people of the country including women; will implement Shar'iah rules in the light of the injunctions of the sacred religion of Islam in order to efficiently maintain internal security and eradicate immortality, injustice, indecency and other vices; will strictly observe the law of punishment and reward and auditing in order to bring about administrative transparency in all government departments. The violators will be dealt with according to the Shar'iah rules.[31]

The Taliban's goals remain to evict foreign troops, to overthrow the Kabul government, to restore to power the IEA, and to implement Shar'iah law. The key messages are (1) Taliban victory in the cosmic conflict is inevitable; (2) Islam cannot be defeated; (3) Taliban fighters are national heroes, willing to sacrifice all for Allah and country; (4) Afghans have a long and honorable history of defeating invading foreign infidels; (5) foreign invaders and their Afghan puppets are attempting to destroy Afghan religion and traditions; and (6) all Afghans have an obligation to join the jihad against the foreigners and apostates.[32]

In the broadest sense the Taliban targets three distinct social identities—religious (Islamic), cultural, and political—that most Afghans share. The Taliban taps into *Pashtunwali* (the way-of-the-Pashtun social code), pride and honor (which extends to non-Pashtun Afghans), and the call for justice (exploiting themes of victimization, independence, and resistance to foreign invaders).[33] As Lt. Col. Ehsan Mehmood Khan noted, "The tradition of Pashtunwali, the Pashtun Social Code, has been combined with Jihad thereby forming a formidable war ideology. This is serving as the nucleus around which everything else is knit and is thus the Centre of Gravity for Taliban Warfare."[34] Again it is nearly impossible for the United States to counter this powerful cultural or sociological dynamic.

Taliban strategy relies on intelligence collection at the local level to pinpoint specific grievances and accusations to incorporate into its messages to strengthen its influence.[35] Unlike the US-led international coalition, the Taliban continually focuses and acts at the village level (*kalay*). The insurgency depends on the narrative of mandatory jihad, particularly in rural areas, and exploits the grievances (real or perceived) of local communities against corrupt and predatory government representatives. The Taliban targets messages and propaganda at the southern and eastern Pashtun-dominated provinces, the location of the Taliban's traditional base of support.

The official website sponsors a series of official militant magazines available for download. Most are published in Pashto, some articles appear in Dari, and one magazine, *al Samood*, is intended for an Arabic-literate audience. Most periodicals are available in slickly produced, full-color hard-copy versions, although primarily through vendors in Peshawar and Quetta, Pakistan.

But most Afghans cannot read and live in isolated rural areas without electricity and limited connectivity to the internet. The communications methods employed by the Taliban in these areas consist of direct contact (oral communications), radio transmissions, and the distribution of *shabnamah* (night letters)—crudely written statements posted on walls or doors inside villages, often in the dead of night.[36] These methods are low-tech, cheap, and extremely effective. Night letters were effective during the Soviet-Afghan War and reappeared following the Taliban's ouster in November 2001. The messages, themes, and intended audiences of these night letters reveal how the Taliban intimidates and influences community decisions. Night letters generally address an entire village or district and often threaten violence or death if demands are not met. Sometimes they "advise" the intended audience—a whole district or village or influential community leaders—on issues of conduct or warn of an impending attack. In theory these communities could be equally susceptible to government- or coalition-sponsored radio programs, repeated face-to-face interactions, or "mobile-mullah" programs. In recent years night letters have not been used as often as they were in earlier years.

Poetry is another important medium of communication because it is primarily a spoken, not written, art and so is accessible to the literate and illiterate alike.[37] Pashto culture emphasizes poetry, Afghans commonly memorize poetry, and educated Afghans consider their country to be a nation of poets.[38] Rhythm and rhyme aid memorization, while short lyrics can embed deep thoughts. The political events of the past three decades have greatly contributed to the dominance of poetry over other literary genres. War, destruction, and the loss of millions of lives have left deep psychological wounds. Poetry has become an effective medium to express feelings of sorrow, anger, pride, hope, desperation, and patriotism. Conflict and political turmoil have politicized poetry. Afghans memorize resonating lyrics reflective of their values, beliefs, and socioeconomic realities. Thus, poetry offers a window into the Afghan mind.

The lyrics surface in daily conversations. To make a point, to offer an example, and even to prove a claim, Afghans often weave a *tak-baiti*, a "one-liner," or a *do-baiti*, a "two-liner," into their speech. Poetry is so prevalent in daily conversation that many lines are synonymous with proverbs and axioms. Unfortunately, these critical pieces of communication are often "lost in translation" during the *shuras*, jirgas, and key meetings between Afghans and US and coalition forces.

Mullah Omar called on the service of Afghan poets to help support the Taliban's military and political objectives in a statement made for the Muslim festival of Eid, released around November 25, 2009: "I also urge the committed and sensible poets to preserve the Jihadic epics and acts of heroism of Mujahideen in their poetry and literary pieces and generate emotions for independence, honor, national unity and Islamic resurgence."[39]

Taliban poets portray their antigovernment efforts as an extension of the efforts to unseat the Marxist government in the early 1980s. Whereas more moderate Afghan poets tend to focus on peace as a theme, Taliban writers emphasize changing the current state of affairs, which revolves around the issue of foreign invasion. They make use of religious terminology far more frequently than do the moderates. Common terms include jihad, crusaders, people of the cross, martyr/*shaheed*, and paradise. They use religious doctrine to justify political and military resistance against the government and coalition forces. They portray cooperation with the state as *be nangi*, a great shame, because the state, in their view, is a puppet of the foreign powers—the infidel invaders. Cooperation with such government means indirect support of the invaders and infidels, making an Afghan supporter of the state *Mulhed*, a "hypocrite." Some argue that being a hypocrite is a graver sin than becoming a *Kafir*, or "infidel."

Taliban authors then leverage guilt and shame to influence readers. Those who cooperate with the government must feel shame both for failing to take action against the infidel invaders and for cooperating with the enemy. The reader must act immediately and join the jihad as his ancestors did when they fought and defeated the Greeks, the Mongols, the Persians, the British, and the Soviets. The authors instigate war and disorder to purify the country of immorality and the irreligiocity of the imposed Western political and economic orders.

Like poetry, chants (*Taranas*) play an important role in Taliban communication with local populations.[40] The chants, communicated in the local language and traditional style, often manipulate traditions, narratives, collective memory of events, and culture to serve Taliban interests. They are melodic, with memorable tunes and often with repeating sections that stick in people's minds. Like advertising jingles, chants are easily memorized, owing to their rhyme, rhythm, and lyrics. They resemble certain types of poetry that are regularly memorized and recited by Afghans. The language of both poetry and chants is the language of *wazn* (balance or rhythm) and *qafia* (rhyme). Abiding by the many other rules of poetry—*badee* (rules for creating a poem) and *arooz* (the art of creating poetic balance and flow)—each verse must maintain a specific *wazn* and continuity in *qafia*. Their combination gives a melodic effect to the lyrics.[41] This enhances both the narrative conveyed and the propaganda value.

In many areas, especially those with a significant Taliban presence, like Loy Kandahar, Taliban chanting has flourished.[42] For example, many Kandahari music shops that used to sell music audiocassettes and musical instruments market Taliban chants. Undoubtedly, the change partly reflects pragmatism, since Kandaharis (and other Afghan urbanites) have been tortured and imprisoned for listening to or participating in other forms of music. In some cases, local singers and musicians have decided to sing Taliban chants, while others have emigrated.[43] The chants have become a source of entertainment and a key component of the Taliban information and propaganda war, powerful tools to instruct and intimidate. Again, the United States cannot respond in kind.

Alemarah, the IEA's official website, first appeared on the World Wide Web in mid-2005 and serves as the Taliban's main source for information operations for both domestic and international audiences. It is a simple website but loaded with religious, cultural, historical, and political messages. Alemarah publishes detailed and up-to-date situation reports on Taliban activities across Afghanistan in five different languages (Pashto, Dari, Urdo, Arabic, and English). Most articles appear in simple syntax. It has sections on Islam, news, commentary, statements, poetry, *Taranas*, articles, books, and magazines and a link for the online Radio Shariat Zhagh (Voice of Shar'iah). Alemarah serves as the virtual public relations center for the Taliban and its viewers.

Although the Taliban's main means of message delivery remains relatively simple—night letters, word of mouth, its website—it has tried to increase its presence on the airwaves. Because the rural population of Afghanistan is generally illiterate, radio programs remain a viable method for communicating. Unlicensed or pirate radio broadcasts conform with the Taliban's reliance on low-tech means of message transmission. The basic equipment can be manufactured or acquired for a few hundred dollars. Most FM radio transmitters come from neighboring countries, such as Pakistan, which is also grappling with a wave of unlicensed Taliban radio programs. The

Pakistan government has confiscated or destroyed several mobile transmission devices belonging to the Pakistani Taliban. The low cost and ready availability of equipment that can be quickly modified and sent back into the field have made disrupting the pirate broadcasts a challenge in both Pakistan and Afghanistan.

Beginning in 2005 the Taliban revitalized its radio program (through pirate broadcasts) in sporadic bursts with the relaunch of Radio Shariat Zhagh from Kandahar, its former stronghold in the south. The spotty signal broadcast for over an hour each night, apparently from mobile transmitters mounted on the back of pickup trucks. In April 2005 Taliban spokesman Mufti Latifullah Hakimi told the Pakistan-based Afghan Islamic Press news agency that Radio Shariat Zhagh was back on the air after a six-month break, although evidence of prior broadcasts was nonexistent after the overthrow of the Taliban in October 2001. The 2005 broadcast consisted of an hourlong program between 0600 to 0700 local time in both Dari and Pashto.

By 2007 media reports indicated Taliban radio programs could be heard in parts of four southeastern provinces—Paktika, Paktia, Khost, and Ghazni—but local officials said the reception remained weak. Similarly, during the ten-month Taliban occupation of Helmand's northern district of Musa Qala between February and December 2007, Radio Shariat Zhagh could be heard throughout the district. Broadcasts included translations of the Koran, calls for jihad, and religious programs. According to a local Taliban spokesman, the radio station had five employees and broadcast on an FM frequency with the traditional Afghan pattern of morning and evening transmissions. By 2009 media reporting concerning the Taliban's radio broadcasts had increased, suggesting an attempt to expand the broadcast area. As late as June 2018 the Taliban was still producing Radio Shariat Zhagh programs in Ghazni Province, prompting an Afghan Air Force aerial bombardment of a suspected broadcasting tower, much to the outrage of local Taliban commanders.[44]

The Taliban has used the internet to expand its broadcast capabilities. In June 2009 the Taliban Pashtu language website Shahamat (Valor), previously at www.shahamat.org, launched an online version of Radio *Shariat Zhagh*. The internet-based radio service streamed news, commentaries, and jihadist songs and updates during daily morning and evening broadcasts.

In February 2011 Alemarah published an interview with the site's editor, Abdul Satar Maiwandi.[45] According to Maiwandi, "Wars today cannot be won without media. Media aims at the heart rather than the body, [and] if the heart is defeated, the battle is won." The interview revealed for the first time the venues and objectives of the Taliban's IO. These included email, texting, tweets, blogs, YouTube, and Facebook. Maiwandi emphasized the importance of both the official Taliban website and expanded use of social media, specifically Facebook and Twitter, to disseminate

Taliban messages. While the Afghan government in Kabul is conspicuously absent from social-networking sites, the Taliban has pioneered their use to reach Afghan youth and young adults. A few years ago the Taliban relied on jihadi forums and blogs, while today it has turned to social-networking sites. It has also studied the impact of social media on the Arab Spring.

Before the US invasion in 2001, there were only 2,000 internet users in the whole of Afghanistan; as of December 31, 2017, the county had 5,700,905 internet users. In addition, there were over 3.2 million Facebook subscribers as of December 2017.[46] This number is expected to increase given the large investment in information technology in Afghanistan.[47]

The Taliban increasingly uses Facebook, where it has a relatively large network of friends across the word. Currently, over 2,000 Facebook members "like" the Islamic State of Afghanistan page, which seems to be the Taliban's official Facebook page; supporters each have hundreds of friends with whom to share pro-Taliban narratives. The official Facebook page provides timely news updates, videos, chants, photos, and conversations on specific topics. In addition, several individual Facebook pages under various names share Taliban-related news coverage and propaganda. As this chapter was being finalized, Facebook authorities apparently took down the most prominent Taliban page. However, it seems that the Taliban continues to network under individuals' names. These individuals' profiles often carry al Qaeda and Taliban content. Presently the size of the Taliban audience is limited perhaps to several thousand people. However, it will most likely increase with the expansion of internet access in Afghanistan.

The Taliban also had an official Twitter account with over 5,600 followers before it was suspended in 2011.[48] The Taliban regularly tweeted news updates concerning its exaggerated "military achievements," such as "9 U.S. invaders killed and wounded, two tanks destroyed in Logar battle," "4 puppets killed in clash with Mujahideen," or "Mujahideen kills 12 U.S.-Afghan cowardly troops in martyr attack."[49]

Conclusion: The Strategic Communication Mismatch

The Taliban uses simple, powerful messages like "force the invaders to withdraw" and "reestablish Shar'iah," while the United States lurches from one package of convoluted messages to another. Complexity is a US, not a Taliban, problem. The simplicity of the Taliban's strategic aims has remained constant since the group's early success in 1994, when it vowed to accomplish (and largely achieved) two highly desired objectives: establish security and instill law and order through swift Islamic-based justice.[50]

The Taliban's messaging spectrum and narrative universe is finite. The number of objectives, messages, and narratives can be identified and framed within a given outline. The Taliban then draws on this information-message-narrative treasure chest and plugs messages in to the many delivery systems available. Despite early misunderstanding of some technology, such as cellular phones and the internet, the resurgent Taliban and other Afghan insurgent groups have leveraged modern communications technology to their advantage. DVDs and CDs, video productions, web pages, text messaging, Twitter, and Bluetooth dissemination of audio and video files are some of the modern delivery systems the Taliban uses to spread its views.

Groups like the Taliban profit from the inability of the United States and the Afghan government to launch a meaningful counterattack against the proliferation of jihadist messages on local and international media outlets. While the Taliban has effectively used narratives and communications media well-known to the average Afghan and has expanded into new media to reflect new realities, the United States and its NATO-ISAF allies have relied on a poorly formulated leaflet program, billboards, and radio messages that in most instances have little resonance with the Afghan population. In September 2017 it was widely reported that US Special Forces developed and air-dropped thousands of leaflets depicting the Taliban as a dog with the Islamic *shahada*, or profession of faith, written on its side.[51] This was extremely offensive to many Muslim Afghans and demonstrated that the US had learned little over the past seventeen years concerning what resonates and what offends Afghans.

The United States continues to focus most of its IO on urban areas. This has proved counterproductive because the war has primarily been a rural insurgency or jihad. The trust and confidence (or in US military parlance, "hearts and minds") to be won are in rural, not urban, Afghanistan, and the United States is a messenger ill-suited to deliver messages to a deeply antiforeign and devoutly Muslim audience.

Notes

This chapter represents an earlier version of sections from a number of chapters in Thomas H. Johnson, *Taliban Narratives: The Power and Use of Stories in the Afghanistan Conflict*, with Matthew C. DuPée and Wali Shaaker (New York: Oxford University Press, 2018).

1. For example, see Anthony H. Cordesman, *Losing the "Forgotten War": The Need to Reshape US Strategy in Afghanistan, Pakistan, and Central Asia* (Washington, DC: Center for Strategic and International Studies, October 6, 2014), http://csis.org /files/publication/141006_Losing_the_Forgotten_War_Final.pdf; and Gian P. Gentile, "A Strategy of Tactics: Population-Centric COIN and the Army," *Parameters*, Autumn 2009, 5–17.

2. See Thomas H. Johnson, *Taliban Narratives: The Power and Use of Stories in the Afghanistan Conflict*, with Matthew C. DuPée and Wali Shaaker (New York: Oxford University Press, 2018).

3. A senior Pentagon official told the senior author of this chapter that the initial US Afghan air operations were delayed several days because the initial US IO campaign had not been finalized. The United States was still behind schedule in completing its initial set of leaflets to be dropped into Afghanistan to correspond with their air campaign.

4. For an example of some of these leaflets, see Psywarrior, "Leaflets Dropped over Afghanistan Operation Enduring Freedom," accessed February 25, 2015, http://www.psywarrior.com/Afghanleaflinks.html.

5. See Johnson, *Taliban Narratives*, for a detailed analysis of US leaflets and their utility.

6. Both authors participated in various aspects of the US and ISAF strategic communication effort in Afghanistan between 2008 and 2012.

7. Francis Scott Main, *Psychological Operations Support to Strategic Communications in Afghanistan* (Carlisle Barracks, PA: US Army War College, 2009), 2.

8. For an excellent discussion of "narratives" and war, see Jill Lepore, *The Name of War: King Phillip's War and the Origins of American Identity* (New York: Alfred A. Knopf, 1998); Douglas Porch, *The Conquest of Morocco* (New York: Farrar, Straus, and Giroux, 2005). For Afghan narratives, see Thomas H. Johnson, "The Taliban Insurgency and an Analysis of *Shabnamah* (Night Letters)," *Small Wars and Insurgencies* 18, no. 3 (September 2007): 317–44.

9. International Crisis Group, *Taliban Propaganda: Winning the War of Words?* Asia Report No. 158 (Brussels: International Crisis Group, 2008).

10. Arturo Munoz, *U.S. Military Information Operations in Afghanistan: Effectiveness of Psychological Operations, 2001–2010* (Santa Monica, CA: RAND, 2012), 33.

11. US Deputy Secretary of Defense, "Implementation of the DOD Strategic Communication Plan for Afghanistan," memorandum, September 12, 2007.

12. US Deputy Secretary of Defense.

13. Authors' field research in Afghanistan, 2008–10.

14. Thomas H. Johnson, "Religious Figures, Insurgency, and Jihad in Southern Afghanistan," in *Who Speaks for Islam? Muslim Grassroots Leaders and Popular Preachers in South Asia*, NBR Special Report #22 (Seattle: National Bureau of Asian Research, February 2010), 41–65.

15. Originally written in *Joint Forces Quarterly* and cited in Daniel Nasaw, "Mullen Blasts US 'Strategic Communication' Efforts in Afghanistan," *Guardian*, August 28, 2009, http://www.theguardian.com/world/2009/aug/28/mullen-afghanistan-communication.

16. Main, *Psychological Operations Support*, 5.

17. For an extensive review of the Haqqani Network and its criminal activities, see Vahid Brown and Don Rassler, *Fountainhead of Jihad: The Haqqani Nexus, 1973–2012* (New York: Columbia University Press, 2013); Thomas Ruttig, "The Haqqani Network as an Autonomous Entity," in *Decoding the New Taliban: Insights from the Afghan Field*, ed. Antonio Guistozzi (New York: Columbia University Press, 2009), 57–88; and Matthew DuPée, "Afghanistan's Conflict Minerals: The Crime-State-Insurgent Nexus," *CTC Sentinel* 5, no. 2 (February 12, 2012), https://www.ctc.usma .edu/posts/afghanistans-conflict-minerals-the-crime-state-insurgent-nexus.

18. Consult the numerous reports of the special inspector general for Afghan reconstruction (SIGAR) for specific details.

19. Chief of Staff, Supreme Headquarters Allied Powers Europe, "NATO/ISAF Strategic Communication Framework 2011," February 24, 2011, https://info.public intelligence.net/NATO-STRATCOM-Afghanistan.pdf.

20. Chief of Staff, Supreme Headquarters Allied Powers Europe.

21. US Army, "Resolute Support," *Stand-To!*, March 13, 2015, http://www.army.mil /standto/archive_2015-03-13/?s_cid=standto.

22. NATO, "RSM Essential Function 8: Strategic Communication," fact sheet, accessed June 18, 2015, https://web.archive.org/web/20150421213218/http://www.rs.nato .int/article/rs-news/rsm-essential-function-8-strategic-communication.html.

23. CIA, "Afghanistan," *The World Factbook*, last modified March 1, 2019, https://www .cia.gov/library/publications/the-world-factbook/geos/af.html.

24. For rich examples of anti-Soviet propaganda produced by the Afghan mujahidin, see Matthew Trevithick, "The Not-So-Funny Papers," *Foreign Policy*, October 26, 2012, https://foreignpolicy.com/slideshow/the-not-so-funny-papers/#4.

25. Matthew C. DuPée, "The Taliban," in *World Almanac of Islamism* (Washington, DC: American Foreign Policy Council, 2013).

26. Thomas H. Johnson's field research in Kandahar, Afghanistan, August 2010.

27. Thomas H. Johnson and Ahwad Waheed, "Analyzing Taliban *Taranas* (Chants): An Effective Afghan Propaganda Artifact," *Small Wars and Insurgencies* 22, no. 1 (March 2011): 3–31.

28. *Suicide Attacks in Afghanistan (2001–2007)* (Kabul: UN Assistance Mission in Afghanistan, September 9, 2007), 68.

29. In 2007–9 the authors spoke to numerous Kandahari businessmen who would regularly use the Taliban justice system, then housed in Zangabad, Panjwai, until it was attacked by US Special Forces, to resolve disputes, especially land and water disputes.

30. Integrity Watch, "Afghans Pay Close to $3b in Bribes Annually," December 6, 2016, https://iwaweb.org/wp-content/uploads/2016/12/Finalized-Press-Release-For-Print -english.pdf.

31. Nick Paton Walsh, "Taliban Back in Town?" CNN, June 22, 2011.

32. Johnson, *Taliban Narratives.*

33. *Pashtunwali* is an informal and unwritten social code based around a series of various social identifiers and values, including *merana* (willpower and tenacity), *melmastia* (hospitality), *namus* (honor/reputation), *himmat* (ambitiousness), *sharam* (shame), and *badal* (literally "exchange," but also used to refer to one seeking revenge).

34. Ehsan Mehmood Khan, "A Strategic Perspective on Taliban Warfare," *Small Wars Journal*, March 22, 2010.

35. Ben Brandt, "The Taliban's Conduct of Intelligence and Counterintelligence," *CTC Sentinel* 4, no. 6 (June 2011): 19–23.

36. While many *shabnamah* are handwritten, typically nearly illegible and rife with bad grammar, some are typed and printed out using modern computer and printer capabilities. See Johnson, "Taliban Insurgency."

37. For a relevant discussion about the role poetry plays in contemporary Afghanistan, see Johnson, *Taliban Narratives.*

38. Mikhail Pelevin and Matthias Weinreich, "The Songs of the Taliban: Continuity of Form and Thought in an Ever-Changing Environment," *Iran and the Caucasus* 16, no. 1 (2012): 45–46.

39. The Eid statement attributed to Mullah Omar was first published by the Taliban's Voice of Jihad website in November 2009. For a replication of the statement, please see Bill Roggio, "Mullah Omar Rejects Negotiations," *Threat Matrix* (blog), November 26, 2009, https://www.longwarjournal.org/archives/2009/11/mullah _omar_rejects_negotiatio.php.

40. For a comprehensive analysis of how the Afghan Taliban harnessed the full potential of chants in their propaganda efforts, see Johnson and Waheed, "Analyzing Taliban Taranas."

41. The Taliban usage of poetry follows the boundaries of Ghazal, which is arguably the most popular classical form of poetry. We suspect the Taliban use similar techniques in their creation of *Taranas.*

42. Loy Kandahar is a common term used by Afghans to describe the contemporary provinces of Kandahar, Helmand, Uruzgan, and Zabul.

43. Kandahar City resident, interview by Thomas H. Johnson, June 2009.

44. "Afghan Taliban Decry Radio Tower Bombing as Attack on Free Speech," Reuters, June 12, 2018.

45. English translation of "Interview with 'Abd al-Sattār Maywand, the Administrator of the Islamic Emirate Website," *Islamic Emirate of Afghanistan's al-Ṣomūd Magazine*, no. 55 (February 17, 2011), https://jihadology.net/2011/02/17/english-translation-of -an-interview-with-abd-al-sattar-maywand-the-administrator-of-the-islamic-emirate -website-from-issue-55-of-the-islamic-emirate-of-afghanistan%E2%80%99s-al -%E1%B9%A3omud-maga/.

46. "Asia," Internet World Stats, accessed March 21, 2019, https://www.internetworld stats.com/asia.htm.

47. Afghan Growth Finance, "SEAF-AGF and RANA Technologies Enterprises Partner to Expand Internet Service in Afghanistan," January 24, 2011, https://www.seaf .com/seaf-agf-rana-technologies-enterprises-partner-to-expand-internet-service-in -afghanistan/.

48. The official Taliban Twitter account is http://twitter.com/#!/alemarahweb, and it was last updated June 19, 2011. (This account is suspended. However, the Abdulqahar Balkhi @balkhi_a account (https://twitter.com/balkhi_a) had 1,424 followers, the zabihullah mujahid @Zmujahid1 account (https://twitter.com/Zmujahid1) had 478 followers, and the qarimuhamadyosufahma @Ahmadi786Qya account (https:// twitter.com/Ahmadi786Qya) had 358 followers, as of June 17, 2015. We suspect the lower range of followers is because most of the Taliban-affiliated accounts are routinely suspended. The @balkhi_a account provides a link to the English version of the Afghan Taliban website (http://shahamat-english.com/).

49. Erin Cunningham, "In Shift, Taliban Embrace New Media," *Global Post*, May 21, 2011, https://www.pri.org/stories/2011-05-21/shift-taliban-embrace-new-media; and Doug Gross, "Taliban Begin Tweeting in English, Add Followers," CNN, May 13, 2011, http://www.cnn.com/2011/TECH/social.media/05/13/taliban.twitter /index.html.

50. Early reports from the time the Taliban was created indicated the movement did not seek wider political authority other than the reestablishment of law and order in Kandahar Province.

51. The *shahada* is the most fundamental expression of Islamic beliefs and one of Islam's key pillars. It simply states, "There is no God but God and Muhammad is his prophet." "US Apologized for Offensive Leaflets in Parwan," *Al Jazeera*, September 6, 2017, https://www.aljazeera.com/news/2017/09/apologises-offensive-leaflets -parwan-170906064404739.html.

14.

The Challenge of Outcommunicating the Islamic State

Haroro J. Ingram and Craig A. Whiteside

The question asked and addressed in this chapter is deceptively simple: In a contest between a state and an armed group—Robert Taber's classic *War of the Flea*—how can a state outcommunicate the armed group? Or to use Taber's framework: How can a state outshout the flea?

On the one hand, it comes as no surprise that the United States has found it lamentably difficult to establish sufficient infrastructure, budget, or personnel to execute an effective strategic communications plan against the Islamic State (IS).[1] In contrast, and perhaps more surprisingly, the flea—IS—developed a resilient infrastructure based on semiautonomous regional and local cells staffed by the most competent individuals in the organization. Moreover, the IS media operation overcame multiple cyberattacks on its delivery systems and physical attacks on its personnel and centers, and by mid-2018, when our analysis ended, IS's media operations were far more effective than those of the states that opposed it.[2]

A quick note on terminology is important at this point: The term "strategic communications" is used in this chapter to describe any message produced and publicly disseminated that is intended to have an operational or strategic effect on target audiences as part of a broader politico-military campaign.[3] Whether the communication is designed to inform, influence, or manipulate is a subjective judgment, which this analysis avoids with the more generic notion of "affect." Used in this way, strategic communications avoid the negative connotations associated with a term such as "propaganda"; the organizational connotations for a term such as "information operations," which is generally associated with the military; and the content limitations associated with specific terms, such as "nonviolent material," or specific types of messaging, such as psychological operations.

Given this context, measuring the efficacy of wartime strategic communications campaigns is extraordinarily difficult, and this difficulty is compounded by the multiple phases of IS's evolution.[4] We use the framework for this book—message, messenger, and medium—to consider the effectiveness of the IS and US government communication programs by assessing whether the messages can *reach* their target audience through appropriate means of communication and maintain their *relevance*. Moreover, the deeper psychological and social impact of messaging depends on *resonance*, its ability to leverage psychosocial factors such as identity and culture. The IS movement and the US State Department both monitor their respective strategic communications campaigns and provide the data for a rudimentary comparison along these lines—reach, relevance, and resonance. We begin the chapter by considering the IS movement's strategic communications, which it monitors closely for effectiveness. In contrast, we then consider the US State Department's "Think Again Turn Away" program, which uses three criteria to measure the efficacy of communication campaigns: reach, relevance, and resonance.[5]

The Expanding Reach, Relevance, and Resonance of IS Communications

What is known today as IS evolved under a series of names from a small group in 1999 into a pseudostate at the forefront of a war resumed in 2014. Its media infrastructure and personnel are part of a continuous organ that dates to late 2003 and that has been instrumental in facilitating and heralding each evolutionary phase of the movement. The IS movement traces its own lineage back to a small group of Salafi jihadists under the leadership of Abu Musab al Zarqawi, a Jordanian who spent time in Afghanistan in the 1990s training with key individuals in the global jihadi movement.[6] Zarqawi and a small cohort of fighters traveled in 2002 to the autonomous Kurdish area of Iraq to get closer to home and prepare for a possible American invasion of Iraq. Zarqawi's vision: the establishment of an Islamic state somewhere in the Levant/Mesopotamia.[7] Following the US invasion in 2003, Zarqawi's group—called Tawhid wal-Jihad in the beginning—began its campaign by detonating several large car bombs on targets chosen to frame the developing resistance in jihadist terms while driving out international agencies and undermining support for the new government, most notably the bombing of the Baghdad UN headquarters on August 19, 2003.[8] At the time the group had no apparatus or formal standing to claim responsibility for these attacks and remained quiet about them despite US accusations that it was responsible.[9]

In January 2004 the group went public when a media representative began posting Zarqawi's statements on jihadist forums, sending out a call for volunteers to join the fight against the "crusaders and apostates."[10] This new campaign was inspired by previous "foreign fighter" flows to jihadist campaigns in Afghanistan, Syria, Algeria, the Balkans, and Chechnya, and Zarqawi hoped to replicate the influx of foreign volunteers while strengthening the international community of those educated and imbued with the Salafi jihadist *manhaj* (method).[11]

A small media unit, consisting of an official spokesman, an unknown number of workers, and a media "emir" in charge, served as the group's outward face on the internet in early 2004. A network of external sympathizers assisted this department, mostly from outside the country, helping spread the group's message in the larger Salafi jihadist milieu.[12] The original Tawhid wal Jihad spokesman was a young Iraqi religious student named Abu Maysara al-Iraqi, who tapped into the quantum growth of the internet to spread the group's message worldwide.[13] Spokesman for a little over two years, he served as the prototype for the rest—trained or self-taught students and teachers of the Salafi tradition able to deliver the "correct" religious message.[14] Within a year of the media unit's creation, the strategic communications problem facing the United States had changed dramatically. During the invasion of Iraq in 2003, the US had an easy time besting Saddam's information minister, whom US officials mockingly called "Baghdad Bob." By mid-2004 US officials charged with pushing Zarqawi's group off the web were flummoxed by an elusive but highly effective millennial-generation Iraqi with part-time internet access in a café.[15]

The catalyst for this shift in the asymmetrical balance between the US and the future core of the Islamic State was the new communications medium of the internet, largely and ironically available because of the new freedoms introduced in Iraq after 2003. Whereas in the late 1990s jihadis had spread their literature manually through audiotapes and CDs, the growth of the internet allowed them to expand both the quantity and quality of their communications.[16] Jihadist theorist Abu Musab al Suri commented on the dynamics of the new media in his tome *Call to Global Islamic Resistance*. He noted that the internet had facilitated a shift from an elite to a mass audience, the messaging focused on a more popular purpose by calling for jihad to protect Muslim communities, the new visual and audio possibilities injected passion and emotion into what had been an academic discussion, and an open distribution system replaced the old clandestine method.[17]

Before 2007 most IS movement statements celebrated the actions of its "knights of monotheism" against cowardly enemies, including the Americans or "crusaders," the "apostate" Iraqi government and Kurdish Peshmerga, and rival Shia militias, such as the Mahdi (devil) Army and the Badr (treachery) Corps. The heavy use of code words that allowed the rapid spread of this line of messaging both confirmed Zarqawi's wisdom in taking on a powerful array of enemies and justified his targeting strategy.[18] The remaining topics consisted of statements by leaders, defenses against external criticism, verbal attacks on rivals, and denials or counteraccusations. Al Qaeda's al-Fajr media office distributed Zarqawi's messages to a global network of supporters.[19] Eventually, to improve the quality of multimedia products, the IS movement created its own production unit, called the al-Furqan media enterprise, in late 2006.[20]

Overshadowing the novelty of a productive young media department was the impact of its early viral videos. Poor in quality, they were popular because of the shock value of their content: decapitation videos featuring the leader of the group butchering captured Westerners. These videos were the movement's attempt to gain attention as it struggled to grow amid the chaos of a civil war. The media strategy succeeded in getting notice, but the strong rebukes from al Qaeda and from both friendly and hostile news networks forced Zarqawi to abandon the experiment.[21] After his death, his successors resurrected this genre of graphic videos showing the killing of their enemies in humiliating ways in 2014, reflecting IS's enduring attitudes and operational codes.

Zarqawi attempted to redress the hostile backlash in Iraq by emphasizing branding, but branding changes risked undermining the group's reputation. Tawhid wal Jihad struggled to recruit in an environment crowded with small, mostly nationally based groups resisting the US-led occupation. To elevate his group's status, Zarqawi negotiated its acceptance as an al Qaeda franchise and changed its name to Tanzim Qaidat al-Jihad fi Bilad al-Rafidayn (Organization of Jihad's Base in Mesopotamia)—better known as al Qaeda in Iraq (AQI).[22] The connection provided instant and global name recognition as well as the funding necessary to become the dominant Salafi jihadist group in Iraq. Zarqawi's AQI became the vanguard of a political front representing a handful of Iraqi resistance groups. AQI then "joined" the political front, Mujahideen Shura Council (MSC), in January 2006. In reality the overwhelming majority of front members belonged to AQI, making this union a bit of a political ploy. To emphasize a transition to something newer and fresher, the name AQI was discarded, and the group became the Islamic State of Iraq (ISI) in October 2006. The new name allowed the group to move beyond criticism of its previous behavior while at the same time suggesting a level of inclusivity and unity that did not truly exist at the time, despite its public incorporation of several smaller groups into the new *dawla Islamiyah*. The move also highlighted its expansion from a small group with local cells into a national organization with regional and local branches focused on state building.[23]

The IS movement created this structure to enforce leader preferences, to prioritize the use of violence, and to control the collection and allocation of resources.[24] Jacob Shapiro describes the organizational structure as an "M-form" hierarchy: a central management structure with functional bureaus that are replicated at each of the lower levels, or what IS calls *wilayets* (provinces). Although the central level controlled planning and shared resources, such as incoming foreign fighters and excess revenue from subordinate units, the geographic units had significant autonomy in implementing the centrally devised plans—allowing for much-needed decentralized execution for an insurgency. After 2006 each *wilayet* included functional bureaus for administration, movement and maintenance, legal matters, military, security, medicine, confiscated property, and media.[25]

A belated US realization of the growing strength of the ISI media program transformed both its spokesmen and its media centers into priority targets.[26] The campaign reached its peak in the summer of 2007, when a series of US raids targeted the upper media structure, killing the official spokesman and capturing the media emir—essentially its chief executive officer. The reported results of the raid, however, demonstrate the growth of the media enterprise in the new Islamic State. One al-Furqan media center near Samarra contained 65 hard drives with 18 terabytes of data, 500 compact discs, and 12 computers. The facility had the capability to mass-produce 156 CDs in eight hours and a fully functioning film studio with modern equipment.[27] Over eight unique media offices at different levels were disrupted throughout Iraq during this frenetic cycle of special operations raids.[28] Although this counterterrorism activity resulted in substantial gaps in video releases, ISI continued to post operational summaries and statements online in friendly forums, demonstrating a resiliency that would fuel its return to relevance in 2013.[29]

In late 2007 the Sahwa (Awakening) movement—a mix of Sunni tribes and resistance groups that flipped to support the government—forced ISI out of Sunni areas and underground. The one place it retained some measure of influence was in and around the northern city of Mosul, Iraq's second most-populous city. Although it no longer could control territory, ISI maintained clandestine cells in its old haunts to continue its terrorist activities, which its various *wilayet*-level and central media offices then publicized throughout Iraq.[30] While ISI admitted that it had suffered a serious setback, its leadership refocused priorities on survival with directed terror attacks designed to keep foes off balance and the narrative alive.[31]

By 2010 the group's leadership losses indicated it was in serious difficulty; in 2009 the US-led coalition reported that just eight of ISI's top forty-two leaders remained at large.[32] Although the decapitation campaign put tremendous pressure on the upper echelons, local groups reorganized and conducted a vicious assassination campaign against the Sahwa to regain their sanctuaries in Sunni areas of Iraq.[33] In turn, this rebuilding phase set the condition for a wider campaign against Iraqi security forces that were trumpeted by the al-Furqan and al-Fajr media centers. The newly invigorated media department created videos, like the *Clanging of the Swords* series (June 2012) and the *Windows upon the Land of Epic Battles* (2013), to immortalize their campaign against the Sahwa and herald their expansion into Syria.[34] The combination of original battle footage and scores with original *nasheeds* (Islamic a cappella songs) made a media splash and highlighted the group's military mastery of its enemies.[35] The ISI leadership correctly predicted that successful operations would help convince many fighters who had abandoned the cause to return.[36]

These successes enabled the media wing to expand operations beyond al-Furqan and al-Fajr media. In 2013 a new organ, al-I'tisam, started disseminating ISI materials on Twitter and other social media platforms with the help of fans who expanded the social network globally.[37] Al-Hayat hosted English translations of ISI materials, an innovation long advocated by jihadists like Abu Musab al Suri. The al-Bayan radio station opened in Mosul during the summer of 2014, along with local kiosks to distribute media to citizens and to screen new releases.[38]

The flood of releases of all formats from IS media outlets in 2015 reflected the existing structure and the long professionalization of its workers and staff combined with new technology that facilitated peer-to-peer interaction and encrypted software. IS's annual report, published in the group's biweekly newsletter *al-Naba*, for 1436 AH (October 2014–October 2015) summarized a prodigious amount of media output during this period (see table 14.1). Popular commentary on the IS strategic communications campaign has disproportionately focused on the ultraviolence in the messaging, slick production, and use of social media as crucial to explain its appeal. Yet the sheer diversity of its messaging, in content but also in medium—ranging from carefully produced hour-long films, such as *Flames of War*, to online magazines, such as the English-language *Dabiq* or the French-language *Daral-Islam*—suggests a different explanation.[39]

IS's strategic communications campaign has a single purpose: to shape perceptions and polarize contested populations in its favor.[40] Some of its messaging appeals to pragmatic concerns, such as the desire for stability, security, and livelihood, by promoting IS's politico-military actions and denigrating those of its opponents. This messaging lures audiences into rational-choice decisions based on a cost-benefit comparison of IS's versus its opponents' ability to deliver benefits. Other IS messaging appeals to perceptual concerns in order to trigger identity-based decision-making. In these cases IS portrays itself as the champion of Sunni Muslims (the in-group identity) and its opponents as the implacable enemies of all Sunnis, responsible for the crises that only IS can solve. By making its enemies responsible for the Sunni plight and making themselves the embodiment of Sunni virtue and the only force capable of protecting it, the messaging provides contested populations with a lens to understand not just the conflict but the world more broadly.

Even more important to IS's success than its media network is its ability to tailor messages to audiences. Typically, it emphasizes pragmatic factors in messaging for local audiences and perceptual factors for regional and global audiences. Even more potently, it fuses appeals to pragmatic and perceptual factors by framing its own victories and its enemies' failings as evidence of God's blessings and wrath, respectively. This

Table 14.1. Islamic State media output

Media source (type, location)	Videos	Audio	Nasheed (religious songs)	Koranic recitations	Magazines	Photo reports	Images
Wilayets (all, provincial media outlets)	710					1,787	14,000
Al Furqan media (video focus, central)	7	6					
Al Hayat Center (foreign lang., central)	15		13		18		
Al Ajnad (audio, central)			45	99			

Source: Thomas Joscelyn, "Graphic Promotes the Islamic State's Prolific Media Machine," Long War Journal, November 25, 2015, http://www.longwarjournal.org/archives/2015/11/graphic-promotes-islamic-states-prolific-media-machine.php.

flexibility allows it to disseminate a vast array of content to a variety of local, regional, and transnational audiences while still working within an overarching purpose. One study highlighted eleven themes that characterize IS's strategic communications: the military, governance, *da'wa* (preaching), *hisba* (governmental accountability), the promotion of the caliphate, enemy attack, news, martyrdom, execution, denial of enemy reports, and miscellaneous topics.[41] Another identified six key themes: brutality, mercy, victimhood, war, belonging, and utopianism.[42] Still another reduced the themes to the interplay four: urgency, agency, authenticity, and victory.[43]

IS's three-tiered strategic communications architecture makes its extraordinary variety of messaging cohere. The architecture consists of central and *wilayat* media units to disseminate official IS messaging, augmented by a broad supporter base, functioning largely online using social media forums that drastically increase the reach of the official messaging. This supporter base even produces its own unofficial messaging that increases the volume and reach of IS communiqués and also, given its popular "supporter-generated" origins, tends to be highly relevant and so resonates with crucial supporter groups.[44]

The combination of an overarching strategic rationale and a facilitating organizational structure has compounded the efficacy of IS's communication efforts. The movement has consistently postured its strategic communications offensively, designing and timing the messaging to shape its target audiences' perceptions as proactively as possible. Its reach comes from a willingness to use all available media, from billboards for local audiences to social media forums for transnational ones, and from an organizational structure that maximizes its ability to reach specific audiences. IS also attracts supporters by drawing on entertaining and emotionally engaging content synchronized with politico-military actions in the field. The increased flow of foreign fighters to IS-controlled areas is estimated at over thirty thousand new members since 2015,[45] and the surge of IS-inspired homegrown terrorists in the West must, at least in part, reflect the efficacy of its strategic communications campaign.[46] These trends also reflect the ineffectiveness of most anti-IS communication efforts, particularly in the spectrum of countermessaging.[47]

The "Counter-ISIL" Strategic Communications Campaign

Most Western anti-IS strategic communications efforts emerged from preexisting initiatives designed to counter al Qaeda and its affiliates over a decade ago. For example, the United Kingdom's Prevent strategy was one of four streams that constituted the UK's overarching Contest counterterrorism strategy, which first emerged from the Home Office in 2003.[48] While a broad range of activities fell under the Prevent work stream established in 2007, a major focus was to counter extremist propaganda by responding "to the ideological challenge we face from terrorism and aspects of extremism."[49] As the IS movement eclipsed al Qaeda as a threat, the priorities of Prevent and Contest shifted to working with a global coalition domestically and internationally to "challenge the poisonous ideology of Daesh" (another name for IS).[50] The UK government's Twitter campaign, UK Against Daesh (@UKagainst-Daesh), represents the front line of its online anti-IS strategic communications efforts with a stated purpose to provide "news & updates on UK Govt & Global Coalition efforts to defeat Daesh & help Syrians & Iraqis. Q&A at end of each month; use #DefeatingDaesh to join conversation."[51]

Across the Atlantic, in September 2011 President Barack Obama established the Center for Strategic Counterterrorism Communications (CSCC) as a key component of the US government's strategic communications efforts targeting Islamic extremism abroad.[52] Although CSCC is a small organization, its primary role has been to coordinate otherwise disparate US government strategic communications efforts and to produce and disseminate countermessaging. Originally, it focused on countering al Qaeda messaging; however, according to founding director Alberto M. Fernandez, between 2011 and 2014 it was "carrying out attributed, targeted counter-messaging against ISIS in Arabic and in English."[53] In 2013 as the IS movement expanded into Syria, it became known variously as ISIS (the Islamic State of Iraq and Syria) and ISIL (the Islamic State of Iraq and the Levant). At that time the US government's priority shifted from al Qaeda to IS, and "exposing ISIL's true nature" through strategic communications became a key component of its strategy.[54]

As the threat of IS-inspired homegrown actors increased and the flow of foreign fighters persisted, the sense of urgency rose. Yet the CSCC suffered from inconsistent strategies and personnel changes—for instance, its director changed for the second time in less than a year with the departure of Fernandez's replacement Rashad Hussain. An independent panel of experts reportedly criticized the credibility of US messaging to Muslim audiences, although it endorsed "State Department initiatives to enlist Middle Eastern allies in the propaganda war as well as a campaign that called attention to often-harrowing accounts from Islamic state defectors."[55]

According to Fernandez, the "efforts to blunt ISIS propaganda have been tentative and ineffective, despite major efforts by countries like Saudi Arabia, the United States and the United Kingdom, and even al-Qaida." Although CSCC is now focused almost entirely on multilingual anti-IS messaging and has received significant attention from the media, Fernandez believes it has had "limited impact."[56] Criticisms of anti-IS efforts have highlighted the comparatively small volume of the messaging, the largely defensive and reactive nature of the messages, the minimal guidance from senior government officials, the small budgetary allocation, and the limited reach of the messaging network.[57]

The US military's information campaign has tried to complement the CSCC's efforts by highlighting on a weekly basis the coalition's military blows to IS in Iraq and Syria. This effort spans television, print, and social media in an attempt to replicate the success of the Gulf War communications strategy. It provides summaries of airstrikes and taped strike footage of IS targets being destroyed. The current US military information campaign aims to whittle away at the legend of IS invulnerability after its blitzkrieg through Syria and Iraq from 2013 to 2014. There is no nuance in this effort, as illustrated by a tweet from the coalition campaign spokesman announcing the death of IS military commander Abu Omar al Shishani: "It's a short career for a leader in #ISIL. You certainly won't make it to retirement."[58] It is worth noting that the successful Gulf War communications campaign targeted US voters, not Arabic-speaking audiences.

The State Department launched its "Think Again Turn Away" Twitter page in December 2013. It has become the central forum for disseminating CSCC anti-IS messaging. The Think Again Turn Away campaign uses social media forums such as Twitter, Facebook, YouTube, and ask.fm.[59] According to the Think Again Turn Away Facebook page, "Our mission is to expose the facts about terrorists and their propaganda. Don't be misled by those who break up families and destroy their true heritage."[60] An analysis of one week of tweets reveals important insights. The State Department channel tweeted 146 times in seven days, in a medium that averages 500 million tweets per day.[61] Almost two-thirds of the tweets concerned IS, while the rest referenced seven other subjects. The tweets were posted generally between the hours of 9 a.m. to 5 p.m. on weekdays and in some cases were mechanically produced every twenty minutes on the mark.

A diversity of subjects could be problematic in a medium such as Twitter, which enables users to focus on certain topics through hashtags that perform an agenda-setting function. This produces what is known as narrowcasting or the transmission of messaging to a specific audience. The assumption that IS supporters and observers are also interested in al Qaeda is not necessarily a faulty one, but it is unlikely that they are also interested in Boko Haram, Al Shabaab, Hezbollah, or the Syrian regime's atrocities. In fact, it is possible that the State Department's Twitter feed might be reinforcing IS messaging against Bashar al Assad.

Subsequent retweets is one measure of reach. The Think Again Turn Away platform has been in existence long enough to have a reasonable following, considering it is a visible feed from a country with a large population. In fact, the tweets are not retweeted frequently, indicating that the audience either finds them uninteresting or does not think they are worth sharing within their own social network. Moreover, the messaging appears ad hoc and devoid of a unifying larger purpose.

Most of the tweets are not original content and merely promote articles in the mainstream media that resonate with the State Department's countering violent extremism (CVE) efforts. They simply highlight the negative effects of extremism around the world. The lack of depth in a medium like Twitter, even with supporting internet links for further exploration, makes the CVE program's effectiveness questionable. Jihadi supporters rely on contemporary interpretations of Islamic values and concepts to justify IS and other group behavior. A Twitter feed that does not attack these interpretations or assumptions—such as the definition of apostates or acceptable collateral damage—might have little influence. The platform's tweets portray the imminent demise of IS and highlight the damage it has caused. Other tweets showcase Western values, such as a free press and women's rights, that seem out of place, disconnected, and unlikely to resonate with potential supporters of IS or other Salafi jihadist groups.

The data set on anti-IS messaging suggests a largely defensive and ad hoc campaign in both the content and targeting of its messaging. Reach depends on producing a large volume of messaging or on having a network willing to disseminate that message through retweets. The data set suggests a significant lack in both areas. The dissemination of tweets containing a short informational message and a link to a mainstream media article reflects assumptions that a universal interpretation of the message exists and that reader curiosity will be sufficient to click on the link. IS's messaging rarely requires its audiences to follow links in order to receive the full story. The combination of unoriginal content, an absence of a central cohesive narrative or strategic rationale unifying the messaging, and difficulty identifying a primary target audience (such as IS supporters, potential IS supports, or the general public) bodes poorly for the relevance and resonance of the anti-IS messaging campaign.

There are enormous differences between IS's and the West's strategic communications campaigns in scope, volume, and quality of the messaging. Western messaging is boring at best. IS, on the other hand, has experimented with not only new media for messaging but also with content that shocks and titillates. The United States dilutes its counter-IS messaging by casting a wide net to cover all groups that commit violence to further extremist ideologies—tweeting about the Lord's Resistance Army one minute and IS the next. In contrast, IS effectively demonizes its enemies as members of a global conspiracy to destroy Muslim greatness and glorifies its own plans for the caliphate. Social media realms like Twitter—a medium IS mastered in 2012—then magnify the focused message by introducing breaking news through handcrafted messages built one follow and one block at a time.[62] It is not even certain that the counter-IS messaging even reaches its intended audience. Perhaps the countermessage serves only to bolster Western morale, an important but secondary purpose.[63]

While it is doubtful that President Obama spent a significant amount of time with his messaging managers, IS's communication managers have access to the inner circle of the leadership, which has entrusted them to execute a decentralized messaging strategy. The IS emirs selected young, charismatic, and technologically capable people to run their media enterprise and to speak and write independently in an organization that has limited communications tools owing to the technological superiority and communications-monitoring capabilities of its adversaries. Their media spokesmen have usually been religious leaders and experts, providing credibility to the core religious themes that dominate IS messaging. The dissemination of IS ideology at all levels gives the messaging a self-instruction role for new and old members alike and allows the *wilayets* to produce their own material with little risk of straying from official doctrine.

While the top leaders of IS have been deeply involved in its strategic communications strategy, professional bureaucrats and political appointees have taken the leading role in the West. Midlevel professionals run the State Department's countermessaging campaign. Such persons are unlikely to take risk. In the one case where the campaign tried to innovate, the leader was replaced.[64] The CSCC's personnel and budget limitations (unchanged during the successive shake-ups) would probably be comparable to those of one of IS's *wilayets*.[65] Whereas IS created its media organization before attempting to build a state, the West has grafted organizations responsible for strategic communications onto larger departments at a time of budgetary austerity.

Conclusion

After the Cold War the West lulled itself into a false sense of security that its soft-power case was self-evident given its high quality of life, human rights, and freedoms. It dismantled its extensive information and outreach programs in the belief that liberal democracy, capitalism, and Western freedoms and values had won, and so governments no longer needed to promote them domestically or abroad.[66] By disengaging from the type of information and outreach efforts that had helped win the Cold War, a vacuum emerged and was filled with other narratives that have not been proactively and systematically challenged. Western democracies' own populations have a distrust and skepticism of any governmental role in mass communications and value promotion. Overly active government involvement in strategic communications is reminiscent of fascism and alienates libertarians, offending both ends of the political spectrum.

Moreover, the compounding negative effects of organizational, leadership, and communications trends have hamstrung Western efforts. Robert Taber's war of the flea metaphor from his classic study on guerrilla warfare comes to mind, the giant destroying himself to kill a flea.[67] Publicly engaging a pseudostate like IS gives the pseudostate legitimacy and sustains the narrative that it can fight and defeat the greatest powers and that despite terrible odds, it is *baqiya* (remaining). *Baqiya* became part of the Islamic State's motto after a 2007 speech by Abu Omar al Baghdadi in reaction to the Sunni Sahwa. Omar insisted that the prowess of the members and the justice of the cause would allow the newly established Islamic State to overcome all obstacles to "remain."

Although the countries countering the IS movement created the communications platforms central to the success of the Islamic State's strategic communications campaign, these same countries have been unable to leverage the platforms nearly as effectively. The brilliance of the IS communication campaign was in its simplicity. IS leaders created a feedback loop based on ancient doctrine, polarizing actions (to associate and disassociate as they describe it), and the packaging of the message and the action into communiqués for the masses.[68] A paradox of globalization has been the rapid spread and democratization of technology that has enabled Salafi militants, who derive governing principles from the ninth century, to dominate in a communications war dependent on the twenty-first-century technology of their adversaries. Globalization has empowered the enemies of the West, even as they rail against it.

And finally, it is vital not to conflate operational battlefield success against IS with strategic communications success against their message. The success of IS, and the lack of confidence to countermessage against the group, led the status quo powers to fall back on the advantages they did have—pressuring social media companies to remove extremist content from the web. It is ironic that of all the strategies tried, curtailing the medium of communication has been the most successful, in part because of the deflating effect of IS's loss of territory in Iraq and Syria in 2018.[69] By late 2014 Twitter was removing IS accounts on a large scale, forcing the group to eventually abandon the forum as a source of regular reporting and outreach.[70] This loss of media was compounded by territorial losses in mid-2018, which degraded the allure of the so-called caliphate and IS's ability to produce the images of utopia that it favored in its caliphate-period propaganda and which may have broken the mystique of the IS movement.[71] However, this outcome should not deflect us from the lessons observed here; the failure of status quo powers to communicate in a strategic manner in the age of the internet will have serious consequences if left unaddressed.

Notes

1. G. Allison and P. Zelikow, *Essence of Decision: Explaining the Cuban Missile Crisis*, 2nd ed. (New York: Longman, 1999), 163–85.

2. William McCants and Charlie Winter, "Experts Weigh In (Part 4): Can the United States Counter ISIS Propaganda?" *Markaz* (blog), July 1, 2015, https://www.brookings.edu/blog/markaz/2015/07/01/experts-weigh-in-part-4-can-the-united-states-counter-isis-propaganda/.

3. C. Paul, *Strategic Communication: Origins, Concepts, and Current Debates* (Santa Barbara, CA: Praeger, 2011), 17–70; C. Paul, "Integrating Apples, Oranges, Pianos, Volkswagens, and Skyscrapers: On the Relationship between Information-Related Capability and Other Lines of Operation," *IO Sphere*, Winter 2014, 3–5; Joint Publication 3-13, *Information Operations* (Washington, DC: Joint Chiefs of Staff, November 20, 2014), chap. 2.

4. T. Rid and M. Hecker, *War 2.0* (Westport, CT: Praeger, 2009); J. Arquilla and D. Borer, eds., *Information Strategy and Warfare* (New York: Routledge, 2007); A. Munoz and E. Dick, *Information Operations: The Imperative of Doctrine Harmonization and Measures of Effectiveness* (Santa Monica, CA: RAND, 2015), 3, http://www.rand.org/pubs/perspectives/PE128.html.

5. H. Ingram, "Three Traits of the Islamic State's Information Warfare," *RUSI Journal* 159, no. 6 (2014).

6. This paper uses the term "IS movement" to cover the arc of the Salafi jihadist groups that merged over time to become the Islamic State, first declared in October 2006, with various name changes until the summer of 2014, when it declared its final evolution as the "Islamic State" with its establishment of a so-called caliphate. When referring to specific events, we use the actual name the group had at the time. This avoids the trap of discussing the group outside a historical perspective. M. Hamid and L. Farrall, *The Arabs at War in Afghanistan* (London: Hurst, 2015), 183, 257.

7. William McCants, *ISIS Apocalypse: The History, Strategy, and Doomsday Vision of the Islamic State* (New York: St. Martin's Press, 2015), 7–11.

8. J. Warrick, *Black Flags: The Rise of ISIS* (New York: Doubleday, 2015), 106–14.

9. Abu Omar al Kurdi, Zarqawi's chief bombmaker in the early years, admitted to making the bomb that destroyed the UN headquarters in Baghdad, killing UN representative Sérgio Vieira de Mello and twenty others. See J. Fairweather, "Top al-Zarqawi Bombmakers Seized, Says Iraq," *Irish Times*, January 25, 2005, https://www.irishtimes.com/news/top-al-zarqawi-bombmaker-seized-says-iraq-1.409061.

10. Zarqawi's first media interaction was an audiotape called "Join the Caravan," released on January 7, 2004. It eulogized his recently deceased partner and called for Muslims to join the jihad in Iraq. For more see A. Cha, "From a Virtual Shadow, Messages of Terror," *Washington Post*, October 2, 2004, http://www.washingtonpost.com/wp-dyn/articles/A1570-2004Oct1.html.

11. Al Qaeda in Iraq, "Biographies of Eminent Martyrs: Saif al Ummah," trans. Evan Kohlmann, retrieved from www.globalterroralert.com.

12. Hanna Rogan, *Al Qaeda's Online Media Strategies: From Abu Reuter to Irhabi 007* (Kjeller, Norway: Norwegian Defense Research Establishment [FFI], 2007), 15.

13. Islamic State of Iraq, "Number Forty-Six of the Biographies of Eminent Martyrs: Abu-Maysarah al-Iraqi," Al-Furqan Establishment, disseminated on jihadist websites by the Al-Fajr Media Center.

14. Abu Turki bin Mubarek al-Binali, "A Biography of IS Spokesman Abu Muhammed al-Adnani as-Shami," ed. and trans. Pieter Vanostaeyen, November 1, 2014, https://pietervanostaeyen.wordpress.com/2014/11/02/a-biography-of-is-spokesman-abu-muhammad-al-adnani-as-shami/.

15. Cha, "From a Virtual Shadow."

16. Rogan, *Al Qaeda's Online Media*, 15.

17. Rogan, 28–29.

18. For an example of this justification of targeting strategy, see Abu Omar al Baghdadi, "Harvest of Prosperity," audiotape released March 17, 2009, al-Fajr Media.

19. A. Zellin, *The State of Global Jihad Online: A Qualitative, Quantitative, and Cross-Lingual Analysis* (Washington, DC: New America Foundation, January 2013), 6, http://www.washingtoninstitute.org/policy-analysis/view/the-state-of-global-jihad-online.

20. Islamic State of Iraq, "Announcement of the Establishment of al Furqan Agency Dedicated to Producing Audio-Visual Productions," Ministry of Information, posted on jihadist website, October 31, 2006.

21. Zawahiri to Abu Musab (al Zarqawi), July 9, 2005, in CTC West Point Archives, https://www.ctc.usma.edu/posts/zawahiris-letter-to-zarqawi-english-translation-2.

22. Abu Musab al Zarqawi, "Pledge of Allegiance to al-Qaeda," *Mu'asker al-Battar*, no. 21 (October 17, 2004). Translated by Jeffrey Pool and available from Jamestown Foundation, http://www.jamestown.org/single/?tx_ttnews[tt_news]=27305#.Vpcp0_GlY7A.

23. B. Fishman, *The Master Plan: ISIS, Al-Qaeda, and the Jihadi Strategy for Final Victory* (New Haven, CT: Yale University Press, 2016), 85–140.

24. Jacob Shapiro, *The Terrorist's Dilemma: Managing Violent Covert Organizations* (Princeton, NJ: Princeton University Press, 2013), 89.

25. B. Bahney, H. Shatz, C. Ganier, R. McPherson, and B. Sude, *An Economic Analysis of the Financial Records of al-Qa'ida in Iraq* (Santa Monica, CA: RAND, 2010), http://www.rand.org/content/dam/rand/pubs/monographs/2010/RAND_MG1026.pdf.

26. Matthew Alexander and John R. Bruning, *How to Break a Terrorist: The U.S. Interrogators Who Used Brains, Not Brutality, to Take Down the Deadliest Man in Iraq* (New York: St. Martin's Griffin, 2011), 88.

27. K. Bergner, "Situational Update," MNF-Iraq, July 18, 2007, www.MNF-Iraq.com.

28. B. Roggio, "US Targets al Qaeda's al Furqan Media Wing in Iraq," *Long War Journal*, October 28, 2007, http://www.longwarjournal.org/archives/2007/10/us_targets_al_qaedas.php.

29. B. Roggio, "Hunting al Qaeda in Iraq's Propaganda Cells," *Long War Journal*, November 28, 2007, http://www.longwarjournal.org/archives/2007/11/hunting_al_qaeda_in.php.

30. C. Whiteside, "War Interrupted: The Roots of Jihadist Resurgence in Iraq," *War on the Rocks*, November 5, 2014, http://warontherocks.com/2014/11/war-interrupted-part-i-the-roots-of-the-jihadist-resurgence-in-iraq/.

31. For a counter to the conventional wisdom that ISI was nonexistent during this time frame, read B. Fishman, *Fall and Rise of Islamic State of Iraq* (Washington, DC: New America Foundation, August 2011), https://static.newamerica.org/attachments/4343-redefining-the-islamic-state/Fishman_Al_Qaeda_In_Iraq.023ac20877a64488b2b791cd7e313955.pdf.

32. "US Says 80% of al Qaeda Leaders in Iraq Removed," BBC News, June 4, 2010, http://www.bbc.co.uk/news/10243585.

33. C. Whiteside, "The Islamic State and the Return of Revolutionary Warfare," *Small Wars and Insurgencies* 27, no. 5 (2016): 743–76, doi:10.1080/09592318.2016.1208287.

34. For more on the Islamic State's counter-Sahwa propaganda campaign, see C. Whiteside, 2018. *Nine Bullets for the Traitors, One for the Enemy: The Slogans and Strategy behind the Islamic State's Campaign to Defeat the Sunni Awakening (2006–2017)* (The Hague: International Centre for Counter-Terrorism, 2018), 9, doi:10.19165/2018.1.07.

35. A. Fernandez, *Here to Stay and Growing: Combating ISIS Propaganda Networks* (Washington, DC: Brookings Institution, October 2015), 8.

36. "Letter to Emir of Faithful, From Abu Ibrahim," Document # AQ-MSLF-D-001-681, n.d. (before 2011), Combat Records Research Center (NDU), Washington, DC.

37. Jessica Stern and J. M. Berger, *ISIS: The State of Terror* (New York: Ecco, 2015), 153.

38. Fernandez, *Here to Stay*.

39. Meira Svirsky, "ISIS Releases '*Flames of War*' Feature Film to Intimidate the West," Clarion Project, September 21, 2014, http://www.clarionproject.org/analysis/isis-releases-flames-war-feature-film-intimidate-west#; *Dabiq*, no. 12 (November 2015), https://azelin.files.wordpress.com/2015/11/the-islamic-state-e2809cdc481biq-magazine-12e280b3.pdf; *Dar al-Islam*, no. 4 (June 2015), https://azelin.files.wordpress.com/2015/06/the-islamic-state-22dc481r-al-islc481m-magazine-422.pdf.

40. H. Ingram, "The Strategic Logic of Islamic State Information Operations," *Australian Journal of International Affairs* 69, no. 6 (2015): 729–52.

41. A. Zelin, "Picture or It Didn't Happen: A Snapshot of the Islamic State's Official Media Output," *Perspectives on Terrorism* 9, no. 4 (2015): 90–94.

42. Charlie Winter, *The Virtual "Caliphate": Understanding Islamic State's Propaganda Strategy* (London: Quilliam, 2015), 22–27, http://www.quilliamfoundation.org/wp/wp-content/uploads/2015/10/FINAL-documenting-the-virtual-caliphate.pdf.

43. Fernandez, *Here to Stay*, 11–12.

44. For more see B. Price, D. Milton, M. al-'Ubaydi, and N. Lahoud, *The Group That Calls Itself a State: Understanding the Evolution and Challenges of the Islamic State* (West Point, NY: Combating Terrorism Center, 2014), https://www.ctc.usma.edu/posts/the-group-that-calls-itself-a-state-understanding-the-evolution-and-challenges-of-the-islamic-state.

45. For more, see Soufan Group, *Foreign Fighters: An Updated Assessment of the Flow of Foreign Fighters into Syria and Iraq* (New York: Soufan Group, December 2015), http://soufangroup.com/wp-content/uploads/2015/12/TSG_ForeignFightersUpdate_FINAL.pdf.

46. For more, see T. Hegghammer and P. Nesser, "Assessing the Islamic State's Commitment to Attacking the West," *Perspectives on Terrorism* 9, no. 4 (2015), http://www.terrorismanalysts.com/pt/index.php/pot/article/view/440.

47. For more on the history of the Islamic State media, see C. Whiteside, *Lighting the Path: The Evolution of the Islamic State Media Enterprise (2003–2016)* (The Hague: International Centre for Counter-Terrorism, 2016), doi:10.19165/2016.1.14.

48. For more on UK's Contest and its Prevent, Pursue, Prepare, and Protect working streams, see *Contest: The United Kingdom's Strategy for Countering Terrorism* (London:

Home Office, July 2011), https://www.gov.uk/government/uploads/system/uploads /attachment_data/file/97995/strategy-contest.pdf.

49. For more, see *2010 to 2015 Government Policy: Counter-Terrorism* (London: Home Office, May 8, 2015), https://www.gov.uk/government/publications/2010-to-2015 -government-policy-counter-terrorism/2010-to-2015-government-policy-counter -terrorism.

50. "Daesh: UK Government Response," GOV.UK, https://www.gov.uk/government /topical-events/daesh/about.

51. UK Against Daesh (@UKagainstDaesh), https://twitter.com/UKagainstDaesh.

52. Executive Order 13584—Developing an Integrated Strategic Counterterrorism Communications Initiative (Washington, DC: White House, Office of the Press Secretary, September 9, 2011), https://www.whitehouse.gov/the-press-office/2011 /09/09/executive-order-13584-developing-integrated-strategic-counterterrorism-c; US Department of State, Center for Strategic Counterterrorism Communications, http://www.state.gov/r/cscc/.

53. Fernandez, *Here to Stay*, 15.

54. White House, "The Administration's Strategy to Counter the Islamic State of Iraq and the Levant (ISIL) and the Updates FY 2015 Overseas Contingency Request," fact sheet, November 7, 2014, https://www.whitehouse.gov/the-press-office/2014 /11/07/fact-sheet-administration-s-strategy-counter-islamic-state-iraq-and-leva.

55. G. Miller, "Panel Casts Doubt on U.S. Propaganda Efforts against ISIS," *Washington Post*, December 2, 2015, https://www.washingtonpost.com/world/national -security/panel-casts-doubt-on-us-propaganda-efforts-against-isis/2015/12/02/ab7f 9a14-9851-11e5-94f0-9eeaff906ef3_story.html. Also see https://foreignaffairs.house .gov/press-release/house-votes-combat-terrorist-use-social-media.

56. Fernandez, *Here to Stay*, 1, 15.

57. For example, E. Schmitt "U.S. Intensifies Effort to Blunt ISIS' Message," *New York Times*, February 16, 2016, http://www.nytimes.com/2015/02/17/world/middleeast /us-intensifies-effort-to-blunt-isis-message.html?_r=0.

58. Steve Warren (@OIRSpox), "It's a short career," Twitter, March 16, 2016, 7:48 a.m., https://twitter.com/OIRSpox/status/710115582247456768?ref_src=twsrc^tfw.

59. Think Again Turn Away (@ThinkAgain_DOS), Twitter, https://twitter.com /ThinkAgain_DOS; Think Again Turn Away, Facebook, https://www.facebook.com /ThinkAgainTurnAway; Think Again Turn Away, YouTube, https://www.youtube .com/user/ThinkAgainTurnAway; Think Again Turn Away, ask.fm, https://ask.fm /ThinkAgainTurnAway.

60. Think Again Turn Away, "Our mission is to expose," Facebook, https://www .facebook.com/ThinkAgainTurnAway/info/.

61. Statistic retrieved from internet live stats blog. "Twitter Usage Statistics," Internet Live Stats, accessed January 29, 2016, http://www.internetlivestats.com/twitter-statistics/#sources.

62. Aaron Zelin, *The State of Global Jihad Online: A Qualitative, Quantitative, and Cross-Lingual Analysis* (Washington, DC: New America Foundation, January 2013), 11.

63. Anthony Pratkanis, "Winning Hearts and Minds: A Social Influence Analysis," in *Information Strategy and Warfare: A Guide to Theory and Practice*, ed. J. Arquilla and D. Borer (New York: Routledge, 2007), 61.

64. Margaret Brennan, "Flaws Seen in US Approach to ISIS Propaganda" CBS News, June 10, 2015, http://www.cbsnews.com/news/flaws-seen-in-u-s-approach-to-isis-propaganda/.

65. Greg Miller and Karen DeYoung, "Obama Administration Plans Shake Up in Propaganda War against ISIS," *Washington Post*, January 8, 2016, https://www.washingtonpost.com/world/national-security/obama-administration-plans-shake-up-in-propaganda-war-against-the-islamic-state/2016/01/08/d482255c-b585-11e5-a842-0feb51d1d124_story.html?tid=pm_world_pop_b.

66. Matthew Armstrong, "No We Do Not Need to Revive the U.S. Information Agency," *War on the Rocks*, November 12, 2015, https://warontherocks.com/2015/11/no-we-do-not-need-to-revive-the-u-s-information-agency/.

67. Robert Taber, *The War of the Flea: A Study of Guerrilla Warfare Theory and Practice* (New York: L. Stuart, 1965).

68. For more on how to reverse engineer an approach to tackle IS countermessaging, see H. J. Ingram, *The Strategic Logic of the "Linkage-Based" Approach to Combating Militant Islamist Propaganda: Conceptual and Empirical Foundations* (The Hague: International Centre for Counter-Terrorism, 2017), doi:10.19165/2017.1.06.

69. A. Alexander, *Digital Decay? Tracing Change over Time among English-Language Islamic State Sympathizers on Twitter* (Washington, DC: Program on Extremism, George Washington University, October 2017), https://extremism.gwu.edu/sites/g/files/zaxdzs2191/f/DigitalDecayFinal_0.pdf.

70. J. M. Berger and J. Morgan, *The ISIS Twitter Census: Defining and Describing the Population of ISIS Supporters on Twitter* (Washington, DC: Brookings Institution, 2015), https://www.brookings.edu/research/the-isis-twitter-census-defining-and-describing-the-population-of-isis-supporters-on-twitter/.

71. Zelin, "Picture or It Didn't Happen"; H. Ingram and C. Whiteside, "In Search of the Virtual Caliphate: Convenient Fallacy, Dangerous Distraction," *War on the Rocks*, September 27, 2017, https://warontherocks.com/2017/09/in-search-of-the-virtual-caliphate-convenient-fallacy-dangerous-distraction/.

15.

Communicating the Global War on Terror from Speeches to Tweets

Andrea J. Dew

This chapter is a tale of three American presidents—President George W. Bush, President Barack Obama, and President Donald Trump—and how they have communicated the longest war in recent American history to audiences domestic and foreign. Assessing a range of public presidential communications—from speeches to tweets—the argument in this chapter is that not only have each of these three presidents struggled to determine and articulate the nature of the war but that as a result, all three presidents and their administrations have struggled to determine clear policy goals and clear overarching strategies to achieve those goals.

The Prussian strategist Carl von Clausewitz, wrote, "The first, the supreme, the most far-reaching act of judgment that the statesman and commander have to make is to establish . . . the kind of war on which they are embarking; neither mistaking it for, nor trying to turn it into, something that is alien to its nature."[1] This is the first of all strategic questions and the most comprehensive. Clausewitz's dictum on the necessity of understanding "the kind of war on which you are embarking" seems so simple from the outside looking in, but for each of the three American presidents discussed in this chapter, even the simplest of tasks has proved deeply complicated.[2]

At eighteen years and counting, the US commitment to fighting the global war on terror—from tweets about troop levels to strategic reviews—remains front-page news debated by politicians and pundits alike.[3] By October 2007 the Bush administration had stationed 166,300 US troops in Iraq.[4] By 2011 the Obama administration had retained 100,000 US troops in Afghanistan.[5] And by spring 2017, during the heated debate over the use of private contractors instead of US troops, the Trump administration struggled to define yet another new strategy for defeating the Taliban while simultaneously directing US troops in Iraq and Syria to fight the Islamic State in Iraq and Syria (ISIS).[6] Moreover, each president has confronted eerily similar challenges—goals to be set, strategies to be aligned, budgets to be passed, alliances to be formed and sustained—in order to vanquish the same enemies in many of the same battlegrounds.

This final chapter on communicating war focuses on the persistent struggle presidents and their policy spokespeople have faced with defining and winning this war given this political and technological context. The chapter considers two entwined challenges: first, how administrations have defined the *nature of the war* and, second, how each administration defined the *nature of the enemy*. The chapter also considers the message, the messenger, and the choice of media that presidents have used—from prime-time television speeches to 140 characters on Twitter—and the way they have framed the ongoing and evolving conflict. Moreover, it tells the tale of how evolving adversaries—in particular al Qaeda, its associated movements, and ISIS—have frustrated and complicated presidential communication about the longest war.

A War against Terror?

In an address before a joint session of Congress on September 20, 2001, President George W. Bush coined the term "Global War on Terror." The Global War on Terror medal, created in 2003, which is awarded to US military personnel who have served in this conflict, helped to perpetuate the name despite multiple attempts to rebrand the war and lower the bar for "victory" by defining down the threshold.

The name, a name, *any* name seemed the least important issue in the immediate aftermath of the terror attacks of September 11, 2001, when the American public was demanding to know the truth behind what had happened: Who was Osama bin Laden, and what was al Qaeda? Who were the hijackers, why did they crash planes into the World Trade Center in New York, why did they drive a plane into the Pentagon in Washington, DC, and what was the target of the plane that crashed in Pennsylvania?[7] And more important, as Fareed Zakaria put it in his *Newsweek* article, "Why Do They Hate Us?"[8]

But nine days later, as speculation continued to swirl, President Bush was ready to communicate something else to audiences domestic and foreign: the US response to the attacks. In his September 20, 2001, speech to a joint session of Congress, he identified al Qaeda as the perpetrator of the attack, framed the nature and scope of the war in extremely broad terms, and set the bar for success extremely high: "Our war on terror begins with Al Qaida, but it does not end there. It will not end until every terrorist group of global reach has been found, stopped, and defeated. . . . We will direct every resource at our command—every means of diplomacy, every tool of intelligence, every instrument of law enforcement, every financial influence, and every necessary weapon of war—to the disruption and to the defeat of the global terror network." And in his conclusion, President Bush put the enemies of the United States on notice: "And we will pursue nations that provide aid or safe haven to terrorism. Every nation, in every region, now has a decision to make: Either you are with us, or you are with the terrorists."[9] At the signing of the "Authorization for the Use of Military Force" on September 18, 2001, the president was equally blunt in asserting the right of the United States to defend itself at home and abroad. Deviating from the equivocating diplomatic and legal environment on terrorism issues of the 1990s, he said that "those who plan, authorize, commit, or aid terrorist attacks against the United States and its interests—including those who harbor terrorists" should be considered "threats to national security," and it was under these authorities that Operation Enduring Freedom began in Afghanistan in October 2001.[10]

Despite this dramatic start, however, the harsh realities of the conflict quickly challenged the goals and the progress of the Global War on Terror. Audacious Central Intelligence Agency and US military special operators delivered swift progress in support of the Northern Alliance's operations against the Taliban regime in Afghanistan in the late autumn and early winter of 2001–2. However, the strategic and operational momentum from the overthrow of the Taliban regime morphed into stalemate around the Afghan mountain range of Tora Bora in 2002 as Osama bin Laden remained at large.[11] From then until his death at the hands of American Special Operations Forces in 2011, bin Laden continued to taunt American policymakers and military forces with his videos and communiques calling on all Muslims to participate in a global jihad against the United States and its allies.[12]

A Religious War? A Clash of Civilizations?

By 2004, as President Bush's sweeping statement on US goals looked frustratingly chimeric, his terminology also came under criticism. How could the United States wage a war against the "tactic" of terrorism? Didn't a "global war" give small terrorist groups too much credit and too much free publicity that amplified their status and message far beyond fringe extremist groups? And by emphasizing "war," didn't this undercut strategic diplomatic, legal, financial, and public communications efforts to address root grievances and build alliances against al Qaeda and its affiliates?[13]

These criticisms were all the more stinging considering the nature of the adversary. As early as 1998, Osama bin Laden's public statement after al Qaeda's bombing attacks on US embassies in Nairobi, Kenya, and Dar-es-Salaam, Tanzania, made it clear that he was involved in a multifaceted conflict and cast the war as a religious clash of ideologies. The organization he fronted, al Qaeda, had developed out of the network of foreign financiers, ideologues, and fighters who had flocked to the

Soviet-Afghan War in the early 1980s. Buoyed by their success against the Soviet Red Army, they turned their attention to other regimes after the Soviet withdrawal from Afghanistan in 1989. Battlefield and strategic interaction further complicated the framing of the long war, not least because bin Laden himself was willing to engage in strategic communication.[14]

Among his many communiqués with his followers and the outside world, bin Laden argued that the continued American presence in the Arabian Peninsula, the continued economic sanctions against Iraq, and American support for Israel constituted "a clear declaration of war on Allah, his messenger, and Muslims." Using this context as justification, bin Laden framed his message as a religious duty: "The ruling to kill the Americans and their allies—civilians and military—is an individual duty for every Muslim who can do it in any country in which it is possible to do it."[15] By 2004 bin Laden— still at large and communicating with his followers—was framing the strategy for the conflict as one of protraction and economic attrition. In his video message played by *Al Jazeera* in October 2004, he argued, "[It is] easy for us to provoke and bait this administration. All that we have to do is to send two mujahidin to the furthest point east to raise a piece of cloth on which is written al Qaeda, in order to make the generals race there and cause America to suffer human, economic, and political losses."[16]

The Bush administration seemed to play into both of these themes—the religious war and the invitation to overreaction—when it launched Operation Iraqi Freedom on March 19, 2003, after a flurry of strategic communication by trusted administration advisers, including Secretary of State Colin Powell. Powell's message, delivered to the United Nations, accused Saddam Hussein's regime of concealing an ongoing pursuit of weapons of mass destruction and contributing to the global war by terrorists because there was a "potentially much more sinister nexus between Iraq and the al-Qaida terrorist network, a nexus that combines classic terrorist organizations and modern methods of murder."[17]

Despite this assessment, however, al Qaeda was an adversary, not an ally, of Saddam's Baathist regime.[18] Indeed, in the immediate aftermath of the 2003 US invasion and ouster of Saddam Hussein, al Qaeda and Zarqawi embraced the opportunity to open a new strategic and operational front against the United States in Iraq. The potent mix of overlapping groups: former regime elements, Sunni tribes, and the newly rebranded "al Qaeda in Mesopotamia" became a multifaceted Sunni insurgency that raged across Iraq until 2010.[19]

In addition to struggling with how to frame the war, the Bush administration experienced numerous self-inflicted mistakes in terms of how to win the war as the invasion of Iraq in 2003 developed into a multifaceted insurgency.[20] In particular, photos of US military police humiliating Iraqi prisoners at Abu Ghraib Prison went viral over the internet. The ensuing scandal exacerbated the perception that the United States and its military contractors were torturing detainees around the world.[21] Bin Laden continued to capitalize on the stories and images as late as 2010, referring to "the crimes at Abu Ghraib and Guantanamo, those ugly crimes which shook the conscience of humanity."[22]

As the Abu Ghraib scandal unfolded, the Bush administration faced a daunting challenge: how to explain the necessity of extreme measures to a domestic audience while shaping perceptions of US actions overseas. In May 2004 President Bush responded with his own strategic communication after a round of interviews with Arab media, including *Al Jazeera*, which had already established itself as part of the new media environment. Bush apologized to King Hussein of Jordan, saying, "I told him I was sorry for the humiliation suffered by the Iraqi prisoners and the humiliation suffered by their families. I told him I was equally sorry that people who have been seeing those pictures didn't understand the true nature and heart of America. I assured him Americans like me didn't appreciate what we saw, that it made us sick to our stomachs."[23] The Bush administration's fumbling of the treatment of prisoners also chipped away at domestic support for the Iraq War. As discussed later in the chapter, ironically, even as the American public was losing faith in the decision to go to war, the Bush administration's strategic messaging in Iraq was becoming more successful with critical local audiences—Sunni Iraqis.

A Gallup poll asking Americans, "Do you think the United States made a mistake in sending troops to Iraq, or not?" reflected early enthusiasm for the war with 75 percent of those polled saying the decision was "not a mistake" in March 2003.[24] That certainly seemed to be the mood in the administration that May, when President Bush landed on USS *Abraham Lincoln*. Against the backdrop of the soon infamous "Mission Accomplished" banner displayed on the warship, he proclaimed, "Major combat operations in Iraq have ended. In the Battle of Iraq, the United States and our allies have prevailed. And now our coalition is engaged in securing and reconstructing that country."[25]

However, as the securing and reconstructing efforts morphed into counterinsurgency operations in Iraq, those who rated the decision "a mistake" grew from 53 percent of Americans polled in March 2004 to 63 percent in July 2009.[26] Likewise, presidential approval ratings slumped rapidly from 71 percent in March 2003 at the outset of Operation Iraqi Freedom to 46 percent in May 2004, when the Abu Ghraib scandal broke, to 31 percent in May 2006 as the insurgency in Iraq intensified.[27]

A Clash of Civilizations or a Law Enforcement Problem?

As the US military struggled to communicate its strategy to Iraqi audiences after 2004, the US government continued to lose ground with its messaging, messengers, and media efforts to broader audiences.[28] As early as November 2001, the Bush administration recognized that anti-American sentiment fed the narrative of al Qaeda and its supporters. An early ill-fated attempt to shape this narrative included hiring ad executive Charlotte Beers as undersecretary for public diplomacy and public affairs to help the State Department "brand America."[29]

Beers, her successor Margaret Tutwiler, and her successor Karen Hughes all ran into the same wall: how to improve perceptions and understanding of America even as Americans continued to fight new wars in a competitive media context. In a 2003 Senate hearing Charlotte Beers could have been writing a script for 2020 when she said, "The gap between who we are and how we wish to be seen, and how we are in fact seen, is frighteningly wide." She added that in Muslim countries such as Egypt, Saudi Arabia, Pakistan, and Indonesia, millions of people had a "gravely distorted, but carefully cultivated images of us—images so negative, so weird, so hostile that I can assure you a young generation of terrorists is being created." Perhaps most ominously, Beers closed by saying, "for some time into the future, we will be dealing with the natural tension between our need for security and our desire to be open and inviting."[30]

One of the more unfortunate terms that added fuel to this fire was "Islamo-fascism." President Bush's administration initially trod carefully with the phrase, which linked the religion of Islam to the political fascist movements of the 1930s. In his speech in October 2005 to the National Endowment for Democracy, he said, "And while the killers choose their victims indiscriminately, their attacks serve a clear and focused ideology, a set of beliefs and goals that are evil but not insane. Some call this evil Islamic radicalism. Others militant jihadism. Still, others Islamo-fascism."[31] But he immediately followed up with language to attempt to separate the violent acts of terrorism from the religion of Islam: "Whatever it's called, this ideology is very different from the religion of Islam. This form of radicalism exploits Islam to serve a violent political vision: the establishment, by terrorism and subversion and insurgency, of a totalitarian empire that denies all political and religious freedom."[32] However, the term "Islamo-fascism" quickly took root in presidential communication and added to the perception that the United States was engaged in an ideological and religious war. Indeed, the summer of Islamo-fascism burned hot and fast. The topic of Republican senator Rick Santorum's July 2006 talk at the National Press Club was "America's War against Islamic Fascism."[33] President Bush called a disrupted terror attack in the United Kingdom in August 2006 "a stark reminder that this nation is at war with Islamic fascists."[34] By the end of August, Secretary of Defense Donald Rumsfeld evoked the 1930s and argued that "we face similar challenges in efforts to confront the rising threat of a new type of fascism" in his American Legion Annual Convention speech.[35]

Not surprisingly, the term drew the ire of critics at home and abroad. In the United States the term became emblematic of the struggle to communicate, influence, and persuade foreign audiences about the intentions of the United States as part of a "war of ideas." As early as October 2003 *Changing Minds and Winning Peace*, a report of the Advisory Group on Public Diplomacy for the Arab and Muslim world, argued, "Americans, on the one hand, and Arabs and Muslims, on the other, are trapped in a dangerously reinforcing cycle of animosity. Arabs and Muslims respond in anger to what they perceive as US denigration of their societies and cultures, and to this Arab and Muslim response Americans react with bewilderment and resentment, provoking a further negative response from Arabs and Muslims."[36]

Even as using Islamo-fascism to describe the enemy was gaining a foothold in official rhetoric, President Bush's administration was trying to address shortfalls in the American "war of ideas" in the 2006 National Security Strategy, stating, "In the long run, winning the war on terror means winning the battle of ideas. . . . While the War on Terror is a battle of ideas, it is not a battle of religions."[37] Bin Laden would clearly argue otherwise, and as the insurgency peaked in Iraq and Afghanistan, the "clash of religions" theme was difficult to discredit. By 2008 the Department of Homeland Security weighed in on the debate with its memo on "Terminology to Define the Terrorists: Recommendations from American Muslims." The report argued that "we must carefully avoid giving bin Laden and other al-Qaeda leaders the legitimacy they crave, but do not possess, by characterizing them as religious figures, or in terms that may make them seem to be noble in the eyes of some." The authors recommended that US administration officials not use the terms "Islamic," "Islamists," or "jihad" or even narrower terms such as "Salafist." Instead, the report recommended talking about Osama bin Laden as a cult leader, emphasizing the negative *takfiri* ideas he espoused, and referring to the broader Muslim community as "mainstream" (not moderate) to differentiate it from bin Laden's cult.[38]

President Obama attempted to both reshape the narrative of the conflict and narrow the political goals in a series of speeches between 2009 and 2013. First, in 2009 he addressed the cadets at West Point to announce an increase of thirty thousand troops to fight in Afghanistan but caveated the announcement by saying, "I set a goal that was narrowly defined as disrupting, dismantling, and defeating al Qaeda and its extremist allies, and pledged to better coordinate our military and civilian effort." He also reassured the cadets that within eighteen months US troops would begin to withdraw.

President Obama's best intentions were thwarted, however, by the magnitude of the task at hand. Not only was the Afghan War difficult to close on schedule, but the president had to manage the fallout from WikiLeaks' July 2010 release of ninety thousand classified documents from Spc. Bradley Manning and Edward Snowden's June

2013 leak of digital surveillance programs.[39] The Manning leaks in particular shone a spotlight on the role US forces played in the death of Reuters journalists in Iraq, and the Snowden leaks exposed the inner deliberations of US diplomats.[40] Moreover, President Obama had to explain to a skeptical US public why secret warrants issued by the Foreign Intelligence Surveillance Court as part of the domestic front of the war on terror were consonant with American core values: "No one expects China to have an open debate about their surveillance programs or Russia to take privacy concerns of citizens in other places into account. . . . But let's remember, we are held to a different standard precisely because we have been at the forefront of defending personal privacy and human dignity. . . . Those values make us who we are."[41]

Even as President Obama attempted to narrow the goals and narrative of the war with the use of "overseas contingency operations" as the new bumper sticker for the conflict, he increasingly authorized the use of drones to kill terrorists overseas. Thus, far from ending the Global War on Terror, he seemed to acknowledge the challenges of reducing the scale and scope of the war at his graduation address at the National Defense University: "Neither I, nor any President, can promise the total defeat of terror. . . . But what we can do—what we must do—is dismantle networks that pose a direct danger to us, and make it less likely for new groups to gain a foothold, all the while maintaining the freedoms and ideals that we defend."[42]

As the Global War on Terror marched into its fifteenth year, the emphasis on communicating to domestic audiences became more pressing, particularly the challenge of preventing domestic radicalization. President Obama had previously used his speech announcing the death of Osama bin Laden in his compound in Pakistan in 2011 to amplify this message:

> I can report to the American people and to the world that the United States has conducted an operation that killed Osama bin Laden, the leader of al Qaeda. . . . We must also reaffirm that the United States is not—and never will be—at war with Islam. I've made clear, just as President Bush did shortly after 9/11, that our war is not against Islam. Bin Laden was not a Muslim leader; he was a mass murderer of Muslims.[43]

By 2016 the Homeland Security Advisory Council at the Department of Homeland Security had tacitly admitted that the US was still struggling with anti-Muslim perceptions and advocated using the phrase "countering violent extremism" to avoid playing into an us-versus-them dynamic that framed the West at war with Islam. In particular the report emphasized that "we are at a particular moment on the world stage with global events driving fear, political and cultural rhetoric leaning on sharp and divisive language, and deep polarization and distrust across communities."[44]

The report reemphasized that the US government was not a legitimate messenger for countering violent extremism at home; instead it needed to empower credible and trusted messengers from local communities to help undermine recruitment by extremist groups. It also captured concerns about "insider threats" and the growing awareness that the threat had changed—new groups such as ISIS had developed sophisticated social media strategies to groom and recruit attackers in American communities.

The Trouble with Tweets

As other chapters in this book have discussed, the names presidents use to label their wars and their enemies indicate both their hopes and their goals. The names have sometimes set political goals, sometimes inflamed passions, and sometimes created more complex political problems for presidents to overcome. Presidential candidate Donald Trump's embrace of social media during the primaries and presidential campaign season from 2015 onward seemed to accomplish all three at once. The former real estate mogul and reality TV personality embraced a range of inflammatory language and rhetoric to incite domestic audiences, taking political advantage of domestic security fears.

The future President Trump started as a staunch social media critic of President Obama's war strategy, tweeting in 2012, "It is time to get out of Afghanistan. We are building roads and schools for people that hate us. It is not in our national interests."[45] In November 2013 Trump kept up the pressure, arguing, "We have wasted an enormous amount of blood and treasure in Afghanistan. Their government has zero appreciation. Let's get out!"[46] And his frustrations peaked in 2014, when he railed against President Obama's strategies: "Now Obama is keeping our soldiers in Afghanistan for at least another year. He is losing two wars simultaneously."[47]

Even as candidate Trump became president-elect and then President Trump, his communication on the domestic threat of terrorism remained consistent. And much of it paralleled the language from the early Bush administration, with a resurgence of "Islamo-fascism." In particular, Trump, his strategist Steve Bannon, and his first National Security Advisor, Michael Flynn, defined the threat as "Islamic" terrorism and linked immigration with terrorism. Trump used his social medium of choice—Twitter—to challenge Hillary Clinton and President Obama's word usage with a series of tweets including this one: "With Hillary and Obama, the terrorist attacks will only get worse. Politically correct fools, won't even call it what it is—RADICAL ISLAM!"[48] Earlier Steve Bannon, the CEO of Breitbart News who became a White House adviser before returning to Breitbart News, said in a presentation for a 2014 conference at the Vatican, "We're now, I believe, at the beginning stages of a global war against Islamic fascism."[49] And as Trump's campaign built momentum, Michael Flynn continued to amplify Trump's messaging. In his book *The Field of Fight: How We Can Win the Global War against Radical Islam and Its Allies*, Flynn challenged the Obama administration's terminology: "We're in a world war against a messianic mass movement of evil people, most of them inspired by a totalitarian ideology; Radical Islam. But we are not permitted to speak or write those two words. . . . We can't beat them if we don't understand them and are afraid to define them."[50]

In 2015–16, during the primaries and general election campaign, Donald Trump went further with this messaging to link immigration to terrorism in a series of speeches and tweets. At a December 2015 campaign rally in Mount Pleasant, South Carolina, he read from his own press release on the issue, saying that he was "calling for a total and complete shutdown of Muslims entering the United States until our country's representatives can figure out what the hell is going on."[51]

By June 2016 Trump had linked immigration to ISIS: "Just announced that as many as 5000 ISIS fighters have infiltrated Europe. Also, many in U.S. I TOLD YOU SO! I alone can fix this problem!"[52] In the same month he returned to his messaging about banning immigrants from some Muslim countries: "In my speech on protecting America I spoke about a temporary ban, which includes suspending immigration from nations tied to Islamic terror."[53] The culmination of this messaging was President Trump's January 27, 2017, Executive Order 13769, titled "Protecting the Nation from Foreign Terrorist Entry into the United States," which narrowed the number of nations down to seven—Iraq, Syria, Iran, Sudan, Libya, Somalia, and Yemen—and suspended "entry into the United States, as immigrants and nonimmigrants, of such persons for 90 days from the date of this order."[54]

Trump's travel ban, which was immediately challenged in US courts, amended in March 2017, and challenged again, reflected his position on immigration and terrorism, which he and his strategists had been talking and tweeting about throughout 2016.[55] He took to Twitter again in the spring of 2017 to defend it, writing, "The threat from radical Islamic terrorism is very real, just look at what is happening in Europe and the Middle-East. Courts must act fast!"[56] He reiterated this linkage in his response to the June 3, 2017, London Bridge attack, in which three attackers connected with Islamist terrorism killed eight people. Trump's initial response was "we need to be smart, vigilant and tough. We need the courts to give us back our rights. We need the Travel Ban as an extra level of safety!"[57]

Although American troops are still deployed in Afghanistan, have redeployed to Iraq, and operate on counterterrorism missions around the globe, Trump's tweets have brought the Global War on Terror full circle to the clash of civilization debates of the 1990s and early 2000s, in which the threat from terrorism was primarily considered a law enforcement problem. After eighteen years of foreign military operations and wars, Trump has repeatedly redefined the nature of the war as fundamentally about defending the American homeland from threats originating from home and abroad. And how to use the US legal system to do so.

Conclusion

This survey of how US presidents have tried to frame America's longest modern war and their struggle to pick their way through communication minefields does not end on an optimistic note. While some might argue that the war is necessary to keep America safe from another 9/11-style attack, undoubtedly the war has been both bad for presidential ratings and bad for the perception of America among the rest of the world.

As Manuel Castells argues in his classic examination of media, *Communication Power*, "the ability to successfully engage in violence or intimidation requires the framing of individual and collective minds."[58] In other words—how presidents *framed* the Global War on Terror was a vital part of establishing their legitimacy in *waging* it at home and abroad. Despite persistent attempts to reorient and reshape the perception of America and its first seven years of the Global War on Terror, President Bush's administration wrapped up its final weeks in Washington, DC, with a deeply mixed score card. As a messenger—at home and abroad—the US president had become a mistrusted purveyor of American values and goals; domestic presidential approval ratings were at a dismal 22 percent in October 2008, lower than even President Nixon's in 1974.[59] In addition, the specter of Abu Ghraib, allegations of the routine use of torture by American intelligence agencies and contractors, and the resurgence of the Taliban in Afghanistan gave the first seven years a distinctly unfinished feeling, which incoming president-elect, Barack Obama, was eager to address.

By the end of President Obama's term in office, however, both the message and media used by the president were deeply controversial. Russia was accused of hacking the communications of at least the Democratic Party in the 2016 election, al Qaeda supporters had YouTube and Twitter accounts shut down by the dozens, and fake news websites had created virtual echo chambers for like-minded citizens that confirmed their worst fears and best hopes.[60] However much legitimacy the messenger accrues, how can an American president possibly compete with this cacophony of voices to communicate the longest war?

In terms of both message and medium, President Trump's choice of Twitter and his political positions on immigration and foreign policy reignited many of the most fundamental and controversial issues of this war even as US troops continue to deploy to Iraq, Afghanistan, and beyond in pursuit of al Qaeda, ISIS, and their supporters. Who is the enemy now? What can Americans do to protect themselves? What will the new "normal" look like? And what affect will this have on America's allies in the Global War on Terror?

In contemplating the future it is worth perhaps returning to the warning of Charlotte Beers—that the United States must balance security and liberty in this protracted struggle—and to the warning in President Obama's speech on American values in 2009: "Now this generation faces a great test in the specter of terrorism. And unlike the Civil War or World War II, we can't count on a surrender ceremony to bring this journey to an end. Right now, in distant training camps and in crowded cities, there are people plotting to take American lives. That will be the case a year from now, five years from now, and—in all probability—10 years from now."[61]

Pew's Spring 2017 Global Attitudes Survey showed that with the exception of perceptions in Russia and Israel, which improved after President Trump took office, the perceptions of America continued to plummet in many of the areas where extremists try to recruit. In the Middle East, for example, "views of America and its leader declined sharply during the Bush era and did not recover with Obama. Just 9 percent of Jordanians, 11 percent of Turks and 15 percent of Lebanese see Trump in a positive light. This is down 34 points in Turkey and 21 points in Lebanon from assessments of Obama."[62]

Even more stark, perhaps, for the domestic audiences of the war on terror is the warning from Obama's graduation address at the National Defense University: "So America is at a crossroads. We must define the nature and scope of this struggle, or else it will define us. We have to be mindful of James Madison's warning that 'No nation could preserve its freedom in the midst of continual warfare.'"[63]

Notes

1. Carl von Clausewitz, Michael Howard, and Peter Paret, *On War* (Princeton, NJ: Princeton University Press, 1984), 88–89.
2. Clausewitz.
3. Alan McLean and Archie Tse, "American Forces in Afghanistan and Iraq," *New York Times*, June 22, 2011.
4. Amy Belasco, *Troop Levels in the Afghan and Iraq Wars, FY2001–FY2012: Cost and Other Potential Issues* (Washington, DC: Congressional Research Service, July 2, 2009), https://fas.org/sgp/crs/natsec/R40682.pdf.
5. Ian S. Livingston and Michael O'Hanlon, *Afghanistan Index* (Washington, DC: Brookings Institution, January 2014), https://www.brookings.edu/wp-content/uploads/2016/07/index20140110.pdf.
6. A searchable archive of President Donald Trump's tweets is available at http://www.trumptwitterarchive.com.

7. For an bipartisan assessment of counterterrorism in the 1990s, see Thomas H. Kean, Lee H. Hamilton, and National Commission on Terrorist Attacks upon the United States, *The 9/11 Commission Report: Final Report of the National Commission on Terrorist Attacks upon the United States* (New York: W. W. Norton, 2004).

8. Fareed Zakaria, "The Politics of Rage: Why Do They Hate Us?" *Newsweek*, October 14, 2001.

9. George W. Bush, "Address before a Joint Session of the Congress on the United States Response to the Terrorist Attacks of September 11," September 20, 2001, in *The American Presidency Project*, ed. Gerhard Peters and John T. Woolley, https://www.presidency.ucsb.edu/node/213749.

10. Bush, "Statement on Signing the Authorization for Use of Military Force," September 18, 2001, in *American Presidency Project*, https://www.presidency.ucsb.edu/node/213941.

11. For two firsthand accounts of the early successes in Afghanistan, see Gary C. Schroen, *First In: An Insider's Account of How the CIA Spearheaded the War on Terror in Afghanistan* (New York: Presidio Press / Ballantine Books, 2005); Gary Berntsen and Ralph Pezzullo, *Jawbreaker: The Attack on Bin Laden and Al Qaeda: A Personal Account by the CIA's Key Field Commander* (New York: Crown Publishers, 2005). On the policymaker's perspective, also see Ivo H. Daalder and James M. Lindsay, *America Unbound: The Bush Revolution in Foreign Policy* (Washington, DC: Brookings Institution, 2003), 108–15.

12. See, for example, Bin Laden, "Your Security Is in Your Own Hands," trans. Octavia Nasr, CNN, October 29, 2004, http://www.cnn.com/2004/WORLD/meast/10/29/bin.laden.transcript/.

13. See, for example, Amy Zalman and Jonathan Clarke, "The Global War on Terror: A Narrative in Need of a Rewrite," *Ethics and International Affairs* 23, no. 2 (Summer 2009), https://www.carnegiecouncil.org/publications/journal/23_2/essays/002; Philip H. Gordon, "Can the War on Terror Be Won?" *Foreign Affairs*, August 20, 2017, https://www.foreignaffairs.com/articles/2007-11-01/can-war-terror-be-won; Michael Stohl, "The Global War on Terror and State Terrorism," *Perspectives on Terrorism* 2, no. 9 (2008), http://www.terrorismanalysts.com/pt/index.php/pot/article/view/48/html; Nick J. Sciullo, "The Ghost in the Global War on Terror: Critical Perspectives and Dangerous Implications for National Security and the Law," *Drexel Law Review* 3 (2011), https://ssrn.com/abstract=1691140.

14. National Commission on Terrorist Attacks upon the United States and Philip Zelikow, *The 9/11 Commission Report: The Attack from Planning to Aftermath: Authorized Text* (New York: W. W. Norton, 2011).

15. Ayman al-Zawahiri Shaykh Usamah Bin-Muhammad Bin-Ladin, Abu-Yasir Rifa'i Ahmad Taha, Shaykh Mir Hamzah, and Fazlur Rahman, "Jihad against Jews and

Crusaders World Islamic Front Statement," news release, February 23, 1998, https:// fas.org/irp/world/para/docs/980223-fatwa.htm.

16. Osama Bin Laden, "Full Transcript of Bin Ladin's Speech," news release, November 1, 2004, http://www.aljazeera.com/archive/2004/11/200849163336457223.html.

17. Colin Powell, "US Secretary of State's Address to the United Nations Security Council," February 5, 2003, https://nsarchive2.gwu.edu//NSAEBB/NSAEBB418/docs /X2a%20-%20Iraq%20Denial%20and%20Deception%20-%20Powell%20UN %20speech%202-5-03.pdf.

18. For a detailed discussion on how and why Saddam Hussein and al Qaeda were linked and not linked, see Michael Isikoff and David Corn, *Hubris: The Inside Story of Spin, Scandal, and the Selling of the Iraq War* (New York: Crown Publishers, 2006), 101–52.

19. On the insurgency, see, for example, Jon Lindsay and Roger Petersen, *Varieties of Insurgency and Counterinsurgency in Iraq, 2003–2009* (Newport, RI: Center on Irregular Warfare and Armed Groups, US Naval War College, 2010); Austin Long, "The Anbar Awakening," *Survival* 50, no. 2 (2008): 67–94; Richard H. Shultz, *Organizational Learning and the Marine Corps: The Counterinsurgency Campaign in Iraq* (Newport, RI: Center on Irregular Warfare and Armed Groups, US Naval War College, 2010).

20. For a few weeks in 2005, the Global War on Terror was briefly rebranded as "a global struggle against violent extremism" (GSAVE) in an attempt to shift emphasis away from military strategies. See Steven Poole, *Unspeak: How Words Become Weapons, How Weapons Become a Message, and How That Message Becomes Reality* (New York: Grove Press, 2006).

21. See discussion on the interrelationship between Abu Ghraib and Guantanamo prisons and the debate on US use of torture in Stephen F. Knott, *Rush to Judgment: George W. Bush, the War on Terror, and His Critics* (Lawrence: University Press of Kansas, 2012), 123–31.

22. Osama Bin Laden, "The Way to Save the Earth," *Inspire Magazine*, no. 1 (2010), https://azelin.files.wordpress.com/2010/06/aqap-inspire-magazine-volume-1-uncor rupted.pdf.

23. George W. Bush, "The President's News Conference with King Abdullah II of Jordan," May 6, 2004, in *American Presidency Project*, https://www.presidency.ucsb.edu /node/214833. See also Bush, "Interview with Alhurra Television," May 5, 2004, in *American Presidency Project*, https://www.presidency.ucsb.edu/node/213964; Bush, "Interview with Al Arabiya Television," May 5, 2004, in *American Presidency Project*, https://www.presidency.ucsb.edu/node/214829; and Bush, "Interview with Al-Ahram International," May 6, 2004, in *American Presidency Project*, https://www .presidency.ucsb.edu/node/213195.

24. Gallup Poll, "Iraq," accessed April 12, 2019, http://www.gallup.com/poll/1633/iraq .aspx.

25. George W. Bush, "President Bush Announces Major Combat Operations in Iraq Have Ended," news release, May 1, 2003, https://georgewbush-whitehouse.archives .gov/news/releases/2003/05/20030501-15.html.

26. Gallup Poll, "Iraq."

27. Gallup Poll, "Presidential Job Approval Center," accessed April 12, 2019, http:// www.gallup.com/interactives/185273/presidential-job-approval-center.aspx.

28. On America's struggle with public diplomacy, see Charles Wolf Jr. and Brian Rosen, *Public Diplomacy How to Think About and Improve It* (Santa Monica, CA: RAND, 2004), https://www.rand.org/content/dam/rand/pubs/occasional_papers/2004 /RAND_OP134.pdf.

29. "White House Hires Legendary Ad Executive Charlotte Beers," *NBC Today Show*, November 7, 2001, https://highered.nbclearn.com/portal/site/HigherEd/browse /?cuecard=5555.

30. *Hearing on American Public Diplomacy and Islam before Committee on Foreign Relations, US Senate*, 108th Cong. (2003) (testimony of Charlotte L. Beers), https://www .foreign.senate.gov/imo/media/doc/BeersTestimony030227.pdf.

31. George W. Bush, "Speech at the National Endowment for Democracy, Washington, DC," October 6, 2005, http://presidentialrhetoric.com/speeches/10.06.05.html.

32. Bush, "Speech at the National Endowment for Democracy."

33. Rick Santorum, "America's War against Islamic Fascism" (speech, National Press Club Newsmaker Luncheon, July 20, 2006), https://www.press.org/sites/default /files/060720rsantorum.pdf.

34. George W. Bush, "President Bush Discusses Terror Plot upon Arrival in Wisconsin," news release, August 10, 2006, https://georgewbush-whitehouse.archives.gov/news /releases/2006/08/20060810-3.html.

35. Donald Rumsfeld, "Address at the 88th Annual American Legion National Convention," news release, August 29, 2006, http://archive.defense.gov/Speeches/Speech .aspx?SpeechID=1033.

36. Advisory Group on Public Diplomacy for the Arab and Muslim World, *Changing Minds and Winning the Peace: A New Strategic Direction for U.S. Public Diplomacy in the Arab and Muslim World* (Washington, DC, 2003), 17.

37. George W. Bush, *The National Security Strategy of the United States of America* (Washington, DC: White House, 2006), http://purl.access.gpo.gov/GPO/LPS67777.

38. Office of Civil Rights and Civil Liberties, Department of Homeland Security, "Terminology to Define the Terrorists: Recommendations from American Muslims," January 2008, https://www.dhs.gov/sites/default/files/publications/dhs_crcl _terminology_08-1-08_accessible.pdf.

39. Paul Lewis, "Bradley Manning Given 35-Year Prison Term for Passing Files to WikiLeaks," *Guardian*, August 21, 2013, https://www.theguardian.com/world /2013/aug/21/bradley-manning-35-years-prison-wikileaks-sentence; Glenn Green-wald, "NSA Collecting Phone Records of Millions of Verizon Customers Daily," *Guardian*, June 6, 2013, https://www.theguardian.com/world/2013/jun/06/nsa -phone-records-verizon-court-order.

40. Mary Beth Sheridan, "Calderon: WikiLeaks Caused Severe Damage to U.S.-Mexico Relations," *Washington Post*, March 3, 2011, http://www.washingtonpost.com/wp -dyn/content/article/2011/03/03/AR2011030302853.html.

41. Barack Obama, "On the Outcome of U.S. Intelligence Programs Review" (speech at the Department of Justice, January 17, 2014), http://www.americanrhetoric.com /speeches/barackobama/barackobamasignalsintelreview.htm.

42. Barack Obama, "Remarks by the President at the National Defense University," news release, May 23, 2013, https://obamawhitehouse.archives.gov/the-press-office /2013/05/23/remarks-president-national-defense-university.

43. "Barack Obama Announces the Death of Osama Bin Laden," May 1, 2011, http:// www.americanrhetoric.com/speeches/barackobama/barackobamaosamabinladen death.htm.

44. Homeland Security Advisory Council, "Countering Violent Extremism (CVE) Sub-committee: Interim Report and Recommendations," June 2016, https://www.dhs .gov/sites/default/files/publications/HSAC/HSAC%20CVE%20Final%20Interim %20Report%20June%209%202016%20508%20compliant.pdf.

45. Donald Trump (@RealDonaldTrump), "It is time to get out of Afghanistan." Twit-ter, February 27, 2012, 11:34 a.m., https://twitter.com/realdonaldtrump/status /174215838814044160.

46. Donald Trump (@RealDonaldTrump), "We have wasted an enormous amount of blood," Twitter, November 21, 2013, 12:06 p.m., https://twitter.com/realdonald trump/status/403615352338128896.

47. Donald Trump (@RealDonaldTrump), "Now Obama is keeping our soldiers," Twitter, December 1, 2014, 1:20 p.m., https://twitter.com/realdonaldtrump/status /539529416037384192.

48. Donald Trump (@RealDonaldTrump), "With Hillary and Obama, the terror-ist attacks," Twitter, July 4, 2016, 8:34 a.m., https://twitter.com/realdonaldtrump /status/749989709275885568.

49. J. Lester Feder, "This Is How Steve Bannon Sees the Entire World," BuzzFeed News, November 16, 2016, https://www.buzzfeed.com/lesterfeder/this-is-how-steve -bannon-sees-the-entire-world?utm_term=.hdd3wyXag#.yfBwn0y4.

50. Michael T. Flynn and Michael Arthur Ledeen, *The Field of Fight: How We Can Win the Global War against Radical Islam and Its Allies* (New York: St. Martin's Press, 2016), 8.

51. Video of President Trump's 2015 rally speech is available at Jenna Johnson, "Trump Calls for 'Total and Complete Shutdown of Muslims Entering the US,'" *Washington Post*, December 7, 2015, https://www.washingtonpost.com/news/post-politics /wp/2015/12/07/donald-trump-calls-for-total-and-complete-shutdown-of-muslims -entering-the-united-states/?utm_term=.3d25e31fc330. Trump's December 2015 statement release on the topic was removed from his campaign website in 2017 during the legal challenges to his controversial travel ban, but he continued to elaborate on this theme throughout 2016 and 2017.

52. Donald Trump (@RealDonaldTrump), "Just announced that as many as 5000," Twitter, March 24, 2016, 8:52 a.m., https://twitter.com/realdonaldtrump/status /713030660475240448.

53. Donald Trump (@RealDonaldTrump), "In my speech on protecting America," Twitter, June 13, 2016, 2:10 p.m., https://twitter.com/realdonaldtrump/status /742464168482201602.

54. Executive Order—Protecting the Nation from Foreign Terrorist Entry into the United States (Washington, DC: White House, Office of the Press Secretary, January 27, 2017), https://www.whitehouse.gov/the-press-office/2017/01/27/executive -order-protecting-nation-foreign-terrorist-entry-united-states.

55. Executive Order—Protecting the Nation from Foreign Terrorist Entry into the United States (Washington, DC: White House, Office of the Press Secretary, March 6, 2017), https://www.whitehouse.gov/the-press-office/2017/03/06/executive-order -protecting-nation-foreign-terrorist-entry-united-states.

56. Donald Trump (@RealDonaldTrump), "The threat from radical Islamic," Twitter, February 6, 2017, 6:49 p.m., https://twitter.com/realdonaldtrump/status /828797801630937089.

57. Donald Trump (@RealDonaldTrump), "We need to be smart, vigilant and tough," Twitter, June 3, 2017, 4:17 p.m., https://twitter.com/realdonaldtrump/status /871143765473406976.

58. Manuel Castells, *Communication Power*, 2nd ed. (Oxford: Oxford University Press, 2013), 416.

59. Pew Research Center, "Presidential Job Approval Ratings from Ike to Obama," January 12, 2016, http://www.pewresearch.org/fact-tank/2016/01/12/presidential-job -approval-ratings-from-ike-to-obama/ft_16-01-06_presapproval_hi_lo/. Nixon had a 24 percent approval rating in August 1974; President Carter, 28 percent; and President George H. W. Bush, 29 percent.

60. Scott Shane, "From Headline to Photograph, a Fake News Masterpiece," *New York Times*, January 18, 2017.

61. Barack Obama, "Speech on American Values and National Security" (speech, National Archives, May 21, 2009), http://www.americanrhetoric.com/speeches /barackobama/barackobamanationalarchives.htm.

62. Bruce Stokes, "Global Confidence in the United States Is Shaken," YaleGlobal Online, August 3, 2017, http://yaleglobal.yale.edu/content/global-confidence-united-states -shaken. Based on data from Richard Wike, Bruce Stokes, Jacob Poushter, and Janell Fetterolf, "U.S. Image Suffers as Publics around World Question Trump's Leader-ship," Pew Research Center, June 26, 2017, http://www.pewglobal.org/2017/06/26 /u-s-image-suffers-as-publics-around-world-question-trumps-leadership/.

63. Barack Obama, "Remarks by the President at the National Defense University," news release, May 23, 2013, https://obamawhitehouse.archives.gov/the-press-office /2013/05/23/remarks-president-national-defense-university.

Conclusion: Tweaking the Tweets

Andrea J. Dew, Marc A. Genest, and S. C. M. Paine

The installation of the tweeter in chief—President Donald Trump—in the White House in 2017 may seem a very long way from the smoke-filled rooms that housed the committees of correspondence. Indeed, the technology, the vast audience, and the speed of modern communications may seem an epoch away from the scratch of quills that crafted the founding revolutionary documents. However, while the channels of communications change, political leaders still need to persuade and shape perceptions. Moreover, as each of the authors demonstrates, the media is an inescapable theater of war for democracies and dictatorships alike. Politicians must craft and then manage messages before, during, and after wars.

How can we assess these messages? How can we understand the impact of a successful and unsuccessful media campaign? How can we shine a light on how communication campaigns work? The framework used in this book examines the message, messenger, and medium and the way they combine to create a platform for the communicator in chief and his proxies to communicate war. In this concluding chapter, we discuss four common threads that three and a half centuries of communicating war provide the United States. First, we consider the role of technology in broadening the audiences of communications and increasing the speed of action, reaction, and interaction in war. This discussion leads to the second major theme: as several authors note, the advantages that emanate from an advanced technological society can be a double-edged sword depending on the nature of the regime—open or closed—and the way it attempts to control media access and content.

Third, we consider how technology and the nature of the regime can shape and be shaped by the audience—the target of presidential communications at home and abroad. In some wars—World War II, for example—a simple message, a credible messenger, and a frightened domestic audience made rallying support for war a relatively straightforward task. In others, including the current US Global War on Terrorism, three separate chapters point out how frustratingly complicated it can be to communicate war to audiences domestic and foreign.

And fourth, we conclude by discussing how political leaders manage the message once released into the world through direct and indirect censorship. In the age of personal drones and Wikileaks, censorship may also seem reassuringly old-fashioned, but closed societies continue to practice it overtly, and the chapters suggest that both indirect censorship and the wave of disinformation is once again the way of the future.

Technology and Communications: Can You Hear Me Now?

Americans pioneered the integration of media campaigns with military operations, and the communications revolution—a combination of message, messenger, medium, and technology—has transformed the media itself into a theater of warfare. In the American Revolution, a nonstate actor developed a highly effective information campaign that swayed audiences on both sides of the Atlantic and ultimately achieved independence for the rebels over the opposition of the preeminent world power. The Americans melded their story line with a combination of conventional and guerrilla operations and coalition-building diplomacy with France to escalate costs beyond what British elites were eventually willing to support. The colonists transformed a legitimate grievance (lack of political representation) into a marketable message (no taxation without representation) delivered by a credible messenger (Samuel Adams and numerous other rebel leaders). The American uprising relied on four pillars that remain essential for any insurgency: they recruited highly skilled leaders, developed powerful messages, created reliable communications networks, and established an organization capable of transforming ideas into successful action.

Since the American Revolution, an ongoing communications revolution has allowed messengers to market their ideas to ever-broader audiences. The development of communications technology has expanded and accelerated from movable-type print we waited a week to have delivered to live color videos playing now on our wrists. Initially, the print media both magnified and amplified speeches, letters, or events by disseminating information to a much wider audience than the original participants. In the early stages of this technological revolution, newspaper coverage of the Battle of New Orleans in the War of 1812 and Abraham Lincoln's speeches in the US Civil War expanded the political impact because papers covered the events on the front pages. The size of the audience, not the intrinsic significance of the event, often determined its importance by swaying public opinion, a sentiment that

President Donald J. Trump, tweeter in chief, seems to share. The expanded audience was also a double-edged sword for politicians. Mass circulation newspapers allowed experienced leaders like President Lincoln to communicate with the public more easily, but the press also provided platforms to rival politicians who sought to undercut Lincoln's policies.

Each technological development broadened both the scope and speed of dissemination, starting with the newspaper, followed in succession by the photograph, the radio, the newsreel, the television, the internet, and most recently social media. Each technological development has reached more distant and larger audiences, amplifying local events into global events and permanent parts of the historical record. These technologies provided a greater completeness of coverage, broadening from words alone to words with still photographs, to subtitled and then full-sound black-and-white motion pictures, to full-color live-streaming over the internet shared from viewers' mobile phones. Politicians increasingly must be performers adept at delivering memorable sound bites tailored to both mass and micro audiences; mastery of the broadcast and the narrowcast are essential skills in communicating war.

Since the advent of television, the US military has had to fight a nonkinetic battle over public perceptions. In the Vietnam War, when military leaders considered the press to be hostile, they blamed the media for their failure to devise a military strategy capable of contributing to national objectives at a sustainable cost. In democracies the sustainment of military operations requires public support—a subject the Vietnam era military failed adequately to appreciate. In contrast, during the Gulf War, stories of US Marine Corps heroism dominated US press accounts. Unlike the other services, the Marines welcomed embedded journalists, who soon empathized with their hosts. The Marines realized that the media is not the enemy but a theater of competition.

There is no way to opt out of the communications revolution, the technologically driven trend toward ever greater and more rapid communications amplification, reaching more distant and more numerous audiences. Leaders who failed to craft a proactive information strategy ceded the message to their rivals, with damaging results. The press abhors a vacuum, and the political opposition soon fills it. This was the case for both William McKinley and the Spanish government when yellow journalism fed by Cuban revolutionaries hijacked public discourse, for Woodrow Wilson in World War I when Theodore Roosevelt dominated the narrative in the US press, for Harry S. Truman in the Korean War when Joseph R. McCarthy dominated the spotlight, and for Lyndon B. Johnson in the Vietnam War when antiwar protestors took to the streets and took possession of the headlines. In all four cases, presidential critics undercut presidential objectives by filling the media void to dominate the story line.

In the case of Truman and Johnson, both feared the escalation of regional wars into global, nuclear Armageddon. Therefore, they deliberately avoided fomenting domestic passions that might have predisposed escalation. They found it impossible to craft a message that would rally Americans behind a protracted war without eliciting public demands for military moves that would have triggered a hostile great-power escalation. As a result, both Truman and Johnson ceded the media theater to the opposing political party, with ruinous consequences. Presidents Dwight D. Eisenhower and John F. Kennedy went a step further: they said virtually nothing about Southeast Asia to prevent it from becoming a public issue. They successfully ducked, but this left Johnson no cover when his escalation made US involvement in Vietnam a controversial strategy.

Technology and Regimes: Open Networks and Closed Societies

Those who fill a vital information void can dominate perceptions long past their natural expiry date. Indeed, the longer the vacuum, the more enduring the influence because the void gives the message time to shape beliefs, which once established endure even as more information becomes available. Moreover, closed societies can leverage the free press of their democratic enemies. Journalists Jack Reed and Edgar Snow had front-row seats at the creation of Soviet Russia and Communist China, two critically important but closed societies. The Communists let Reed and Snow in, but no other foreigners ever received such access again. Reed and Snow fed an eager Western readership on partial truths: each gave the best case for the Communists and the worst case for their enemies, yielding a warped interpretation. For decades, theirs were the only detailed narratives concerning the secretive Soviet and Chinese leadership, so their positive spin on what they witnessed had enormous influence.

Reed and Snow gained access because Leon Trotsky and Mao Zedong chose them as their foreign messengers to reach out to an international audience. Likewise, the North Vietnamese selected American journalists to deliver their message to American voters. In societies with a free press, journalists are credible messengers, particularly if they have no idea that they are unwittingly serving foreign ambitions. Once such tales take root, they are difficult to uproot. In the case of China, not until images from the Tiananmen Massacre in 1989, another media event, did the human costs of Communism suddenly become clear and myths constructed a half century prior collapsed. In the case of Reed, Snow, and the US press during the Vietnam War, journalists unwittingly delivered the mail sent by repressive societies, and by reiteration, seemed to confirm the accuracy of the Communists' desired message.

To be sure, this strategy does not always deliver the desired results. In the Spanish-American War, Cuban revolutionaries lobbied Congress and furnished stories of Spanish war crimes to US newspaper publishers eager to sell copy. This whipped up public demands, not for the aid that the revolutionaries desired but for direct military intervention that resulted not in independence but in a change from Spanish to US dominance.

In contrast to closed societies, not only the official policies but also the mistakes of democracies are usually on public display. After Wikileaks and the Snowden leaks, President Obama, who had campaigned in support of radical transparency, soon found himself justifying unfettered US government access to American phone calls and emails. During the George W. Bush administration, photographs from Abu Ghraib Prison and the allegations of torture played into the hands of the critics of the war and American power just at a time when American legitimacy and leadership in the world were being challenged. As President Bush pointed out, both incidents caused a profound dislocation between the Americans' image of themselves, their values, and the way the rest of the world perceived them. Meanwhile, the inmates of Abu Ghraib, who went on to become the core leadership of ISIS, did not have to face up to their strategy of atrocities against civilians.

US enemies have also tried to make the public communications bonanza of the US electoral cycle work to their advantage, beginning with Emilio Aguinaldo, who timed his 1890 military campaign in the Philippines to coincide with US elections but failed to dissuade voters from supporting the war. Three-quarters of a century later, the advent of radio and television changed the power dynamic. The North Vietnamese also timed their military offensives to coincide with the US electoral cycle to highlight the costs of the war to voters as they voted. A preponderance of antiwar officials won the elections. Most recently, Russian president Vladimir Putin allegedly had the computer accounts of the Democratic National Committee and others hacked to throw the 2016 US presidential election.[1]

Audience and Message: Listening with Prejudice

In our tweet-ridden social media world, it seems evident that media campaigns require a message tailored to resonate with a specific audience. However, the chapters in this book reveal the unique challenges that American presidents have faced in crafting a message for domestic and foreign audiences. All the authors indicate that the primary audience for the most efficient media campaigns is the home audience, in no small measure because it is the one most susceptible to the influence of the indigenous messenger. Indeed, Americans were most effective when they attempted to sway other Americans in the American Revolution, the War of 1812, the US Civil War, the Philippine-American War, and World War II. However, they were least effective, and probably counterproductive, when they tried to influence Muslims in the Middle East and Central Asia.

The most powerful messages are simple. "No taxation without representation" in the American Revolution; "unconditional surrender" in World War II; national liberation in China and Vietnam; and "drive Saddam from Kuwait" in the Gulf War are all simple, clear messages that resonated with domestic audiences.[2] The most powerful messages also were not received wisdom delivered top-down from a hierarchical authority but mediated between messenger and audience. The key to these simple and powerful messages was that they "both shaped and reflected public opinion" as illustrated by the Philippine-American War (see chapter 5) and later by Franklin Roosevelt's fireside chats to prepare voters for US entry into World War II.

Some audiences are crosscutting: a message popular with one may alienate another or a crucial message for one may undermine influence over another. When Nixon won the presidency on a platform of withdrawing from Vietnam, he lost all leverage over the North Vietnamese government, which waited him out until he folded. Moreover, the sensitivities of foreign audiences are not always evident. In 2011 the Obama administration decided not to base missiles in Poland and unwittingly announced the policy change on the seventieth anniversary of the Russian invasion of Poland. While the announcement was intended to convey improved security for Poland, instead Poles perceived US abandonment, given the timing coinciding with the anniversary of their country's destruction by Stalinist Russia and Nazi Germany.[3]

While the message must be mediated for the domestic audience, attempts at deterrence must be calibrated to the enemy audience. It is hard to know when calibrated messages work, since they deter the undesired event that never happens, leaving analysts without evidence. President Dwight Eisenhower tried to calibrate a message of nuclear threats to wind down the Korean War. There is no conclusive evidence that he was successful, while there is much evidence that Johnson's and Nixon's calibrated signaling through bombing was ineffective. Regardless of the bombing intensity, the North Vietnamese stuck to their objective until they achieved it, while the United States left the Vietnam War emptyhanded and Arlington Cemetery significantly expanded.

The chapters also show that a successfully mediated message requires a messenger acceptable to the intended audience. In both the Philippine-American War and World War II, the receptive audience was domestic, and the messenger was the duly elected president, who calibrated his narrative to what the traffic would bear. In a sense the leader led without seeming to lead. In contrast, in the Middle East, non-Muslim messengers are generally unacceptable and American presidents are certainly not trusted messengers. When Charlotte Beers, a legendary advertising executive, was hired in 2001 to "sell America," her domestic campaign featuring American Muslims was controversial, and internationally US actions undercut her messaging. US information campaigns aimed at influencing the citizens of Afghanistan and Iraq found few takers. They have failed primarily because, for too many Afghans, the Taliban's simple message that the Americans were in Afghanistan to conquer the country and destroy Islam rang true. Similarly, despite the headlines, ISIS attempts to foment terrorism in the West also have found few takers. Such export messages in the age of nationalism have proved difficult to market.

Religious and ideological messages have had the greatest portability across borders because of their ability to mitigate nationalism, as was the case for Reed and Snow. For many years, Communism drew many followers. Now militant versions of Islam find supporters among expatriate communities. ISIS has relied on a simple, self-reinforcing message concerning polarizing actions in support of ancient doctrine targeting fellow Arab Sunni Muslims. Those compelled to live the dream have been less enthusiastic. But figuring out how to communicate and inoculate Western expatriate communities against radical and extremist ideologies remains a difficult challenge. Consider the Bush and Obama administrations' careful parsing of words to demonstrate that America was not at war with the religion of Islam. Or how President Trump's tweets were used to reignite the passions, hatred, and enmity over "radical Islam" in 2016 and 2017 to justify his travel ban targeting predominantly Muslim countries.[4]

Managing the Message: Tweaking Those Tweets

Crafting a political message to explain war to a domestic audience becomes even more challenging once those powerful ideas are set loose in the world. Then, managing the nuances and ramifications of those ideas becomes ever more complicated. Moreover, for every president in this book, management of the message also entailed dealing with key domestic political rivals. President Theodore Roosevelt in the Philippine-American War, Franklin Roosevelt in World War II, and George H. W. Bush in the Gulf War dominated the narrative. McKinley covered up the slaughter in the Philippines, and his successor, Theodore Roosevelt, proclaimed victory and then left with Americans feeling victorious. For the duration of World War II, Franklin Roosevelt carefully kept a potential presidential rival, Gen. Douglas MacArthur, far from Washington, DC, in Asia, where MacArthur could not easily influence domestic politics. Roosevelt also appointed Republicans to key posts in his administration to gain bipartisan support for his wartime leadership.

In contrast, Wilson stuck to party-line appointments and, most fatefully, turned down his predecessor Theodore Roosevelt's request for command, leaving an articulate and fierce political enemy in Washington and communication out of control with a rogue former president tearing down national policy. Ultimately, Wilson and Roosevelt knocked each other out politically, with the result that the United States failed to go far enough militarily—Theodore Roosevelt's hue and cry—by not deploying Allied troops on German soil to make defeat in World War I undeniable to German citizens. Meanwhile, Roosevelt's avalanche of criticisms helped undermine Wilson's plans for US membership and leadership in the League of Nations. The combination of insufficient troops in Germany and a crippled international organization precluded enforcement of the peace, leaving the way open for a second world war.

The most obvious way to manage the message is to censor, but in the world of Wikileaks and private drones, it may no longer be possible for open societies to contain battlefield information to the battlefield. Moreover, competing goals create deep tensions between the need to keep secrets and the need to explain actions. Although military and intelligence bureaucracies try to control the release of information to keep the enemy in the dark, politicians even in dictatorships need the press to transmit desired messages to rally public support, maintain morale, influence allies, cow critics, and also cross-check the story line provided by their militaries. Political leaders in democracies rely even more heavily on the press to reach voters to remain in office. Therefore, as shown in the US Civil War, civil and military leaders can have very different perspectives on censorship.

US censorship did not begin until after the War of 1812. During the American Civil War both sides censored; in World War I the United States immediately passed the Espionage and Sedition Acts; likewise in World War II it quickly established the Office of Censorship. But in the Korean War, it did not impose mandatory censorship until the Chinese rout of UN forces. Moreover, in the Vietnam War, the United States did not censor, and the government lost control of the message, while in the Gulf War the government did not censor either but forced the press to operate in pools or embedded with forces, producing effects equivalent to censorship. The insurgencies after the US invasions of Iraq and Afghanistan have made reporting so dangerous that censorship is often superfluous.

Censorship cannot keep up with the pace of technological change even in police states. Most recently, the United States has become a hacker's paradise with government and personal files downloaded by enemy intelligence services from the Wikileaks website. Hackers dumped terabytes of sensitive information on the internet. Thus far, dissemination has won out over attempts to control information. But the sheer volume of available data has exceeded the ability of the press to analyze it, while the proliferation of blogs and websites likewise exceeds readers' ability to follow them all.

Discrete censorship has been more politically effective than attempts to impose unenforceable blanket rules. Even in the US Civil War, neither the Confederate nor Union governments could control the flow of information despite attempts at censorship on both sides. At that time, the generals discovered that the most efficient place to prevent leakage of battlefield information was to control press access to the battlefield. Censorship (de jure in World War II with an Office of Censorship and de facto with press pool rules in the Gulf War) took place on the battlefield. Limiting access to the battlefield allowed the government to precensor or delay information while the reporters were still on the battlefield, not at home after objectionable coverage had appeared in print as occurred, most controversially, in World War I, with the very undemocratic prosecution of the left-wing press. Unlike Woodrow Wilson's heavy-handed approach, voters rarely directly felt Franklin Roosevelt's censorship by stealth, which also did not damage domestic institutions because it naturally disappeared when the war ended. The military maintained battlefield secrecy without injuring democracy at home. Moreover, embedding the press with military units leveraged journalists' instinctual empathy for those whose lives they followed. The war coverage during the Gulf War, as in World War II, was overwhelmingly positive. Like President Franklin D. Roosevelt, President George H. W. Bush managed both the message and the messenger without seeming to control the message.

As the chapters in this book illustrate, in the twenty-first century, social media elevates politicians, platforms, and pundits alike, providing a cacophony of voices and opinions that presidents and tyrants alike must cut through to persuade. Disinformation is a particularly powerful tool for dictatorships not subject to domestic fact-checking: the Korean and Vietnamese Communists, for example, detailed the well-known faults of the adversaries in their respective civil wars, while their brutality at home went unexamined. In the hands of a ruthless regime, disinformation exploits power disparities, allowing them to target the flaws of others without facing similar scrutiny of their own perhaps even more significant deficiencies.

Thus, management of the message is often harder for a liberal democracy with a free press than for a dictatorship, which maintains tight control over its media outlets. Dictatorships routinely deny information both to their citizens and to others. Differences in press freedom permit closed societies to launch powerful disinformation campaigns, like those waged by Vladimir Putin in his so-called gray zone warfare against his Western neighbors. According to Paul A. Goble, a special adviser on Soviet nationality issues and Baltic affairs to Secretary of State James Baker, disinformation is "the clever combination of what is true, what people want to be true, and what is demonstrably false but which many will not notice if it is cleverly presented. . . . It is implemented with a clear understanding that a combination of truth and falsehood is useful and effective."[5]

*   *   *

The chapters in this book have covered all of America's foreign wars and a full range of war communication: from civilian leaders justifying American entry into war, politicians bent on undermining rival political parties, newspapers adjusting spin to sell copy, and individual journalists intent on making a name for themselves to nonstate actors hoping to build a following as the route to power. All have sought to use information and emerging technology to garner public support and gain political advantage over domestic and foreign adversaries. In the eighteenth century, the press fed information to governments. By the nineteenth century, political leaders and interest groups had mastered leaking information to the press. In the twentieth century, professional journalists filtered the information that reached the public. The twenty-first century began with foreign espionage services and super-empowered hackers sidestepping the filters to feed hacked information directly to the blogosphere and to circulate false news stories through the social media. Bloggers and bots now occupy territory once dominated by professional journalists.

This survey of three centuries of American war also shows that changes in communications technology have broken down international borders. On the one hand, hacked government emails dumped on the internet have left the United States reeling. On the other hand, the United States has unprecedented access to closed societies. In the past, radio transmissions subject to persistent jamming, such as Voice of America, were the state-of-the-art means to reach audiences behind the Iron Curtain. These efforts began in the 1940s, but the Iron Curtain did not part until 1991. Now email can instantaneously deliver messages to individuals to sow distrust at will in kleptocracies, and the internet can be used to provide accurate news to those fed a diet of disinformation by their governments. Disinformation targeted at social media accounts, however, can potentially throw elections in democracies.

Dictatorships depend on information control to retain power, but the world of information control is more difficult to achieve than in the past. In the long run, hacking may turn out to be more damaging to those who depend on monopolizing information than for those who have long accepted openness and a diversity of opinion. Back in the day, the Soviet Union used Reed in the hopes of spreading Communism to the West, and Mao Zedong used Snow initially in the hopes of gaining Western financial and military support for China's fight against Japan. Over the long-term their efforts to manipulate Western voters contributed to a backlash of anticommunist hatred.

There are three key lessons that we can take away from this study of the evolving role that information, rhetoric, and communications technology have played in shaping the American political landscape during times of war. First, the battles waged in print and later in electronic outlets have played a vital role in all of America's wars. From Samuel Adams' exploitation of the *Boston Gazette* to Abraham Lincoln's Gettysburg Address to the ongoing battle waged on social media between the United States and Islamic State, the war of words has affected the outcomes of war. Second, while communications technology has let established political leaders influence vast audiences, it has simultaneously enabled nonstate actors and individuals to compete in shaping the wartime political landscape and allowed state and nonstate actors to conduct espionage and information campaigns on an unprecedented scale. Finally, technological innovations have changed how wars are covered, strengthened the power of those savvy in the use of social media, and super-empowered individuals to shape public and elite perceptions of the legitimacy of wars and their conduct.

Notes

1. Adam Entous, Ellen Nakashima, and Greg Miller, "Secret CIA Assessment Says Russia Was Trying to Help Trump Win the White House," *Washington Post*, December 9, 2016, https://www.washingtonpost.com/world/national-security/obama-orders-review-of-russian-hacking-during-presidential-campaign/2016/12/09/31d6b300-be2a-11e6-94ac-3d324840106c_story.html?utm_term=.bcb90c2d8491; W. J. Hennigan, "Obama Orders Full Review of Russian Hacking during the 2016 Election," *Los Angeles Times*, December 10, 2016, http://touch.latimes.com/#section/-1/article/p2p-92089929/.

2. George W. Bush, "Address to the Nation on the Invasion of Iraq," January 16, 1991, http://www.americanrhetoric.com/speeches/ghwbushiraqinvasion.htm.

3. Rosa Brooks, "Ten Years On: The Evolution of Strategic Communication and Information Operations since 9/11" (testimony before the House Armed Services Subcommittee on Evolving Threats and Capabilities, July 12, 2011), 3.

4. Donald Trump (@RealDonaldTrump), "With Hillary and Obama, the terrorist attacks will only get worse. Politically correct fools, won't even call it what it is—RADICAL ISLAM!" Twitter, July 4, 2016, 8:34 a.m., https://twitter.com/realdonaldtrump/status/749989709275885568.

5. Paul Goble, "Hot Issue—Lies, Damned Lies and Russian Disinformation," *Hot Issues*, August 13, 2014, http://www.jamestown.org/single/?tx_ttnews%5btt_news%5d=42745&tx_ttnews%5bbackPid%5d=7&cHash=6ccbe7697870188378d5960d23bb0f3a#.U-1YD82Av8l.

Contributors

Judith Baroody began her professional life as an award-winning reporter before joining the US Foreign Service. Rising to the rank of minister-counselor, she served in Syria, Israel, Morocco, Cyprus, Chile, Iraq, and France before retiring in 2017. She also taught diplomatic history at American University in Washington, DC, and national security strategy at the National War College.

Troy Bickham is professor of history at Texas A&M University. His books include *The Weight of Vengeance: The United States, the British Empire, and War of 1812* (Oxford University Press, 2012).

Michael G. Carew is professor emeritus at Baruch College, City University of New York. His books include *The Impact of the First World War on U.S. Policymakers: American Strategic and Foreign Policy Formulation, 1938–1942* (Lexington Books, 2014) and *The Power to Persuade: FDR, the Newsmagazines, and Going to War, 1939–1941* (Roman and Littlefield, 2005).

Steven Casey is professor in international history at the London School of Economics and is a specialist in US foreign policy. His latest book, *The War Beat, Europe: The American Media at War against Nazi Germany,* (Oxford University Press, 2017) won the American Journalism Historians Association prize for best book in journalism and mass media history.

Andrea J. Dew is the Maritime Irregular Warfare Forces Chair, the founding codirector of the Center on Irregular Warfare and Armed Groups (CIWAG), and an associate professor of strategy and policy at the US Naval War College. Her publications include *Insurgents, Terrorists, and Militias: The Warriors of Contemporary Combat* (Columbia University Press, 2007) and *Deep Currents and Rising Tides: The Indian Ocean and International Security* (Georgetown University Press, 2013).

Matthew C. DuPée has a master's degree in South Asia security studies from the Naval Postgraduate School in Monterey, California. His studies focus on licit and illicit aspects of the extractives industry, organized crime, and insurgency. He has written extensively for *World Politics Review* (https://www.worldpoliticsreview.com /authors/447/matthew-c-dupee).

Bruce A. Elleman is the William V. Pratt Professor of International History at the US Naval War College. He is the author of twenty-five books on Chinese history, naval operations, and Taiwan, including *China's Naval Operations in the South China Sea: Evaluating Legal, Strategic and Military Factors* (2018) and *International Competition in China, 1899–1991* (2015).

Marc A. Genest is the Forrest Sherman Professor of Public Diplomacy in the Strategy and Policy Department and the founding codirector of the Center on Irregular Warfare and Armed Groups (CIWAG) at the Naval War College. Dr. Genest's publications include *Negotiating in the Public Eye: The Impact of the Press on the Intermediate-Range Nuclear Force Negotiations* and *Conflict and Cooperation: Evolving Theories of International Relations*.

Michelle D. Getchell is an assistant professor at the US Naval War College. She earned her PhD in history at the University of Texas at Austin, where she focused on US foreign policy, Soviet studies, Latin America, and the international history of the Cold War. She is the author of *The Cuban Missile Crisis and the Cold War: A Short History with Documents* (Hackett Publishing, 2018) and is working on a monograph examining US–Soviet–Latin American relations during the Cold War.

Haroro J. Ingram is a research fellow at the George Washington University Program on Extremism and an associate fellow at the International Centre for Counterterrorism (ICCT)—The Hague. He researches the role of propaganda in the strategies of violent nonstate political movements and is the author of *The ISIS Reader: Milestone Texts of the Islamic State Movement* (C. Hurst & Co. Publishers, 2019).

Thomas H. Johnson is a research professor of National Security Affairs at the Naval Postgraduate School (Monterey, California). He has conducted research and published widely on Afghanistan and South Asia for three decades. In 2009, he served as the Senior Political and Counterinsurgency Advisor to Gen. Jonathan Vance, Commander of Canadian Forces in Afghanistan (Task Force Kandahar).

David Kaiser was a professor in the Strategy and Policy Department of the US Naval War College from 1990 until 2012 and has taught at Carnegie Mellon, Williams College, and Harvard University. His book, *American Tragedy: Kennedy, Johnson, and the Origins of the Vietnam War*, was winner of the 2001 ForeWord Magazine Book of the Year Award (History Category).

Martin J. Manning was a librarian in the Bureau of Public Diplomacy and Public Affairs, US Department of State, Washington, DC, where he was curator of the US Information Agency archives. His published works include *Greenwood's Historical Dictionary of American Propaganda* and *Encyclopedia of Media and Propaganda in Wartime America* (ABC-CLIO, 2010).

S. C. M. Paine, William S. Sims University Professor of History and Grand Strategy at the US Naval War College, has written a dozen books on the relations among Russia, China, and Japan and on naval operations, including the award-winning *Wars for Asia, 1911–1949* (Cambridge, 2012).

David J. Silbey is currently adjunct associate professor and associate director of Cornell in Washington. His publications include *A War of Frontier and Empire: The Philippine-American War, 1899–1902* (Hill and Wang, 2008) and *The Boxer Rebellion and the Great Game in China: A History* (Hill and Wang, 2013). He is series editor for Cornell University Press's Battlegrounds: Cornell Studies in Military History.

J. Lee Thompson served as president of the Western Conference on British Studies from 2004 to 2006 and since 2006 has been a visiting fellow at Wolfson College, Cambridge University. A Lamar University Distinguished Faculty Lecturer for 2007, he is also a fellow of the Royal Historical Society. His publications include *Theodore Roosevelt and the Great War* (Palgrave Macmillan, 2013).

Craig A. Whiteside is an associate professor at the Naval War College in Monterey, California, and has published extensively on a variety of topics regarding the Islamic State movement, including a media history, *The ISIS Reader: Milestone Texts of the Islamic State Movement* (C. Hurst & Co. Publishers, 2019). He is a fellow at the George Washington University Program on Extremism and the Naval War College's Center on Irregular Warfare and Armed Groups.

Index